Junior Worldmark Encyclopedia of the States, Fifth Edition

Junior Worldmark Encyclopedia of the States, Fifth Edition

VOLUME 2: INDIANA–NEBRASKA

U·X·L
An imprint of Thomson Gale,
a part of The Thomson Corporation

Detroit • New York • San Francisco
New Haven, Conn. • Waterville, Maine • London

Junior Worldmark Encyclopedia of the States, Fifth Edition

Project Editor
Jennifer York Stock

Editorial
Julie Mellors

Rights and Acquisitions
Margaret Chamberlain-Gaston, Robert McCord, Sue Rudolph

Imaging and Multimedia
Dean Dauphinais, Lezlie Light

Product Design
Jennifer Wahi

Composition
Evi Seoud

Manufacturing
Rita Wimberly

LIBRARY OF CONGRESS CATALOGING-IN-PUBLICATION DATA

Junior Worldmark encyclopedia of the states / [edited by] Timothy L. Gall and Susan Bevan Gall. --5th ed.
    p. cm.
  Includes bibliographical references and index.
    ISBN 978-1-4144-1106-4 (set: hardcover) -- ISBN 978-1-4144-1107-1 (v. 1: hardcover) -- ISBN 978-1-4144-1108-8 (v. 2: hardcover) -- ISBN 978-1-4144-1109-5 (v. 3: hardcover) -- ISBN 978-1-4144-1110-1 (v. 4: hardcover)
    1. United States--Encyclopedias, Juvenile. 2. U.S. states--Encyclopedias, Juvenile. I. Gall, Timothy L. II. Gall, Susan B.
  G63.J86 2007
  903--dc22

                   2007002388

ISBN-13:

978-1-4144-1106-4 (set)
978-1-4144-1107-1 (v. 1)
978-1-4144-1108-8 (v. 2)
978-1-4144-1109-5 (v. 3)
978-1-4144-1110-1 (v. 4)

ISBN-10:

1-4144-1095-6 (set: hardcover)
1-4144-1107-3 (v. 1: hardcover)
1-4144-1108-1 (v. 2: hardcover)
1-4144-1109-X (v. 3: hardcover)
1-4144-1110-3 (v. 4: hardcover)

This title is also available as an ebook
ISBN 13: 978-1-4144-2959-5 (set), ISBN 10: 1-4144-2959-2 (set)
Contact your Thomson Gale representative for ordering information
Printed in the United States of America

10 9 8 7 6 5 4 3 2 1

Table of Contents

Reader's Guide

Junior Worldmark Encyclopedia of the States, Fifth Edition, presents profiles of the 50 states of the nation, the District of Columbia, Puerto Rico, and the US dependencies, arranged alphabetically in four volumes. *Junior Worldmark* is based on the seventh edition of the reference work, *Worldmark Encyclopedia of the States.* The *Worldmark* design organizes facts and data about every state in a common structure. Every profile contains a map, showing the state and its location in the nation.

For this fifth edition of *Junior Worldmark,* facts were updated and many new photographs were added depicting the unique economic and social features of the individual states. In addition, the page design has been changed to improve aesthetics and usability of the set.

Each state's political history is documented in the updated table listing the governors who have served the state since the founding of the nation. The population profiles give users of *Junior Worldmark* access to the latest population data for the states.

A subject index to all four volumes appears at the end of volume four.

Sources

Due to the broad scope of this encyclopedia many sources were consulted in compiling the information and statistics presented in these volumes. Of primary importance were the publications of the US Bureau of the Census. The most recent agricultural statistics on crops and livestock were obtained from files posted by the US Department of Agriculture on its worldwide web site at http://www.econ.ag.gov. Finally, many fact sheets, booklets, and state statistical abstracts were used to update data not collected by the federal government.

Profile Features

The *Junior Worldmark* structure—40 numbered headings—allows student researchers to compare two or more states in a variety of ways.

Each state profile begins by listing the origin of the state name, its nickname, the capital, the date it entered the union, the state song and motto, and a description of the state coat of arms. The profile also presents a picture and textual description of both the state seal and the state flag (color versions of the flags and seals can be found on the endpages of each volume). Next, a listing of the official state animal, bird, fish, flower, tree, gem, etc. is given. The introductory information ends with the standard time given by time zone in relation to Greenwich mean time (GMT). The world is divided into 24 time zones, each one hour apart. The Greenwich meridian, which is 0 degrees, passes through Greenwich, England, a suburb of London. Greenwich is at the center of the initial time zone, known as Greenwich mean time (GMT). All times given are converted from noon in this zone. The time reported for the state is the official time zone.

The body of each country's profile is arranged in 40 numbered headings as follows:

1 Location and Size. The state is located on the North American continent. Statistics are given on area and boundary length. Size comparisons are made to the other 50 states of the United States.

2 Topography. Dominant geographic features including terrain and major rivers and lakes are described.

3 Climate. Temperature and rainfall are given for the various regions of the state in both English and metric units.

4 Plants and Animals. Described here are the plants and animals native to the state.

5 Environmental Protection. Destruction of natural resources—forests, water supply, air—is described here. Statistics on solid waste production, hazardous waste sites, and endangered and extinct species are also included.

6 Population. Census statistics, including the seven categories identifying race introduced with the 2000 census of population, are provided. Population density and major urban populations are summarized.

7 Ethnic Groups. The major ethnic groups are ranked in percentages. Where appropriate, some description of the influence or history of ethnicity is provided.

8 Languages. The regional dialects of the state are summarized as well as the number of people speaking languages other than English at home.

9 Religions. The population is broken down according to religion and/or denominations.

10 Transportation. Statistics on roads, railways, waterways, and air traffic, along with a listing of key ports for trade and travel, are provided.

11 History. Includes a concise summary of the state's history from ancient times (where appropriate) to the present.

12 State Government. The form of government is described, and the process of governing is summarized. A table listing the state governors, updated to 2006, accompanies each entry.

13 Political Parties. Describes the significant political parties through history, where appropriate, and the influential parties as of 2006.

14 Local Government. The system of local government structure is summarized.

15 Judicial System. Structure of the court system and the jurisdiction of courts in each category is provided. Crime rates as reported by the Federal Bureau of Investigation (FBI) are also included.

16 Migration. Population shifts since the end of World War II are summarized.

17 Economy. This section presents the key elements of the economy. Major industries and employment figures are also summarized.

18 Income. Personal income and the poverty level are given as is the state's ranking among the 50 states in per person income.

19 Industry. Key industries are listed, and important aspects of industrial development are described.

20 Labor. Statistics are given on the civilian labor force, including numbers of workers, leading areas of employment, and unemployment figures.

21 Agriculture. Statistics on key agricultural crops, market share, and total farm income are provided.

22 Domesticated Animals. Statistics on livestock—cattle, hogs, sheep, etc.—and the land area devoted to raising them are given.

23 Fishing. The relative significance of fishing to the state is provided, with statistics on fish and seafood products.

24 Forestry. Land area classified as forest is given, along with a listing of key forest products and a description of government policy toward forest land.

25 Mining. Description of mineral deposits and statistics on related mining activity and export are provided.

26 Energy and Power. Description of the state's power resources, including electricity produced and oil reserves and production, are provided.

27 Commerce. A summary of the amount of wholesale trade, retail trade, and receipts of service establishments is given.

28 Public Finance. Revenues, ex-penditures, and total and per person debt are provided.

29 Taxation. The state's tax system is explained.

30 Health. Statistics on and description of such public health factors as disease and suicide rates, principal causes of death, numbers of hospitals and medical facilities appear here. Information is also provided on the percentage of citizens without health insurance within each state.

31 Housing. Housing shortages and government programs to build housing are described.

Statistics on numbers of dwellings and median home values are provided.

32 **Education.** Statistical data on educational achievement and primary and secondary schools is given. Per person state spending on primary and secondary education is also given. Major universities are listed, and government programs to foster education are described.

33 **Arts.** A summary of the state's major cultural institutions is provided together with the amount of federal and state funds designated to the arts.

34 **Libraries and Museums.** The number of libraries, their holdings, and their yearly circulation is provided. Major museums are listed.

35 **Communications.** The state of telecommunications (television, radio, and telephone) is summarized. Activity related to the Internet is reported where available.

36 **Press.** Major daily and Sunday newspapers are listed together with data on their circulations.

37 **Tourism, Travel, and Recreation.** Under this heading, the student will find a summary of the importance of tourism to the state, and factors affecting the tourism industry. Key tourist attractions are listed.

38 **Sports.** The major sports teams in the state, both professional and collegiate, are summarized.

39 **Famous People.** In this section, some of the best-known citizens of the state are listed. When a person is noted in a state that is not the state of his of her birth, the birthplace is given.

40 **Bibliography.** The bibliographic and web site listings at the end of each profile are provided as a guide for further reading.

Because many terms used in this encyclopedia will be new to students, each volume includes a glossary and a list of abbreviations and acronyms. A keyword index to all four volumes appears in Volume 4.

Acknowledgments

Junior Worldmark Encyclopedia of the States, Fifth Edition, draws on the seventh edition of the *Worldmark Encyclopedia of the States.* Readers are directed to that work for a complete list of contributors, too numerous to list here. Special acknowledgment goes to the government officials throughout the nation who gave their cooperation to this project.

Comments and Suggestions

We welcome your comments on the *Junior Worldmark Encyclopedia of the States, Fifth Edition,* as well as your suggestions for features to be included in future editions. Please write to: Editors, *Junior Worldmark Encyclopedia of the States,* U•X•L, 27500 Drake Road, Farmington Hills, Michigan 48331-3535; or call toll-free: 1-800-877-4253.

Guide to State Articles

All information contained within a state article is uniformly keyed by means of a number to the left of the subject headings. A heading such as "Population," for example, carries the same key numeral (6) in every article. Therefore, to find information about the population of Alabama, consult the table of contents for the page number where the Alabama article begins and look for section 6.

Introductory matter for each state includes:
Origin of state name
Nickname
Capital
Date and order of statehood
Song
Motto
Flag
Official seal
Symbols (animal, tree, flower, etc.)
Time zone

Sections listed numerically
1 Location and Size
2 Topography
3 Climate
4 Plants and Animals
5 Environmental Protection
6 Population
7 Ethnic Groups
8 Languages
9 Religions
10 Transportation
11 History
12 State Government
13 Political Parties
14 Local Government
15 Judicial System
16 Migration
17 Economy
18 Income
19 Industry
20 Labor
21 Agriculture
22 Domesticated Animals

23 Fishing
24 Forestry
25 Mining
26 Energy and Power
27 Commerce
28 Public Finance
29 Taxation
30 Health
31 Housing
32 Education
33 Arts
34 Libraries and Museums
35 Communications
36 Press
37 Tourism, Travel, and
   Recreation
38 Sports
39 Famous Persons
40 Bibliography

Alphabetical listing of sections
Agriculture 21
Arts 33
Bibliography 40
Climate 3
Commerce 27
Communications 35
Domesticated Animals 22
Economy 17
Education 32
Energy and Power 26
Environmental Protection 5
Ethnic Groups 7
Famous Persons 39
Fishing 23
Forestry 24

Health 30
History 11
Housing 31
Income 18
Industry 19
Judicial System 15
Labor 20
Languages 8
Libraries and Museums 34
Local Government 14
Location and Size 1
Migration 16
Mining 25
Plants and Animals 4
Political Parties 13
Population 6
Press 36
Public Finance 28
Religions 9
Sports 38
State Government 12
Taxation 29
Topography 2
Tourism, Travel, and
   Recreation 37
Transportation 10

Explanation of symbols
A fiscal split year is indicated by a stroke (e.g. 1999/00).
Note that 1 billion = 1,000 million = 10^9.
The use of a small dash (e.g., 1998–99) normally signifies the full period of calendar years covered (including the end year indicated).

Indiana

State of Indiana

ORIGIN OF STATE NAME: Named "land of Indians" for the many Indian tribes that formerly lived in the state.

NICKNAME: The Hoosier State.

CAPITAL: Indianapolis.

ENTERED UNION: 11 December 1816 (19th).

OFFICIAL SEAL: In a pioneer setting, a farmer fells a tree while a buffalo flees from the forest and across the prairie; in the background, the sun sets over distant hills. The words "Seal of the State of Indiana 1816" surround the scene.

FLAG: A flaming torch representing liberty is surrounded by 19 gold stars against a blue background. The word "Indiana" is above the flame.

MOTTO: The Crossroads of America.

SONG: "On the Banks of the Wabash, Far Away."

FLOWER: Peony.

TREE: Tulip poplar.

BIRD: Cardinal.

ROCK OR STONE: Indiana limestone.

LEGAL HOLIDAYS: New Year's Day, 1 January; Birthday of Martin Luther King Jr., 3rd Monday in January; Good Friday, Friday before Easter, March or April; Primary Election Day, 1st Tuesday after 1st Monday in May in even-numbered years; Memorial Day, last Monday in May; Independence Day, 4 July; Labor Day, 1st Monday in September; Columbus Day, 2nd Monday in October; Election Day, 1st Tuesday after 1st Monday in November in even-numbered years; Veterans' Day, 11 November; Thanksgiving Day, 4th Thursday in November;

Lincoln's Birthday, 12 February (observed the day after Thanksgiving); Christmas Day, 25 December; Washington's Birthday, 3rd Monday in February (observed the day after Christmas).

TIME: 7 AM EST = noon GMT; 6 AM CST = noon GMT.

---

1 Location and Size

Situated in the eastern north-central United States, Indiana is the smallest of the 12 Midwestern states and ranks 38th in size among the 50 states. Indiana's total area is 36,185 square miles (93,720 square kilometers), of which land takes up 35,932 square miles (93,064 square kilometers) and inland water the remaining 253 square miles (656 square kilometers). The state extends about 160 miles (257 kilometers) east–west and about 280 miles (451 kilometers) north–south. The total boundary length of Indiana is 1,696 miles (2,729 kilometers).

2 Topography

Indiana has two principal types of terrain: slightly rolling land in the northern half of the state, and rugged hills in the southern, extending to the Ohio River. The highest point in the state is a hill in Franklin Township that is 1,257 feet (383 meters) above sea level. The lowest point, on the Ohio River, is 320 feet (98 meters).

Four-fifths of the state's land is drained by the Wabash River and by its tributaries, the White, Eel, Mississinewa, and Tippecanoe rivers. The northern region is drained by the Maumee, Calumet, and Kankakee rivers. In the southwest, the two White River forks empty into the Wabash, and in the southeast, the Whitewater River flows into the Ohio.

In addition to Lake Michigan on the northwestern border, there are more than 400 lakes in the northern part of the state. The largest lakes include Wawasee, Maxinkuckee, Freeman, and Shafer. There are mineral springs at French Lick and West Baden in Orange County and two large caves at Wyandotte and Marengo in adjoining Crawford County.

3 Climate

Temperatures vary from the extreme north to the extreme south of the state. The annual mean temperature in the north is 49°F–58°F (9°C–12°C). In the south, the mean temperature is 57°F (14°C) in the south. The average temperatures in January range between 17°F (–8°C) and 35°F (2°C). Average temperatures during July vary from 63°F (17°C) to 88°F (31°C). The record

---

Indiana Population Profile

Total population estimate in 2006:	6,313,520
Population change, 2000–06:	3.8%
Hispanic or Latino†:	4.6%
Population by race	
One race:	98.5%
White:	86.1%
Black or African American:	8.6%
American Indian /Alaska Native:	0.2%
Asian:	1.2%
Native Hawaiian / Pacific Islander:	0.0%
Some other race:	2.4%
Two or more races:	1.5%

Population by Age Group

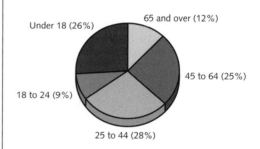

Under 18 (26%)
65 and over (12%)
45 to 64 (25%)
18 to 24 (9%)
25 to 44 (28%)

Major Cities by Population

City	Population	% change 2000–05
Indianapolis	784,118	0.3
Fort Wayne	223,341	8.6
Evansville	115,918	-4.7
South Bend	105,262	-2.3
Gary	98,715	-3.9
Hammond	79,217	-4.6
Bloomington	69,017	-0.4
Muncie	66,164	-1.9
Lafayette	60,459	7.2
Carmel	59,243	57.0

Notes: †A person of Hispanic or Latino origin may be of any race. NA indicates that data are not available.
Sources: U.S. Census Bureau. *American Community Survey* and *Population Estimates.* www.census.gov/ (accessed March 2007).

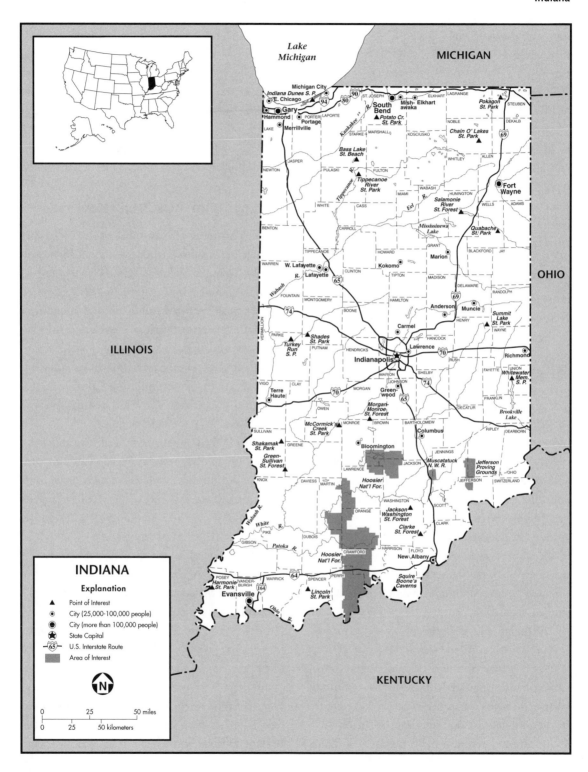

INDIANA

Explanation

▲ Point of Interest
⊙ City (25,000-100,000 people)
◉ City (more than 100,000 people)
★ State Capital
─65─ U.S. Interstate Route
▨ Area of Interest

Ⓝ

0   25   50 miles
0   25   50 kilometers

high for the state was 116°F (47°C), set on 14 July 1936 at Collegeville, and the record low was -36°F (-38°C) on 19 January 1994 at New Whiteland.

Rainfall is distributed fairly evenly throughout the year, although drought sometimes occurs in the southern region. The average annual precipitation in the state is 40 inches (102 centimeters), ranging from about 35 inches (89 centimeters) near Lake Michigan to 45 inches (114 centimeters) along the Ohio River. The annual snowfall in Indiana averages less than 22 inches (56 centimeters). The average wind speed in the state is 8 miles per hour (13 kilometers per hour), but gales sometimes occur along the shores of Lake Michigan. There are occasional tornadoes in the interior.

4 Plants and Animals

There are 124 native tree species, including 17 varieties of oak, as well as black walnut, sycamore, and the tulip tree (yellow poplar), which is the state tree. Fruit trees—apple, cherry, peach, and pear—are common. American elderberry and bittersweet are common shrubs, while various jack-in-the-pulpits and spring beauties are among the indigenous wildflowers. The peony is the state flower. As of April 2006, Mead's milkweed and Pitcher's thistle were considered threatened, and running buffalo clover was considered endangered.

Although the presence of wolves and coyotes has been reported occasionally, the red fox is Indiana's only common carnivorous mammal. Other native mammals include the common cottontail, muskrat, and raccoon. Many waterfowl and marsh birds, including the black duck and great blue heron, inhabit northern Indiana,

while the field sparrow, yellow warbler, and red-headed woodpecker nest in central Indiana. Catfish, pike, bass, and sunfish are native to state waters. As of April 2006, the US Fish and Wildlife Service listed 21 Indiana animal species as threatened or endangered. Among these are the bald eagle, Indiana and gray bats, gray wolf, piping plover, and two species of butterfly.

5 Environmental Protection

The Department of Natural Resources regulates the use of Indiana's lands, waters, forests, and wildlife resources. The Indiana Department of Environmental Management (IDEM) seeks to protect public health through the implementation and management of various environmental programs. In addition, the following boards exist to aid in environmental involvement: Air Pollution Control Board, Water Pollution Control Board, Pollution Prevention Control Board, and the Solid Waste Management Board.

The IDEM offers technical assistance to industries for the installation of pollution prevention equipment, and encourages consumers to rethink their use and disposal of hazardous household goods and chemicals. In 2003, the Environmental Protection Agency's database listed 210 hazardous waste sites in the state, 29 of which were on the National Priorities List.

Some of the state's most serious environmental challenges lie in Lake and Porter counties in Northwest Indiana. A century of spills, emissions and discharges to the environment there require comprehensive, regionally coordinated programs. The Northwest Indiana Remedial Action Plan (RAP) is a three-phased program designed especially for the Grand Calumet River and the Indiana Harbor Ship Canal. Both waterways are

Indiana Population by Race

Census 2000 was the first national census in which the instructions to respondents said, "Mark one or more races." This table shows the number of people who are of one, two, or three or more races. For those claiming two races, the number of people belonging to the various categories is listed. The U.S. government conducts a census of the population every ten years.

	Number	Percent
Total population	6,080,485	100.0
One race	6,004,813	98.8
Two races	71,132	1.2
White *and* Black or African American	19,187	0.3
White *and* American Indian/Alaska Native	18,053	0.3
White *and* Asian	9,131	0.2
White *and* Native Hawaiian/Pacific Islander	843	—
White *and* some other race	15,756	0.3
Black or African American *and* American Indian/Alaska Native	1,883	—
Black or African American *and* Asian	959	—
Black or African American *and* Native Hawaiian/Pacific Islander	156	—
Black or African American *and* some other race	2,432	—
American Indian/Alaska Native *and* Asian	298	—
American Indian/Alaska Native *and* Native Hawaiian/Pacific Islander	30	—
American Indian/Alaska Native *and* some other race	458	—
Asian *and* Native Hawaiian/Pacific Islander	512	—
Asian *and* some other race	1,291	—
Native Hawaiian/Pacific Islander *and* some other race	143	—
Three or more races	4,540	0.1

Source: U.S. Census Bureau. *Census 2000: Redistricting Data*. Press release issued by the Redistricting Data Office. Washington, D.C., March, 2001. A dash (—) indicates that the percent is less than 0.1.

heavily contaminated, and if left in their current state, would certainly degrade the waters of Lake Michigan, the primary source of drinking water for the Northwest Indiana area.

6 Population

In 2006, Indiana ranked 15th in population among the 50 states, with an estimated total of 6,313,520 residents. In 2004, the population density was 173.9 persons per square mile (67.1 persons per square kilometer). The population is projected to reach 6.5 million by 2015, and 6.7 million by 2025. In 2005, Indianapolis, the capital and largest city, had a population of 784,118. Other major cities with their 2005 populations were Fort Wayne, 223,341; Evansville, 115,918;

and South Bend, 105,262. In 2004, the median age was 35.7 years. In 2005, about 12% of all residents were 65 or older, and about 26% were 18 or younger.

7 Ethnic Groups

According to the 2000 census, the state had 510,034 blacks, representing about 8.4% of the total population. In that same year, about 214,536 Hispanics and Latinos lived within the state, representing approximately 3.5% of the population. In 2006, Hispanics and Latinos accounted for 4.6% of the state's population. The Asian population was estimated at 59,126, in 2000, including 14,685 Asian Indians, 12,531 Chinese, 6,674 Filipinos, 7,502 Koreans, 5,065 Japanese, and

4,843 Vietnamese. Pacific Islanders numbered 2,005. There were 15,815 Native Americans, many of whom are descendants of a variety of Algonkian-speaking tribes, such as Delaware, Shawnee, and Potawatomi. As of 2000, foreign-born Hoosiers numbered 186,534, about 3% of the total state population.

8 Languages

Most Indiana speech is basically that of the South Midland pioneers from south of the Ohio River. Between the Ohio River and Indianapolis, South Midland speakers use the term *clabber cheese* instead of cottage cheese, *frogstools* rather than toadstools, and *goobers* instead of peanuts. North of Indianapolis, speakers with a Midland Pennsylvania background wish on the *pullybone* of a chicken, may use a *trestle* (sawhorse), and are likely to get their hands *greezy* rather than *greasy*.

In 2000, of all Hoosiers five years old and older, 93.5% spoke only English at home. Other languages spoken at home (and number of speakers) include Spanish (185,576), German (44,142), French (18,065), and Polish (7,831). Chinese, Indic, Greek, Italian, and Korean were also reported.

9 Religions

The first branch of Christianity to gain a foothold in Indiana was Roman Catholicism, introduced by the French settlers in the early 18th century. The first Protestant church was founded near Charlestown by Baptists from Kentucky in 1798. In 1807, Quakers built their first meetinghouse at Richmond. The Shakers, established a short-lived community in Sullivan County in 1808.

In 2004, the Roman Catholic Church was the largest single denomination in the state, with about 765,699 adherents. The largest Protestant denominations were the United Methodist Church (with 212,667 adherents) in that same year. Other denominations included (with 2000 membership data) the Church of Christ (205,408 adherents), the Southern Baptist Convention (124,452), the American Baptist Church (115,101), and the Lutheran Church—Missouri Synod (111,522). The estimated Jewish population of the state in 2000 was 18,000. The Muslim community had about 11,000 members. There were also over 17,000 Mennonites, and over 19,000 members of Amish communities statewide. About 57% of the population (over 3.4 million people) were not counted as members of any religious organization.

10 Transportation

Indiana's central location in the country and its position between Lake Michigan to the north and the Ohio River to the south gave the state its motto, "The Crossroads of America." Historically, the state took advantage of its strategic location by digging canals to connect Indiana rivers and by building roads and railroads to provide farmers access to national markets.

In 2003, there were 37 railroads operating on 5,136 miles (8,269 kilometers) of railroad track. As of 2006, regularly scheduled Amtrak passenger trains served Indianapolis, Hammond/Whiting, South Bend, and seven other stations in the state. Indianapolis and other major cities have public transit systems subsidized heavily by the state and federal governments. The South

Shore commuter railroad connects South Bend, Gary, and East Chicago with Chicago, Illinois.

Major highways include the east–west National Road (US 40), and the north–south Michigan road (US 421). In 2003, there were 94,597 miles (152,301 kilometers) of public roads in the state. In 2004, motor vehicle registrations totaled 5.587 million, including 3.043 million passenger cars and 2.382 million trucks.

Water transportation has been important from the earliest years of European settlement. The Wabash and Erie Canal, constructed in the 1830s from Fort Wayne east to Toledo, Ohio, and southwest to Lafayette, was vital to the state's market economy. The transport of freight via Lake Michigan and the Ohio River helped to spark Indiana's industrial development. A deep-water port on Lake Michigan, which became operational in 1970, provided access to world markets via the St. Lawrence Seaway. Indiana Harbor and the port of Gary are leading ports.

In 2005, there were 629 public and private use aviation facilities in the state, including 492 airports, 121 heliports, 3 STOLports (Short Take-Off and Landing), and 13 seaplane bases. The state's main airport is Indianapolis International Airport. In 2004, it handled 3,992,097 boardings.

11 History

The first Native Americans to be seen by Europeans in present-day Indiana were probably the Miami and Potawatomi tribes. The first European penetration was made in the 1670s by the French explorers Father Jacques Marquette and Robert Cavelier, Sieur de la Salle. After the founding of Detroit, Michigan, in 1701, the Maumee-Wabash river route to the lower Ohio

was discovered. The first French fort was built farther down the Wabash among the Wea tribe, near present-day Lafayette, in 1717.

By 1765, Indiana had fallen to the English. The pre-Revolutionary turmoil in the colonies on the Atlantic was hardly felt in Indiana. However, the region did not escape the Revolutionary War itself. Colonel George Rogers Clark, acting for Virginia, captured Vincennes from a British garrison early in 1779. Following the war, the area northwest of the Ohio River was granted to the new nation by treaty in 1783.

The first US town plotted in Indiana was Clarksville, established in 1784. A government for the region was established by the Continental Congress under the Northwest Ordinance of 1787. Known as the Northwest Territory, it included present-day Indiana, Ohio, Illinois, Michigan, Wisconsin, and part of Minnesota. After continued Native American unrest, General Anthony Wayne was put in command of an enlarged army, which ended the disturbance in 1794 at Fallen Timbers (near Toledo, Ohio).

Statehood In 1800, as Ohio prepared to enter the Union, the rest of the Northwest Territory was set off and called Indiana Territory, with its capital at Vincennes. After Michigan Territory was detached in 1805, and Illinois Territory in 1809, Indiana assumed its present boundaries (having added about 10 miles to its northern border in 1816). William Henry Harrison was appointed first governor and, with a secretary and three appointed judges, constituted the government of Indiana Territory. When the population totaled 60,000—as it did in 1815—the voters were allowed to elect delegates to write a state constitution and to apply for admission to the Union. Indiana became the 19th state on 11 December 1816.

After the War of 1812, new settlers began pouring into the state from the upper South and in fewer numbers from Ohio, Pennsylvania, New York, and New England. In 1816, Thomas Lincoln brought his family from Kentucky, and his son Abe grew up in southern Indiana from age 7 to 21. Unlike most other frontier states, Indiana was settled from south to north. Central and northern Indiana were opened up as land was purchased from the Native Americans. Railroads began to tie Indiana commercially with the East. Irish immigrants dug canals and laid the rails, and German immigrants took up woodworking and farming. Levi Coffin, a Quaker who moved to Fountain City in 1826, operated the Underground Railroad, a network of people dedicated to help escaping slaves from the South.

Civil War   Hoosiers (as Indianans are called) showed considerable sympathy with the South in the 1850s. However, Indiana remained staunchly in the Union under Governor Oliver P. Morton, sending some 200,000 soldiers to the Civil War. The state suffered no battles, but General John Hunt Morgan's Confederate cavalry raided the southeastern sector of Indiana in July 1863.

After the Civil War, small local industries expanded rapidly. Discovery of natural gas in several northeastern counties in 1886, and the resultant low fuel prices, spurred the growth of energy-intensive glass factories. As America became captivated by the automobile, a racetrack for testing cars was built outside Indianapolis in 1908, and the famous 500-mile (805-kilometer) race on Memorial Day weekend began in 1911.

Five years earlier, US Steel had constructed a steel plant at the south end of Lake Michigan. The town built by the company to house the workers was called Gary, and it grew rapidly with the help of the company and the onset of World War I.

World Wars Although many Hoosiers of German and Irish descent favored neutrality when World War I began, Indiana industries boomed with war orders, and public sympathy swung heavily toward the Allies. Indiana furnished 118,000 men and women to the armed forces and suffered the loss of 3,370.

After 1920, only about a dozen makes of cars were still being manufactured in Indiana, and those factories steadily lost out to the three largest car makers in Detroit. Auto parts continued to be a big business, however, along with steelmaking and oil-refining in the Calumet region. Elsewhere there was manufacturing of machinery, farm implements, railway cars, furniture, and pharmaceuticals. Meat-packing, coal-mining, and limestone-quarrying continued to be important. With increasing industrialization, cities grew, particularly in the northern half of the state, and the number of farms diminished. The balance of rural and urban population, about even in 1920, tilted in favor of urban dwellers.

World War II had a greater impact on Indiana than did World War I. Most factories converted to production of war materials, and 300 of them held defense orders in 1942. Military training facilities were created. Camp Atterbury covered 100 square miles (259 square kilometers) in Bartholomew County, and two air stations trained aviators. Two large ammunition depots loaded and stored shells, and the enor-

Indiana Governors: 1816–2007

Years	Governor	Party		Years	Governor	Party
1816–1822	Johathan Jennings	Dem-Rep		1913–1917	Samuel Moffett Ralston	Democrat
1822	Ratliff Boone	Jackson Democrat		1917–1921	James Putnam Goodrich	Republican
1822–1825	William Hendricks	Dem-Rep		1921–1924	Warren Terry McCray	Republican
1825–1831	James Brown Ray	Anti–Jacksonian/Indep		1924–1925	Emmett Forest Branch	Republican
1831–1837	Noah Noble	Nat-Rep/Whig		1925–1929	Edward L. Jackson	Republican
1837–1840	David Wallace	Whig		1929–1933	Harry Guyer Leslie	Republican
1840–1843	Samuel Bigger	Whig		1933–1937	Paul Vories McNutt	Democrat
1843–1848	James Whitcomb	Democrat		1937–1941	Mourice Clifford Townsend	Democrat
1848–1849	Paris Chipman Dunning	Democrat		1941–1945	Henry Frederick Schricker	Democrat
1849–1857	Joseph Albert Wright	Unionist		1945–1949	Ralph Fesler Gates	Republican
1857–1860	Ashbel Parsons Willard	Democrat		1949–1953	Henry Frederick Schricker	Democrat
1860–1861	Abram Adams Hammond	Democrat		1953–1957	George North Craig	Republican
1861	Henry Smith Lane	Republican		1957–1961	Harold Willis Handley	Republican
1861–1867	Oliver Hazzard Perry Morton	Republican		1961–1965	Matthew Empson Welsh	Democrat
1867–1873	Conrad Baker	Republican		1965–1969	Roger Douglas Branigin	Democrat
1873–1877	Thomas Andrews Hendricks	Democrat		1969–1973	Edgar Doud Whitcomb	Republican
1877–1880	James Douglas Williams	Democrat		1973–1981	Otis Ray Bowen	Republican
1880–1881	Isaac Pusey Gray	Democrat		1981–1989	Robert Dunkerson Orr	Republican
1881–1885	Albert Gallatin Porter	Republican		1989–1997	Evan Bayh	Democrat
1885–1889	Isaac Pusey Gray	Democrat		1997–2003	Frank O'Bannon	Democrat
1889–1891	Alvin Peterson Hovey	Republican		2003–2004	Joseph Kernan	Democrat
1891–1893	Ira Joy Chase	Republican		2004–	Mitch Daniels	Republican
1893–1897	Claude Matthews	Democrat				
1897–1901	James Atwell Mount	Republican				
1901–1905	Winfield Taylor Durbin	Republican		Democratic Republican – Dem-Rep		
1905–1909	James Franklin Hanly	Republican		Independent – Indep		
1909–1913	Thomas Riley Marshall	Democrat		National Republican – Nat-Rep		

mous Jefferson Proving Grounds tested ammunition and parachutes.

Post-War Period After the war, many small local industries were taken over by national corporations, and their plants were expanded. By 1984, the largest employer in Indiana was General Motors, with 47,800 employees in six cities. Inland Steel, with 18,500 workers, was second, followed by US Steel with 13,800 workers.

Nostalgia for an older, simpler, rural way of life pervades much Hoosier thinking. The state's conservation efforts were guided by Richard Lieber, a state official from 1933 to 1944, promoted the preservation of land for state parks and recreational areas, as well as for state and federal forests.

Hoosiers enjoy politics and participate intensively in conventions and elections. The percentage of registered voters who vote has generally exceeded the national average by a wide margin. The state legislature was dominated by rural interests until a 1966 reorganization gave urban counties more representation.

In October 1999, Indiana saw its first African American, Justice Robert D. Rucker, named to the state's supreme court.

On 8 September 2003, Indiana's governor Frank O'Bannon, who had named Justice Rucker to the state's highest court, suffered a massive stroke and died five days later. O'Bannon was

Indiana Presidential Vote by Political Parties, 1948–2004

YEAR	INDIANA WINNER	DEMOCRAT	REPUBLICAN	PROGRESSIVE	PROHIBITION
1948	Dewey (R)	807,833	821,079	9,649	14,711
1952	*Eisenhower (R)	801,530	1,136,259	1,222	15,335
1956	*Eisenhower (R)	783,908	1,182,811	—	6,554
1960	*Nixon (R)	952,358	1,175,120	—	6,746
1964	*Johnson (D)	1,170,848	911,118	—	8,266
				AMERICAN IND.	
1968	*Nixon (R)	806,659	1,067,885	243,108	4,616
				PEOPLE'S	**SOC. WORKERS**
1972	*Nixon (R)	708,568	1,405,154	4,544	5,575
				AMERICAN	
1976	Ford (R)	1,014,714	1,185,958	14,048	5,695
				CITIZENS	**LIBERTARIAN**
1980	*Reagan (R)	844,197	1,255,656	4,852	19,627
1984	*Reagan (R)	841,481	1,377,230	—	6,741
				NEW ALLIANCE	
1988	*Bush (R)	860,643	1,297,763	10,215	—
				IND. (PEROT)	
1992	Bush (R)	848,420	989,375	455,934	7,936
1996	Dole (R)	887,424	1,006,693	224,299	15,632
					REFORM
2000	*Bush, G. W. (R)	901,980	1,245,836	18,531	16,959
2004	*Bush, G. W. (R)	969,011	1,479,438	—	—

* Won US presidential election.

replaced by Lieutenant Governor Joe Kernan, who was defeated in November 2004 by Republican Mitch Daniels Jr.

Upon taking office in 2005, Daniels moved to fix the state's $700 million budget shortfall. Daniels called for strict spending controls, and a one-time, one-year tax hike of 1% on all residents with incomes of $100,000 or more.

12 State Government

Indiana's first constitution, which took effect in 1816, prohibited slavery and recommended a free public school system, including a state university. The constitution did not allow for amendment, so a new one was adopted in 1851, which is still in force. It had been amended 46 times as of January 2005.

The Indiana General Assembly consists of a fifty-member Senate elected to four-year terms, with half the senators elected every two years, and a one hundred-member House of Representatives elected to two-year terms. The state's chief executive is the governor, elected to a four-year term. The governor may call special sessions of the legislature and may veto bills passed by the legislature, but his veto can be overridden by a majority vote in each house.

Indiana's other top elected officials are the lieutenant governor, secretary of state, treasurer, auditor, attorney general, and superintendent of public instruction. Each is elected to a four-year term. The lieutenant governor is constitutionally empowered to preside over the state senate and to act as governor if that office should become vacant, or the governor is unable to discharge his duties. Legislation may be introduced in either house of the General Assembly, although bills for raising revenue must originate in the House of Representatives.

As of December 2004, the governor's salary was $95,000, and the legislative salary was $11,600.

13 Political Parties

After voting Republican in four successive presidential elections, Indiana voted Democratic in 1876 and became a swing state. More recently, a Republican trend has been evident, as the state voted Republican in 16 out of 17 presidential elections between 1940 and 2004.

In 2004, Indiana gave 60% of the vote to Republican George W. Bush and 39% to Democrat John Kerry. In that same year, Governor Joseph E. Kernan was defeated by Republican Mitch Daniels, but Democrat Evan Bayh was reelected to the US Senate. The state's other senate seat was held by Republican Richard Lugar, who won re-election to the Senate in 2006. Indiana's delegation to the US House of Representatives following the 2006 elections included five Democrats and four Republicans. Following the 2006 elections, the state senate had 33 Republicans and 17 Democrats. In the state house of representatives, there were 51 Democrats and 49 Republicans. Following the 2006 elections, there were 27 women serving in the state legislature, or 18%. In 2004 there were 4,009,000 registered voters in the state. There is no party registration in the state.

14 Local Government

Indiana's 92 counties have traditionally provided law enforcement in rural areas, operated county courts and institutions, maintained county roads, administered public welfare programs, and collected taxes. In 1984, counties were given the power to impose local income taxes. The county's business is conducted by a board of county commissioners, consisting of three members elected to four-year terms.

Townships (1,008 in 2002) provide assistance for the poor, and assess taxable property. Each township is administered by a trustee elected to a four-year term. Indiana had 567 municipal governments in 2005. They are governed by elected city councils. In 2005, Indiana had 294 public school districts and 1,125 special districts.

15 Judicial System

The Indiana supreme court consists of 5 justices who are appointed by the governor. The state court of appeals consists of 15 justices. The court exercises appeals jurisdiction under rules set by the state supreme court. Superior courts, probate courts, and circuit courts all function as general trial courts and are presided over by 279 judges who serve a term of 6 years. Indiana had 24,008 prisoners in its state and federal correctional facilities as of 31 December 2004. Indiana in 2004, had a violent crime rate (murder/nonnegligent manslaughter, forcible rape, robbery, aggravated assault) of 325.4 incidents per 100,000 people statewide. Indiana has a death penalty, of which lethal injection is the sole method of execution. As of 1 January 2006, there were 26 inmates on death row.

16 Migration

Indiana's early settlers were predominantly northern Europeans who migrated from eastern and southern states. The principal migratory pattern since 1920 has been within the state, from the farms to the cities. Since World War II, Indiana has lost population through a growing migratory movement to other states, mostly to Florida and the Southwest.

Between 1990 and 1998, the state had a net gain of 76,000 persons through domestic migration and a net gain of 25,000 in international migration. In 1998, 3,981 foreign immigrants arrived in Indiana. In the period 2000–05, some 55,656 people arrived in the state from other countries, while 17,000 people left the state to move to other states, giving the state a net gain of 38,656 people.

17 Economy

Indiana is both a leading agricultural and industrial state. The state's industrial development in Indianapolis, Gary, and other cities was based on its plentiful natural resources—coal, natural gas, timber, stone, and clay—and on good transportation facilities. The northwestern corner of the state is the site of one of the world's greatest concentrations of heavy industry, especially steel.

Until the end of the 20th century, manufacturing continued to grow, and between 1997 and 2000 accounted for about 30% of Indiana's total economic output. In the national recession of 2001, however, manufacturing output fell 9.2%. Many jobs were lost, although the unemployment rate remained below the national average. Indiana's gross state product (GSP) in 2004 was $227.569 billion, of which industry accounted for 27.8% of GSP, followed by real estate at 9.7%, and health care and social services at 7% of GSP. Of the 125,746 businesses in the state that had employees, 97.6% were small companies.

18 Income

In 2004, Indiana had a per capita (per person) personal income of $30,204, which was under the national average of $33,050. For the three-year period 2002 through 2004, the median household income was $43,003, compared to the national average of $44,473. For the same period, 10.2% of the state's residents lived below the federal poverty level, compared to the national average of 12.4%.

19 Industry

The industrialization of Indiana that began in the Civil War era was spurred by technological advances in processing agricultural products, manufacturing farm equipment, and improving transportation facilities. Meat-packing plants, textile mills, furniture factories, and wagon works—including Studebaker wagons—were soon followed by metal foundries, machine shops, farm implement plants, and various other durable-goods plants.

In 2004, the shipment value of all products manufactured in Indiana was $183.563 billion. Among the leading industry groups were transportation equipment, primary metal products, chemicals, food products, and fabricated metal products. Indiana is also a leading producer of compact discs, elevators, storage batteries, small motors and generators, mobile homes, household furniture, burial caskets, and musical instruments. Most manufacturing plants are located in and around Indianapolis and in the Calumet region.

In 2004, the state's manufacturing sector employed 534,942 people.

20 Labor

In April 2006, the civilian labor force in Indiana numbered 3,252,000, with approximately 159,500 workers unemployed, yielding an unemployment rate of 4.9%, compared to the national average of 4.7% for the same period. Preliminary nonfarm employment data for April 2006 showed that 5.1% of the labor force was employed in construction; 19.2% in manufacturing; 19.6% in trade, transportation, and public utilities; 4.7% in financial activities; 9.2% in professional and business services; 12.8% in educational and health services; 9.4% in leisure and hospitality services; and 14.3% in government.

Most industrial workers live in Indianapolis and the Calumet area of northwestern Indiana. The American Federation of Labor (AFL) first attempted to organize workers at the US Steel Company's plant in Gary in 1919, but a strike to get union recognition failed. By 1936, however, the Congress of Industrial Organizations (CIO) had won bargaining rights, and the 40-hour workweek from US Steel and union organization spread to other industries throughout the state.

In 2005, a total of 346,000 of Indiana's 2,789,000 employed wage and salary workers were members of a union. This represented 12.4% of those employed, and just above the national average of 12%. The majority of the workers belonged to unions affiliated with the AFL-CIO.

The Oliver chilled plow was developed by James Oliver, an industrialist who came to South Bend, Indiana, in the 1850s. A superior farm plow made of chilled and hardened steel, it revolutionized farming in the later half of the 19th century. NORTHERN INDIANA HISTORICAL SOCIETY.

21 Agriculture

Agriculture in Indiana is a large and diverse industry that plays a vital role in the economy. The state had 59,300 farms containing 15,000,000 acres (6,800,000 hectares) of farmland. In 2005, cash receipts from the sale of all commodities (crops and livestock) reached $5.4 billion. In the same year, Indiana ranked 16th in the United States in cash receipts from the sale of all commodities.

Over 80% of Indiana's farm operators live on the farm, while more than 55% of farmers have a principal occupation other than farming.

Corn and soybeans are Indiana's two main crops. In 2004 the state produced 929.04 million bushels of corn for grain, ranking fifth in the United States. Indiana also grew 287.04 million bushels of soybeans, the third most in the nation. Other principal field crops in 2004 included spearmint, peppermint, and cantaloupes.

22 Domesticated Animals

Indiana dairy farmers produced an estimated 2.9 billion pounds (1.3 billion kilograms) of milk from 149,000 milk cows in 2003. The state's poultry farmers sold an estimated 24.8 million pounds (11.3 million kilograms) of chicken, and an estimated 396.8 million pounds (179.985 million kilograms) of turkey during 2003. Indiana had an estimated 850,000 cattle and calves worth around $799 million in 2005.

23 Fishing

Fishing is not of commercial importance in Indiana, although fishing for bass, pike, perch, catfish, and trout is a popular sport with Indiana anglers. In 2004, there were 522,389 sport fishing licenses issued by the state. There are eight state fish hatcheries.

24 Forestry

About 20% of Indiana's total land area was forested in 2004. Indiana has 4,501,000 acres (1,822,000 hectares) of forestland, of which 96%, or 4,342,000 acres (1,757,000 hectares), is considered commercial timberland. Some 75% of the commercial forestland is located in the southern half of Indiana, where oak, hickory, beech, maple, yellow poplar, and ash predominate in the uplands. Soft maple, sweetgum, pin oak, cottonwood, sycamore, and river birch are the most common species found in wetlands and drainage corridors.

Indiana's wood-using industries manufacture everything from the "crinkle" center lining in cardboard boxes to the finest furniture in the world. Other wood products include pallets, desks, fancy face veneer, millwork, flooring, mobile homes, and recreational vehicle components. In 2004, Indiana produced 333 million board feet of lumber. Indiana has always been noted for the quality of its hardwood forests and the trees it produces.

25 Mining

The value of nonfuel mineral production in Indiana in 2004 was $764 million. Nationally, Indiana ranked 22nd in value of nonfuel mineral production. In 2004, cement (portland and masonry) was Indiana's top nonfuel mineral by value, followed by crushed stone, construction sand and gravel, and lime, which together accounted for 92% of all nonfuel mineral output by the states. The state's top two mineral commodities by output were crushed stone (2001 estimated output 56 million metric tons) and cement (portland cement production was estimated at 2.86 million metric tons).

26 Energy and Power

Indiana is largely dependent on fossil fuels for its energy supplies. In recent years, petroleum has become an important power source for automobiles, home heating, and electricity. Nevertheless, coal has continued to be the state's major source of power, meeting about half of Indiana's energy needs.

The Indianapolis skyline featuring the Indiana Convention Center & RCA Dome. The RCA Dome is the home of the Indianapolis Colts professional football team. ROB BANAYOTE.

The state has no nuclear power plants. Electric power produced in Indiana in 2003 totaled 124.888 billion kilowatt hours, with total net summer generating capacity at 25.640 million kilowatts. Of the total produced, 94.3% came from coal-fired plants.

As of 2004, Indiana's proven reserves of crude oil totaled 11 million barrels, with production at 5,000 barrels per day in that same year. Natural gas production in 2004 totaled 1.464 billion cubic feet (0.041 billion cubic meters). Data was unavailable as to the state's proven reserves of natural gas.

In 2004 there were 29 producing coal mines in Indiana, of which 7 were underground and 22 were strip (surface) mines. Indiana's coal production in that same year totaled 35.11 million tons. Recoverable reserves totaled 398 million tons in 2004.

27 Commerce

Indiana's wholesale trade sector in 2002 had sales of $79.8 billion, while the state's retail trade sector had sales that same year of $67.2 billion. Indiana ranked 11th among the 50 states in exports during 2005, when its goods shipped abroad were valued at $21.4 billion.

28 Public Finance

The State Budget Agency acts as a watchdog over state financial affairs. The agency prepares the budget for the governor and presents it to the

General Assembly. The fiscal year runs from 1 July to 30 June of the following year.

The total revenues for 2004 were $26.9 billion, with total expenditures that same year of were $25.37 billion. The largest general expenditures were for education ($9.04 billion), public welfare ($5.67 billion), and highways ($1.9 billion). The total indebtedness of the state government in 2004 stood at $13.07 billion, or $2,100.50 per person.

29 Taxation

Indiana has a general state sales tax of 6%. As of 1 January 2006, the state had a single individual income tax rate of 3.4%, and a flat corporate tax rate of 8.5%. Indiana also imposes an excise tax on cigarettes and gasoline. Food is not subject to the state sales tax, if it is consumed off premises (such as at home).

In 2005, state tax collections totaled $12.854 billion, with 38.9% generated by the state sales taxes, 32.8% by the state personal income tax, 17.1% by state excise taxes, 6.4% by the state corporate income tax, and 4.8% from other taxes. Indiana ranked 31st among the 50 states in per capita (per person) tax burden at $2,049, compared to the national average of $2,192.

30 Health

In October 2005, Indiana had an infant death rate estimated at 7.9 per 1,000 live births. In 2003, the state's crude death rate stood at 9.1 per 1,000 inhabitants. The principal causes of death were heart disease, cerebrovascular diseases, chronic lower respiratory diseases, and diabetes. About 24.8% of the state's residents were smokers in 2004. The rate of HIV-related deaths stood at 1.9 per 100,000 population. The reported AIDS case rate was about 6.3 per 100,000 people in 2004.

Indiana's 112 community hospitals had about 18,900 beds in 2003. There were 834 nurses per 100,000 people in 2005, and 222 physicians per 100,000 people in 2004. In that same year, Indiana had 2,939 dentists. In 2003, the average expense of community hospital care was $1,352 per day. In 2004, about 14% of the population was uninsured.

31 Housing

In 2004, the state had an estimated 2,690,619 housing units, of which 2,412,885 were occupied, 71.8% by the owner. About 21% of all units were built before 1939. About 71.5% of all units were single-family, detached homes. Most units relied on utility gas and electricity for heating, but about 1,030 units were equipped for solar power. It was estimated that 158,051 units lacked telephone service, while 10,304 lacked complete plumbing facilities, and 12,973 lacked complete kitchen facilities. The average household size was 2.51 people.

In 2004, the construction of 39,200 privately owned housing units were authorized. The median home value was $110,020. The median monthly cost for mortgage owners was $963. Renters paid a median of $589 per month.

32 Education

Although the 1816 constitution recommended establishment of public schools, the state legislature did not provide funds for education. The constitution of 1851 more specifically outlined the state's responsibility to support a system of free public schools. In 2004, of those aged 25 years and over, 87.2% were high school graduates, and 21.1% had completed four or more years of college.

Total enrollment in public schools was estimated at 1,009,000 in fall 2003, and was expected to reach 1,029,000 by fall 2014. Enrollment in nonpublic schools in fall 2003 was 109,101. Expenditures for public education in 2003/04 were estimated at $10 billion.

As of fall 2002, there were 342,064 students enrolled in college or graduate school. In 2005, Indiana had 101 degree-granting institutions. Indiana University, the state's largest institution of higher education, was founded in 1820. It is one of the largest state universities in the United States, with a total of eight campuses. The Bloomington campus has a nationally recognized music program. Other major state universities include Purdue University (Lafayette), Ball State University (Muncie), and Indiana State University (Terre Haute). Well-known private universities in the state include Notre Dame (at South Bend) and Butler (Indianapolis). Small private colleges and universities include DePauw (Greencastle), Earlham (Richmond), Hanover (Hanover), and Wabash (Crawfordsville).

33 Arts

The earliest center for artists in Indiana was the Art Association of Indianapolis, founded in 1883. Around 1900, art colonies sprang up in Richmond, Muncie, South Bend, and Nashville. Indianapolis remains the state's cultural center. Since 1969, the Indiana Arts Commission has taken art and artists into many Indiana communities. The commission also sponsors biennial awards to artists in the state.

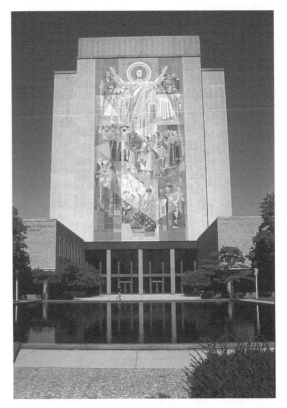

University of Notre Dame, Hesburgh Library. SOUTH BEND/MISHAWAKA CONVENTION AND VISITORS BUREAU.

The state's first resident theater company was established in Indianapolis in 1840 and the first theater building, the Metropolitan, was opened there in 1858. Ten years later, the Academy of Music was founded as the center for dramatic activities in Indianapolis. In 1875, the Grand Opera House opened there and the following year it was joined by the English Opera House. Amateur theater has been popular since the 1915 founding of the nation's oldest amateur drama group, the Little Theater Society, which later became the Civic Theater of Indianapolis.

Music has flourished in Indiana. Connersville reportedly was the first American city to establish a high school band, while Richmond claims the first high school symphony orchestra. The Indianapolis Symphony Orchestra was founded in 1930. There are 23 other symphony orchestras in the state. Indianapolis Opera was founded in 1975. The annual Indiana Fiddlers' Gathering, founded in 1973, is a three-day festival featuring the bluegrass, swing fiddle, string band, and Celtic and other ethnic music.

The Indiana Humanities Council sponsors programs that include Habits of the Heart, a youth volunteer leadership development program, and History Alive, an educational program featuring live portrayals of famous historical figures.

34 Libraries and Museums

In 2001 there were 239 public library systems in Indiana, with a total of 430 libraries, of which 191 were branches. The largest book collections are at public libraries in Indianapolis, Fort Wayne, Gary, Evansville, Merrillville, and Hammond. The total book stock of all Indiana public libraries was 22.14 million volumes in 2001, with a total circulation of 62.7 million.

The Indiana State Library has a large collection of documents about Indiana's history and a large genealogical collection. The Indiana University Library has special collections on American literature and history and an extensive collection of rare books. The University of Notre Dame has a noteworthy collection on medieval history. Also of note are the General Lew Wallace Study Museum in Crawfordsville, and the Elwood Haynes Museum of early technology in Kokomo.

In 2000, Indiana had 179 museums. Many county historical societies maintain smaller museums, such as the Wayne County Historical Museum. Indiana's historic sites include the Lincoln Boyhood National Memorial near Gentryville, the Levi Coffin Home (one of the Underground Railroad stops) in Fountain City, and the Benjamin Harrison Memorial Home in Indianapolis.

35 Communications

In 2004, about 91.8% of all households had telephone service. The state's first radio station was licensed in 1922 at Purdue University, Lafayette. Indiana had 20 major AM, 102 major FM radio stations, and 30 television stations as of 2005. Powerful radio and television transmissions from Chicago and Cincinnati also blanket the state. In 1999, the Indianapolis area had 963,320 television households, 65% of which received cable. A total of 73,696 Internet domain names were registered in the state in 2000.

In 2003, computers were in 59.6% of all Indiana households, while 51% had Internet access. As of June 2004, there were over 2.8 million mobile telephone service subscribers.

36 Press

In 2005, the state had 24 morning dailies, 44 evening dailies, and 25 Sunday papers. In 2005, the morning *Indianapolis Star* had a daily circulation of 252,021 (Sunday circulation, 358,261), while the circulation of Gary's *Post-Tribune* averaged 65,621 daily and 73,795 on Sundays.

A number of national magazines are published in Indiana, including *Children's Digest* and *The Saturday Evening Post*.

Many Hoosier authors were first published by Indiana's major book publisher, Bobbs-Merrill. Indiana University Press is an important publisher of scholarly books.

37 Tourism, Travel & Recreation

In 2004, there were about 57.7 million visitors to the state, who spent $6.5 billion. The tourist industry supported about 94,000 full-time jobs.

About 70% of visitors participate in outdoor activities, many within one of three national parks. Summer resorts are located in the north, along Lake Michigan and in Steuben and Kosciusko counties, where there are nearly 200 lakes. Popular tourist sites include the reconstructed village of New Harmony, site of famous communal living experiments in the early 19th century; the Indianapolis Motor Speedway and Museum; and the George Rogers Clark National Historic Park at Vincennes.

Among the natural attractions are the Indiana Dunes National Lakeshore on Lake Michigan; the state's largest waterfall, Cataract Falls, near Cloverdale; and the largest underground cavern, at Wyandotte.

Indiana has 23 state parks, comprising 59,292 acres (21,800 hectares). The largest state park is Brown County (15,543 acres—6,290 hectares), near Nashville. There are 15 state fish and wildlife preserves, totaling about 75,200 acres (30,400 hectares).

38 Sports

Professional teams in Indiana include the Indiana Pacers of the National Basketball Association, the Indiana Fever of the Women's National

A kayaker looking at Century Center, South Bend. SOUTH BEND/MISHAWAKA CONVENTION AND VISITORS BUREAU.

Basketball Association, and the National Football League's Colts, who moved to Indianapolis from Baltimore in 1984. There are also several minor league baseball, basketball, and hockey teams in the state.

The state's biggest annual sports event is the Indianapolis 500. The race is now part of a three-day Indiana festival held over Memorial Day weekend that attracts crowds of over 300,000 spectators, the largest crowd for any sporting event anywhere in the world.

The state's most popular amateur sport is basketball. The high school tournaments for both boys and girls are big events. Basketball is also popular at the college level, with teams from Indiana University, Purdue University, and Indiana State holding a number of championship titles. Evansville College won the NCAA Division II championships three times.

College football is also popular. The Fighting Irish football team from the University of Notre Dame competes as an independent team. They have won ten bowl games. Football teams from Indiana University and Purdue University compete in the Big Ten. The team from Indiana State University is part of the Missouri Valley Conference.

The Little 500, a 50-mile (80-kilometer) bicycle race, is held each spring at Indiana University's Bloomington campus.

Other annual sporting events include the National Muzzle-loading Rifle Association Championship Shoot, which is held in Friendship in September, and the Sugar Creek canoe race, which is held in Crawfordsville in April.

39 Famous Indianans

Indiana has contributed one US president and five vice-presidents to the nation. Benjamin Harrison (b.Ohio, 1833–1901), the 23rd president, was a Republican who served one term (1889–1893) and then returned to Indianapolis, where his home is now a national historic landmark. Three vice-presidents were Indiana residents: Thomas Hendricks (b.Ohio, 1819–1885), who served only eight months under President Cleveland and died in office; Schuyler Colfax (b.New York, 1823–1885), who served under President Grant; and Charles Fairbanks (b.Ohio, 1852–1918), who served under Theodore Roosevelt. Two vice-presidents were native sons: Thomas Marshall of North Manchester (1854–1925), who served two four-year terms with President Wilson;

James Whitcomb Riley (1849–1916) was one of Indiana's best known poets. EPD PHOTOS.

and J(ames) Danforth Quayle of Indianapolis (b.1947), who served with President George H. W. Bush during 1989–93.

Only one Hoosier, Sherman Minton (1890–1965), has served on the US Supreme Court. Ambrose Burnside (1824–1881), and Lew Wallace (1827–1905) were Union generals during the Civil War.

Harold C. Urey (1893–1981) won the Nobel Prize in chemistry in 1934, and Wendell Stanley (1904–1971) won it in 1946. The Nobel Prize in economics was awarded to Paul Samuelson (b. 1915) in 1970. Booth Tarkington (1869–1946) won the Pulitzer Prize for fiction in 1918 and

1921. A. B. Guthrie (1901–1991) won it for fiction in 1950. Aviation pioneer Wilbur Wright (1867–1912) was born in Millville.

Juvenile writer Annie Fellows Johnston (1863–1931) produced the "Little Colonel" series. Other notable Indiana novelists include Theodore Dreiser (1871–1945), Jessamyn West (1907–1984), and Kurt Vonnegut (b.1922).

Composers of Indiana origin have worked mainly in popular music: Cole Porter (1893–1964) and Howard Hoagland "Hoagy" Carmichael (1899–1981). Entertainers from Indiana include David Letterman (b.1947) and singer Michael Jackson (b.1958).

Hoosier sports heroes include Knute Rockne (b.Norway, 1888–1931), famed as a football player and coach at Notre Dame. Larry Bird (b.1956) was college basketball's player of the year at Indiana State University in 1978/79 and went on to play for the Boston Celtics of the NBA in the 1980s; in 1998 he became head coach of the NBA's Indiana Pacers.

40 Bibliography

BOOKS

Brill, Marlene Targ. *Indiana*. New York: Marshall Cavendish Benchmark, 2006.

Bristow, M. J. *State Songs of America*. Westport, CT: Greenwood Press, 2000.

Brown, Jonatha A. *Indiana*. Milwaukee, WI: Gareth Stevens, 2006.

Fish, Bruce. *Indy Car Racing*. Philadelphia, PA: Chelsea House, 2000.

Heinrichs, Ann. *Indiana*. New York: Children's Press, 2000.

McAuliffe, Bill. *Indiana Facts and Symbols*. Rev. ed. Mankato, MN: Capstone, 2003.

Murray, Julie. *Indiana*. Edina, MN: Abdo Publishing, 2006.

Nelson, Julie. *Indianapolis Colts*. Mankato, MN: Creative Education, 2000.

WEB SITES

Government of Indiana. *www.IN.gov.* www.in.gov (accessed March 1, 2007).

Indiana Traveler: Regional Tourism Office & Information Links. www.indianatraveler.com/tourism.htm (accessed March 1, 2007).

Iowa

State of Iowa

ORIGIN OF STATE NAME: Named for Iowa Indians of the Siouan family.

NICKNAME: The Hawkeye State.

CAPITAL: Des Moines.

ENTERED UNION: 28 December 1846 (29th).

OFFICIAL SEAL: A sheaf and field of standing wheat and farm utensils represent agriculture; a lead furnace and a pile of pig lead are to the right. In the center stands a citizen-soldier holding a US flag with a liberty cap atop the staff in one hand and a rifle in the other. Behind him is the Mississippi River with the steamer *Iowa* and mountains; above him an eagle holds the state motto. Surrounding this scene are the words "The Great Seal of the State of Iowa" against a gold background.

FLAG: There are three vertical stripes of blue, white, and red; in the center a spreading eagle holds in its beak a blue ribbon with the state motto.

MOTTO: Our Liberties We Prize and Our Rights We Will Maintain.

SONG: "The Song of Iowa."

FLOWER: Wild rose.

TREE: Oak.

BIRD: Eastern goldfinch.

ROCK OR STONE: Geode.

LEGAL HOLIDAYS: New Year's Day, 1 January; Birthday of Martin Luther King Jr., 3rd Monday in January; Memorial Day, last Monday in May; Independence Day, 4 July; Labor Day, 1st Monday in September; Veterans' Day, 11 November; Thanksgiving Day, 4th Thursday in November; Christmas Day, 25 December.

TIME: 6 AM CST = noon GMT.

1 Location and Size

Located in the western north-central United States, Iowa is the smallest of the Midwestern states west of the Mississippi River and ranks 25th in size among the 50 states. The total area of Iowa is 56,275 square miles (145,752 square kilometers), of which land takes up 55,965 square miles (144,949 square kilometers) and inland water 310 square miles (803 square kilometers). The state extends 324 miles (521 kilometers) east-west and 210 miles (338 kilometers) north-south. Its total boundary length is 1,151 miles (1,853 kilometers).

2 Topography

The physical terrain of Iowa consists of a gently rolling plain that slopes from the highest point of 1,670 feet (509 meters) in the northwest to the lowest point of 480 feet (146 meters) in the southeast at the mouth of the Des Moines River. Iowa has the richest and deepest topsoil in the United States. The major rivers are the Mississippi River and the Missouri River. Iowa has 13 natural lakes. The largest are Spirit Lake, at about 9 miles (14 kilometers) long and West Okoboji Lake, at 6 miles (10 kilometers) long. Both are near the state's northwest border.

3 Climate

Iowa lies in the humid continental zone and generally has hot summers, cold winters, and wet springs. Temperatures vary widely during the year, with an annual average of 49°F (9°C). Des Moines, in the central part of the state, has a normal daily maximum temperature of 86°F (30°C) in July and a normal daily minimum of 11°F (-4°C) in January. The record low temperature for the state of Iowa is -47°F (–44°C), set as Washta on 12 January 1912. That record was matched on 3 February 1996 in Elkader. The record high is 118°F (48°C), set at Keokuk on 20 July 1934. Annual precipitation averages 32.4 inches (82 centimeters) in Des Moines. Average snowfall statewide is 33.2 inches (84 centimeters).

4 Plants and Animals

Although most of Iowa is under cultivation, such unusual wild specimens as bunchberry and bearberry can be found in the northeast. Other notable plants are pink lady's slipper and twin-

Iowa
Population Profile

Total population estimate in 2006:	2,982,085
Population change, 2000–06:	1.9%
Hispanic or Latino†:	3.7%
Population by race	
One race:	98.9%
White:	93.5%
Black or African American:	2.2%
American Indian /Alaska Native:	0.2%
Asian:	1.5%
Native Hawaiian / Pacific Islander:	0.0%
Some other race:	1.5%
Two or more races:	1.1%

Population by Age Group

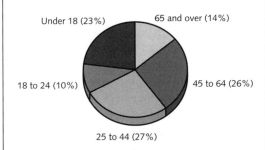

Under 18 (23%)
65 and over (14%)
18 to 24 (10%)
45 to 64 (26%)
25 to 44 (27%)

Major Cities by Population

City	Population	% change 2000–05
Des Moines	194,163	-2.3
Cedar Rapids	123,119	2.0
Davenport	98,845	0.5
Sioux	83,148	-2.2
Waterloo	66,483	-3.3
Iowa	62,887	1.1
Council Bluffs	59,568	2.2
Dubuque	57,798	0.2
West Des Moines	52,768	13.7
Ames	52,263	3.0

Notes: †A person of Hispanic or Latino origin may be of any race. NA indicates that data are not available. **Sources:** U.S. Census Bureau. *American Community Survey* and *Population Estimates.* www.census.gov/ (accessed March 2007).

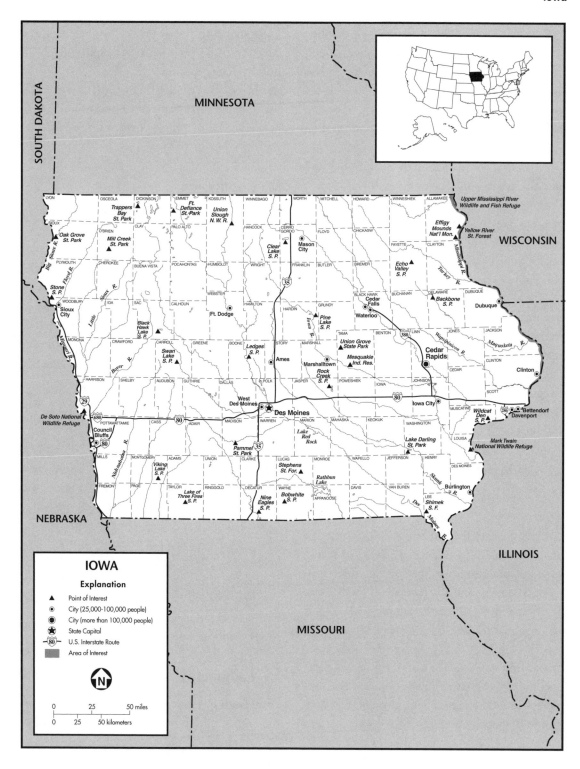

IOWA

Explanation

▲ Point of Interest

⊙ City (25,000-100,000 people)

◉ City (more than 100,000 people)

★ State Capital

—⟨80⟩— U.S. Interstate Route

▨ Area of Interest

Ⓝ

0   25   50 miles

0   25   50 kilometers

leaf. More than 80 native plants have become extinct in the area and at least 35 others are confined to a single location. The federal government classified five plant species as threatened as of April 2006. Among these are the northern wild monkshood and the eastern and western prairie fringed orchids.

Common Iowa mammals include red and gray foxes, raccoon, opossum, and woodchuck. Common birds include the cardinal, rose-breasted grosbeak, and eastern goldfinch (the state bird). Game fish include rainbow trout, smallmouth bass, and walleye. In all Iowa has 140 native fish species.

Rare animals include the pygmy shrew, ermine, black-billed cuckoo, and crystal darter. As of April 2006, the US Fish and Wildlife Service listed eight threatened or endangered species, including the Indiana bat, bald eagle, Higgins' eye pearlymussel, piping plover, Topeka Shiner, Iowa Pleistocene snail, pallid sturgeon, and least tern.

5 Environmental Protection

Conservation measures in Iowa are generally directed toward preventing soil erosion and preserving watershed runoff. Other concerns include with improving air quality, preventing chemical pollution, and preserving water supplies. In 1997, wetlands covered 1.2% of Iowa. The Wetlands Reserve Program of 1990 was created to reclaim some of the state's lost wetlands.

The Department of Water, Air and Waste Management, established in 1983, regulates operation of the state's 2,900 public water supply systems. The department also enforces laws prohibiting open dumping of solid wastes, monitors the handling of hazardous wastes, estab-

lishes standards for air quality, and regulates the emission of air pollutants from more than 600 industries and utilities.

In 2003, Iowa had 172 hazardous waste sites listed in the Environmental Protection Agency's database, 11 of which were on the National Priorities List in 2006.

6 Population

In 2005, Iowa ranked 30th of the 50 states in population with an estimated total of 2,982,085 residents. In 2004, population density was 52.9 persons per square mile (20.4 persons per square kilometer). The median age of all residents in 2004 was 38. In 2005, about 14% of the people were 65 or older while just over 23% were 18 or younger. In 2005, the largest cities and their estimated populations were Des Moines, 194,163 and Cedar Rapids, 123,119.

7 Ethnic Groups

In the 2000 census, Iowa had 61,853 black Americans, 8,989 Native Americans, and 82,473 Hispanics and Latinos living in the state. Among Iowans of European descent, there were 1,046,153 Germans, representing about 35.7% of the population. Other groups included 395,905 Irish residents and 277,487 English residents. The foreign-born population numbered 91,085. The primary countries of origin included Germany, Mexico, Laos, Canada, Korea, and Vietnam.

8 Languages

Iowa English reflects the three major migration streams: Northern in the half of the state above Des Moines, North Midland in the southern half,

Iowa Population by Race

Census 2000 was the first national census in which the instructions to respondents said, "Mark one or more races." This table shows the number of people who are of one, two, or three or more races. For those claiming two races, the number of people belonging to the various categories is listed. The U.S. government conducts a census of the population every ten years.

	Number	Percent
Total population	2,926,324	100.0
One race	2,894,546	98.9
Two races	29,959	1.0
White *and* Black or African American	7,856	0.3
White *and* American Indian/Alaska Native	7,075	0.2
White *and* Asian	4,369	0.1
White *and* Native Hawaiian/Pacific Islander	468	—
White *and* some other race	7,049	0.2
Black or African American *and* American Indian/Alaska Native	577	—
Black or African American *and* Asian	266	—
Black or African American *and* Native Hawaiian/Pacific Islander	46	—
Black or African American *and* some other race	634	—
American Indian/Alaska Native *and* Asian	198	—
American Indian/Alaska Native *and* Native Hawaiian/Pacific Islander	24	—
American Indian/Alaska Native *and* some other race	299	—
Asian *and* Native Hawaiian/Pacific Islander	275	—
Asian *and* some other race	750	—
Native Hawaiian/Pacific Islander *and* some other race	73	—
Three or more races	1,819	0.1

Source: U.S. Census Bureau. *Census 2000: Redistricting Data.* Press release issued by the Redistricting Data Office. Washington, D.C., March, 2001. A dash (—) indicates that the percent is less than 0.1.

and a slight South Midland trace in the extreme southeastern corner. Northern words that contrast with Midland words include: *crab* for *crawdad, corn on the cob* for *roasting ears, barnyard* for *barn lot*, and *gopher* for *ground squirrel*. In 2000, 94.2% of all Iowans aged five or more spoke only English at home. Other languages reported by Iowans, and the number speaking each at home, included Spanish, 79,491; German, 17,262; and French, 7,476.

9 Religions

The first church building in Iowa was constructed by Methodists in Dubuque in 1834. A Roman Catholic church was built in Dubuque the following year. Mainline Protestantism is predominant in the state even though the largest single Protestant denomination is the Evangelical Free Church of America, which had about 268,211 members in 2000. Other major Protestant denominations include the United Methodist Church (with 195,024 adherents in 2004), the Lutheran Church—Missouri Synod (120,075 adherents in 2000), the Presbyterian Church USA (69,974 adherents in 2000), and the United Church of Christ (36,326 adherents in 2005). Roman Catholic Church membership was about 506,698 in 2004. The Jewish community had about 6,400 members in 2000. Muslims numbered about 4,717. Nearly 41.5%

Des Moines has the largest skywalk system per capita in the world. GREATER DES MOINES CONVENTION AND VISITORS BUREAU.

(over 1.2 million) of the state population did not specify a religious affiliation.

10 Transportation

The early settlers came to Iowa by way of the Ohio and Mississippi rivers and the Great Lakes, then traveled overland on trails via wagon and stagecoach. The need of Iowa farmers to haul their products to market over long distances prompted the development of the railroads.

In 2003, Iowa had 4,248 miles (6,839 kilometers) of track. Amtrak operates the long-distance California Zephyr (Chicago to Oakland, California) and Southwest Chief (Chicago to Los Angeles, California), serving six major stations in Iowa.

Iowa had 113,377 miles (182,462 kilometers) of public roadway in 2004. In 2004, there were 3,461,000 registered vehicles in the state, including 1,872,000 automobiles, 1,448,000 trucks, and around 1,000 buses. There were 2,003,723 licensed drivers.

Iowa is bordered by two great navigable rivers, the Mississippi and the Missouri. They provided excellent transport facilities for the early settlers via keelboats and paddle-wheel steamers. Today, rivers remain an important part of Iowa's intermodal transportation system, providing shippers a gateway to an extensive inland waterway system that has access to ports in St. Paul, Chicago, Pittsburgh, Houston, and New Orleans. Most docks in Iowa are privately owned and all are privately operated.

Iowa's busiest airfield is Des Moines Municipal Airport, which handled 975,859 passengers in 2004.

11 History

The first permanent settlers of the land were the Woodland Indians, who built villages in the forested areas along the Mississippi River and introduced agriculture. Not until June 1673 did the first known white men, explorer Louis Jolliet and the Catholic priest Jacques Marquette, come to the territory. Iowa was part of the vast Louisiana Territory that extended from the Gulf of Mexico to the Canadian border and was ruled by the French until the title was transferred to Spain in 1762.

Napoleon took the territory back in 1800 and then promptly sold all of Louisiana Territory to the amazed American envoys who had come to Paris seeking only the purchase of New Orleans and the mouth of the Mississippi. After Iowa had thus come under US control in 1803, the Lewis and Clark expedition worked its way up the Missouri River to explore the newly purchased land.

Placed under the territorial jurisdiction of Michigan in 1834, and then two years later under the newly created Territory of Wisconsin, Iowa became a separate territory in 1838. The first territorial governor, Robert Lucas, began planning for statehood by drawing aggressive boundary lines that extended county boundaries and local government westward and northward. Under the Missouri Compromise, Iowa came into the Union with Florida as its slaveholding counterpart. A serious dispute, concerning how large the state would be, delayed Iowa's admission into the Union until 28 December 1846.

State Development The settlement of Iowa was rapidly accomplished. With one-fourth of the nation's fertile topsoil located within its borders, Iowa was a powerful magnet that drew farmers by the thousands from many areas. The settlers were overwhelmingly Protestant in religion and remarkably uniform in ethnic and cultural backgrounds. Fiercely proud of its claim to be the first free state created out of the Louisiana Purchase, Iowa was an important center of abolitionist sentiment throughout the 1850s. The Underground Railroad for fugitive slaves from the South ran across the southern portion of Iowa to the Mississippi River. When the Civil War came, Iowa overwhelmingly supported the Union cause.

The railroad had been lavishly welcomed by Iowans in the 1850s. By the 1870s, Iowa farmers were battling the railroad interests for effective regulatory legislation. The National Grange (an association of farmers) was powerful enough in Iowa to push through the so-called Granger laws regulating the railroads. Following World War I, conservatives regained control of the ruling Republican Party and remained in control until the 1960s. Then new liberal leadership was forced on the party after the disastrous 1964 presidential campaign of Barry Goldwater and effective opposition from a revitalized Democratic Party led by Harold Hughes.

After Hughes gave up the governorship in 1969 to become a US senator, he was succeeded in office by Robert Ray, a liberal Republican who dominated the state throughout the 1970s. Iowa's economy suffered in the 1980s from a combination of high debt and interest rates, numerous droughts, and low crop prices. Businesses departed or shrank their work forces.

The five-domed state capitol in Des Moines has a 23-karat gold center dome. GREATER DES MOINES CONVENTION AND VISITORS BUREAU.

By the 1990s, however, the companies that had survived were in a much stronger position, and Iowa began enjoying a period of cautious prosperity. The state's unemployment rate in 1992 was 4.7%, lower than the national average. By 1999, it had dropped to 2.5%, the lowest rate in the nation. In Iowa, as elsewhere in the Midwest, high-tech and service industries continued to pull workers away from farming—and away from the state, causing many to worry about a disappearing way of life.

By 2003, the United States economy was slowly recovering from its 2001 recession, and Iowa was also feeling the effects. In 2005, the state was pursuing a comprehensive economic growth strategy focusing on renewable energy, life sciences, financial services, advanced man-

ufacturing, and improving cultural and recreational opportunities. The governor made Iowa's energy independence a goal, and to that effect, the state from 2000 to 2005 nearly tripled its ethanol production and by 2006 was projected to be the nation's leading producer of ethanol.

In 1993, unusually heavy spring and summer rains produced record floods along the Mississippi River by mid-July. The entire state of Iowa was declared a disaster area. The floods forced 11,200 people to evacuate their homes and caused $2.2 billion in damages.

12 State Government

The state legislature, or general assembly, consists of a 50-member senate and a 100-member house of representatives. Senators serve four-year

Iowa Governors: 1846–2007

1846–1850	Ansel Briggs	Democrat		1925–1931	John Hammill	Republican
1850–1854	Stepehn P. Hempstead	Democrat		1931–1933	Daniel Webster Turner	Republican
1854–1858	James Wilson Grimes	Whig		1933–1937	Clyde LaVerne Herring	Democrat
1858–1860	Ralph Phillips Lowe	Republican		1937–1939	Nelson George Kraschel	Democrat
1860–1864	Samuel Jordan Kirkwood	Republican		1939–1943	George Allison Wilson	Republican
1864–1868	William Milo Stone	Republican		1943–1945	Bourke Blakemore Hickenlooper	Republican
1868–1872	Samuel Merrill	Republican		1945–1949	Robert Donald Blue	Republican
1872–1876	Cyrus Clay Carpenter	Republican		1949–1954	William S. Beardsley	Republican
1876–1877	Samuel Jordan Kirkwood	Republican		1954–1955	Leo Elthon	Republican
1877–1878	Joshua G. Newbold	Republican		1955–1957	Leo Arthur Hoegh	Republican
1878–1882	John Henry Gear	Republican		1957–1961	Herschel Celiel Loveless	Democrat
1882–1886	Buren Robinson Sherman	Republican		1961–1963	Norman Arthur Erbe	Republican
1886–1890	William Larrabee	Republican		1863–1969	Harold Everett Hughes	Democrat
1890–1894	Horace Boies	Democrat		1969	Robert David Fulton	Democrat
1894–1896	Frank Darr Jackson	Republican		1969–1983	Robert D. Day	Republican
1896–1898	Francis Marion Drake	Republican		1983–1999	Terry Edward Branstad	Republican
1898–1902	Leslie Mortier Shaw	Republican		1999–2006	Thomas J. Vilsack	Democrat
1902–1908	Albert Baird Cummins	Republican		2006–	Chester Culver	Democrat
1908–1909	Warren Garst	Republican				
1909–1913	Beryl Franklin Carroll	Republican		Democratic Republican – Dem-Rep		
1913–1917	George W. Clarke	Republican		Independent – Indep		
1917–1921	William Lloyd Harding	Republican		National Republican – Nat-Rep		
1921–1925	Nathan Edward Kendall	Republican				

terms, with half the members elected every two years; representatives serve two-year terms. Each house may introduce or amend legislation, with a simple majority vote required for passage. The governor's veto of a bill may be overridden by a two-thirds majority in both houses. The state's elected executives are the governor, lieutenant governor, secretary of state, auditor, treasurer, attorney general, and secretary of agriculture.

As of December 2004, the governor's salary was $107,482, and the legislative salary was $21,380.54.

13 Political Parties

For 70 years following the Civil War, a majority of Iowa voters supported the Republicans over the Democrats in nearly all state and national elections. During the Great Depression of the 1930s, Iowa briefly turned to the Democrats, supporting Franklin D. Roosevelt in two presidential elections. However, from 1940 through 1984, the majority of Iowans voted Republican in 10 of 12 presidential elections. Democrats carried the state in four recent presidential contests (1988, 1992, 1996, 2000), but turned Republican again in 2004. Republicans won 35 of the 45 gubernatorial elections from 1900 through 2002 and controlled both houses of the state legislature for 112 of the 130 years from 1855 to 1984.

In the 2000 elections, Iowa gave Democrat Al Gore 49% of the vote, while Republican George W. Bush received 48%. In 2004, Bush increased his support to 50% to Democrat John Kerry's 49%. As of the 2006 elections, Democrats had a 3–2 edge in the US House delegation, while a Democrat and a Republican both served in

Iowa Presidential Vote by Political Parties, 1948–2004

YEAR	IOWA WINNER	DEMOCRAT	REPUBLICAN	PROGRESSIVE	PROHIBITION	SOCIALIST LABOR
1948	*Truman (D)	522,380	494,018	12,125	3,382	4,274
1952	*Eisenhower (R)	451,513	808,906	5,085	2,882	—
						CONSTITUTION
1956	*Eisenhower (R)	501,858	729,187	—	—	3,202
1960	Nixon (R)	550,565	722,381	—	—	—
1964	*Johnson (D)	733,030	449,148	—	1,902	—
				SOC. WORKERS	**AMERICAN IND.**	
1968	*Nixon (R)	476,699	619,106	3,377	66,422	—
				AMERICAN		**PEACE & FREEDOM**
1972	*Nixon (R)	496,206	706,207	22,056	—	1,332
						LIBERTARIAN
1976	Ford (R)	619,931	632,863	—	3,040	1,452
				CITIZENS		
1980	*Reagan (R)	508,672	676,026	2,191	—	12,324
1984	*Reagan (R)	605,620	703,088	—	—	—
1988	Dukakis (D)	670,557	545,355	755	540	2,494
				IND. (PEROT)		
1992	*Clinton (D)	586,353	504,891	253,468	3,079	1,177
1996	*Clinton (D)	620,258	492,644	105,159	—	2,315
				REFORM		
2000	Gore (D)	638,517	634,373	29,374	5,731	190
2004	*Bush, G. W. (R)	741,898	751,957	—	—	—

* Won US presidential election.

the US Senate—Republican Charles Grassley, who won election to a fifth term in 2004, and Democrat Tom Harkin, who won reelection for a fourth term in 2002. Democrat Chet Culver won election as governor in 2006. Following the 2006 elections, there were 30 Democrats and 20 Republicans in the state senate, and 54 Democrats, 45 Republicans, and 1 Independent in the state house. There were 30 women serving in the state legislature following the 2006 elections, or 20%.

Iowa's presidential caucuses are held in January of presidential campaign years (ahead of New Hampshire, which also has a primary in January). This is earlier than any other state, thus giving Iowans a degree of influence in national politics.

14 Local Government

The state's 99 counties are governed by boards of supervisors. County officials enforce state laws, collect taxes, supervise welfare activities, and manage roads and bridges. Local government was exercised by 948 municipal units in 2005. The mayor-council system functioned in the great majority of these municipalities. The power to tax is authorized by the state general assembly. In 2005, there were 374 public school districts and 542 special districts.

15 Judicial System

The Iowa supreme court consists of seven justices appointed by the governor, who select one of their number as chief justice. The court exercises appeals jurisdiction in civil and criminal cases, supervises the trial courts, and establishes the rules of civil and appeals procedure. The supreme court transfers certain cases to the six-member court of appeals. The state is divided into eight judicial districts, each with a chief justice. Iowa's violent crime rate (murder, rape, robbery, aggravated assault) in 2004 was 270.9 per 100,000 population. Crimes against property (burglary, larceny/theft, and motor vehicle theft) in 2004 totaled 2,905.3 reported incidents per 100,000 people. Iowa does not have a death penalty. As of 31 December 2004, there were 8,525 prisoners in federal and state institutions.

16 Migration

Iowa was opened, organized, and settled by a generation of native migrants from other states. Around the 1850s, the largest group of foreign immigrants were Germans who had fled military conscription. The next largest group had sought to escape the hardships of potato famine in Ireland or of agricultural and technological displacement in Scotland, England, and Wales. They were joined in the by Dutch immigrants seeking religious liberty and by Norwegians and Swedes. During and immediately after the Civil War, some former slaves fled the South for Iowa, and more blacks settled in Iowa cities after 1900. But many of the migrants who came to Iowa did not stay long. Some Iowans left to join the gold rush and others settled lands in the West.

In the period 2000–05, a net total of 29,386 moved into the state from other countries and a net 41,140 people moved to other states, for a net loss of 11,754 people.

17 Economy

Iowa's economy is based on agriculture. Although the value of the state's manufactures exceeds the value of its farm production, manufacturing is basically farm-centered. The major industries are food processing and the manufacture of agriculture-related products, such as farm machinery.

Technological progress in agriculture and the growth of manufacturing industries have enabled Iowans to enjoy general prosperity since World War II. In the early 1980s, however, high interest rates and falling land prices created serious economic difficulties for farmers and contributed to the continuing decline of the farm population. By the early 1990s, the state had recovered. The national recession of 2001 had a relatively mild effect on Indiana's unemployment rate. Agricultural production was positive in 2002, largely because Iowa escaped the drought that was harming other states in the region.

18 Income

In 2005, Iowa ranked 30th among the 50 states and the District of Columbia with a gross state product (GSP) of $114 billion. In 2004, Iowa had a per capita personal income of $31,058. This ranked 28th in the United States; the national average was $33,050. The three-year average median household income for 2002–04 was $43,042, compared to the national average of $44,473. For the period 2002–04, 9.7% of the state's residents lived below the federal poverty level, as compared to 12.4% nationwide.

19 Industry

Because Iowa was primarily a farm state, the first industries were food processing and the manufacture of farm implements. These industries have retained a key role in the economy. In recent years, Iowa has added a variety of others—including pens, washing machines, and even mobile homes.

The estimated total value of shipments by manufacturers was $79.47 billion in 2004.

20 Labor

In April 2006, the seasonally adjusted civilian labor force in Iowa numbered 1,674,200, with approximately 59,800 workers unemployed. Iowa's unemployment rate of 3.6% was below the overall US rate of 4.7%. As of April 2006, approximately 5% of the labor force was employed in construction; 15.5% in manufacturing; 20.5% in trade, transportation, and public utilities; 6.6% in financial activities; 16.4% in government; 7.6% in professional and business services; 13.2% in education and health services; and 8.7% in leisure and hospitality services.

The labor movement generally has not been strong in Iowa, and labor unions have had little success in organizing farm laborers. The Knights of Labor, consisting mostly of miners and railroad workers, was organized in Iowa in 1876. But the Knights practically disappeared after 1893, when the American Federation of Labor (AFL) established itself in the state among miners and other workers. The Congress of Industrial Organizations (CIO) succeeded in organizing workers in public utilities, meat packing, and light industries in 1937. After 1955, when the AFL and CIO merged, the power and influence of labor unions increased in the state.

In 2005, 157,000 of Iowa's 1,369,000 employed wage and salary workers were members of unions. This represented 11.5% of those so employed. The national average is 12%.

21 Agriculture

Iowa recorded a gross farm income of $14.2 billion in 2005, the third highest in the United States. Nearly half of all cash receipts from marketing came from the sale of livestock and meat products. During 2000–04, Iowa ranked first in output of corn for grain and soybeans and fifth for oats.

Two important 20th-century developments were the introduction in the 1920s of hybrid corn and the utilization on a massive scale of soybeans as a feed grain (during World War II). In 2004, Iowa had 89,700 farms, with an average size of 353 acres (143 hectares) per farm. Nearly all of Iowa's land is tillable and about nine-tenths of it is given to farmland. Corn is grown practically everywhere; wheat is raised in the southern half of the state and in counties bordering the Mississippi and Missouri rivers.

In 2004, production of corn for grain totaled 2.24 billion bushels, soybeans totaled 497.4 million bushels, oats totaled 10.1 million bushels, and hay totaled 6.24 million tons.

22 Domesticated Animals

Iowa had an estimated 3.6 million cattle and calves in 2005, worth around $3.2 billion. In 2004, Iowa was ranked first among the 50 states in the number of hogs and pigs with 16.1 million, worth around $1.77 billion.

Pigs, calves, lambs, and chickens are raised throughout the state, particularly in the Mississippi and Missouri river valleys, where good pasture and water are plentiful. Iowa farmers are leaders in applying modern livestock breeding methods to produce lean hogs, tender corn-fed cattle, and larger-breasted chickens and turkeys. In 2003, Iowa farmers produced an estimated 30.7 million pounds (14 million kilograms) of sheep and lambs, which grossed a total of around $31.6 million. Also during 2003, Iowa farmers produced 267.7 million pounds (121.6 million kilograms) of turkeys, worth $96.4 million. In the same year an estimated 10.4 billion eggs were produced, worth around $460.5 million.

Iowa dairy farmers produced 3.8 billion pounds (1.7 million kilograms) of milk from 201,000 dairy cows in 2003.

23 Fishing

Fishing has very little commercial importance in Iowa. Game fishing in the rivers and lakes, however, is a popular sport. In 2004, there were 429,689 sport fishermen licensed in the state.

24 Forestry

Lumber and woodworking were important to the early settlers, but the industry has since declined in commercial importance. In 2004, Iowa had 2.7 million acres (1.1 million hectares) of forestland, which represents 7.5% of the state's land area, up from 1.6 million acres (650,000 hectares) in 1974. The state's lumber industry produced 78 million board feet of lumber in 2004.

25 Mining

The value of nonfuel mineral production in Iowa was estimated at $478 million in 2003. The top products were crushed stone, construction sand and gravel, cement, crude gypsum, which collectively accounted for 97% of the total mineral value produced. In 2001, Iowa ranked second in production of crude gypsum. In 2003, Iowa was a significant producer of crushed stone (34.7 million metric tons), portland cement, and construction sand and gravel (13 million metric tons). The state is also a producer of common clays.

26 Energy and Power

Although Iowa's fossil fuel resources are extremely limited, the state's energy supply has been adequate for consumer needs. In 2000, Iowa consumed 372 million Btu (93.7 million kilocalories) per capita, to rank 19th among the states. In 2003, the state's production of electricity (utility and nonutility) totaled 42.1 billion kilowatt hours. The total installed capacity was 10 million kilowatts. Coal-fired plants supplied the vast majority of generated power (85%), with nuclear power plants in second place (9.5%). The remainder came from gas, hydroelectric power, and other sources. Iowa has one single-unit nuclear plant, the Duane Arnold plant in Palo.

Extensive coalfields in southeastern Iowa were first mined in 1840. The state's annual bituminous coal production reached nearly 9 million tons in 1917–18. Coal output in 1994 was only 46,000 tons. Recoverable coal reserves totaled 1.1 billion tons in 2001. As of 2004, Iowa had

Des Moines skyline. GREATER DES MOINES CONVENTION AND VISITORS BUREAU.

no production of crude oil or natural gas. There are no refineries in Iowa.

27 Commerce

Iowa had 2002 wholesale sales of $33.5 billion and retail sales of $31.1 billion. The most valuable categories of goods traded were agricultural raw materials, durable goods, groceries and related products, and farm supplies. Iowa's exports of goods originating within the state had an estimated value of $7.3 billion in 2005.

28 Public Finance

The public budget is prepared by the Department of Management with the governor's approval and is adopted or revised by the general assembly. The fiscal year runs from 1 July to 30 June.

Iowa's fiscal year 2004 budget included revenues of $15.3 billion and expenditures of $13.4 billion. The largest general expenditures were for education ($4.67 billion), public welfare ($3.1 billion), and highways ($1.36 billion). The state had an outstanding debt of $4.8 billion, or $1,644.98 per capita (per person).

29 Taxation

Iowa's personal income tax schedule has nine brackets. In 2006, the lowest bracket was at 0.36% and the highest was at 8.98%. Iowa's corporate income tax ranges from 6% to 12%. Iowa's retail sales tax is 5%, with exemptions for basic foods and prescription drugs. Some local governments have local-option sales taxes of up to 2%. There are also state excise taxes on motor fuels, tobacco products, amusements, pari-mutuels, insurance premiums, and other selected items. The state directly controls alcohol sales. Other state taxes include license fees and stamp taxes. Property taxes are all local. Localities collect over 40% of the taxes in Iowa.

Total state tax collections in Iowa came to over $5.7 billion in 2005, with 39.2% generated by the state income tax, 29.9% by the state sales tax, 15.7% by state excise taxes, 3.2% by the state corporate income tax, and other taxes 11.9%. The state placed 33rd in the nation in terms of tax burden in 2005.

30 Health

In October 2005, the infant mortality rate was 5.2 per 1,000 live births. The overall death rate was 9.5 per 1,000 people in 2003. The leading causes of death were heart disease and cerebrovascular disease. About 20.8% of all Iowans ages 18 and older were smokers in 2004. The mortality rate from HIV infection was 1 per 100,000 persons, the lowest in the nation. In 2004, the reported AIDS case rate was at about 2.2 per 100,000 population.

Iowa's 116 community hospitals have about 11,000 beds. In 2004, Iowa had 218 doctors per 100,000 people and 1,009 nurses per 100,000 people in 2005. In 2004, there were 1,546 dentists in the state. In 2001, the average expense for hospital care was $1,437.60 per inpatient day. In 2004, about 10% of the population was uninsured.

31 Housing

In 2004, there were 1,292,976 housing units in Iowa, of which 1,175,771 were occupied; 73.8% were owner-occupied, placing the state fourth in the nation in the percentage of homeownership. About 74.7% of all units were single-family, detached homes. About 31.5% of all units were built in 1939 or earlier. Most households relied on utility gas and electricity for heating. It was estimated that 52,215 lacked telephone service, 4,728 lacked complete plumbing facilities, and 5,037 lacked complete kitchen facilities. Average household size was 2.42 people.

In 2004, 16,300 privately owned housing units were authorized for construction. Median home value was $95,901. The median monthly cost for mortgage owners was $942. Renters paid a median of $533 per month.

32 Education

In 2004, 89.8% of Iowans age 25 and older were high school graduates and 24.3% had obtained a bachelor's degree or higher.

Total enrollment in public schools was estimated at 482,000 in fall 2002 but expected to drop to 452,000 by fall 2014. Enrollment in private schools in fall 2003 was 45,309. Expenditures for public education in 2003/04 were estimated at $4.28 billion.

As of fall 2002, there were 202,546 students enrolled in institutions of higher education. As of 2005, Iowa had 63 degree-granting institutions. Iowa has three state universities and 35 private colleges. Since the public community college system began offering vocational and technical training in 1960, total enrollment has increased rapidly and the number of different career programs has grown. Iowa's small liberal arts colleges and universities include Briar Cliff College, Coe College, Cornell College, Drake University,

Grinnell College, Iowa Wesleyan College, Loras College, and Luther College.

33 Arts

There is an opera company in Des Moines, and there are art galleries, little theater groups, symphony orchestras, and ballet companies in the major cities and college towns. The Des Moines Arts Center is a leading exhibition gallery for native painters and sculptors. The Des Moines Arts Festival, established in 1998, has drawn an attendance of nearly 800,000 people each year. The 2002 ArtFair SourceBook ranked it as the Sixth Best Fine Arts Festival in the nation. There are regional theater groups in Des Moines, Davenport, and Sioux City. The Writers' Workshop at the University of Iowa has an international reputation.

The Iowa Arts Council (IAC) was established as a state agency in 1967. In 1986, the IAC became a division of the Department of Cultural Affairs, which also includes the State Historical Society of Iowa. Humanities Iowa, founded in 1971, sponsors over $1.5 million of programs each year. Iowa's arts programs have a total audience of nearly seven million people. There are over 36,000 contributing artists for the programs. The state offers arts education to about 120,000 schoolchildren. There are over 800 art associations in Iowa.

34 Libraries and Museums

As of the end of fiscal year 2001 (June), Iowa had 537 public library systems, with a total of 561 libraries, of which 24 were branches. That year, the public library system had total book and serial publication holdings of 11.45 million volumes and a circulation of nearly 25.5 million. Among the principal libraries in Iowa are the State Library in Des Moines, the State Historical Society Library in Iowa City, the libraries of the University of Iowa (also in Iowa City), and the Iowa State University Library in Ames.

Iowa had 134 museums and zoological parks in 2000. The Herbert Hoover National Historical Site, in West Branch, houses the birthplace and grave of the 31st US president and a library and museum with papers and memorabilia.

35 Communications

In 2004, about 95.4% of all occupied units had telephones. In June of that year, there were 1,445,711 mobile phone subscribers. In 2003, 64.7% of Iowa households had a computer and 57.1% had Internet access. The first commercial radio station west of the Mississippi, WDC at Davenport, began broadcasting in 1921. In 2005 there were 110 major radio stations, including 37 AM stations and 73 FM stations. In the same year, Iowa had a total of 21 network television stations.

36 Press

In 2005, Iowa had 37 dailies (21 evening, 16 morning) and 12 Sunday papers. The *Des Moines Register* remained the leader, with a morning circulation of 152,800 and a Sunday circulation of 243,302 as of 2002. Other major newspapers and their estimated daily circulations at 2002 include the Cedar Rapids *Gazette* (63,493), Dubuque *Telegraph Herald* (28,621), Sioux City *Journal* (41,182), and the Waterloo *Courier* (42,679). Also published in Iowa were over 100 periodi-

From 1960 until her retirement in 2006, Norma Duffield Lyon ("Duffy") of Toledo produced butter sculptures for the Iowa State Fair. It takes about 16 hours to sculpt a life-size cow out of more than a quarter-ton of low-moisture sweet butter. The finished product is displayed during the fair in a refrigerated showcase in the Agriculture Building. IOWA STATE FAIR. PHOTO BY STEVE POPE.

cals, among them *Better Homes and Gardens* and *Successful Farming*.

37 Tourism, Travel & Recreation

The Mississippi and Missouri rivers offer popular water sports facilities for both out-of-state visitors and resident vacationers. Notable tourist attractions include the Effigy Mounds National Monument (near Marquette), which has hundreds of prehistoric Indian mounds and village sites. Tourist sites in the central part of the state include the state capitol and the Herbert Hoover National Historic Site (West Branch), with its Presidential Library and Museum.

Iowa has about 85,000 acres (34,400 hectares) of lakes and reservoirs and 19,000 miles (30,600 kilometers) of fishing streams. There are 52 state parks and 7 state forests.

In 2005, there were about 30.5 million visitors to the state. This showed an increase from 17.1 million in 2001. Travel generated expenditures of about $4.3 billion in 2002; in 2005, the figure was $5 billion. In 2005, there were over 62,290 travel-related jobs in the state.

38 Sports

Iowa has no major league professional sports teams, but do sponsor the Iowa Barnstormers in the Arena Football League. Minor league baseball and basketball teams make their home in Des Moines, Cedar Rapids, Clinton, Sioux City, Burlington, and the Quad Cities. High school and college basketball and football teams draw thousands of spectators, particularly to the state high school basketball tournament at Des Moines in March. Large crowds also fill stadiums and fieldhouses for the University of Iowa games in Iowa City and Iowa State University games in Ames.

In intercollegiate football competition, the University of Iowa Hawkeyes belong to the Big Ten Conference. They have a legendary wrestling program that has won the NCAA Championship 20 times. The Iowa State University Cyclones are in the Big Twelve Conference. A popular track-and-field meet for college athletes is the Drake Relays, held every April in Des Moines.

Horse racing is popular at state and county fairgrounds, as is stock car racing at small-town tracks. The Register's Annual Great Bicycle Ride Across Iowa is held in July. There are rodeos in Sidney and Fort Madison and the National Balloon Classic is held in Indianola. Iowa has over 350 golf courses, eight major ski areas, and is the nation's leading state in pheasant hunting.

39 Famous Iowans

Among Iowa's most influential governors were the first territorial governor, Robert Lucas (b.Virginia, 1781–1853); William Larrabee (b.Connecticut, 1832–1912); and Harold Hughes (1863–1969). Iowa has produced a large number of radical dissenters and social reformers. Abolitionists, strong in Iowa before the Civil War, included Josiah B. Grinnell (b.Vermont, 1821–1891), and Asa Turner (b.Massachusetts, 1799–1885).

George D. Herron (b.Indiana, 1862–1925) made Iowa a center of the Social Gospel movement before helping to found the Socialist Party. William "Billy" Sunday (1862–1935) was an evangelist with a large following among rural Americans. John L. Lewis (1880–1969), head of the United Mine Workers, founded the Congress of Industrial Organizations (CIO).

Iowa can claim two winners of the Nobel Peace Prize: religious leader John R. Mott (b.New York, 1865–1955), and agronomist and plant geneticist Norman E. Borlaug (b.1914). Distinguished scientist George Washington Carver (b.Missouri 1864–1943) was an Iowa resident.

Iowa writers of note include Hamlin Garland (b.Wisconsin, 1860–1940) and Wallace Stegner (1909–1993). Two Iowa playwrights, Susan Glaspell (1882–1948) and her husband, George Cram Cook (1873–1924), were instrumental in founding influential theater groups. Columnists Abigail Van Buren (Pauline Esther Friedman, b.1918) and her twin sister Ann Landers (Esther Pauline Friedman Lederer, 1918–2002) are from Sioux City. Iowans who have contributed to America's musical heritage include popular composers Meredith Willson (1902–1984) and Peter "PDQ Bach" Schickele (b.1935), jazz musician Leon "Bix" Beiderbecke (1903–1931), bandleader Glenn Miller (1904–1944), and opera singer Simon Estes (b.1938). Iowa's artists of note include Grant Wood (1892–1942), whose *American Gothic* is one of America's best-known paintings.

Iowa's contributions to the field of popular entertainment include William F. "Buffalo Bill" Cody (1846–1917); circus promoter Charles Ringling (1863–1926) and his four brothers;

and one of America's best-loved movie actors, John Wayne (Marion Michael Morrison, 1907–1979). Johnny Carson (1925–2005), host of the *Tonight Show* for 30 years, was born in Corning. Iowa sports figures of note are baseball Hall of Famers Adrian C. "Cap" Anson (1851–1922) and Robert "Bob" Feller (b.1918), and football All-American Nile Kinnick (1918–1944).

40 Bibliography

BOOKS

Bristow, M. J. *State Songs of America.* Westport, CT: Greenwood Press, 2000.

Dykstra, Mary. *Iowa.* Milwaukee, WI: Gareth Stevens, 2006.

Genoways, Ted, and Hugh H. Genoways, eds. *A Perfect Picture of Hell: Eyewitness Accounts by Civil War Prisoners from the 12th Iowa.* Iowa City: University of Iowa Press, 2001.

Kule, Elaine A. *Iowa Facts and Symbols.* Rev. ed. Mankato, MN: Capstone, 2003.

Morrice, Polly Alison. *Iowa.* 2nd ed. New York: Marshall Cavendish Benchmark, 2007.

Murray, Julie. *Iowa.* Edina, MN: Abdo Publishing, 2006.

WEB SITES

Iowa Tourism Office. *Iowa: Life Changing.* traveliowa.com (accessed March 1, 2007).

State of Iowa. *Official Web Site of the State of Iowa.* www.iowa.gov/state/main/index.html (accessed March 1, 2007).

Kansas

State of Kansas

ORIGIN OF STATE NAME: Named for the Kansa (or Kaw) Indians, the "people of the south wind."

NICKNAME: The Sunflower State; the Jayhawker State.

CAPITAL: Topeka.

ENTERED UNION: 29 January 1861 (34th).

OFFICIAL SEAL: A sun rising over mountains in the background symbolizes the east; commerce is represented by a river and a steamboat. In the foreground, agriculture, the basis of the state's prosperity, is represented by a settler's cabin and a man plowing a field. Beyond this is a wagon train heading west and a herd of buffalo fleeing from two Indians. Around the top is the state motto above a cluster of 34 stars; the circle is surrounded by the words "Great Seal of the State of Kansas, January 29, 1861."

FLAG: The flag consists of a dark blue field with the state seal in the center; a sunflower on a bar of twisted gold and blue is above the seal; the word "Kansas" is below it.

MOTTO: *Ad astra per aspera* (To the stars through difficulties).

SONG: "Home on the Range."

MARCH: "The Kansas March."

FLOWER: Wild native sunflower.

TREE: Cottonwood.

ANIMAL: American buffalo.

BIRD: Western meadowlark.

INSECT: Honeybee.

REPTILE: Ornate box turtle.

LEGAL HOLIDAYS: New Year's Day, 1 January; Birthday of Martin Luther King Jr., 3rd Monday in January; Memorial Day, last Monday in May; Independence Day, 4 July; Labor Day, 1st Monday in September; Columbus Day, 2nd Monday in October; Veterans' Day, 11 November; Thanksgiving Day, 4th Thursday in November; Christmas Day, 25 December.

TIME: 6 AM CST = noon GMT; 5 AM MST = noon GMT.

1 Location and Size

Located in the western north-central United States, Kansas is the second-largest Midwestern state (following Minnesota) and ranks 14th among the 50 states. The total area of Kansas is 82,277 square miles (213,097 square kilometers), of which 81,778 square miles (211,805 square kilometers) are land, and the remaining 499 square miles (1,292 square kilometers) inland water. The state has a maximum extension east-west of about 411 miles (661 kilometers) and an extreme north-south distance of about 208 miles (335 kilometers). Kansas has a total boundary length of 1,219 miles (1,962 kilometers).

2 Topography

Three main land regions define the state. The eastern third consists of the Osage Plains, Flint Hills, Dissected Till Plains, and Arkansas River Lowlands. The central third comprises the Smoky Hills to the north and several lowland regions to the south. To the west are the Great Plains, divided into the Dissected High Plains and the High Plains. Kansas generally slopes eastward from a maximum elevation of 4,039 feet (1,232 meters) at Mt. Sunflower on the Colorado border to 679 feet (207 meters) by the Verdigris River at the Oklahoma border.

More than 50,000 streams run through the state and there are hundreds of artificial lakes. Major rivers include the Missouri, the Arkansas, and the Kansas.

Extensive beds of prehistoric ocean fossils lie in the chalk beds of two western counties, Logan and Gove.

3 Climate

Kansas's continental climate is highly changeable. The average mean temperature is 55°F (13°C). The record high in the state is 121°F (49°C), recorded near Alton on 24 July 1936. The record low is -40°F (-40°C), recorded at Lebanon on 13 February 1905. The normal annual precipitation ranges from slightly more than 40 inches (101.6 centimeters) in the southeast to as little as 16 inches (40.6 centimeters) in the west. The

Kansas
Population Profile

Total population estimate in 2006:	2,764,075
Population change, 2000–06:	2.8%
Hispanic or Latino†:	8.4%
Population by race	
One race:	97.8%
White:	85.2%
Black or African American:	5.5%
American Indian /Alaska Native:	0.9%
Asian:	2.0%
Native Hawaiian / Pacific Islander:	0.0%
Some other race:	4.1%
Two or more races:	2.3%

Population by Age Group

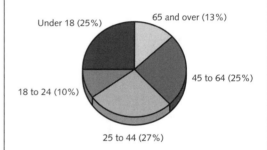

Under 18 (25%)
65 and over (13%)
45 to 64 (25%)
25 to 44 (27%)
18 to 24 (10%)

Major Cities by Population

City	Population	% change 2000–05
Wichita	354,865	3.1
Overland Park	164,811	10.6
Kansas City	144,210	-1.8
Topeka	121,946	-0.4
Olathe	111,334	19.8
Lawrence	81,816	2.1
Shawnee	57,628	20.1
Manhattan	48,668	8.6
Salina	45,956	0.6
Lenexa	43,434	7.9

Notes: †A person of Hispanic or Latino origin may be of any race. NA indicates that data are not available.
Sources: U.S. Census Bureau. *American Community Survey* and *Population Estimates*. www.census.gov/ (accessed March 2007).

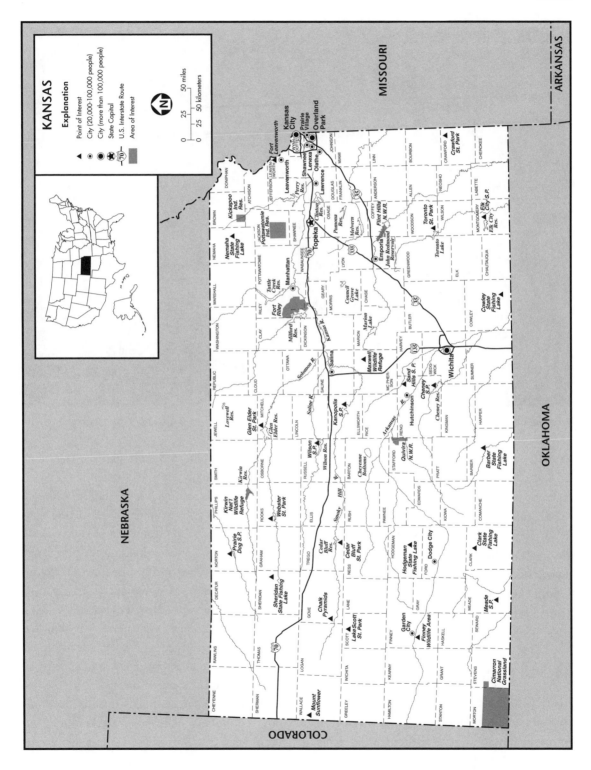

KANSAS

Explanation

Point of Interest ▲

City (20,000–100,000 people) ⊙

City (more than 100,000 people) ◉

State Capital ✪

U.S. Interstate Route 🛣70

Area of Interest ▮

0   25   50 miles

0   25   50 kilometers

National Weather Service meteorologists in Wichita, Kansas, track tornadoes on their computers. © JIM REED/CORBIS.

overall annual precipitation for the state averages 27 inches (68.6 centimeters), although years of drought have not been uncommon. Tornadoes are a regular fact of Kansas life. The annual mean snowfall ranges from about 36 inches (91.4 centimeters) in the extreme northwest to less than 11 inches (27.9 centimeters) in the far southeast. Dodge City is said to be the windiest city in the United States, with an average wind speed of 14 miles per hour (23 kilometers per hour).

4 Plants and Animals

There are 194 species of grasses covering the state of Kansas. Bluestem, both big and little, grows in most parts of the state. Other grasses include buffalo grass, blue and hairy gramas, and alkali sacaton. One native conifer, eastern red cedar, is found generally throughout the state. Hackberry, black walnut, and sycamore grow in the east, while box elder and cottonwood predominate in western Kansas. There are no native pines. The wild native sunflower, the state flower, is found throughout the state. Other characteristic wildflowers include wild daisy, ivy-leaved morning glory, and smallflower verbena. As of 2006, the western prairie fringed orchid and Mead's milkweed were listed as threatened species and are protected under federal statutes.

Kansas's native mammals include the common cottontail, black-tailed jackrabbit, and black-tailed prairie dog. The white-tailed deer is

Kansas Population by Race

Census 2000 was the first national census in which the instructions to respondents said, "Mark one or more races." This table shows the number of people who are of one, two, or three or more races. For those claiming two races, the number of people belonging to the various categories is listed. The U.S. government conducts a census of the population every ten years.

	Number	Percent
Total population	2,688,418	100.0
One race	2,631,922	97.9
Two races	53,344	2.0
White *and* Black or African American	9,970	0.4
White *and* American Indian/Alaska Native	17,539	0.7
White *and* Asian	5,781	0.2
White *and* Native Hawaiian/Pacific Islander	613	—
White *and* some other race	12,631	0.5
Black or African American *and* American Indian/Alaska Native	1,951	0.1
Black or African American *and* Asian	661	—
Black or African American *and* Native Hawaiian/Pacific Islander	132	—
Black or African American *and* some other race	1,514	0.1
American Indian/Alaska Native *and* Asian	242	—
American Indian/Alaska Native *and* Native Hawaiian/Pacific Islander	41	—
American Indian/Alaska Native *and* some other race	581	—
Asian *and* Native Hawaiian/Pacific Islander	433	—
Asian *and* some other race	1,104	—
Native Hawaiian/Pacific Islander *and* some other race	151	—
Three or more races	3,152	0.1

Source: U.S. Census Bureau. *Census 2000: Redistricting Data.* Press release issued by the Redistricting Data Office. Washington, D.C., March, 2001. A dash (—) indicates that the percent is less than 0.1.

the state's only big-game animal. There are 12 native species of bat, 2 varieties of shrew and mole, and 3 types of pocket gopher. The western meadowlark is the state bird. Kansas has the largest flock of prairie chickens remaining on the North American continent. In April 2006 the US Fish and Wildlife Service named 12 Kansas animal species as threatened or endangered. Among these are the Indiana and gray bats, bald eagle, Eskimo curlew, Topeka Shiner, and black-footed ferret.

5 Environmental Protection

Water quality is the most crucial environmental problem for Kansas. Protection of the water supply is a primary focus of the state's environmental efforts. Maintenance of air quality is also a primary effort and the state works actively with the business community to promote pollution prevention.

Strip mining for coal is decreasing in southeast Kansas, and the restoration of resources damaged by previous activities is ongoing.

The state has sufficient capacity for handling solid waste, although the total number of solid waste facilities has decreased in recent years. In 2003, Kansas had 307 hazardous waste sites listed in the Environmental Protection Agency's database, 10 of which were on the National Priorities List as of 2006.

6 Population

In 2006, Kansas ranked 33rd in population among the states with an estimated total of 2,764,075 residents. The population is projected to reach 2.91 million by 2025. The population density in 2004 was 33.4 persons per square mile (12.89 persons per square kilometer). In 2004, the median age of all residents was 36.1. In 2005, about 13% of the population was 65 years old or older while 25% were 18 or younger. The largest cities in 2005 with their estimated populations were Wichita, 354,865; Overland Park, 164,811; and Kansas City, 144,210.

7 Ethnic Groups

According to the census, there were 24,936 Native Americans living in Kansas in 2000. The same year, black Americans in Kansas numbered 154,198, or 5.7% of the population. There were 188,252 Hispanics and Latinos and 46,806 Asian residents. The largest group of Asians was the Vietnamese with 11,623 residents. There were 8,153 Asian Indians and 7,624 Chinese, as well as sizable communities of Laotians and Cambodians. The census also reported that a total of 80,271 residents (2% of the population) were foreign born. The most common lands of origin were Mexico, Germany, and Vietnam. Among the Europeans who reported descent from a single ancestry group, the leading nationalities were German, English, and Irish.

8 Languages

Regional features of Kansas speech are almost entirely those of the Northern and North Midland dialects. Kansans typically play as children on a *teetertotter* (seesaw), make *white bread* sandwiches, and carry water in a *pail*. The migration by Southerners in the mid-19th century is evidenced in southeastern Kansas by such South Midland terms as *pullybone* (wishbone) and *light bread* (white bread). In 2000, about 2,281,705 Kansans (91.3% of the residents five years old or older) spoke only English at home. Other languages (and the number of speakers) were Spanish (137,247), German (16,821), Vietnamese (10,393), and French (6,591).

9 Religions

Isaac McCoy, a Baptist minister, was instrumental in founding the Shawnee Baptist Mission in Johnson County in 1831. Mennonites were drawn to the state by a law passed in 1874 allowing exemptions from military service on religious grounds. Religious freedom is specifically granted in the Kansas constitution, and a wide variety of religious groups is represented in the state.

The leading Protestant denominations are the United Methodist Church, with 162,202 adherents in 2004; the Southern Baptist Convention, 101,696 adherents in 2000; the American Baptist Church, 64,312 in 2000; the Lutheran Church—Missouri Synod, 62,712 in 2000; and the Christian Church (Disciples of Christ), 56,908 in 2000. Roman Catholics constitute the largest single religious group in the state, with 409,906 adherents in 2004. The estimated Jewish population in 2000 was 14,500. There were over 18,000 Mennonites throughout the state and about 3,470 Muslims. About 50.6% of the population (or over 1.3 million people) were not counted as members of any religious organization.

10 Transportation

In the heartland of the nation, Kansas is at the crossroads of US road and railway systems. In 2001, Kansas had 25,638 bridges (third in the nation behind Texas and Ohio). In 2004, the state had 135,017 miles (217,377 kilometers) of public roads. There were 845,000 automobiles, 1.71 million trucks, and some 1,000 buses registered in 2004.

In the late 1800s, the two major railroads, the Kansas Pacific (now the Union Pacific) and the Santa Fe (now the Burlington Northern-Santa Fe) acquired more than 10 million acres (4 million hectares) of land in the state and then advertised for immigrants to come and buy it. By 1872, the railroads stretched across the state, creating in their path the towns of Ellsworth, Newton, Caldwell, Wichita, and Dodge City. One of the first "cow towns" was Abilene, the terminal point for all cattle shipped to the East.

In 2003, the state had 6,269 route miles (10,093 kilometers) of railroad track. An Amtrak passenger train (the Southwest Chief) crosses Kansas en route from Chicago to Los Angeles.

In 2005, the state had 370 airports. The busiest airport is Kansas City International, with 5,040,595 passengers in 2004. Approximately two-thirds of all business and private aircraft in the United States are built in Kansas.

River barges move bulk commodities along the Missouri River. The chief river ports are Atchison, Leavenworth, Lansing, and Kansas City.

11 History

Plains tribes—the Wichita, Pawnee, Kansa, and Osage—were living or hunting in Kansas when the earliest Europeans arrived. Around 1800, they were joined on the Central Plains by the nomadic Cheyenne, Arapaho, Comanche, and Kiowa. The first European, explorer Francisco Coronado, entered Kansas in 1541. Between 1682 and 1739, French explorers established trading contacts with the Native Americans. France ceded its claims to the area to Spain in 1762 but received it back from Spain in 1800.

Most of Kansas was sold to the United States by France as part of the Louisiana Purchase of 1803. (The extreme southwestern corner was gained after the Mexican War.) Early settlement of Kansas was sparse, limited to a few thousand Native Americans—including Shawnee, Delaware, Ojibwa, and Wyandot. These tribes were forcibly removed from their lands and relocated in what is now eastern Kansas.

The Santa Fe Trail was opened to wagon traffic in 1822, and for 50 years that route, two-thirds of which lay in Kansas, was of commercial importance to the West. During the 1840s and 1850s, thousands of migrants crossed northeastern Kansas on the California-Oregon Trail. Kansas Territory was created by the Kansas-Nebraska Act (30 May 1854). Almost immediately, disputes arose as to whether Kansas would enter the Union as a free or slave state. Both free-staters and pro-slavery settlers were brought in, and a succession of governors tried to mediate between the two groups.

Statehood Kansas entered the Union on 29 January 1861 as a free state, and Topeka was named the capital. Although Kansas lay west of the major Civil War action, more than two-thirds of its adult males served in the Union Army and gave it the highest military death rate among the northern states. Following the Civil

The John Ritchie House (left) and the Hale Ritchie House, a stop on the Underground Railroad. AP IMAGES.

War, settlement expanded in Kansas, particularly in the central part of the state. White settlers encroached on the hunting grounds of the Plains tribes, and their settlements were attacked in retaliation. Most of the Native Americans were eventually removed to the Indian Territory in what is now Oklahoma.

By 1872, both the Union Pacific and the Santa Fe railroads had crossed Kansas, and other lines were under construction. Rail expansion brought more settlers, who established new communities. It also led to the great Texas cattle drives that meant prosperity to a number of Kansas towns—including Abilene, Ellsworth, Wichita, Caldwell, and Dodge City—from 1867 to 1885. This was when Bat Masterson, Wyatt Earp, and Wild Bill Hickok reigned in Dodge City and Abilene—the now romantic era of the Old West.

A strain of hard winter wheat that proved particularly well-suited to the state's soil was brought to Kansas in the 1870s by Russian Mennonites fleeing czarist rule, and Plains agriculture was transformed. Significant changes in agriculture, industry, transportation, and communications came after 1900. Mechanization became commonplace in farming, and vast areas were opened to wheat production, particularly during World War I. The Progressive movement of the early 1900s focused attention on control of monopolies, public health, labor legislation, and more representative politics.

The Modern Age Kansas suffered through the Great Depression of the 1930s. The state's western region, part of the Dust Bowl, was hardest hit. Improved weather conditions and the demands of World War II revived Kansas agriculture in the 1940s. The World War II era also saw the development of industry, especially in transportation. Other heavy industry grew, and mineral production—oil, natural gas, salt, coal, and gypsum—expanded greatly.

Since World War II, Kansas has become increasingly urban. Agriculture has become highly commercialized, and there are dozens of large industries that process and market farm products and supply materials to crop producers. Livestock production, especially in closely controlled feedlots, is a major enterprise. Recent governors have worked to expand international exports of Kansas products, and by 1981/82, Kansas ranked seventh among the states in agricultural exports, with sales of more than $1.6 billion.

The late 1980s and early 1990s brought dramatic extremes of weather. A severe drought in 1988 drove up commodity prices and depleted grain stocks. From April through September of 1993, Kansas experienced the worst floods of the century. Some 13,500 people evacuated their homes, and the floods caused $574 million dollars worth of damage.

In 1999, the Kansas Board of Education voted 6–4 to adopt standards that downplayed the importance of evolution and omitted the Big Bang theory of the universe's origin from the curriculum. The standards drew national attention.

The bronze sculpture Ad Astra on top of the dome of the Kansas state capitol is silhouetted against a full moon. AP IMAGES.

The decision was later reversed. In 2005, the Kansas Board of Education resumed hearings to determine whether evolution should once again be eliminated from state science standards.

The Kansas economy improved by 2003, following the 2001 US recession. From 2003–05, Wichita's aircraft industry was shored up, business development in small Kansas towns was increasing, and heavy investments were made in bioscience research at universities and medical centers.

12 State Government

The form of Kansas's constitution was a matter of great national concern, because the question of whether Kansas would be a free or a slave state was in doubt throughout the 1850s. After three draft constitutions failed to win popular support or congressional approval, a fourth version, which banned slavery, was ratified in 1859 and signed by President James Buchanan in 1861.

Kansas Governors: 1861–2007

1861–1863	Charles Lawrence Robinson	Republican	1925–1929	Benjamin Sanford Paulen	Republican
1863–1865	Thomas Carney	Republican	1929–1931	Clyde Martin Reed	Republican
1865–1868	Samuel Johnson Crawford	Republican	1931–1933	Harry Hines Woodring	Democrat
1868–1869	Nehemiah Green	Republican	1933–1937	Alfred Mossman Landon	Republican
1869–1873	James Madison Harvey	Republican	1937–1939	Walter Augustus Huxman	Democrat
1873–1877	Thomas Andrew Osborn	Republican	1939–1943	Payne Harry Ratner	Republican
1877–1879	George Tobey Anthony	Republican	1943–1947	Andrew Frank Schoeppel	Republican
1879–1883	John Pierce St. John	Republican	1947–1950	Frank Carlson	Republican
1883–1885	George Washington Glick	Democrat	1950–1951	Frank Leslie Hagaman	Republican
1885–1889	John Alexander Martin	Republican	1951–1955	Edward Ferdinand Arn	Republican
1889–1893	Lyman Underwood Humphrey	Republican	1955–1957	Frederick Lee Hall	Republican
1893–1895	Lorenzo Dow Lewelling	Populist	1957	John Berridge McCuish	Republican
1895–1897	Edmund Needham Morrill	Republican	1957–1961	George Docking	Democrat
1897–1899	John Whitnah Leedy	Populist	1961–1965	John Anderson, Jr.	Republican
1899–1903	William Eugene Stanley	Republican	1965–1967	William Henry Avery	Republican
1903–1905	Willis Joshua Bailey	Republican	1967–1975	Robert Blackwell Docking	Democrat
1905–1909	Edward Wallis Hoch	Republican	1975–1979	Robert Frederick Bennett	Republican
1909–1913	Walter Roscoe Stubbs	Republican	1979–1987	John Carlin	Democrat
1913–1915	George Hartshorn Hodges	Democrat	1987–1991	John Michael Hayden	Republican
1915–1919	Arthur Capper	Republican	1991–1995	Joan Finney	Democrat
1919–1923	Henry Justin Allen	Republican	1995–2002	Bill Graves	Republican
1923–1925	Johathan McMillan Davis	Democrat	2002–	Kathleen Sebelius	Democrat

This constitution is in force today, with its 92 amendments (as of 2005).

The Kansas legislature consists of a 40-member senate and a 125-member house of representatives. Officials elected statewide include the governor, lieutenant governor, secretary of state, attorney general, treasurer, and commissioner of insurance. Members of the state Board of Education are elected by districts. The governor cannot serve more than two consecutive terms. Candidates for governor need meet no age, citizenship, or residency requirements as qualifications for office. A bill becomes law when it has been approved by 21 senators and 63 representatives and signed by the governor. A veto can be overridden by two-thirds of the members of both houses.

As of December 2004, the governor's salary was $98,331, and the legislative salary was $78.75 per day during regular sessions.

13 Political Parties

Although the Republicans remain the dominant force in state politics, the Democrats controlled several state offices in the early 2000s. The most recent Democratic governor was Kathleen Sebelius, elected in 2002 and reelected in 2006. Republicans have regularly controlled the state legislature, however. In 2004 there were 1,694,000 registered voters. In 1998, 29% of registered voters were Democratic, 45% Republican, and 26% unaffiliated or members of other parties.

In the 2004 election, President George W. Bush won 62% of the vote to Democrat John Kerry's 36%. In the 2000 election, Republican George W. Bush won 58% of the vote while Democrat Al Gore received 37%. In the 1996 elections, native Kansan and Republican Bob Dole, first elected to the US Senate in 1968

Kansas Presidential Vote by Political Parties, 1948–2004

YEAR	KANSAS WINNER	DEMOCRAT	REPUBLICAN	PROGRESSIVE	SOCIALIST	PROHIBITION
1948	Dewey (R)	351,902	423,039	4,603	2,807	6,468
1952	*Eisenhower (R)	273,296	616,302	6,038	530	6,038
1956	*Eisenhower (R)	296,317	566,878	—	—	3,048
1960	Nixon (R)	363,213	561,474	—	—	4,138
1964	*Johnson (D)	464,028	386,579		1,901	5,393
				AMERICAN IND.		
1968	*Nixon (R)	302,996	478,674	88,921	—	2,192
1972	*Nixon (R)	270,287	619,812	21,808	—	4,188
				LIBERTARIAN		
1976	Ford (R)	430,421	502,752	4,724	3,242	1,403
1980	*Reagan (R)	326,150	566,812	7,555	14,470	—
1984	*Reagan (R)	333,149	677,296	—	3,329	—
1988	*Bush (R)	422,636	554,049	3,806	12,553	—
				IND. (PEROT)		
1992	Bush (R)	390,434	449,951	312,358	4,314	—
1996	Dole (R)	387,659	583,245	92,639	4,557	—
					REFORM	LIBERTARIAN
2000	*Bush, G. W. (R)	399,276	622,332	36,086	7,370	4,525
2004	*Bush, G. W. (R)	434,993	736,456	—	9,348	4,013

* Won US presidential election.

and elected Senate majority leader in 1984, was reelected in 1992. He reclaimed the post of Senate majority leader when the Republicans gained control of the Senate in the elections of 1994. In a surprise move in May 1996, Dole suddenly retired from the Senate to concentrate on his presidential campaign. In November, the race to fill his remaining term was won by Republican Sam Brownback. Brownback won his first full term in 1998, and was reelected in 2004. Kansas's other Republican Senator is Pat Roberts, reelected in 2002. Following the 2006 election, Republicans and Democrats each held two US congressional seats. In the state legislature following those elections, there were 30 Republicans and 10 Democrats in the state senate and 77 Republicans and 48 Democrats in the state house. Fifty-three women were elected to the state legislature in 2006, or 32.1%.

14 Local Government

As of 2005, Kansas had 105 counties, 627 incorporated cities, 1,533 special districts, and 304 school districts. In 2002, there were 1,299 townships. Each county government is headed by elected county commissioners. Other county officials include the county clerk, treasurer, register of deeds, attorney, sheriff, clerk of district court, and appraiser. Most cities are run by mayor-council systems.

15 Judicial System

The supreme court, the highest court in the state, is composed of a chief justice and six other justices. An intermediate-level court of appeals consists of a chief judge and six other judges. There are 31 district courts. Kansas had a death penalty until 17 December 2004, when the state's death penalty statutes were declared unconstitutional.

However, as of 1 January 2006, eight inmates remained on death row. Kansas's violent crime rate (murder, rape, robbery, aggravated assault) was 374.5 per 100,000 inhabitants in 2004. Crimes against property (burglary, larceny/theft, and motor vehicle theft) that year totaled 3,973.5 reported incidents per 100,000 people. The state had a prison population of 8,966 as of 31 December 2004.

16 Migration

By the 1770s, Kansas was inhabited by a few thousand Indians, mainly from five tribes: the Kansa (Kaw), the Osage, the Pawnee, the Wichita, and Comanche. The first wave of white migration came during the 1850s with the arrival of New England abolitionists who settled in Lawrence, Topeka, and Manhattan. They were followed by a much larger wave of emigrants from the eastern Missouri and the upper Mississippi Valley, drawn by the lure of wide-open spaces and abundant economic opportunity.

The population swelled as a result of the Homestead Act of 1862, which offered land to anyone who would improve it and live on it for five years. The railroads promoted the virtues of Kansas overseas and helped sponsor immigrant settlers. More than 30,000 blacks, mostly from the South, arrived during 1878–80. Crop failures caused by drought in the late 1890s led to extensive out-migration from the western half of the state. Another period of out-migration occurred in the early 1930s, when massive dust storms drove people off the land.

Between 1990 and 1998, the state had a net loss of 13,000 in domestic migration and a gain of 24,000 in international migration. In the period 2000–05, a net total of 38,222 people moved into the state from other countries and 57,763 moved out of the state to other states, for a net loss of 19,541 people.

17 Economy

Agricultural products and meat-packing industries are rivaled by the large aircraft industry centered in Wichita. Four Kansas companies, all located in Wichita, manufacture 70% of the world's general aviation aircraft. Kansas leads all states in wheat production. The Kansas City metropolitan area is a center of automobile production and printing. Metal fabrication, printing, and mineral products are the main industries in the nine southeastern counties.

The national recession of 2001 had a relatively mild impact on the Kansas economy. Despite layoffs in 2001 and 2002, total job creation was positive, in contrast to the nation as a whole. Farming was affected by drought conditions, which persisted into the winter of 2002–2003. Kansas's gross state product (GSP) in 2004 totaled $98.9 billion, of which manufacturing accounted for 15%, followed by real estate (8.8%) and health care and social services (7%).

18 Income

In 2005, Kansas had a gross state product (GSP) of $105 billion, ranking the state 32nd among the 50 states and the District of Columbia in highest GSP. In 2004, Kansas had a per capita (per person) income of $31,078. The three-year average median household income for 2002–04 was $43,725, compared to the national average of $44,473. During the same period, 10.7% of the state's residents lived below the federal poverty level, compared to 12.4% nationwide.

19 Industry

Food products, transportation equipment, printing and publishing, petroleum and coal products, and chemicals accounted for about 70% of the estimated value of shipments, which totaled $56.46 billion in 2004. Kansas is a world leader in aviation, claiming a large share of both US and world production and sales of commercial aircraft. Wichita is a manufacturing center for Boeing, Cessna, Learjet, and Raytheon, which combined manufacture approximately 70% of the world's general aviation aircraft.

20 Labor

In April 2006, the civilian labor force in Kansas numbered 1,481,300, with approximately 67,400 workers unemployed, yielding an unemployment rate of 4.6%, compared to the national average of 4.7% for the same period. In April 2006, 4.9% of the labor force was employed in construction; 19.3% in manufacturing; 19.3% in trade, transportation, and public utilities; 9.8% in professional and business services; 12.4% in education and health services; 8.4% in leisure and hospitality services; and 18.9% in government.

In 2005, 85,000 of Kansas's 1,210,000 employed wage and salary workers were members of unions. This represented 7% of those so employed. The national average is 12%.

21 Agriculture

Known as the breadbasket of the nation, Kansas typically produces more wheat than any other state. It ranked fifth in total farm income in 2005, with cash receipts of $9.7 billion. Between 1940 and 2002, the number of farms declined from 159,000 to 64,500. Income from crops in 2005 totaled $3.1 billion. Other leading crops are alfalfa, hay, oats, barley, popcorn, rye, dry edible beans, corn and sorghums for silage, red clover, and sugar beets.

22 Domesticated Animals

Kansas dairy farmers have an estimated 111,000 milk cows that produced 2.11 billion pounds (0.96 billion kilograms) of milk. In 2001, Kansas poultry farmers sold an estimated 2.2 million pounds (1 million kilograms) of chicken and 434 million eggs worth around $13.6 million.

In 2005, Kansas farmers had an estimated 6.65 million cattle and calves worth $5.51 billion (second in the United States). Kansas farmers had an estimated 1.72 million hogs and pigs worth around $160 million in 2004. An estimated 6.9 million pounds (3.1 million kilograms) of sheep and lambs were produced by Kansas farmers in 2003 and sold for $6.1 million.

23 Fishing

There is little commercial fishing in Kansas. Sport fishermen can find bass, crappie, catfish, perch, and pike in the state's reservoirs and artificial lakes. In 2004, there were 265,238 fishing licenses issued by the state. The Kansas Department of Wildlife and Parks' objectives for fisheries include provision of 11.7 million angler trips annually on Kansas reservoirs, lakes, streams, and private waters, while maintaining the quantity and quality of the catch. There are four state hatcheries.

24 Forestry

Kansas was at one time so barren of trees that early settlers were offered 160 acres (65 hectares) free if they would plant trees on their land. This program was rarely implemented, however, and today much of Kansas is still treeless.

Kansas has 1,545,000 acres (625,000 hectares) of forestland, 2.9% of the total state area. There are 1,491,000 acres (491,000 hectares) of commercial timberland, of which 96% are privately owned.

25 Mining

The value of nonfuel mineral production in Kansas was estimated at $754 million in 2004. The leading nonfuel mineral commodities were grade-A helium, portland cement, salt, and crushed stone. Kansas continued to rank first in the nation in producing crude helium and grade-A helium, fifth in salt production, and eighth in the production of gypsum. Production of portland cement in 2004 was 2.69 million metric tons and crushed stone was 19.8 million metric tons.

26 Energy and Power

In 2003, Kansas's electrical output was 46.56 billion kilowatt hours, 75.4% of which was coal-fired. The installed electrical generating capacity (utility and nonutility) was 10.88 million kilowatts. In 2000, the state ranked 18th in energy consumption per capita, with 385 million Btu (97 million kilocalories).

In 2004, Kansas was the nation's eighth-leading oil producer. Output in 2004 totaled 92,000 barrels of crude petroleum per day. There were proven reserves of 245 million barrels in 2004. Natural gas marketed production was 397.1 billion cubic feet (11.2 billion cubic meters) in 2004. Proven reserves that year totaled 4,652 billion cubic feet (132.1 billion cubic meters). Kansas had only one producing coal mine in 2004, a surface mine. Coal production that year totaled 71,000 tons. The state has one single-unit nuclear plant, the Wolf Creek plant in Burlington.

27 Commerce

The state's wholesale sales totaled $44.1 billion in 2002; retail sales totaled $26.5 billion. Kansas's agricultural and manufactured goods have an important role in US foreign trade. Exports of goods originating in Kansas totaled $6.7 billion in 2005.

28 Public Finance

The state budget is prepared by the Division of the Budget and is submitted by the governor to the legislature for approval. The fiscal year runs from 1 July to 30 June.

The state revenues for fiscal year 2004 were $11.04 billion and expenditures were $11.20 billion. The largest general expenditures were for education ($4.44 billion), public welfare ($2.47 billion), and highways ($1.22 billion). The total indebtedness of state government exceeded $4.57 billion, or about $1,672.06 per capita (per person).

29 Taxation

The state individual income tax schedule has three brackets, 3.5%, 6.25%, and 6.45%. The corporate tax rate is 4.0%. In 2005, the state sales tax rate was at 5.3%. Prescription drugs are exempted from the sales tax. Local-option sales taxes can range up to 3%. The state also collects a full set of excise taxes—on motor fuels, insurance premiums, alcoholic beverages, tobacco products, amusements, pari-mutuels, public utilities and other selected items.

The Kansas inheritance tax is 10% on amounts up to $100,000 and 15% on amounts above $200,000. Other taxes include various license fees, a state property tax, severance taxes for oil and coal, and an oil and gas conservation tax. Property taxes are mainly collected at the local level and are the largest source of income for local governments.

Total state tax collections in Kansas came to $5.59 billion in 2005, with 36.6% generated by the state income tax, 35.6% by the state sales tax, 14.1% by state excise taxes, 1.1% by property taxes, 4.4% by the state corporate income tax, and 8.2% by other taxes. Kansas ranked 32nd in the country in terms of state and local tax burden in 2005.

30 Health

In October 2005, the infant mortality rate was 6.3 per 1,000 live births. The overall death rate in 2003 was 9 deaths per 1,000 population. Heart disease was the leading cause of death in the state. About 19.8% of all Kansans ages 18 and older were smokers in 2004. The rate of HIV-related deaths stood at 1.4 per 100,000 population in 2004.

Kansas's 134 community hospitals had about 10,600 beds in 2003. In 2004, Kansas had 235 doctors per 100,000 resident population and 923 nurses per 100,000 population in 2005. In 2004, there was a total of 1,360 dentists in the state. In 2003, the average expense for community hospital care was $952 per inpatient day. In 2004, at least 11% of the adult population was uninsured.

The University of Kansas has the state's only medical and pharmacology schools. The university's Mid-America Cancer Center and Radiation Therapy Center are the major cancer research and treatment facilities in the state. Topeka, a major US center for psychiatric treatment, is home to the world-famous Menninger Clinic, where research and treatment is sponsored in part by The Menninger Foundation.

31 Housing

Kansas has relatively old housing stock. According to a 2004 survey, about 20% of all housing units were built in 1939 or earlier and 49.6% were built between 1940 and 1979. The overwhelming majority (73.8%) were one-unit, detached structures and 69.5% were owner-occupied. The total number of housing units in 2004 was 1,185,114, of which 1,076,366 were occupied. Most units relied on utility gas and electricity for heating. It was estimated that 46,269 units lacked telephone service, 3,554 lacked complete plumbing facilities, and 5,093 lacked complete kitchen facilities. The average household size was 2.47 people.

In 2004, 13,300 privately owned units were authorized for construction. The median home value was $102,458. The median monthly cost for mortgage owners was $1,013. Renters paid a median of $567 per month.

32 Education

In 1954, Kansas was the focal point of a US Supreme Court decision that had enormous implications for public education. The court ruled, in *Brown v. Board of Education of Topeka*, that Topeka's "separate but equal" elementary schools for black and white students were inherently unequal and it ordered the school system to integrate. In 2004, 89.6% of those age 25 and older were high school graduates and some 30% had obtained a bachelor's degree or higher.

Total public school enrollment was estimated at 471,000 in fall 2002. Enrollment in nonpublic schools in fall 2003 was 41,762. Expenditures for public education in 2003/04 were estimated at more than $3.96 million.

As of fall 2002, there were 188,049 students enrolled in institutions of higher education. In 2005, Kansas had 63 degree-granting institutions. There are 9 state universities, 27 two-year community colleges, and 21 private nonprofit four-year institutions. In addition, Kansas has a state technical institute, a municipal university (Washburn University, Topeka), and an American Indian university. Kansas State University was the nation's first land-grant university. Washburn University and the University of Kansas have the state's two law schools. The oldest higher-education institution in Kansas is Highland Community College, which was chartered in 1857. The oldest four-year institution is Baker University, a United Methodist institution, which received its charter just three days after Highland's was issued.

33 Arts

The Kansas Arts Commission is a state arts agency governed by a 12-member panel of commissioners appointed for four-year rotating terms by the governor. The Arts Commission is in partnership with the regional Mid-America Arts Alliance. The Kansas Humanities Council, founded in 1972, sponsors programs involving over 500,000 people each year.

The largest and most active arts organizations in the state is the Wichita Symphony Orchestra, established in 1944. The Topeka Performing Arts Center presents concerts and shows of a variety of music. Topeka also hosts a symphony.

34 Libraries and Museums

Kansas had 321 public library systems in 2001, with a total of 373 libraries of which 53 were branches. That year, the state's public library system had 10.4 million volumes and a circulation of 21.48 million. The Dwight D. Eisenhower Library in Abilene houses the collection of papers and memorabilia from the 34th president. There is also a museum there. The Menninger Foundation Museum and Archives in Topeka maintains various collections pertaining to psychiatry. The Kansas State Historical Society Library (Topeka) contains the state's archives.

There were about 188 museums, historical societies, and art galleries scattered across the state in 2000. Among the art museums are the Mulvane Art Center in Topeka, the Helen Foresman Spencer Museum of Art at the University of Kansas (Lawrence), and the Wichita Art Museum. The Dalton Museum in Coffeyville displays memorabilia from the famed Dalton family of desperadoes. La Crosse is the home of the Barbed Wire Museum, displaying more than 500 varieties of barbed wire. The Emmett Kelly Historical Museum in Sedan honors the world-famous clown born there. The US Cavalry Museum is on the grounds of Ft. Riley.

35 Communications

In 2004, about 94.8% of all households had telephone service. By June of that year, there were 1,345,160 mobile telephone subscribers. In 2003, 63.8% of Kansas households had a computer, and 54.3% had Internet access. The state had 15 major AM and 54 major FM radio stations, 14 major commercial television stations, and 4 public television stations in 2005.

36 Press

The first newspaper in the state was the *Shawnee Sun*, a Shawnee-language newspaper founded by missionary Jotham Meeker in 1833. In 2005, Kansas had 43 daily newspapers and 14 Sunday papers. Leading newspapers and their daily circulations in 2005 were the *Wichita Eagle* (96,506) and the *Topeka Capital-Journal* (89,469). The *Kansas City Star* (from Missouri) is widely read in both the Kansas and Missouri metropolitan areas.

37 Tourism, Travel & Recreation

Kansas has 23 state parks, 24 federal reservoirs, 48 state fishing lakes, and more than 100 privately owned campsites. There are two national historic sites, Fort Larned and Fort Scott, both 19th century frontier army bases.

The most popular tourist attraction, with over 2.4 million visitors in 2002, is Cabela's (Kansas City), a 190,000 square-foot showroom and shopping center featuring a mule deer museum, a 65,000 gallon aquarium, a gun library, and Yukon base camp grill. The next ranking visitor sites in 2002 were Harrah's Prairie Band Casino (Mayetta), the Kansas City Speedway, Sedgwick County Zoo (Wichita), Woodlands Race Tracks (Kansas City), New Theatre Restaurant (Overland Park), Exploration Place (Wichita) and the Kansas Cosmosphere and Space Center (Hutchinson).

The state fair is held in Hutchinson. Topeka features a number of tourist attractions, including the Kansas Museum of History and the Menninger Foundation. Dodge City offers a reproduction of Old Front Street as it was when the town was the "cowboy capital of the world." In Hanover stands the only remaining original and unaltered Pony Express station. A recreated "Little House on the Prairie," near the childhood home of author Laura Ingalls Wilder, is 13 miles (21 kilometers) southwest of Independence. The Eisenhower Center in Abilene contains the 34th president's family home, library, and museum.

38 Sports

There are no major professional sports teams in Kansas. The minor league Wichita Wranglers play in the AA Texas League. There is also a minor league hockey team in Wichita. During spring, summer, and early fall, horses are raced at Eureka Downs. The national Greyhound Association Meet is held in Abilene.

The University of Kansas and Kansas State both play collegiate football in the Big Twelve Conference. The National Junior College Basketball Tournament is held in Hutchinson each March. The Kansas Relays take place at Lawrence in April. The Flint Hills Rodeo

Dwight D. Eisenhower (1890–1969), shown here with his wife, Mamie, was born in Texas but grew up in Abilene, Kansas. He was elected the 34th president in 1952 and was reelected in 1956. NATIONAL ARCHIVES.

in Strong City is one of many rodeos held statewide.

A sporting event unique to Kansas is the International Pancake Race, held in Liberal each Shrove Tuesday. Women wearing housedresses, aprons, and scarves run along an S-shaped course carrying skillets and flipping pancakes as they go.

39 Famous Kansans

Kansas claims only one US president and one US vice president. Dwight D. Eisenhower (b.Texas, 1890–1969) was elected the 34th president in 1952 and was reelected in 1956.

Charles Curtis (1860–1936) was vice president during the Herbert Hoover administration. Two Kansans have been associate justices of the US Supreme Court: David J. Brewer (1837–1910) and Charles E. Whittaker (1901–1973).

Prominent US senators include Robert "Bob" Dole (b.1923), who was the Republican candidate for vice-president in 1976, twice served as Senate majority leader, and was his party's presidential candidate in 1996; and Nancy Landon Kassebaum Baker (b.1932), who was first elected to the US Senate in 1978 but retired in 1997. Gary Hart (b.1936) was a senator and a presidential candidate in 1984 and 1988.

Other prominent Kansan political figures included Alfred M. Landon (1887–1984), a former governor who ran for US president on the Republican ticket in 1936; and Carrie Nation (b. Kentucky, 1846–1911), the prohibition activist.

Leaders in medicine and science include the Menninger doctors—C. F. (1862–1953), William (1899–1966), and Karl (1893–1990)—who established the Menninger Foundation, a leading center for mental health; and Clyde Tombaugh (1906–1997), who discovered the planet Pluto. Kansas also had several pioneers in aviation including Clyde Cessna (b.Iowa, 1880–1954), Walter Beech (1891–1950), and Amelia Earhart (1898–1937). William Coleman (1870–1957) was an innovator in lighting, and Walter Chrysler (1875–1940) was a prominent automotive developer.

Most famous of Kansas writers was William Allen White (1868–1944), whose son William L. White (1900–1973) also had a distinguished literary career. Damon Runyon (1884–1946) was a popular journalist and storyteller, and Gordon Parks (1912–2006) made his mark in literature, photography, and music. Mort Walker (Mortimer Walker Addison, b.1923) is a famous cartoonist. William Inge (1913–1973) was a prize-winning playwright who contributed to the Broadway stage.

Notable painters include John Noble (1874–1934) and John Steuart Curry (1897–1946). Jazz great Charlie "Bird" Parker (Charles Christopher Parker, Jr., 1920–1955) was born in Kansas City.

Stage and screen notables include Joseph "Buster" Keaton (1895–1966), Louise Brooks (1906–1985), Edward Asner (b.1929), and Kirstie Alley (b.1955). The clown Emmett Kelly (1898–1979) was a Kansan.

Glenn Cunningham (1909–1988) and Jim Ryun (b.1947) both set running records for the mile. Also prominent in sports history were James Naismith (b.Ontario, Canada, 1861–1939), the inventor of basketball, and baseball pitcher Walter Johnson (1887–1946).

40 Bibliography

BOOKS

Averill, Thomas Fox. *Soldier of Democracy: A Biography of Dwight Eisenhower.* New York: Doubleday, 1945, 1952.

Bjorklund, Ruth. *Kansas.* New York: Benchmark Books, 2000.

Bristow, M. J. *State Songs of America.* Westport, CT: Greenwood Press, 2000.

Deady, Kathleen W. *Kansas Facts and Symbols.* Rev. ed. Mankato, MN: Capstone, 2003.

Murray, Julie. *Kansas.* Edina, MN: Abdo Publishing, 2006.

Nelson, Julie. *Kansas City Chiefs.* Mankato, MN: Creative Education, 2000.

Zeinert, Karen. *Tragic Prelude: Bleeding Kansas.* North Haven, CT: Linnet, 2001.

WEB SITES

Kansas Travel and Tourism. *Kansas: As Big as You Think.* www.travelks.com (accessed March 1, 2007).

State of Kansas Web Site www.state.ks.us (accessed March 1, 2007).

Kentucky

Commonwealth of Kentucky

ORIGIN OF STATE NAME: Possibly derived from the Wyandot Indian word *Kah-ten-tah-teh* (land of tomorrow).

NICKNAME: The Bluegrass State.

CAPITAL: Frankfort.

ENTERED UNION: 1 June 1792 (15th).

OFFICIAL SEAL: In the center are two men exchanging greetings; above and below them is the state motto. On the periphery are two sprigs of goldenrod and the words "Commonwealth of Kentucky."

FLAG: A simplified version of the state seal on a blue field.

MOTTO: United We Stand, Divided We Fall.

SONG: "My Old Kentucky Home."

COLORS: Blue and gold.

FLOWER: Goldenrod.

TREE: Tulip poplar.

ANIMAL: Gray squirrel.

BIRD: Cardinal.

FISH: Bass.

INSECT: Viceroy butterfly.

FOSSIL: Brachiopod.

LEGAL HOLIDAYS: New Year's Day, 1 January, plus one extra day; Birthday of Martin Luther King Jr., 3rd Monday in January; Washington's Birthday, 3rd Monday in February; Good Friday, March or April, half-day holiday; Memorial Day, last Monday in May; Independence Day, 4 July; Labor Day, 1st Monday in September; Veterans' Day, 11 November; Thanksgiving Day, 4th Thursday in November, plus one extra day; Christmas Day, 25 December, plus one extra day.

TIME: 7 AM EST = noon GMT; 6 AM CST = noon GMT.

1 Location and Size

Located in the eastern south-central United States, the Commonwealth of Kentucky is the smallest of the eight south-central states and ranks 37th in size among the 50 states. The total area of Kentucky is 40,409 square miles (104,659 square kilometers), of which land makes up 39,669 square miles (102,743 square kilometers) and inland water 740 square miles (1,917 square kilometers). The state extends about 350 miles (563 kilometers) east-west and 175 miles (282 kilometers) north-south. Its total boundary length is 1,290 miles (2,076 kilometers). Because of a double bend in the Mississippi River, about 10 square miles (26 square kilometers) of southwest Kentucky is separated from the rest of the state by a narrow strip of Missouri.

2 Topography

The eastern quarter of the state is dominated by the Cumberland Plateau, which is on the western border of the Appalachians. At its western edge, the plateau meets the uplands of the Lexington Plain (known as the Bluegrass region) to the north and the hilly Pennyroyal to the south. These two regions, which together make up nearly half the state's area, are separated by a narrow curving plain known as the Knobs, because of the shapes of its eroded hills. The most level area of the state consists of the western coalfields bounded by the Pennyroyal to the east and the Ohio River to the north. In the far west are the coastal plains of the Mississippi River, a region commonly known as the Purchase, having been purchased from the Chickasaw Indians.

The highest point in Kentucky is Black Mountain on the southeastern boundary in Harlan County, at 4,139 feet (2,162 meters). The lowest point is 257 feet (78 meters), along the Mississippi River in Fulton County.

The only large lakes in Kentucky are artificial. The biggest is Cumberland Lake, at 79 square miles (205 square kilometers). Kentucky Lake, Lake Barkley, and Dale Hollow Lake straddle the border with Tennessee.

Kentucky claims at least 3,000 miles (4,800 kilometers) of navigable rivers. Among the most important of Kentucky's rivers are the Kentucky (259 miles/417 kilometers), the Cumberland, the Tennessee, the Big Sandy, Green, Licking, and Tradewater rivers. Completion in 1985 of the Tennessee-Tombigbee Waterway, linking the Tennessee and Tombigbee rivers in Alabama,

Kentucky Population Profile

Total population estimate in 2006:	4,206,074
Population change, 2000–06:	4.1%
Hispanic or Latino†:	1.7%
Population by race	
One race:	98.9%
White:	89.9%
Black or African American:	7.2%
American Indian /Alaska Native:	0.2%
Asian:	0.9%
Native Hawaiian / Pacific Islander:	0.1%
Some other race:	0.7%
Two or more races:	1.0%

Population by Age Group

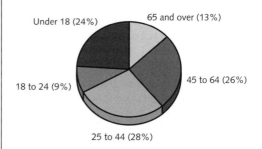

Under 18 (24%)
65 and over (13%)
45 to 64 (26%)
18 to 24 (9%)
25 to 44 (28%)

Major Cities by Population

City	Population	% change 2000–05
Louisville/Jefferson	556,429	NA
Lexington-Fayette	268,080	2.9
Owensboro	55,459	2.6
Bowling Green	52,272	6.0
Covington	42,811	-1.3
Richmond	30,893	13.8
Hopkinsville	28,821	-4.2
Henderson	27,666	1.1
Frankfort	27,210	-1.9
Florence	26,349	11.9

Notes: †A person of Hispanic or Latino origin may be of any race. NA indicates that data are not available. **Sources:** U.S. Census Bureau. *American Community Survey* and *Population Estimates*. www.census.gov/ (accessed March 2007).

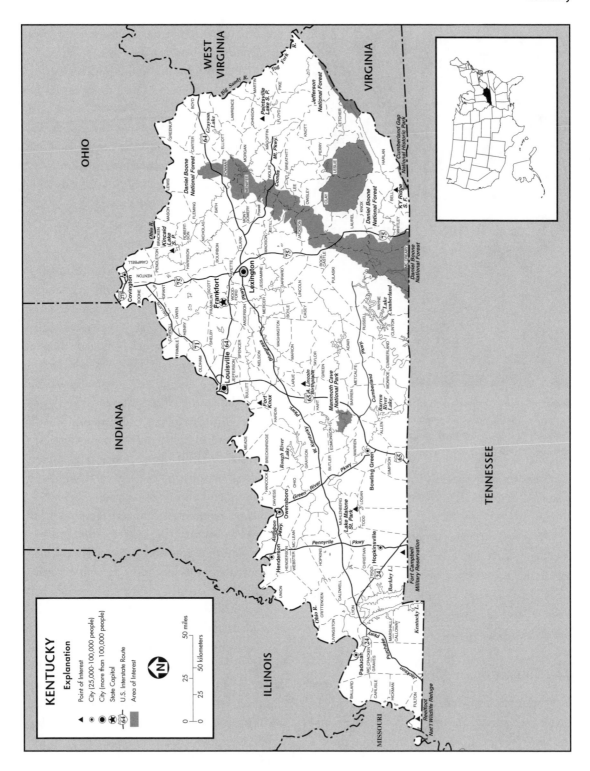

Mammoth Cave National Park, visited each year by over 1.8 million people, contains an estimated 150 miles (241 kilometers) of underground passages. WWW. KENTUCKYTOURISM.COM.

gave Kentucky's Appalachian coalfields direct water access to the Gulf of Mexico for the first time.

Drainage through porous limestone rock of the Pennyroyal has created underground passages, the best known of which is Mammoth Cave, now a national park. The Cumberland Falls, 92 feet (28 meters) high and 100 feet (30 meters) wide, are located in Whitely County.

3 Climate

Kentucky has a moderate, relatively humid climate, with abundant rainfall. The southern and lowland regions are slightly warmer than the uplands. In Louisville, the normal monthly mean temperature ranges from 33°F (1°C) in January to 76°F (24°C) in July. The record high for the state was 114°F (46°C), set in Greensburg on 28 July in 1930. The record low, -37°F (-40°C), was set in Shelbyville of 19 January 1994. The average daily relative humidity in Louisville ranges from 58% to 81%. The normal annual precipitation is 44.5 inches (113 centimeters). Snowfall totals about 18 inches (46 centimeters) a year.

4 Plants and Animals

Kentucky's forests are mostly of the oak and hickory variety, with some beech and maple areas. Four species of magnolia are found and the tulip poplar, eastern hemlock, and eastern white pine are also common. Kentucky's famed bluegrass is actually blue only in May, when dwarf iris and wild columbine are in bloom. Rare plants include the swamp loosestrife and showy gentian. In April 2006, the US Fish and Wildlife Service listed eight Kentucky plant species as threatened or endangered, including Braun's rock-cress, Cumberland sandwort, running buffalo clover, and Short's goldenrod.

Game mammals include the raccoon, muskrat, and opossum. The eastern chipmunk and flying squirrel are common small mammals. At least 300 bird species have been recorded, including blackbirds, cardinals (the state bird), and robins. More than 100 types of fish have been identified.

Rare animal species include the swamp rabbit, black bear, raven (Corvus corax), and mud darter. In April 2006, there were 31 animal species listed as threatened or endangered, including three species of bat (Indiana, Virginia big-eared, and gray), bald eagle, puma, piping plo-

Kentucky Population by Race

Census 2000 was the first national census in which the instructions to respondents said, "Mark one or more races." This table shows the number of people who are of one, two, or three or more races. For those claiming two races, the number of people belonging to the various categories is listed. The U.S. government conducts a census of the population every ten years.

	Number	Percent
Total population	4,041,769	100.0
One race	3,999,326	98.9
Two races	39,863	1.0
White *and* Black or African American	11,084	0.3
White *and* American Indian/Alaska Native	12,842	0.3
White *and* Asian	4,728	0.1
White *and* Native Hawaiian/Pacific Islander	633	—
White *and* some other race	6,166	0.2
Black or African American *and* American Indian/Alaska Native	1,174	—
Black or African American *and* Asian	571	—
Black or African American *and* Native Hawaiian/Pacific Islander	141	—
Black or African American *and* some other race	1,126	—
American Indian/Alaska Native *and* Asian	174	—
American Indian/Alaska Native *and* Native Hawaiian/Pacific Islander	30	—
American Indian/Alaska Native *and* some other race	233	—
Asian *and* Native Hawaiian/Pacific Islander	251	—
Asian *and* some other race	592	—
Native Hawaiian/Pacific Islander *and* some other race	118	—
Three or more races	2,580	0.1

Source: U.S. Census Bureau. *Census 2000: Redistricting Data.* Press release issued by the Redistricting Data Office. Washington, D.C., March, 2001. A dash (—) indicates that the percent is less than 0.1.

ver, Kentucky cave shrimp, and three species of pearly mussel.

5 Environmental Protection

The National Resources and Environmental Protection Cabinet is the primary state agency for the environment. The Environmental Quality Commission, a watchdog group for environmental concerns, is a citizen's group of seven members appointed by the governor.

The most serious environmental concern in Kentucky is repairing and minimizing damage to land and water from strip-mining.

Also active in environmental matters is the Department of Environmental Protection, consisting of four divisions. The Division of Water administers the state's Safe Drinking Water and Clean Water acts and regulation of sewage disposal. The Division of Waste Management oversees solid waste disposal systems in the state. The Air Pollution Control Division monitors industrial discharges into the air and other forms of air pollution. A special division is concerned with Maxey Flats, a closed nuclear waste disposal facility in Fleming County, where leakage of radioactive materials was discovered.

Flooding is a chronic problem in southeastern Kentucky, where strip-mining has exacerbated soil erosion.

In 2003, Kentucky had 149 hazardous waste sites, 14 of which were on the National Priorities List, as of 2006.

6 Population

In 2005, Kentucky ranked 26th in population among the 50 states, with an estimated total of 4,206,074 residents. The projected population for 2025 is 4.48 million. The population density in 2004 was 104.7 persons per square mile (40.49 persons per square kilometer). In that same year, the median age was 37.3. In 2005, those 65 years or older accounted for 13% of all residents, while 24% of all residents were 18 years old or younger.

As of 2005, Louisville-Jefferson County had an estimated population of around 556,429 people. Lexington-Fayette had an estimated population of about 268,080. The population of Louisville metropolitan area (includes portions of Kentucky and Indiana) was estimated at 1,200,847.

7 Ethnic Groups

According to the 2000 census, the number of black Americans in Kentucky stood at 295,994 residents, representing 7.3% of the population. In 2006, the percentage of black residents was 7.2%. In 2000, the state's Asian population was estimated at 29,744, and the Native American population was estimated at 8,616. In that same year, there were also 3,818 Koreans, 6,771 Asian Indians, 3,683 Japanese, 3,596 Vietnamese, and 5,397 Chinese. A total of 59,939 residents (1.5%) were Hispanic or Latino in 2000, with 31,385 reporting Mexican ancestry and 6,469 of Puerto Rican ancestry. In 2006, the Hispanic or Latino population accounted for 1.7% of all Kentucky residents. Pacific Islanders numbered 1,460, in 2000, while there were 80,271 foreign-born residents in that same year (about 2% of the total population). Among persons reporting a single ancestry a total of 391,542 were English, 514,955 were German, 424,133 were Irish, and 66,147 were French.

8 Languages

Speech patterns in the state generally reflect the Virginia and Kentucky backgrounds of the first settlers. South Midland features are best preserved in the mountains, but some common to Midland and Southern are widespread. Other regional features are typically both South Midland and Southern. After a vowel, the /r/ sound may be weak or missing. In southern Kentucky, earthworms are called *redworms*, a burlap bag is a *tow sack*, and green beans are called *snap beans*. Subregional terms appear in abundance. In the east, kindling is *pine* and a seesaw is a *ridyhorse*. In central Kentucky, a moth is a *candlefly*.

In 2000, of all residents five years old and older, 96.1% spoke only English at home. Other languages spoken at home included Spanish, German, Korean, and Chinese.

9 Religions

Throughout its history, Kentucky has been predominantly Protestant. The New Light Baptists immigrated from Virginia to Kentucky under the leadership of Lewis Craig and built the first church in the state near Lancaster in 1781. The first Methodist Church was established near Danville in 1783. In 1784, the Roman Catholics also built a church.

As of 2000, Evangelical Protestantism was predominant with the single largest denomination within the state being the Southern Baptists

Convention with 979,994 adherents. The next largest Protestant denomination was the United Methodist Church with 208,720 adherents, but reported only 152,727 members in 2003. In 2000, the Christian Churches and Churches of Christ with 106,638 adherents. The Roman Catholic Church had about 382,042 members in 2004. There were an estimated 11,350 Jews in Kentucky in 2000, and about 4,696 Muslims. Over 1.8 million people (46.6% of the population) were not counted as members of any religious organization in the 2000 survey.

10 Transportation

As of 2003, Kentucky had 2,823 miles (4,545 kilometers) of railroad track, with five Class I railroads operating in the state. Rail service to the state, nearly all of which was freight, was provided by 15 railroads. As of 2006, there were four Amtrak stations in Kentucky.

The trails of Indians and buffalo became the first roads in Kentucky. Throughout the 19th century, counties called on their citizens to maintain some roads although maintenance was haphazard. The best roads were the toll roads. This system came to an end as a result of the "toll-gate war" of the late 19th and early 20th centuries, a rebellion in which masked Kentuckians, demanding free roads, raided tollgates and assaulted their keepers. In 1912, a state highway commission was created, and by 1920, roads had improved considerably. In 2004, Kentucky had 77,366 miles (124,559 kilometers) of public roads and 2.8 million licensed drivers. In the same year, there were some 1.855 million automobiles, about 1.415 million trucks, and around 2,000 buses registered in the state.

The Ohio River and its tributaries, along with the Mississippi, were Kentucky's primary commercial routes for trade with the South and the West, until railroads became more popular. Louisville, on the Ohio River, is the chief port. Paducah is the outlet port for traffic on the Tennessee River.

In 2005 there were 149 airports, 58 heliports and 1 STOLport (Short Take-Off and Landing) in Kentucky. The largest of these is Cincinnati/Northern Kentucky International Airport, with 10,864,547 passenger boardings in 2004.

11 History

No Native American nations resided in central and eastern Kentucky when these areas were first explored by British-American surveyors Thomas Walker and Christopher Gist in 1750 and 1751. The dominant Shawnee and Cherokee tribes utilized the region as a hunting ground, returning to homes in the neighboring territories of Ohio and Tennessee. The first permanent colonial settlement in Kentucky was established at Harrodstown (now Harrodsburg) in 1774.

North Carolina speculator Richard Henderson, assisted by famed woodsman Daniel Boone, purchased a huge tract of land in central Kentucky from the Cherokee and established Fort Boonesborough. Henderson sought approval for creation of a 14th colony, but the plan was blocked by Virginians, who in 1776 incorporated the region as the County of Kentucky.

Kentucky became the principal gateway for migration into the Mississippi Valley. By the late 1780s, its settlements were growing, and it was obvious that Kentucky could not long remain

Kentucky Governors: 1792–2007

Years	Governor	Party	Years	Governor	Party
1792–1796	Isaac Shelby	Dem-Rep	1899–1900	William Sylvester Taylor	Republican
1796–1804	James Garrard	Dem-Rep	1900	William Goebel	Democrat
1804–1808	Christopher Greenup	Republican	1900–1907	John Crepps Wickliffe Beckham	Democrat
1808–1812	Charles Scott	Dem-Rep	1907–1911	Augustus Everett Willson	Republican
1812–1816	Isaac Shelby	Dem-Rep	1911–1915	James Bennett McCreary	Democrat
1816	George Madison	Dem-Rep	1915–1919	Augustus Owsley Stanley	Democrat
1816–1820	Gabriel Slaughter	Dem-Rep	1919	James Dixon Black	Democrat
1820–1824	John Adair	Dem-Rep	1919–1923	Edwin Porch Morrow	Republican
1824–1828	Joseph Desha	Dem-Rep	1923–1927	William Jason Fields	Democrat
1828–1832	Thomas Metcalfe	Nat-Rep	1927–1931	Flem Davis Sampson	Republican
1832–1834	John Breathitt	Democrat	1831–1835	Ruby Laffoon	Democrat
1834–1836	James Turner Morehead	Democrat	1835–1839	Albert Benjamin Chandler	Democrat
1836–1839	James Clark	Whig	1839–1843	Keen Johnson	Democrat
1839–1840	Charles Anderson Wickliffe	Whig	1943–1947	Simeon Slavens Willis	Republican
1840–1844	Robert Perkins Letcher	Whig	1947–1950	Earle Chester Clements	Democrat
1844–1848	William Owsley	Whig	1950–1955	Lawrence Winchester Wetherby	Democrat
1848–1850	John Jordan Crittenden	Whig	1955–1959	Albert Benjamin Chandler	Democrat
1850–1851	John Larue Helm	Democrat	1959–1963	Bertram Thomas Combs	Democrat
1851–1855	Lazarus Whitehead Powell	Democrat	1963–1967	Edward Thompson Breathitt	Democrat
1855–1859	Charles Slaughter Morehead	American	1967–1971	Louie Broady Nunn	Republican
1859–1862	Beriah Magoffin	Democrat	1971–1974	Wendell Hampton Ford	Democrat
1862–1863	James Fisher Robinson	Democrat	1974–1979	Julian Morton Carroll	Democrat
1863–1867	Thomas E. Bramlette	Union-Dem	1979–1983	John Young Brown, Jr.	Democrat
1867	John Larue Helm	Democrat	1983–1987	Martha Layne Collins	Democrat
1867–1871	John White Stevenson	Democrat	1987–1991	Wallace G. Wilkinson	Democrat
1871–1875	Preston Hopkins Leslie	Democrat	1991–1995	Brereton Chandler Jones	Democrat
1875–1879	James Bennett McCreary	Democrat	1995–2003	Paul E. Patton	Democrat
1879–1883	Luke Pryor Blackburn	Democrat	2003–	Ernie Fletcher	Republican
1883–1887	James Procter Knott	Democrat			
1887–1891	Simon Bolivar Buckner	Democrat		Democratic Republican – Dem-Rep	
1891–1895	John Young Brown	Democrat		National Republican – Nat-Rep	
1895–1899	William O'Connell Bradley	Republican		Union Democrat – Union-Dem	

under the control of Virginia. In June 1792, Kentucky entered the Union as the 15th state.

State Development Kentucky became a center for breeding and racing fine thoroughbred horses, an industry that still thrives today. More important was the growing and processing of tobacco, which accounted for half the agricultural income of Kentucky farmers by 1860. Finally, whiskey began to be produced in vast quantities by the 1820s, culminating in the development of a fine, aged amber-red brew known throughout the world as bourbon, after Bourbon County.

During the Civil War, Kentuckians were forced to choose sides between the Union, led in the North by Kentucky native Abraham Lincoln, and the Confederacy, led in the South by Kentucky native Jefferson Davis. Although the state legislature finally opted for the Union side, approximately 30,000 men went south to Confederate service, while up to 100,000—including nearly 24,000 black soldiers—served in the Union army.

In the decades following the war, railroad construction increased threefold and exploitation of timber and coal reserves began in eastern Kentucky. By 1900, Kentucky ranked first among southern states in per capita (per person) income. However, wealth remained very unevenly distributed—a third of all Kentucky farmers were landless tenants. The gubernatorial election scandal of 1899, in which Republican William S. Taylor was charged with fraud and reform-minded Democrat William Goebel was assassinated, polarized the state. Outside investment plummeted, and Kentucky fell into a prolonged economic depression. By 1940, the state ranked last among the 48 states in per capita income and was burdened by an image of poverty and feuding clans. The Great Depression hit the state hard, though an end to Prohibition revived the inactive whiskey industry.

Post-World War II Kentucky has changed greatly since World War II. Between 1945 and 1980, the number of farms decreased by 53%, while the number of manufacturing plants increased from 2,994 to 3,504 between 1967 and 1982. Although Kentucky remains one of the poorest states in the nation, positive change is evident even in relatively isolated rural communities, the result of better roads, education, television, and government programs.

In the early 1990s, public corruption became a major issue in Kentucky politics. In a sting operation code-named Boptrot, legislators were filmed by hidden cameras accepting payments from lobbyists. Fifteen state legislators, lobbyists, and public figures were convicted or charged with bribery, extortion, fraud, and racketeering. An investigation carried out at the same time charged the husband of former Governor Martha Layne Collins, Dr. William Collins,

with collecting $1.7 million in bribes while his wife was in office.

In 1990, the Kentucky Supreme Court ruled that the state's public education system was unconstitutional and ordered the state legislature to develop a new system of school administration and funding. The legislature responded with the Kentucky Education Reform Act, which it passed that same year and was implemented over the next five years.

In 2003, Republican Ernie Fletcher was elected governor, and by 2005, had moved to make the state more business-friendly through the creation of a more flexible tax code, improvements in the quality of education, encouraging more healthy lifestyles, and other governmental and administrative reforms.

12 State Government

The state legislature, called the General Assembly, consists of the House of Representatives, which has 100 members elected for 2-year terms, and the Senate with 38 members elected for staggered 4-year terms. Except for revenue-raising measures, which must be introduced in the House of Representatives, either chamber may introduce or amend a bill. Most bills may be passed by majority votes equal to at least two-fifths of the membership of each house. A majority of the members of each house is required to override the governor's veto. The elected executive officers of Kentucky include the governor and lieutenant governor (elected jointly), secretary of state, attorney general, treasurer, auditor of public accounts, and commissioner of agriculture. All serve 4-year terms and may succeed themselves only once.

Kentucky Presidential Vote by Political Parties, 1948–2004

YEAR	KENTUCKY WINNER	DEMOCRAT	REPUBLICAN	DEMOCRAT	PROHIBITION	STATES' RIGHTS PROGRESSIVE	SOCIALIST
1948	*Truman (D)	466,756	341,210	10,411	1,245	1,567	1,284
1952	Stevenson (D)	495,729	495,029	—	1,161	—	—
1956	*Eisenhower (R)	476,453	572,192	—	2,145	—	—
1960	Nixon (R)	521,855	602,607	—	—	—	—
				STATES' RIGHTS			
1964	*Johnson (D)	669,659	372,977	3,469	—	—	—
				AMERICAN IND.			SOC. WRKRS
1968	*Nixon (R)	397,541	462,411	193,098	—	—	2,843
					AMERICAN	PEOPLE'S	
1972	*Nixon (R)	371,159	676,446	—	17,627	1,118	—
1976	*Carter (D)	615,717	531,852	2,328	8,308	—	—
						LIBERTARIAN	CITIZENS
1980	*Reagan (R)	617,417	635,274	—	—	5,531	1,304
1984	*Reagan (R)	539,539	821,702	—	—	1,776	599
1988	*Bush (R)	580,368	734,281	4,994	1,256	2,118	—
				IND. (PEROT)			
1992	*Clinton (D)	665,104	617,178	203,944	430	4,513	989
1996	*Clinton (D)	636,614	623,283	120,396	—	4,009	—
				LIBERTARIAN	REFORM		
2000	*Bush, G. W. (R)	638,898	872,492	2,896	4,173	23,192	—
2004	*Bush, G. W. (R)	712,733	1,069,439	—	—	2,619	—

*Won US presidential election.

As of December 2004, the governor's salary was $127,146, and most legislators received less than $14,000 per year based upon salaries of $166.34 per day when the legislature is in session.

13 Political Parties

Regional divisions in party affiliation during the Civil War era, based upon sympathy with the South (Democrats) or with the Union (Republicans), have persisted in the state's voting patterns. In general, in the 21st century, the poorer mountain areas tend to vote Republican, while the more affluent lowlanders in the Bluegrass and Pennyroyal areas tend to vote Democratic.

In 1983, Martha Layne Collins, a Democrat, defeated Republican candidate Jim Bunning to become Kentucky's first woman governor. In 2004 there were 2,819,000 registered voters. In 1998, the party affiliation of registered voters was 61% Democratic, 32% Republican, and 7% unaffiliated or members of other parties. Republican Ernie Fletcher was elected governor in 2003. Republican George W. Bush defeated Democrat Al Gore 57% to 41% in the 2000 US presidential campaign. Bush also defeated Democrat John Kerry 59.5% to 39.7% in the 2004 presidential election.

Following the 2006 midterm elections, Republicans held 21 seats in the state senate, while Democrats held 16, and 1 was held by an independent. However in the state house, the Democrats continued to dominate, with 61 seats, to the Republicans' 39. Sixteen women were elected to the state legislature in 2006, or 11.6%. At the national level, Kentucky was represented by Republican senators Mitch McConnell (reelected in 2002) and Jim Bunning (elected in 1998 and reelected in 2004). In the US House of Representatives, there were two Democrats and four Republicans following the 2006 elections.

14 Local Government

The chief governing body of Kentucky's counties is the fiscal court. Elected officials include magistrates, commissioners, and sheriffs. As of 2005, the state had 120 counties and 424 cities. Cities are assigned by the General Assembly to one of six classes on the basis of population. Kentucky has two first-class cities, Louisville and Lexington. The mayor or other chief executive officer in the top three classes must be elected. In the bottom classes, the executive may be either elected by the people, or appointed by a city council or commission. Other units of local government in Kentucky included 720 special-purpose districts and 176 public school districts in 2005.

15 Judicial System

Judicial power in Kentucky is vested in a unified court of justice. The highest court is the supreme court, consisting of a chief justice and six associate justices. It has appeals jurisdiction and also bears responsibility for the budget and administration of the entire system. The court of appeals consists of 14 judges, 2 elected from each supreme court district.

Circuit courts, with original and appeals jurisdiction, are held in each county. There are 56 judicial circuits. Under the revised judicial system, district courts, which have limited and original jurisdiction, replaced various local and county courts. In 2004, Kentucky had a vio-

lent crime (murder/nonnegligent manslaughter, forcible rape, robbery, aggravated assault) rate of 244.9 crimes per 100,000 people. As of 31 December 2004, there were 17,814 prisoners in Kentucky's state and federal prisons. The state has a death penalty, of which the sole method of execution is lethal injection for those sentenced after 31 March 1998. Those inmates sentenced before that date may select electrocution, instead of lethal injection. From 1976 through 5 May 2006, the state had executed only 2 persons. As of 1 January 2006, there were 37 inmates on death row.

16 Migration

During the frontier period, Kentucky first attracted settlers from eastern states, especially Virginia and North Carolina. Prominent among early foreign immigrants were people of English and Scotch-Irish ancestry, who tended to settle in the Kentucky highlands, which resembled their Old World homelands.

Kentucky's black population increased rapidly during the first 40 years of statehood through slavery. By the 1830s, however, many Kentucky owners either moved to the Deep South or sold their slaves to new owners in that region. During the 1850s, nearly 16% of Kentucky's slave population, more than 43,000 people, were sold or moved from the state. A tiny percentage of Kentucky's blacks, probably fewer than 200, emigrated to Liberia under the auspices of the Kentucky Colonization Society.

Until the early 1970s there was a considerable out-migration of whites, especially from eastern Kentucky to industrial areas of Ohio, Indiana, and other nearby states. Between 1990 and 1998, Kentucky had net gains of 90,000 in

Bowling Green is the only place where the Chevy Corvette is manufactured. The Corvette Museum is located across the street from the manufacturing plant. WWW. KENTUCKYTOURISM.COM.

domestic migration and 14,000 in international migration. In the period 2000–05, net international migration into the state totaled 27,435 people, while net domestic migration totaled 32,169, for a net gain of 59,604 people.

17 Economy

Although agriculture is still important in Kentucky, manufacturing has grown rapidly since World War II, and was by the mid-1980s, the most important area of the economy as a source of both employment and personal income. Kentucky leads the nation in the production of coal and whiskey, and ranks second in

tobacco output. In contrast to the generally prosperous Bluegrass area and the growing industrial cities, eastern Kentucky, highly dependent on coal mining, is one of the poorest regions in the United States.

During the 1990s, declines in the tobacco, textiles, apparel, and coal mining areas were compensated for by job growth in motor vehicle manufacturing, fabricated metals, and appliances. The national recession of 2001 negatively impacted the economy, however, as manufacturing declined. Nonetheless, Kentucky was one of only five states where employment grew more than 1% in 2002.

Kentucky's gross state product (GSP) in 2004 totaled $136.446 billion, of which manufacturing accounted for the largest portion at 21% of GSP, followed by real estate at 9%, and health care and social services at 7.6% of GSP. Of the 83,046 businesses in the state that had employees, 97% were small companies.

18 Income

In 2004, Kentucky had a per capita (per person) personal income of $27,265, which ranked the state 44th among the 50 states and the District of Columbia, compared to the national average of $33,050. Median household income for the three-year period 2002–04 was $37,396 in Kentucky, compared to the national average of $44,473. For that period, 15.4% of the state's residents lived below the federal poverty level, compared to 12.4% nationwide.

19 Industry

Manufacturing industries are concentrated in Louisville and Jefferson County, and other cities along the Ohio River. Kentucky is the leading producer of bourbon whiskey, and is one of the largest producers of trucks in the nation, with assembly plants at Louisville, as well as for automobiles at Bowling Green and Georgetown. The shipment value of manufactured products in 2004 was $97.253 billion. Of that total, transportation equipment accounted for the largest share at $34.220 billion, followed by primary metals at $9.178 billion.

In 2004, a total of 246,749 people were employed in Kentucky's manufacturing sector. Of that total, the transportation equipment manufacturing sector accounted for the largest portion at 50,032, followed by food manufacturing at 22,863.

20 Labor

In April 2006, the seasonally adjusted civilian labor force in Kentucky numbered 2,022,000, with approximately 123,600 workers unemployed, yielding an unemployment rate of 6.1%, compared to the national average of 4.7% for the same period. According to early data on nonfarm employment for that same period, about 4.7% of the labor force was employed in construction; 14.1% in manufacturing; 20.7% in trade, transportation, and public utilities; 4.8% in financial activities; 9.4% in professional and business services; 12.9% in educational and health services; 9.2% in leisure and hospitality services; and 17% in government.

Although a small number of trade unions existed in Kentucky before the 1850s, it was not until after the Civil War that substantial unionization took place. During the 1930s, there were long, violent struggles between the United Mine Workers (UMW) and the mine owners of eastern Kentucky. The UMW won bargaining rights in 1938, but after World War II the displacement of workers because of mechanization, a drastic drop in the demand for coal, and evidence of mismanagement and corruption within the UMW served to undercut the union's position. Increased demand for coal in the 1970s led to a substantial increase in jobs for miners and the UMW, under different leaders, began a new drive to organize the Cumberland Plateau.

In 2005, a total of 164,000 of Kentucky's 1,696,000 employed wage and salary workers were members of a union. This represented 9.7% of those so employed, under the national average of 12%.

21 Agriculture

With cash receipts totaling $3.9 billion, Kentucky ranked 24th among the 50 states in farm marketings in 2005. Kentucky tobacco, first marketed in New Orleans in 1787, quickly became the state's most important crop. Corn has long been one of the state's most important crops, not only for livestock feed, but also as a major ingredient in the distilling of whiskey.

In 2004 there were approximately 85,000 farms in Kentucky, with an average size of 162 acres (66 hectares). In that same year, Kentucky farms produced some 234.5 million pounds (106.36 million kilograms) of tobacco, the second most in the nation. Other leading field crops in 2004 included corn for grain, soybeans, wheat, sorghum, and barley.

22 Domesticated Animals

The Bluegrass region, which offers excellent pasturage and drinking water, has become renowned as a center for horse breeding, including thoroughbreds, quarter horses, American saddle horses, Arabians, and standardbreds. In 2004, sales of horses accounted for 23% of Kentucky's farm receipts.

In 2005, Kentucky had an estimated 2.25 million cattle and calves worth $1.82 billion. In 2004, Kentucky farmers had an estimated 350,000 hogs and pigs, worth around $27.6 million. Kentucky also produced an estimated 1.46 billion pounds (0.66 billion kilograms) of milk from 116,000 dairy cows in 2003.

23 Fishing

Fishing is of little commercial importance in Kentucky. In 2004, Kentucky had 580,917 fishing license holders. In 2005, there were 60 catfish farms operating within the state. The Wolf Creek National Fish Hatchery in Jamestown raises rainbow and brown trout and stocks 90 different areas within the state.

24 Forestry

In 2004 there were 11,391,000 acres (4,828,000 hectares) of forested land in Kentucky, which is 47% of the state's land area, with over 90% of the forestland classified as commercially viable for timber production.

The most heavily forested areas are in the river valleys of eastern Kentucky, in the Appalachians. In 2004, Kentucky produced 662 million board feet of lumber, nearly all of it in hardwoods. The Division of Forestry of the Department of Natural Resources manages approximately 30,000 acres (12,300 hectares) of state-owned forestland and operates two forest tree nurseries producing 7 to 9 million seedling trees a year.

There are two national forests (the Daniel Boone and the Jefferson on Kentucky's eastern border) enclosing two national wilderness areas. These two national forests had a combined area of 1,415,744 acres (572,952 hectares) in 2005. Gross acreage of all Kentucky lands in the National Forest System was 2,212,000 acres (895,400 hectares) in 20031. National parks in the state include the Mammoth Cave National Park, and the Cumberland Gap National Historical Park on Kentucky's eastern border.

25 Mining

The value of nonfuel mineral production in Kentucky in 2003 was estimated at $559 million. Nationally, Kentucky ranked 24th in nonfuel mineral production, by value. According to preliminary figures, in 2003, crushed stone accounted for about 57% of nonfuel mineral production value, followed by lime, cement (portland and masonry), and construction sand and gravel. Nationally, the state ranked third in ball clays and in lime, and tenth in common clay. According to early data for 2003, the state produced 8.8 million metric tons of construction sand and gravel, valued at $35.2 million.

26 Energy and Power

In 2003, Kentucky had 62 electric power service providers. In that same year, total net summer generating capacity was 19.068 million kilowatts, with total production at 91.718 billion kilowatt hours. Of the total amount generated, 91.6% came from coal-fired plants, with hydroelectric power accounting for 4.3% of production and 3.2% from petroleum-fired plants. The remaining production came from generating plants using natural gas, or other renewable energy sources.

Most of Kentucky's coal came from the western fields of the interior coal basin until late in the 19th century, when the lower-sulfur Cumberland Plateau coal reserves of the Appalachian region were discovered. In 2004, eastern Kentucky produced 90,871,000 tons of coal, while western Kentucky produced 23,373,000 tons. In that same year, Kentucky had 419 active coal mines, of which 196 were surface (strip) mines and 223 were underground. Recoverable coal reserves as of 2004 stood at 1.129 billion tons.

In 2004, Kentucky produced an average of 7,000 barrels per day of crude petroleum. The state's proven oil reserves in that same year stood at 27 million barrels. Kentucky had 18,075 producing oil wells in 2004. In 2003, Kentucky marketed 87.608 billion cubic feet (2.49 billion cubic meters) of natural gas. As of 31 December 2004, the state had proven reserves of dry or consumer-grade natural gas of 1.880 billion cubic feet (0.157 billion cubic meters).

As of 2005, Kentucky had two operating refineries with a combined crude oil refining capacity of 227,500 barrels per day.

27 Commerce

In 2002, Kentucky's wholesale trade sector had sales totaling $51.8 billion, while the state's retail sector had sales totaling $40.06 billion, that same year. Motor vehicle and motor vehicle parts dealers accounted for the largest portion of retail sales in the state in 2002, at $9.5 billion, followed by general merchandise stores at $7.6 billion. Kentucky's exports to foreign countries in 2005 totaled $14.8 billion.

28 Public Finance

The Kentucky biennial state budget is prepared by the Governor's Office for Policy and Management late in each odd-numbered year and submitted by the Governor to the General Assembly for approval. The fiscal year runs from July 1 to June 30.

Total revenues in 2004 totaled $20.180 billion, while total expenditures amounted to $20.072 billion. The largest general expenditures were for education ($6.39 billion), public welfare ($5.27 billion), and highways ($1.7 billion). The total state debt at the end of 2004 stood at $8.1 billion, or $1,959.55 per capita (per person).

29 Taxation

As of 1 January 2006, Kentucky's personal income tax consisted of a six-bracket schedule ranging from 2% to 6%. Corporate income is taxed according to a schedule ranging from 4% to 7%. Kentucky also levies a 6% sales and use tax, that exempts food, if it is eaten off-premises (such as at home). Gasoline and cigarettes are subject to a state excise tax.

State tax collections in Kentucky for 2005 totaled $9.1 billion, of which 33.4% was generated by the state's personal income tax, followed by 28.5% from the state general sales and use tax, 18.2% by state excise taxes, 5.2% by state property taxes, and 5.3% by the state's corporate income tax. In 2005, the per capita (per person) tax burden amounted to $2,179 as compared to the national average of $2,192.

30 Health

In 2003, Kentucky's overall death rate was 9.8 deaths per 1,000 inhabitants, while the infant mortality rate, as of October 2006, was estimated at 6.6 per 1,000 live births. As of 2002, Kentucky's death rates for major causes of death (per 100,000 people) were 285.8 from heart diseases, 230.6 from cancer, 62.4 from cerebrovascular diseases, 58.7 from chronic lower respiratory diseases, and 30.9 from diabetes. Of all Kentuckians, 27.4% were smokers in 2004, the highest in the nation. There were 2.4 HIV-related deaths per 100,000 population. In 2004, the reported AIDS case rate was 6.1 per 100,000 people.

Kentucky's 103 community hospitals had about 14,900 beds in 2003. In 2005, there were 904 nurses per 100,000 people, while in 2004 there were 233 physicians per 100,000 population, and a total of 2,325 dentists throughout the state. The average expense for community hospital care was $1,106 per inpatient day in 2003. In 2004, about 14% of the population was uninsured.

31 Housing

In 2004, Kentucky had 1,842,971 housing units, of which 1,647,464 were occupied. About 70.1% were owner-occupied. About 67% of all units were single-family, detached homes, and 13.9% were mobile homes. Though most units relied on utility gas or electricity for heating, about 11,533 units used coke or coal and 37,785 relied on wood. It was estimated that 109,895 units lacked telephone service, 13,677 lacked complete plumbing facilities, and 9,421 lacked complete kitchen facilities. The average household size was 2.45 people.

In 2004, a total of 22,600 privately owned units were authorized for construction. The median home value was $98,438. The median monthly cost for mortgage owners was $888. Renters paid a median of $503 per month.

32 Education

In 2004, a total of 81.8% of all adults in Kentucky had completed high school, which was below the national average of 84%. Also, 21% of all adults had completed four or more years of college, compared to the national average of 26%.

Total public school enrollment was estimated at 650,000 in fall 2003, but is expected to rise to decline to 618,000 by fall 2014. Enrollment in private schools in fall 2003 was 71,067. Expenditures for public education in 2003/2004 were estimated at $5.4 billion.

As of fall 2002, there were 225,489 students enrolled in institutions of higher education. Kentucky had 77 degree-granting institutions, as of fall 2005. Kentucky's higher education facilities included 8 public and 26 private 4-year colleges and universities, and 26 public 2-year schools. The University of Kentucky, established in 1865 at Lexington, is the state's largest public institution. The University of Louisville (1798) is also state supported.

33 Arts

The Kentucky Arts Council (est. 1965) is authorized to promote the arts through such programs as Arts in Education and the State Arts Resources Program. Ongoing programs include the Craft Marketing Program, which promotes the state's craft industry, and the Folklife Program, a partnership with the Kentucky Historical Society.

Kentucky Chautauqua, an ongoing program of the Kentucky Humanities Council, sponsors impersonations of ten historical characters from Kentucky's past who travel across the state for presentations. The Arts Kentucky is a statewide membership organization for artists, performers, craftspeople, and community arts groups.

The Actors Theater of Louisville holds a yearly festival of new American plays. In 2006, the festival celebrated its 30th anniversary. The Kentucky Center for the Arts in Louisville, dedicated in 1983, serves as home to the Louisville Orchestra (est. 1937), the Louisville Ballet (est. 1952), and the Kentucky Opera. As of 2006, the Louisville Ballet has entertained over 75,000 people, annually, and reached more than 15,000 children each year, through its education programs. Bluegrass, a form of country music performed on fiddle and banjo, and played at a rapid tempo, is named after the style pioneered by Kentuckian Bill Monroe and his Blue Grass Boys.

34 Libraries and Museums

In the year ending in June 2001, there were 116 public library systems in Kentucky, with a total of 189 libraries, of which 73 were branches. In that same year, there were over 7.89 million volumes, and a circulation of 20.8 million. The regional library system included university libraries and the state library at Frankfort, as well as city and county libraries. The Kentucky Historical Society in Frankfort also maintains a research library of more than 85,000 volumes.

The state has over 107 museums. The Kentucky Historical Society in Frankfort maintains the State History Museum and supports a mobile museum system that brings exhibits on Kentucky history to schools, parks, and local gatherings, and aids over 400 local historical organizations. Art museums include the University of Kentucky Art Museum and the Headley-Whitney Museum, both in Lexington. The Muhammad Ali Center in Louisville opened 21 November 2005.

Among Kentucky's horse-related museums are the Kentucky Derby Museum in Louisville, and the International Museum of the Horse in Lexington. The John James Audubon Museum is located in Audubon State Park at Henderson. Leading historical sites include Abraham Lincoln's birthplace at Hodgenville and the Mary Todd Lincoln and Henry Clay homes in Lexington.

35 Communications

In 2004, only 91.4% of all occupied housing units in the state had a telephone. In 2005, Kentucky had 73 major radio stations (15 AM and 58 FM), as well as 29 major television broadcasting stations, with 17 public broadcasting stations. There were 576,850 television households, 65% of which received cable. In 2003, computers were in 58.1% of all households in the state, while 49.6% had access to the Internet.

36 Press

In 2005, Kentucky had 23 daily newspapers (10 morning, 13 evening), and 14 Sunday papers. The leading Kentucky newspapers, with their 2005 daily circulations, were the Louisville *Courier-Journal* (207,655) and the Lexington *Herald-Leader* (114,234). Both were morn-

Natural Bridge State Resort, located in the Daniel Boone National Forest, is home to the great natural sandstone arch that spans 78 feet (24 meters) in length and 65 feet (20 meters) in height. WWW.KENTUCKYTOURISM.COM.

ing and Sunday papers. Magazines included *Kentucky Living* and *Kentucky Monthly*.

37 Tourism, Travel & Recreation

The economic impact of tourism within the state reached about $10 billion, and supported more than 164,000 travel-related jobs.

One of the state's top tourist attractions is Mammoth Cave National Park, which contains over 365 miles of explored underground passages. Other units of the national park system in Kentucky include Abraham Lincoln's birthplace in Hodgenville, and Cumberland Gap National

Historical Park, which extends into Tennessee and Virginia. The state operates 17 resort parks (open year-round). The state also operates 24 recreational parks and 22 historic sites. The Kentucky State Fair is held every August at Louisville.

38 Sports

There are no major league professional sports teams in Kentucky. There is a minor league baseball team in Louisville that plays in the AAA International League. There are also two minor league hockey teams in Kentucky that play in the American Hockey League.

The first known horse race in Kentucky was held in 1783. The annual Kentucky Derby, first run on 17 May 1875, has become the single most famous event in US thoroughbred racing. Held on the first Saturday in May at Churchill Downs in Louisville, the Derby is one of three races for three-year-olds constituting the Triple Crown. Keeneland Race Course in Lexington is the site of the Blue Grass Stakes and other major thoroughbred races. The Kentucky Futurity, an annual highlight of the harness racing season, is usually held on the first Friday in October at the Red Mile in Lexington.

Rivaling horse racing as a spectator sport is collegiate basketball. The University of Kentucky Wildcats, who play in the Southeastern Conference, have won the NCAA Division I basketball championships six times, and the National Invitation Tournament twice. The University of Louisville Cardinals play in Conference USA. Kentucky Wesleyan, at Owensboro, was the NCAA Division II titleholder seven times, including 1999 and 2001.

Hillerich & Bradsby, makers of the "Louisville Slugger" baseball bat. LOUISVILLE AND JEFFERSON COUNTY CONVENTION AND VISITORS BUREAU.

39 Famous Kentuckians

Kentucky has been the birthplace of one US president, four US vice-presidents, the only president of the Confederacy, and several important jurists, statesmen, writers, artists, and sports figures. Abraham Lincoln, (1809–1865) the 16th president of the United States, was born in Hodgenville. His wife, Mary Todd Lincoln (1818–1882), was a native of Lexington. Kentucky-born US vice-presidents have all been Democrats. The best known were Adlai Stevenson (1835–1914), who served with Grover Cleveland, and Alben W. Barkley (1877–1956) who, before his election with President Harry S Truman in 1948, was a US senator and longtime Senate majority leader.

Frederick M. Vinson (1890–1953) was the only Kentuckian to serve as chief justice of the United States. Noteworthy associate justices were John Marshall Harlan (1833–1911), famous for his dissent from the segregationist *Plessy v. Ferguson* decision (1896); and Louis B. Brandeis (1856–1941), the first Jew to serve on the Supreme Court and a champion of social reform.

A figure prominently associated with frontier Kentucky is the explorer and surveyor Daniel Boone (b.Pensylvania, 1734–1820). Other frontiersmen include Kit Carson (1809–1868) and Roy Bean (1825?–1903).

Other personalities of significance include James G. Birney (1792–1857) and Cassius Marcellus Clay (1810–1903), both major anti-

Churchill Downs in Louisville, home of the Kentucky Derby. LOUISVILLE AND JEFFERSON COUNTY CONVENTION AND VISITORS BUREAU.

slavery spokesmen. Clay's daughter, Laura (1849–1941), and Madeline Breckinridge (1872–1920) were important contributors to the women's suffrage movement. Carry Nation (1846–1911) was a leader of the temperance movement. During the 1920s, Kentuckian John T. Scopes (1900–1970) gained fame as the defendant in the "monkey trial" in Dayton, Tennessee. Scopes was charged with teaching Darwin's theory of evolution.

Thomas Hunt Morgan (1866–1945), honored for his work in heredity and genetics, and chemist William N. Lipscomb (b.Ohio, 1919) were Nobel Prize winners. Notable businessmen include "Colonel" Harland Sanders (b.Indiana, 1890–1980), founder of Kentucky Fried Chicken restaurants. Robert Penn Warren (1905–1989), a novelist, poet laureate, and critic, won the Pulitzer Prize three times and was the first author to win the award in both the fiction and poetry categories.

Among Kentuckians well recognized in the performing arts are film innovator D. W. Griffith (David Lewelyn Wark Griffith, 1875–1948); Academy Award-winning actress Patricia Neal (b.1926); and country music singers Loretta Lynn (b.1932) and her sister, Crystal Gayle (Brenda Gail Webb, b.1951). Kentucky's sports figures include basketball coach Adolph Rupp (b.Kansas, 1901–1977); shortstop Harold ("Pee Wee") Reese (1919–1999); football great Paul Hornung (b.1935); and world heavyweight boxing champions Jimmy Ellis (b.1940) and Muhammad Ali (Cassius Clay, b.1942).

40 Bibliography

BOOKS

Bristow, M. J. *State Songs of America.* Westport, CT: Greenwood Press, 2000.

Deady, Kathleen W. *Kentucky Facts and Symbols.* Rev. ed. Mankato, MN: Capstone, 2003.

Lantier, Patricia. *Kentucky.* Milwaukee, WI: Gareth Stevens, 2006.

Murray, Julie. *Kentucky.* Edina, MN: Abdo Publishing, 2006.

Williams, Suzanne M. *Kentucky.* New York: Children's Press, 2001.

WEB SITES

Commonwealth of Kentucky. *Kentucky.gov* www.kentucky.gov (accessed March 1, 2007).

Official Kentucky Department of Travel. *Kentucky: Unbridled Spirit.* www.kytourism.com (accessed March 1, 2007).

Louisiana

State of Louisiana

ORIGIN OF STATE NAME: Named in 1682 for France's King Louis XIV.

NICKNAME: The Pelican State.

CAPITAL: Baton Rouge.

ENTERED UNION: 30 April 1812 (18th).

OFFICIAL SEAL: In the center, a pelican and its young are as depicted on the flag; the state motto encircles the scene, and the words "State of Louisiana" surround the whole.

FLAG: On a blue field, fringed on three sides, a white pelican feeds her three young, symbolizing the state providing for its citizens; the state motto is inscribed on a white ribbon.

MOTTO: Union, Justice, and Confidence.

SONG: "Give Me Louisiana;" "You are My Sunshine;" "State March Song."

COLORS: Gold, white, and blue.

FLOWER: Magnolia; Louisiana iris (wildflower).

TREE: Bald cypress.

BIRD: Eastern brown pelican.

CRUSTACEAN: Crawfish.

INSECT: Honeybee.

DOG: Catahoula leopard.

GEM: Agate.

FOSSIL: Petrified palmwood.

LEGAL HOLIDAYS: New Year's Day, 1 January; Birthday of Martin Luther King Jr., 3rd Monday in January; Mardi Gras Day, Tuesday before Ash Wednesday, February; Good Friday, Friday before Easter, March or April; Independence Day, 4 July; Huey Long's Birthday, 30 August, by proclamation of the governor; Labor Day, 1st Monday in September; Election Day, 1st Tuesday in November in even-numbered years; Veterans' Day, 11 November; Thanksgiving Day, 4th Thursday in November; Christmas Day, 25 December. Legal holidays in Baton Rouge parish also include Inauguration Day, once every four years in January.

TIME: 6 AM CST = noon GMT.

1 Location and Size

Situated in the western south-central United States, Louisiana ranks 31st in size among the 50 states. The total area of Louisiana is 47,751 square miles (123,675 square kilometers), including 44,521 square miles (115,309 square kilometers) of land and 3,230 square miles (8,366 square kilometers) of inland water. The state extends 237 miles (381 kilometers) east-west and 236 miles (380 kilometers) north-south. Louisiana is shaped roughly like a boot, with the heel in the southwest corner and the toe at the extreme southeast. The state's total boundary length is 1,486 miles (2,391 kilometers).

2 Topography

Louisiana lies wholly within the Gulf Coastal Plain. The alluvial plains of the Red and Mississippi rivers occupy the north-central third of the state. East and west of these plains are the upland districts, characterized by rolling hills sloping gently toward the coast. The coastal-delta section, in the southernmost portion of the state, consists of the Mississippi Delta and the coastal lowlands. The highest elevation in the state, at 535 feet (163 meters), is Driskill Mountain in Bienville Parish. The lowest point, at 8 feet (2 meters) below sea level, is in New Orleans.

Louisiana has the most wetlands of all the states, about 11,000 square miles (28,000 square kilometers) of floodplains and 7,800 square miles (20,200 square kilometers) of coastal swamps, marshes, and estuarine waters. The largest lake, actually a coastal lagoon, is Lake Pontchartrain, with an area of more than 620 square miles (1,600 square kilometers). Toledo Bend Reservoir, an artificial lake along the Louisiana-Texas border, has an area of 284 square miles (736 square kilometers). The most important rivers are the Mississippi, Red, Pearl, Atchafalaya, and Sabine. Louisiana has nearly 2,500 coastal islands.

3 Climate

Louisiana has a relatively constant semitropical climate. The temperature in New Orleans ranges from 53°F (11°C) in January to 82°F (27°C) in July. The all-time high temperature is 114°F (46°C), recorded at Plain Dealing on 10

Louisiana
Population Profile

Total population estimate in 2006:	4,287,768
Population change, 2000–06:	-4.1%
Hispanic or Latino†:	2.8%
Population by race	
One race:	98.9%
White:	63.7%
Black or African American:	32.5%
American Indian /Alaska Native:	0.6%
Asian:	1.3%
Native Hawaiian / Pacific Islander:	0.0%
Some other race:	0.8%
Two or more races:	1.1%

Population by Age Group

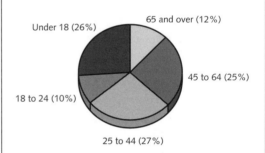

Under 18 (26%)
65 and over (12%)
45 to 64 (25%)
18 to 24 (10%)
25 to 44 (27%)

Major Cities by Population

City	Population	% change 2000–05
New Orleans	454,863	-6.2
Baton Rouge	222,064	-2.5
Shreveport	198,874	-0.6
Lafayette	112,030	1.6
Lake Charles	70,555	-1.7
Kenner	69,911	-0.9
Bossier	60,505	7.2
Monroe	51,914	-2.2
Alexandria	45,693	-1.4
New Iberia	32,495	-0.4

Notes: †A person of Hispanic or Latino origin may be of any race. NA indicates that data are not available.
Sources: U.S. Census Bureau. *American Community Survey* and *Population Estimates*. www.census.gov/ (accessed March 2007).

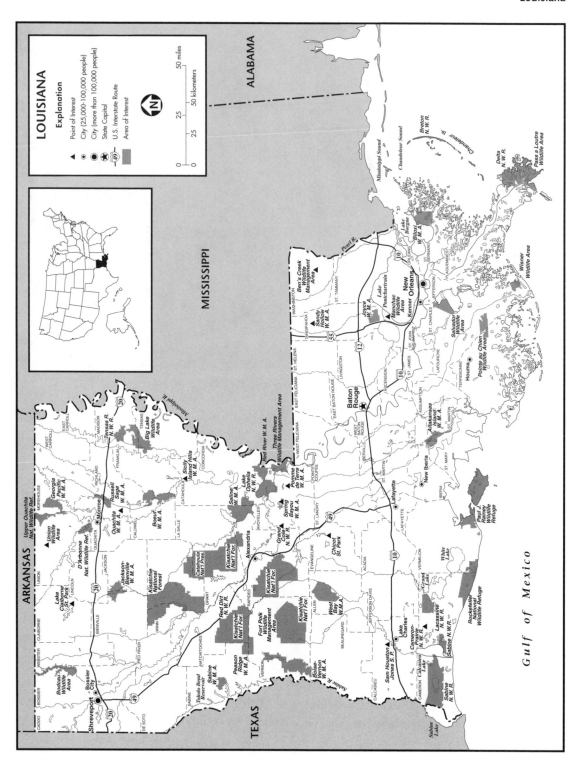

Swamp of the Atchafalaya River. Louisiana has the most wetlands of all the states. LOUISIANA OFFICE OF TOURISM.

August 1936. The all-time low, -16°F (-27°C), was set at Minden on 13 February 1899. New Orleans has an average annual rainfall of 61.6 inches (156 centimeters). Snow falls occasionally in the north, but rarely in the south. During the summer and fall, tropical storms and hurricanes frequently batter the state, especially along the coast.

The 2005 hurricane season devastated much of the Gulf region, primarily through Hurricane Katrina. Katrina made landfall at Buras on 29 August 2005 as a Category 4 storm. The combination of high winds and flooding led to levee damage around New Orleans, allowing flood waters to cover about 80% of the city, with depths as high as 20 feet (6.3 meters). One month later, Hurricane Rita made landfall near Johnson's Bayou as a Category 3 storm. As of early 2006, over 1,300 deaths had been reported as a result of Hurricane Katrina, well over one million people were displaced, and the cost of rebuilding was estimated at over $150 billion.

4 Plants and Animals

Forests in Louisiana consist of four major types: shortleaf pine uplands, pine flats and hills, hardwood forests, and cypress and tupelo swamps. Important commercial trees also include beech, eastern red cedar, and black walnut. Among the state's wildflowers are the ground orchid and several hyacinths. Spanish moss grows profusely in the southern regions but is rare in the north. Louisiana quillwort and American chaffseed were listed as endangered in 2006.

Louisiana Population by Race

Census 2000 was the first national census in which the instructions to respondents said, "Mark one or more races." This table shows the number of people who are of one, two, or three or more races. For those claiming two races, the number of people belonging to the various categories is listed. The U.S. government conducts a census of the population every ten years.

	Number	Percent
Total population	4,468,976	100.0
One race	4,420,711	98.9
Two races	44,657	1.0
White *and* Black or African American	7,099	0.2
White *and* American Indian/Alaska Native	11,666	0.3
White *and* Asian	5,345	0.1
White *and* Native Hawaiian/Pacific Islander	466	—
White *and* some other race	11,212	0.3
Black or African American *and* American Indian/Alaska Native	2,675	0.1
Black or African American *and* Asian	1,133	—
Black or African American *and* Native Hawaiian/Pacific Islander	270	—
Black or African American *and* some other race	2,504	0.1
American Indian/Alaska Native *and* Asian	335	—
American Indian/Alaska Native *and* Native Hawaiian/Pacific Islander	28	—
American Indian/Alaska Native *and* some other race	450	—
Asian *and* Native Hawaiian/Pacific Islander	349	—
Asian *and* some other race	974	—
Native Hawaiian/Pacific Islander *and* some other race	151	—
Three or more races	3,608	0.1

Source: U.S. Census Bureau. *Census 2000: Redistricting Data.* Press release issued by the Redistricting Data Office. Washington, D.C., March, 2001. A dash (—) indicates that the percent is less than 0.1.

Louisiana's varied habitats—tidal marshes, swamps, woodlands, and prairies—offer a diversity of animals. Deer, squirrel, and bear are hunted as game, while muskrat, mink, and skunk are commercially valuable furbearers. Prized game birds include quail, turkey, and various waterfowl, of which the mottled duck and wood duck are native. Coastal beaches are inhabited by sea turtles. Whales may be seen offshore. Freshwater fish include bass, crappie, and bream. As of April 2006, 23 animal species were on the US Fish and Wildlife Service's threatened and endangered species list, including the Louisiana black bear, bald eagle, Alabama heelsplitter, and red-cockaded woodpecker.

5 Environmental Protection

In 1984, Louisiana consolidated much of its environmental protection efforts into a new state agency—The Department of Environmental Quality (DEQ). Among its responsibilities are maintenance of air and water quality, solid-waste management, hazardous waste disposal, and control of radioactive materials. According to the Louisiana Environmental Action Plan (LEAP to 2000 Project), toxic air pollution, industrial and municipal wastewater discharges, and coastal wetland loss head the list of state residents' environmental concerns.

Louisiana's problem in protecting its wetlands differs from that of most other states in that its wetlands are more than wildlife refuges—they are central to the state's agriculture and fishing industries. Assessment of the environmental impact of various industries on the wetlands has been conducted under the Coastal Zone Management Plan of the Department of Natural Resources.

The two largest wildlife refuges in the state are the Rockefeller Wildlife Refuge, comprising 84,000 acres (34,000 hectares) in Cameron and Vermilion parishes, and the Marsh Island Refuge, 82,000 acres (33,000 hectares) of marshland in Iberia Parish. Both are managed by the Department of Wildlife and Fisheries.

With approximately 100 major chemical and petrochemical manufacturing and refining facilities located in Louisiana, many DEQ programs deal with the regulation of hazardous waste generation, management and disposal, and chemical releases to the air and water. In 2003, Louisiana had 155 hazardous waste sites, 11 of which were included on the National Priorities List in 2006, included in the Environmental Protection Agency's database.

Among the most active citizen's groups on environmental issues are the League of Women Voters, the Sierra Club (Delta Chapter), and the Louisiana Environmental Action Network (LEAN). Curbside recycling programs exist in 28 parishes.

6 Population

In 2005, Louisiana ranked 25th in population in the United States with an estimated total of 4,287,768 residents. Louisiana's population density in 2004 was 104.2 persons per square mile (40.2 persons per square kilometer). In 2004, the median age was 35.2. In 2005, about 26% of the population was 18 years of age and younger and 12% was 65 and older. New Orleans is the largest city, with a 2005 estimated population of 454,863 (down from 462,269 in 2004), followed by Baton Rouge, 222,064; and Shreveport, 198,874.

7 Ethnic Groups

According to the 2000 census, black Americans made up about 32.5% of the population (the second-highest percentage among the 50 states), with a total of 1,451,944 people. They include descendants of "free people of color," some of whom were craftsmen and rural property owners before the Civil War. Many of these, of mixed blood, are referred to locally as "colored Creoles" and have constituted a black elite in both urban and rural Louisiana.

Two groups that have been highly identified with the culture of Louisiana are Creoles and Acadians (also called Cajuns). Both descend primarily from early French immigrants to the state. The Cajuns trace their origins from the rural people from Acadia (Nova Scotia). The first Creoles were city people from France, Nova Scotia, or Hispaniola. The term Creole also applies to the relatively few early Spanish settlers and their descendants. Although Acadians have intermingled with Spaniards and Germans, they still speak a French patois and retain a distinctive culture and cuisine. In 2000, 179,739 residents claimed Acadian ancestry.

Also in 2000, 107,738 residents were of Hispanic or Latino descent. There were 25,477 Native Americans and 54,758 Asians, including 24,358 Vietnamese. Pacific Islanders numbered 1,240.

A total of 115,885 Louisianians (2.6% of the population) were foreign born. The largest ancestry groups were from France, Germany, Ireland, and the United Kingdom.

8 Languages

Louisiana English is predominantly Southern. Notable features of the state's speech patterns are that the words *pen* and *pin* sound the same and, in New Orleans, the so-called Brooklyn pronunciation of *bird* is /boyd/. A pecan sugar candy is well known as a *praline*. Louisiana has a large French-speaking area. West of New Orleans the French dialect called Acadian (Cajun) is used as the first language. From it, and from early colonial French, English has taken such words as *pirogue* (dugout canoe), *armoire* (wardrobe), and *lagniappe* (extra gift).

In 2000, 3,771,003 Louisiana residents (90.8% of the population five years old and older) spoke only English at home. Other languages spoken at home (with number of speakers) included French or French Patois (194,314), Spanish or Spanish Creole (105,189), and Vietnamese (23,326).

9 Religions

Spanish missionaries brought Roman Catholicism to Louisiana in the early 16th century. Until the Louisiana Purchase, the public practice of any but the Catholic religion was prohibited, and Jews were entirely banned. Joseph Willis, a mulatto preacher, organized the first Baptist church west of the Mississippi, at Bayou Chicot in 1812. After the Civil War, blacks withdrew from white-dominated churches to form their own religious groups, mainly Baptist and Methodist.

As of 2004, the Roman Catholic Church was the largest Christian denomination, with 1,312,237 adherents. The leading Protestant denominations (with 2000 membership data) were the Southern Baptist Convention, 768,587; the Assemblies of God, 49,041; and the Episcopal Church, 33,653. The United Methodist Church had 127,059 members in 2004. There were about 16,500 Jews residing in Louisiana in 2000. The Muslim community had about 13,050 members. Voodoo, in some cases blended with Christian ritual, is more widespread in Louisiana than anywhere else in the United States, although the present number of practitioners is impossible to ascertain. Over 1.8 million people (about 41.2% of the population) did not claim any religious affiliation in the 2000 survey.

10 Transportation

New Orleans has long been a major center of domestic and international freight traffic. Several short-run railroads were built in Louisiana during the 1830s. The first of these, and the first rail line west of the Alleghenies, was the Pontchartrain Railroad, which opened, using horse-drawn vehicles, in 1831. By the late 1800s, New Orleans was connected with New York, Chicago, and California. Railroads soon rivaled the Mississippi River in the movement of goods to and from New Orleans. In 2003, there were six Class I line-haul railroads in Louisiana and total railroad mileage was 3,426 route miles (5,515 kilometers). As of 2006, Amtrak provides passenger links with Los Angeles, Chicago, and New York and carries passengers from seven stations through the state.

At the end of 2004, Louisiana had a total of 60,941 miles (98,115 kilometers) of public roads. Also in 2004, there were about 1,926,000 automobiles and 1,747,000 trucks registered in the state and 3,169,627 drivers' licenses were in force.

Early in the nation's history, the Mississippi River emerged as the principal route for north–south traffic and New Orleans soon became the South's main port. The advent of the steamboat in 1812 solved the problem of upstream navigation, which previously had required three or four months for a distance that could be covered downstream in 15 days. An important breakthrough in international transportation was the deepening of the channel at the mouth of the Mississippi by means of jetties, the first of which were completed in 1879. The port of New Orleans is served by more than 100 steamship lines, 20 common carrier lines, and about 100 contract carrier barge lines. The Louisiana Offshore Oil Port (LOOP), the first deepwater oil port in the United States, was opened in 1981. Other large ports include Baton Rouge and the Port of Plaquemines.

In 2005, Louisiana had 242 private and public airfields. The busiest was the Louis Armstrong New Orleans International Airport. In 2004, the airport had 4,839,400 passengers. Louisiana also had 237 heliports and 16 seaplane bases.

11 History

When European exploration and settlement of North America began, Louisiana was inhabited by a number of different Native American groups, including various tribes of the Caddo people, small Tunican-speaking groups, the Atakapa group, and the Chitimacha. The Spaniard Hernando de Soto was probably the first to penetrate the state's present boundaries, in 1541. Robert Cavelier, Sieur de la Salle reached the mouth of the Mississippi on 9 April 1682, named the land there Louisiana in honor of King Louis XIV, and claimed it for France. In 1714, Louis Juchereau de St. Denis established Natchitoches, the first permanent European settlement in Louisiana; Iberville's brother, the Sieur de Bienville, established New Orleans four years later.

Although Louisiana did not thrive economically under French rule, French culture was firmly implanted there and absorbed by non-French settlers, especially Germans from Switzerland and the Rhineland. In 1762, France ceded Louisiana to Spain. Governed by Spaniards, the colony was much more prosperous. New settlers—including Acadian refugees from Nova Scotia—added to the population. The territory grew to about 50,000 inhabitants by 1800, when Napoleon forced the Spanish government to return Louisiana to France. Three years later, Napoleon sold Louisiana to the United States to keep it from falling into the hands of Great Britain.

President Thomas Jefferson concluded what was probably the best real estate deal in history, purchasing 800,000 square miles (2,100,000 square kilometers) for $15,000,000 and thus more than doubling the size of the United States at a cost of about three cents per acre. The next year, that part of the purchase south of 33°n was separated from the remainder and designated the Territory of Orleans. When its population reached the level required for statehood in 1810, the people of the territory drew up a constitu-

A blue cannon and the Chalmette Monument at Chalmette National Historic Park in New Orleans. © ROBERT HOLMES/ CORBIS.

tion, and Louisiana entered the Union on 30 April 1812.

State Development American control of Louisiana was threatened soon afterward when British troops tried to take New Orleans in 1814 but were soundly defeated by a mixed contingent of forces under the command of Andrew Jackson. From 1815 to 1861, Louisiana was one of the most prosperous states in the South, producing sugar and cotton, and raising hogs and cattle. Wealthy planters, whose slaves made up almost half the population, dominated Louisiana politically and economically. When the secession crisis came in 1861, they led Louisiana into the

Confederacy and, after four bloody years, to total defeat.

After the Civil War, Radical Republican governments elected by black voters ruled the state, but declining support from the North and fierce resistance from Louisiana whites brought the Reconstruction period to an end. Blacks and their few white allies lost control of state government and, in 1898, blacks were deprived almost entirely of their voting rights by a new state constitution drawn up primarily for that purpose. This constitution also significantly reduced the number of poorer whites who voted in Louisiana elections. Just as before the Civil War, large landowners—combined with New Orleans bankers,

Aerial view of Hurricane Katrina damage in New Orleans, August 30, 2005. © SMILEY N. POOL/DALLAS MORNING NEWS/CORBIS.

businessmen, and politicians—dominated state government, effectively blocking political and social reform.

Not until 1928, with the election of Huey P. Long as governor, did the winds of major change strike Louisiana. The years from 1928 through 1960 could well be called the Long Era. Three Longs dominated state politics for most of the period: Huey, who became governor but was assassinated in 1935; his brother Earl, who served as governor three times; and his son Russell, who became a powerful US senator. From a backward agricultural state, Louisiana evolved into one of the world's major petrochemical-manufacturing centers. What had been one of the most frugal states became one of the most liberal in wel-

fare spending, care for the aged, highway building, and education. The state could afford these expanding programs because of ever-increasing revenues from oil and gas.

In the mid-1980s, the major problems confronting the state were racial and labor tensions, inadequate disposal sites for industrial waste, and (despite important new discoveries) the depletion of oil and gas resources. In 1989, racial tensions took a new turn when white supremacist David Duke, running as a Republican, narrowly won a seat in the Louisiana state legislature. He then ran for the US Senate—with a showing of 44 percent among voters—and, in 1991, for governor. (He was defeated by former governor Edwin Edwards.) In opposing affirmative action,

Duke appealed to whites' frustrations with the high unemployment brought on by the collapse of oil prices in the mid- and late-1980s, when the number of jobs in the state declined by 8%.

For most of the 1990s, in spite of an increase in service-sector and high-tech jobs, Louisiana had more people living in poverty than any other state. Louisiana had for decades been among the nation's poorest; the percentage of residents living in poverty in 1998 was 19.1%, making it the second-poorest state in the nation. Other problems confronting the state at the turn of the century included racial tensions, disposing of toxic wastes from the petrochemical industry, depletion of oil and gas resources, and the ongoing struggle to institute good government.

On 29 August 2005, Hurricane Katrina landed on the state, in what was one of the worst natural disasters in US history. New Orleans had been evacuated, but some 150,000 people were unable to leave before the storm hit. A day after the storm appeared to have bypassed the city's center, levees were breached by the storm surge and water submerged the city. The costs of the hurricane and flooding were exceedingly high in terms of both loss of life and economic damage: more than 1,400 people died in Louisiana (80% of them in New Orleans) and damages were estimated to reach $150 billion. Race and class issues also came to the fore, as the majority of New Orleans residents unable to evacuate the city and affected by the catastrophe were poor and black.

12 State Government

Louisiana has had 11 constitutions (more than any other state), the most recent of which went

Governor Kathleen Blanco stands in front of the state capitol building just weeks before her inauguration in January 2004. AP IMAGES.

into force in 1974. By January 2005, it had been amended 129 times.

The state legislature consists of a 39-member senate and a 105-member house of representatives. All legislators are elected for four-year terms. Major elected executive officials include the governor and lieutenant governor (independently elected), secretary of state, attorney general, and treasurer, all elected for four-year terms.

To become law, a bill must receive majority votes in both the senate and the house and be

Louisiana Governors: 1812–2007

1812–1816	William Charles Cole Claiborne	Dem-Rep
1816–1820	Jacques PhilippeVillere	Dem-Rep
1820–1824	Thomas Bolling Robertson	Dem-Rep
1824	Henry Schuyler Thibodeaux	Dem-Rep
1824–1828	Henry Johnson	Dem-Rep
1828–1829	Pierre Auguste Charles Derbigny	Nat-Rep
1829–1830	Armand Beauvais	Nat-Rep
1830–1831	Jacques Dupre	Nat-Rep
1831–1835	Andre Bienvenu Roman	Whig
1835–1839	Edward Douglass White, Sr.	Whig
1839–1843	Andre Bienvenu Roman	Whig
1843–1846	Alexandre Mouton	Democrat
1846–1850	Isaac Johnson	Democrat
1850–1853	Joseph Marshall Walker	Democrat
1853–1856	Paul Octave Herbert	Democrat
1856–1860	Robert Charles Wickliffe	Democrat
1860–1862	Thomas Overton Moore	Democrat
1862–1864	Gen. George Foster Shepley	Military
1864–1865	Henry Watkins Allen	Democrat
1864–1865	Michael Hahn	State Rights Free Trader
1865–1867	James Madison Wells	Democrat
1867–1868	Benjamin Franklin Flanders	Military-Rep
1868	Joshua Baker	Military-Dem
1868–1872	Henry Clay Warmouth	Republican
1872–1873	Pinkney Benton Pinchback	Republican
	John McEnery (elected but ruled out)	
1873–1877	William Pitt Kellogg (de facto)	Republican
1877–1880	Francis Redding Tillou Nicholls	Democrat
1880–1881	Louis Alfred Wiltz	Democrat
1881–1888	Samuel Douglas McEnery	Democrat
1888–1892	Francis Redding Tillou Nicholls	Democrat
1892–1900	Murphy James Foster	Anti–Lottery-Dem
1900–1904	William Wright Heard	Democrat
1904–1908	Newton Crain Blanchard	Democrat
1908–1912	Jared Young Sanders	Democrat
1912–1916	Luther Egbert Hall	Democrat
1916–1920	Ruffin Golson Pleasant	Democrat
1920–1924	John Milliken Parker	Democrat
1924–1926	Henry Luce Fugua	Democrat
1926–1928	Oramel Hinckley Simpson	Democrat
1928–1932	Huey Pierce Long	Democrat
1932	Alvin Olin King	Democrat
1932–1936	Oscar Kelly Allen	Democrat
1936	James Albert Noe	Democrat
1936–1939	Richard Webster Leche	Democrat
1939–1940	Earl Kemp Long	Democrat
1940–1944	Sam Houston Jones	Democrat
1944–1948	James Houston Davis	Democrat
1948–1952	Earl Kemp Long	Democrat
1952–1956	Robert Floyd Kennon	Democrat
1956–1960	Earl Kemp Long	Democrat
1960–1964	James Houston Davis	Democrat
1964–1972	John Julian McKeithen	Democrat
1972–1980	Edwin Washington Edwards	Democrat
1980–1984	David Conner Treen	Republican
1984–1988	Edwin Washington Edwards	Democrat
1988–1992	Charles Elson Roemer III	Republican
1992–1996	Edwin Washington Edwards	Democrat
1996–2004	Michael J. Foster	Republican
2004–	Kathleen Blanco	Democrat

Democratic Republican – Dem-Rep
National Republican – Nat-Rep

signed by the governor; or be left unsigned but not vetoed by the governor; or be passed again by two-thirds votes of both houses over the governor's veto. Appropriation bills must originate in the house but may be amended by the senate. The governor has an item veto on appropriation bills. Constitutional amendments require approval by two-thirds of the elected members of each house and ratification by a majority of the people voting on it at the next general election.

The governor's salary as of December 2004 was $94,532, and the legislative salary was $16,800.

13 Political Parties

The major political organizations are the Democratic Party and the Republican Party, each affiliated with the national party. However, differences in culture and economic interests have made Louisiana's politics extremely complex. After an extended period of Democratic dominance under the Long family, the 1960s and 1970s saw a resurgence of the Republican Party and the election in 1979 of David C. Treen, the state's first Republican governor since Reconstruction. However, Treen was succeeded

Louisiana Presidential Vote by Political Parties, 1948–2004

YEAR	LOUISIANA WINNER	DEMOCRAT	REPUBLICAN	STATES' RIGHTS DEMOCRAT	PROGRESSIVE	AMERICAN INDEPENDENT
1948	Thurmond (SRD)	136,344	72,657	204,290	3,035	—
1952	Stevenson (D)	345,027	306,925	—	—	—
				UNPLEDGED		
1956	*Eisenhower (R)	243,977	329,047	44,520	—	—
				Nat'l. States' Rights		
1960	*Kennedy (D)	407,339	230,980	169,572	—	—
1964	Goldwater (R)	387,068	509,225	—	—	—
1968	Wallace (AI)	309,615	257,535	—	—	530,300
				AMERICAN	**SOC. WORKERS**	
1972	*Nixon (R)	298,142	686,852	44,127	12,169	—
				LIBERTARIAN	**COMMUNIST**	
1976	*Carter (D)	661,365	587,446	3,325	7,417	10,058
				CITIZENS		
1980	*Reagan (R)	708,453	792,853	8,240	1,584	10,333
1984	*Reagan (R)	651,586	1,037,299	1,876	9,502	—
				POPULIST	**NEW ALLIANCE**	
1988	*Bush (R)	717,460	883,702	4,115	18,612	2,355
				IND. (PEROT)	**AMERICA FIRST**	
1992	*Clinton (D)	815,971	733,386	3,155	211,478	18,545
1996	*Clinton (D)	927,837	712,586	7,499	123,293	—
				REFORM	**CONSTITUTIONAL**	
2000	*Bush, G. W. (R)	792,344	927,871	14,356	20,473	5,483
2004	*Bush, G. W. (R)	820,299	1,102,169	—	—	5,203

* Won US presidential election.

by Democrats Edwin Edwards in 1983 and Charles Roemer in 1987, and Edwards again in 1991. In November 2003, Democrat Kathleen Babineaux Blanco was elected Louisiana's first female governor.

In 2004 there were 2,806,000 registered voters. In 1998, 62% of registered voters were Democratic, 21% Republican, and 16% unaffiliated or members of other parties. Louisiana's US senators are Republican David Vitter and Democrat Mary Landrieu. Following the 2006 elections Louisiana's delegation of US representatives consisted of two Democrats and five Republicans. Following those elections, 24 of the state senators were Democrats and 15 were Republicans; 63 of the state representatives were Democrats, 41 were Republicans, and 1 was an Independent. Twenty-five women were elected to the state legislature in the 2006 elections, or 17.4%. In the 2004 presidential election, Louisianans gave Republican George W. Bush 56% of the vote, while Democrat John Kerry received 42%.

14 Local Government

The church districts, called parishes, into which Louisiana was divided in the late 17th century remain the primary political divisions in the state, serving functions similar to those of counties in other states. In 2005 there were 64 parishes, many of them governed by police jury. Other parish officials are the sheriff, clerk of court, assessor, and coroner. As of 2005, Louisiana also had 302 municipal governments. Prominent local officials include the mayor, chief of police, and a council or board of aldermen. In 2005, there were 78 public school districts in the state.

15 Judicial System

The highest court in Louisiana is the supreme court, with appeals jurisdiction. There are five appeals circuits in the state, each divided into three districts. Each of the state's district courts serves at least one parish and has at least one district judge, elected for a six-year term. District courts have original jurisdiction in criminal and civil cases. City courts are the principal courts of limited jurisdiction.

According to the FBI Crime Index in 2004, Louisiana had a violent crime rate (murder, rape, robbery, aggravated assault) of 638.7 reported incidents per 100,000 people. Crimes against property (burglary, theft/larceny, and motor vehicle theft) in 2004 totaled 4,410.2 reported incidents per 100,000 people. As of 31 December 2004, 36,939 prisoners were in Louisiana's state and federal prisons. Louisiana has a death penalty law—27 people were executed between 1976 and 5 May 2006. As of 1 January 2006, 85 persons were under sentence of death.

16 Migration

Louisiana was settled by an unusually diverse assortment of immigrants. The Company of the Indies, which administered Louisiana from 1717 until 1731, at first began importing French convicts, vagrants, and prostitutes because of the difficulty of finding willing colonists. Next the company turned to struggling farmers in Germany and Switzerland, who proved to be more suitable and productive settlers. The importation of slaves from Africa and the West Indies began early in the 18th century.

Attracted by generous land grants, perhaps 10,000 Acadians, or Cajuns (people of French descent who had been exiled from Nova Scotia, called Acadia, during the 1740s), migrated to Louisiana after the French and Indian War. They settled in the area of Lafayette and Breaux Bridge and along Bayou Lafourche and the Mississippi River.

Beginning in World War II, large numbers of both black and white farm workers left Louisiana and migrated north and west. Between 1990 and 1998, the state had a net loss of 117,000 in domestic migration and a net gain of 25,000 in international migration. In 1998, 2,193 foreign immigrants arrived in Louisiana. In the period 2000–05, net international migration was 20,174 and net internal migration was -89,547, for a net loss of 69,373 people.

17 Economy

With the rise of the petrochemical industry, Louisiana's economy has regained much of the vitality it enjoyed before the Civil War. Today, Louisiana ranks second only to Texas in the value of its mineral products.

Louisiana is primarily an industrial state, but its industries are to a large degree based on its natural resources, principally oil, natural gas, water, and timber. Industrial expansion suffered a severe blow in the early 1980s, when the price of oil dropped from $37 a barrel in 1981 to $15 a barrel in 1986. Energy-related industries, such as barge-building, machinery-manufacturing, and rig/platform production suffered.

In the early 1990s, the chemical industry expanded, but by the late 1990s, a high exchange value of the dollar reversed the chemical industry's growth. In response, Louisiana built several riverboat casinos and a land-based casino which added many jobs to the economy.

Although the economy was negatively impacted by the 2001 national recession, the oil and natural gas industries grew. Offsetting a decline in manufacturing was growth in services. Of Louisiana's gross state product (GSP) of $152.9 billion in 2004, mining (about 99% of which was oil and gas production) contributed 12.8%, followed by real estate (10% of GSP), and manufacturing (7.5% of GSP).

18 Income

In 2005, Louisiana had a gross state product (GSP) of $166 billion, which ranked the state 24th among the 50 states and the District of Columbia in terms of highest GSP. In 2004, Louisiana's per capita income was $27,297, 43rd in the United States, where the national average was $33,050. The three year average median household income for 2002–04 was $35,523 compared to the national average of $44,473. For the period 2002–04, 17% of the state's residents lived below the federal poverty level, compared with 12.4% nationwide.

19 Industry

A huge and still-growing petrochemical industry has become a dominant force in the state's economy. Other expanding industries are wood products and, especially since World War II,

shipbuilding. In 2004, the total value of shipments of manufactured goods was $124.3 billion. Petroleum and coal products manufacturing accounted for the largest share at $53.36 billion, followed by chemical manufacturing at $39.91 billion. The state's main industrial regions are along the Mississippi River from north of Baton Rouge to New Orleans, and also include the Monroe, Shreveport, Morgan City, and Lake Charles areas.

20 Labor

In April 2006, the civilian labor force in Louisiana numbered 1,872,700, with approximately 90,100 workers unemployed, yielding an unemployment rate of 4.8%, compared to the national average of 4.7% for the same period. Some 6% of the labor force was employed in construction; 8.1% in manufacturing; 20.5% in trade, transportation, and public utilities; 5.3% in financial activities; 9.6% in professional and business services; 11.9% in education and health services; 9.6% in leisure and hospitality services; and 21% in government.

During the antebellum period, Louisiana had both the largest slave market in the United States (in New Orleans) and the largest slave revolt in the nation's history, in St. Charles and St. John the Baptist parishes in January 1811. New Orleans also had a relatively large free black population and many of the slaves in the city were skilled workers, some of whom were able to earn their freedom by outside employment. Major efforts to organize Louisiana workers began after the Civil War. In the mid-1880s, the Knights of Labor began to organize the cane workers. The Brotherhood of Timber Workers began organizing in 1910 but had little to show for their efforts except the scars of violent conflict with the lumber-mill owners.

In 2005, 114,000 of Louisiana's 1,778,000 employed wage and salary workers were members of unions. This represented 6.4% of those so employed. The national average was 12%.

21 Agriculture

With a farm income of over $2.1 billion in 2005, Louisiana ranked 34th among the 50 states. Nearly every crop grown in North America can be raised somewhere in Louisiana. In the south are strawberries, oranges, and sweet potatoes; in the southeast, sugarcane; and in the southwest, rice and soybeans. Soybeans are also raised in the cotton-growing area of the northeast. Oats, alfalfa, corn, potatoes, and peaches are among the other crops grown in the north.

As of 2004, there were an estimated 27,200 farms covering 7.85 million acres (3.18 million hectares) with an average farm size of 290 acres (117 hectares). In 2004, Louisiana ranked second in the United States in sugar cane production, third in the value of its rice production, and eighth for upland cotton.

22 Domesticated Animals

Cattle are raised mainly in the southeast (between the Mississippi and Pearl rivers), in the north-central region, and in the west. In 2005, there were an estimated 860,000 cattle and calves worth $670.8 million. In 2004, Louisiana had an estimated 16,000 hogs and pigs worth around $1.7 million. Dairy farmers had an estimated 43,000 milk cows, which produced 519 million pounds (236 million kilograms) of milk in 2003. Also during 2003, poultry farmers produced an estimated 7.5 million pounds (3.4 million kilograms) of chicken, which sold for $631,000, and an estimated 487 million eggs worth around $35.9 million.

23 Fishing

In 2004, Louisiana was second behind only Alaska in the size and value of its commercial landings, with nearly 1.1 billion pounds (500 million kilograms) valued at $274.4 million. Leading ports in volume were Empire-Venice (third in the nation), Intracoastal City (fifth in the nation), and Cameron (sixth in the nation). In value, Empire-Venice was sixth in the nation with $60.2 million and Dulac-Chauvin was 11th with $42.8 million.

The most important species caught in Louisiana are shrimp, hard blue crab, and oysters. In 2002, the state commercial fleet had 8,874 boats and 2,084 vessels. In 2003, there were 90 processing and 114 wholesale plants in the state.

Louisiana produces most of the US crawfish harvest. In 2004, 1,126 crawfish farms covered some 118,250 acres (47,856 hectares), producing 69.5 million pounds (28.1 million kilograms). Catfish are also cultivated in Louisiana, on 38 farms covering some 7,600 acres (3,075 hectares) in 2005.

The Natchitoches National Fish Hatchery focuses on paddlefish, striped bass, and pallid sturgeon, but also raises largemouth bass, bluegill, and catfish in limited quantities.

Louisiana had 639,139 sport fishing license holders in 2004.

24 Forestry

As of 2004, there were 14,017,000 acres (5,673,000 hectares) of forestland in Louisiana, representing almost half the state's land area and 2% of all US forests. The principal forest types are loblolly and shortleaf pine in the northwest, longleaf and slash pine in the south, and hardwood in a wide area along the Mississippi River. In 2004, more than 99% of Louisiana's forests were commercial timberland, over 90% of it was privately owned. Lumber production totaled 1.52 billion board feet in 2004.

Louisiana has one national forest, Kisatchie, with a gross area of 1,022,373 acres (413,754 hectares) within its boundaries. Gross acreage of National Forest System lands in the state was 2,049,000 acres (829,000 hectares) in 2005. Near the boundaries of Kisatchie's Evangeline Unit is the Alexander State Forest, established in 1923.

25 Mining

Louisiana's nonfuel mineral value totaled an estimated $331 million in 2003. The leading mineral commodity, accounting for roughly half of all nonfuel mineral production in 2003, was salt, accounting for about 41% of all nonfuel mineral production (by value) that year. It was followed by construction sand and gravel, crushed stone, industrial sand and gravel, and lime. Louisiana is the leading state in salt and sulfur production. Salt brine is produced in Ascension, Assumption, Calcasieu, Iberville, and Lafourche parishes. Rock salt is produced in Iberia and St. Mary parishes. In 2003, the state ranked 34th in the nation in mineral value.

26 Energy and Power

In 2000, Louisiana's total per capita energy consumption was 887 million Btu (223.5 million kilocalories), ranking it second among the 50 states. In 2003, power plants in Louisiana had a total installed capacity (utility and nonutility) of 25.7 million kilowatts. In the same year, total electrical generation was 94.8 billion kilowatt hours.

As of 2006, Louisiana had two nuclear power plants: Waterford 3 in St. Charles Parish and River Bend I in West Feliciana Parish. Louisiana produced 228,000 barrels per day of crude oil during 2004, the fourth-highest total among the 31 oil producing states and about 4% of the US total. As of 2004, remaining proven reserves of oil in Louisiana amounted to 427 million barrels, about 2% of the US total and seventh among the 31 oil producing states.

Marketed production of natural gas in 2004 was 1.357 trillion cubic feet (38.5 billion cubic meters), leaving proven reserves of 9.58 trillion cubic feet (272.2 billion cubic meters). There were 20,734 producing gas wells in 2004. Energy conservation plans in Louisiana call for development of untapped energy sources, such as the state's lignite and geothermal reserves.

27 Commerce

In 2002, Louisiana had wholesale sales of $47.1 billion, and retail sales of $41.8 billion. In 2005, Louisiana exported $19.2 billion in merchandise abroad.

28 Public Finance

The budget is prepared by the state executive budget director and submitted annually by the governor to the legislature for amendment and approval. The fiscal year runs from 1 July through 30 June.

Revenues for fiscal year 2004 were $23.73 billion and expenditures were $20.47 billion. The largest general expenditures were for education ($6.43 billion), public welfare ($4.12 billion), and hospitals ($1.64 billion). Louisiana had a total debt of $10.18 billion, or about $2,259.36 per capita (per person).

29 Taxation

In 2005, Louisiana ranked 36th in the nation in terms of combined state and local tax burden, at $1,910 per person. (The national average was $2,192 per person). Louisiana's individual income tax has three brackets ranging from 2% to 6%. The corporate income tax has five brackets ranging from 4% to 8%. Federal taxes paid are deductible from state taxes for both individual and corporate income taxes. The state's sales and use tax is levied at 4% with exemptions for food for home consumption, electricity, natural gas and water, and prescription drugs. Parishes and municipalities may impose additional sales taxes up to combined rates of 6.25%. The state imposes a full range of selective sales taxes including excises on motor fuels, tobacco products, soft drinks, alcoholic beverages, amusements, parimutuels, public utilities, insurance premiums, and other selected items.

Other state taxes include various license fees. The Louisiana Stadium and Exposition District and the New Orleans Exhibition Hall Authority impose a tax on hotel and motel room occupancy in the greater New Orleans area. In addition, local taxing authorities may impose a tax on hotel and motel room occupancy. Taxes on beer and chain stores contribute to local revenues, as does the property tax.

Total state tax collections in Louisiana in 2005 came $8.639 billion, of which 33.1% was generated by the state general sales and use tax, 20% by state excise taxes, 27.7% by the state income tax, 4% by the state corporate income tax, 0.5% by property taxes, and 14.6% by other taxes.

30 Health

In October 2005, Louisiana's infant mortality rate was 9.5 per 1,000 live births. The overall death rate was 9.5 per 1,000 population in 2003. Leading causes of death were heart disease, cancer, accidents and adverse effects, and motor vehicle accidents. Of the population age 18 and older, 23.4% were smokers in 2004. In 2002, Louisiana had the second-highest diabetes death rate in the nation, following West Virginia. The state also had the second-highest homicide death rate, following the District of Columbia. The death rate from HIV infection was 8.1 per 100,000 people. In 2004, the reported AIDS case rate was at about 22.4 per 100,000 people, the fifth-highest in the nation.

Louisiana's 127 community hospitals had about 17,800 beds in 2003. The average expense for community hospital care was $1,177 per inpatient day in 2003. In 2004, Louisiana had 262 doctors per 100,000 people, and 873 nurses per 100,000 people in 2005. In 2004, there were a total of 2,040 dentists in the state. In

2004, approximately 19% of the population was uninsured.

31 Housing

The Native Americans of Louisiana built huts with walls made of clay kneaded with Spanish moss and covered with cypress bark or palmetto leaves. The earliest European settlers used split cypress boards filled with clay and moss. A few early 18th-century houses with clay and moss walls remain in the Natchitoches area. Examples of later architectural styles also survive, including buildings constructed of bricks between heavy cypress posts, covered with plaster and plantation houses from the Greek Revival period of antebellum Louisiana.

In 2004, Louisiana had 1,919,859 housing units, of which 1,713,680 were occupied. About 66.2% were owner-occupied. An estimated 65.7% of all units were single-family, detached homes. Most units relied on utility gas or electricity for heating. It was estimated that 121,505 units lacked telephone service, 7,424 lacked complete plumbing facilities, and 8,581 lacked complete kitchen facilities. The average household size was 2.56 people.

In 2004, 23,000 privately owned units were authorized for construction. The median home value was $95,910. The median monthly cost for mortgage owners was $902. Renters paid a median of $540 per month.

32 Education

As of 2004, still only 78.7% of adult Louisianians had completed high school, well below the national average of 84%. Some 22.4% had completed four or more years of college, below the national average of 26%.

Total public school enrollment was estimated at 730,000 in fall 2002 but was expected to drop to 707,000 by fall 2014. Enrollment in nonpublic schools in fall 2003 was 140,492. Expenditures for public education in 2003/04 were estimated at $5.7 billion.

As of fall 2002, there were 232,140 students enrolled in college or graduate school. As of 2005, Louisiana had 90 degree-granting institutions. There are 16 public four-year schools, 46 public two-year institutions, and 10 private four-year nonprofit institutions. The center of the state university system is Louisiana State University (LSU), founded at Baton Rouge. LSU also has campuses at Alexandria, Eunice, and Shreveport, and includes the University of New Orleans. Tulane University, founded in New Orleans in 1834, is one of the most distinguished private universities in the South, as is Loyola University, also in New Orleans. Southern University Agricultural and Mechanical System at Baton Rouge (est. 1881) is one of the largest predominantly black universities in the country and has other campuses in New Orleans and Shreveport. Another mainly black institution is Grambling State University (est. 1901). The state Council for the Development of French in Louisiana (CODOFIL) organizes student exchanges with Quebec, Belgium, and France and aids Louisianians studying French abroad.

33 Arts

The Louisiana Division of the Arts (est. 1977) is an agency of the state Office of Cultural Development, Department of Culture, Recreation and Tourism. In the aftermath of

Hurricanes Katrina and Rita of 2005, the LDOA worked with the Louisiana Partnership for the Arts to assess the impact these disasters had on the art communities. Arts projects are funded in every parish (county) in the state through the LDOA Decentralized Arts Funding Program. In 2005, Louisiana arts organizations received 24 grants totaling $1,150,000 from the National Endowment for the Arts.

The Louisiana Endowment for the Humanities was established in 1971. Ongoing programs include *Relic: Readings in Literature and Culture* and *Prime Time Family Reading Time*, an annual program presented through local libraries.

New Orleans has long been one of the most important centers of artistic activity in the South. The earliest theaters were French. The American Theater, which opened in 1824, attracted many of the finest actors in America. Showboats traveled the Mississippi and other waterways, bringing dramas, musicals, and minstrel shows to river towns and plantations as early as the 1840s, with their heyday being the 1870s and 1880s.

Principal theaters included the New Orleans Theater of the Performing Arts, the Saenger Theater in New Orleans, Le Petit Theatre du Vieux Carre, and the Tulane Theater. Junebug Productions is a black touring company based in New Orleans. Louisiana State University (LSU) at Baton Rouge has theaters for both opera and drama. Baton Rouge, Shreveport, Monroe, Lake Charles, and Hammond are among the cities with little theaters and Baton Rouge, Lafayette, and Lake Charles have ballet companies. There are symphony orchestras in most of the larger cities, the Louisiana Philharmonic Orchestra (LPO) being the best known. Although Hurricane Katrina battered the state, devastating New Orleans in 2005, the LPO returned to the city with a spring concert season during March, April, and May 2006.

It is probably in music that Louisiana has made its most distinctive contributions to culture. Jazz was born in New Orleans around 1900. It was the music played by brass bands at carnivals and at black funerals and its immediate precursor was the highly syncopated music known as ragtime. Early jazz in the New Orleans style is called Dixieland. Louis Armstrong pioneered the transformation of jazz from the Dixieland ensemble style to a medium for solo improvisation. Traditional Dixieland may still be heard in New Orleans at Preservation Hall, Dixieland Hall, and the New Orleans Jazz Club. In 2005, many of the buildings that housed these organizations and clubs were either severely damaged or destroyed by the forces of Hurricane Katrina. Despite having to close buildings, groups like the Hall Jazz Band of the Preservation Hall continued touring; the Preservation hall celebrated its 45th anniversary on tour in 2006.

Equally distinctive is Cajun music, dominated by the sound of the fiddle and accordion. The French Acadian Music Festival, held in Abbeville, takes place in April.

Visual arts in the state flourish, especially in New Orleans, home to the Ogden Museum of Southern Art. Prompted by the devastation of Hurricane Katrina, the museum showcased several special exhibits including, *Come Hell and High Water: Portraits of Hurricane Katrina Survivors, New Housing Prototypes for New Orleans*, and *Louisiana Story: A Photographic Journey*.

34 Libraries and Museums

In 2001, Louisiana had 65 public library systems, with a total of 329 libraries, of which 264 were branches. That year, the public library system had about 10.8 million volumes and a circulation of 18.37 million. The New Orleans Public Library features a special collection on jazz and folk music. The libraries at Grambling State University, Xavier University of Louisiana at New Orleans, and the Amistad Collection at Tulane University have research materials on black American studies.

As of 2000, Louisiana had 89 museums, historic sites, and public gardens, as well as 27 art collections. Leading art museums are the New Orleans Museum of Art, the Lampe Gallery in New Orleans, and the R. W. Norton Art Gallery at Shreveport. The art museum of the Louisiana Arts and Science Center at Baton Rouge is located in the renovated Old Illinois Central Railroad Station. The Bayou Folk Museum at Cloutierville is in the restored home of author Kate Chopin. Among the state's scientific museums are the Lafayette Natural History Museum, Planetarium, and Nature Station, and the Museum of Natural Science in Baton Rouge. Audubon Park and Zoological Gardens are in New Orleans.

35 Communications

As of 2004, 90.9% of Louisiana's occupied housing units had telephones. By June of that year there were 2,547,153 mobile telephone subscribers. In 2003, 52.3% of Louisiana households had a computer, and 44.1% had Internet access. In 2005, the state had 77 major radio broadcasting stations (15 AM and 62 FM) as well as 32 television stations.

36 Press

In 2005, Louisiana had a total of 15 morning dailies, 11 evening dailies, and 21 Sunday papers. The principal dailies with their approximate 2005 daily circulations are *The New Orleans Times-Picayune* (252,799), *The Baton Rouge Advocate* (87,026), and *The Shreveport Times* (62,551). Two influential literary magazines originated in the state. The *Southern Review was* founded at Louisiana State University in the 1930s by Robert Penn Warren and Cleanth Brooks. The *Tulane Drama Review*, founded in 1955, moved to New York University in 1967 but is still known by its original acronym, *TDR*.

37 Tourism, Travel & Recreation

In 2000, there were about 15.4 million visitors to the state of Louisiana. Initial reports for 2001 estimated a total travel-related economic impact of $9 billion, including support for 124,200 jobs. The two most popular activities for tourists are shopping and gambling.

New Orleans is one of the major tourist attractions. Known for its fine restaurants, serving such distinctive fare as gumbo, jambalaya, and crayfish, along with an elaborate French-inspired haute cuisine, New Orleans also offers jazz clubs, the graceful buildings of the French Quarter, and a lavish carnival called Mardi Gras ("Fat Tuesday"). Beginning on the Wednesday before Shrove Tuesday (preceding Lent), parades and balls, staged by private organizations called *krewes*, are held almost nightly.

A Mardi Gras float decoration. AP IMAGES.

In 2005 Hurricane Katrina devastated New Orleans and surrounding areas, and tourism was virtually eliminated. As of 2006, only the French Quarter of New Orleans was able to support some tourism. A Mardi Gras celebration was held, but it was shortened from its usual month to a week.

Among the many other annual events that attract visitors to the state are the Natchitoches Christmas Festival, which includes 170,000 Christmas lights and spectacular fireworks displays. Louisiana has 34 state parks and recreation sites covering a total area of 39,000 acres (15,800 hectares).

38 Sports

Louisiana has two major league professional sports teams: the Saints of the National Football League and the Hornets of the National Basketball Association. The Hornets were formerly located in Charlotte, North Carolina. Both the Saints and Hornets are located in New Orleans. The Super Bowl has been held in New Orleans six times. It has been played in the Louisiana Superdome, the largest indoor arena in the United States.

New Orleans also has a minor league baseball team, the Zephyrs, of the AAA Pacific Coast League. In Shreveport, the Captains compete in the AA Texas League. There are several other minor league baseball and hockey teams scattered throughout the state.

Horseracing is popular in the state. The principal tracks are the Louisiana Jockey Club at the Fair Grounds in New Orleans and Evangeline Downs at Lafayette. Gambling has long been widespread in Louisiana, particularly in the steamboat days, when races along the Mississippi drew huge wagers.

From the 1880s to World War I, New Orleans was the nation's boxing capital. In 1893, the city was the site of the longest bout in boxing history, between Andy Bowen and Jack Burke, lasting 7 hours and 19 minutes—110 rounds—and ending in a draw.

The TPC of Louisiana at Fairfield is a newly constructed championship-level golf course that became the home of the PGA's HP Classic in 2005.

In college football, teams from Tulane University and Louisiana State University (LSU) have been successful. The LSU Tigers baseball team won the College World Series four times in the 1990s. The LSU Tigers have had a number of famous basketball alumni, including "Pistol" Pete Maravich and Shaquille O'Neal.

39 Famous Louisianians

Zachary Taylor (b.Virginia, 1784–1850) is the only US president to whom Louisiana can lay claim. Taylor owned a large plantation north of Baton Rouge, which was his residence before his election to the presidency in 1848. Edward Douglass White (1845–1921) served as chief justice of the US Supreme Court.

Also prominent in Louisiana history was Robert Cavelier, Sieur de la Salle (b.France, 1643–1687), who was the first to claim the region for the French crown. Jean Étienne Boré (1741–1820) laid the foundation of the Louisiana sugar industry by developing a process for granulating sugar from cane; Norbert Rillieux (1806–1894), a free black man, developed the much more efficient vacuum pan process of refining sugar.

Biochemist Andrew Victor Schally (b.Poland, 1926) shared the Nobel Prize for medicine in 1977 for his research on hormones. Among other distinguished Louisiana professionals have been historian T. Harry Williams (1909–1979), who won the Pulitzer Prize for his biography of Huey Long; architect Henry Hobson Richardson (1838–1886); and heart specialist Michael De Bakey (b.1908).

Louisiana's important writers include George Washington Cable (1844–1925), an early advocate of racial justice; Kate O'Flaherty Chopin (b.Missouri, 1851–1904); playwright and memoirist Lillian Hellman (1905–1984); and novelists Walker Percy (b.Alabama 1916–1990), Truman Capote (1924–1984), Shirley Ann Grau (b.1929), and John Kennedy Toole (1937–1969). The latter two were both winners of the Pulitzer Prize.

Louisianians in the arts include composer Louis Moreau Gottschalk (1829–1869); jazz musicians Jelly Roll Morton (Ferdinand Joseph La Menthe, 1885–1941) and Louis "Satchmo" Armstrong (1900–1971), gained nationwide popularity. Other prominent Louisianians in music are gospel singer Mahalia Jackson (1911–1972); pianist-singer-songwriter Antoine "Fats" Domino (b.1928); and pop singer Jerry Lee Lewis (b.1935).

Louisiana baseball heroes include Hall of Famer Melvin Thomas "Mel" Ott (1909–1958). Terry Bradshaw (b.1948) quarterbacked the Super Bowl champion Pittsburgh Steelers during the 1970s. Player-coach William F. "Bill" Russell (b.1934) led the Boston Celtics to 10 National Basketball Association championships between 1956 and 1969. Chess master Paul Morphy (1837–1884) was born in New Orleans.

40 Bibliography

BOOKS

Bristow, M. J. *State Songs of America*. Westport, CT: Greenwood Press, 2000.

Corrick, James A. *The Louisiana Purchase*. San Diego: Lucent Books, 2000.

Gaines, Ann. *The Louisiana Purchase in American History*. Berkeley Heights, NJ: Enslow, 2000.

Kein, Sybil, ed. *Creole: The History and Legacy of Louisiana's Free People of Color*. Baton Rouge: Louisiana State University Press, 2000.

Lantier, Patricia. *Louisiana*. Milwaukee, WI: Gareth Stevens, 2006.

LeVert, Suzanne. *Huey Long: the Kingfish of Louisiana*. New York: Facts on File, 1995.

LeVert, Suzanne. *Louisiana*. New York: Marshall Cavendish Benchmark, 2006.

McAuliffe, Emily. *Louisiana Facts and Symbols*. Rev. ed. Mankato, MN: Capstone, 2003.

Murray, Julie. *Louisiana*. Edina, MN: Abdo Publishing, 2006.

WEB SITES

Louisiana Secretary of State. *All Around Louisiana*. www.sec.state.la.us/around/all.htm (accessed March 1, 2007).

Official Web Site of the State of Louisiana. *Louisiana.gov*. Available www.state.la.us (accessed March 1, 2007).

Maine

State of Maine

ORIGIN OF STATE NAME: Derived either from the French for a historical district of France, or from the early use of "main" to distinguish coast from islands.

NICKNAME: The Pine Tree State.

CAPITAL: Augusta.

ENTERED UNION: 15 March 1820 (23rd).

OFFICIAL SEAL: Same as the coat of arms.

FLAG: The coat of arms is on a blue field, with a yellow fringed border surrounding three sides.

COAT OF ARMS: A farmer and sailor support a shield on which are depicted a pine tree, a moose, and water. Under the shield is the name of the state; above it are the state motto and the North Star.

MOTTO: *Dirigo* ("I direct" or "I lead").

SONG: "State of Maine Song."

FLOWER: White pine cone, tassel; wintergreen (herb).

TREE: White pine.

ANIMAL: Moose.

BIRD: Chickadee.

FISH: Landlocked salmon.

CRUSTACEAN: Blue crab.

INSECT: Honeybee.

MINERAL: Tourmaline.

LEGAL HOLIDAYS: New Year's Day, 1 January; Birthday of Martin Luther King Jr., 3rd Monday in January; Washington's Birthday, 3rd Monday in February; Patriots' Day, 3rd Monday in April; Memorial Day, last Monday in May; Independence Day, 4 July; Labor Day, 1st Monday in September; Columbus Day, 2nd Monday in October; Veterans Day, 11 November; Thanksgiving Day, 4th Thursday in November and day following; Christmas Day, 25 December.

TIME: 7 AM EST = noon GMT.

1 Location and Size

Situated in the extreme northeastern corner of the United States, Maine is the nation's most easterly state, the largest in New England, and 39th in size among the 50 states. The total area of Maine is 33,265 square miles (86,156 square kilometers), including 30,995 square miles (80,277 square kilometers) of land and 2,270 square miles (5,879 square kilometers) of inland water. Maine extends 207 miles (333 kilometers) east-west and 322 miles (518 kilometers) north-south. Hundreds of islands dot Maine's coast. The largest is Mt. Desert Island. Others include Deer Isle, Vinalhaven, and Isle au Haut.

Maine's total boundary length is 883 miles (1,421 kilometers).

2 Topography

Maine is divided into four main regions: coastal lowlands, the piedmont, mountains, and uplands. Maine's mountain region, the Longfellow range, is at the northeastern end of the Appalachian Mountain system. This zone contains nine peaks over 4,000 feet (1,200 meters), including Mt. Katahdin, which at 5,267 feet (1,606 meters) is the highest point in the state. The summit of Katahdin marks the northern terminus of the 2,000-mile (3,200-kilometer) Appalachian Trail. Maine's uplands form a high, relatively flat plateau. The eastern part of this zone is the Aroostook potato-farming region and the western part is heavily forested.

Of Maine's more than 2,200 lakes and ponds, the largest are Moosehead Lake, 117 square miles (303 square kilometers), and Sebago Lake, 13 miles (21 kilometers) by 10 miles (16 kilometers). Of the more than 5,000 rivers and streams, the Penobscot, Androscoggin, Kennebec, and Saco rivers are the most important. The longest river in Maine is the St. John, but it runs for most of its length in the Canadian province of New Brunswick.

3 Climate

Maine has three climatic regions: the northern interior zone, comprising roughly the northern half of the state between Quebec and New Brunswick; the southern interior zone; and the coastal zone. The northern zone is both drier and cooler in all four seasons than either of the other zones, while the coastal zone is more moderate

Maine Population Profile

Total population estimate in 2006:	1,321,574
Population change, 2000–06:	3.7%
Hispanic or Latino†:	0.9%
Population by race	
One race:	99.0%
White:	96.6%
Black or African American:	0.7%
American Indian /Alaska Native:	0.5%
Asian:	0.8%
Native Hawaiian / Pacific Islander:	0.0%
Some other race:	0.4%
Two or more races:	1.0%

Population by Age Group

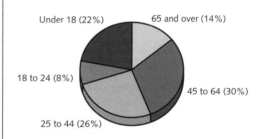

Under 18 (22%)
65 and over (14%)
18 to 24 (8%)
45 to 64 (30%)
25 to 44 (26%)

Major Cities by Population

City	Population	% change 2000–05
Portland	63,889	-0.6
Lewiston	36,050	1.0
Bangor	31,074	-1.3
South Portland	23,742	1.8
Auburn	23,602	1.7
Biddeford	22,072	5.4
Augusta	18,626	0.4
Saco	18,230	8.4
Westbrook	16,108	-0.2
Waterville	15,621	0.1

Notes: †A person of Hispanic or Latino origin may be of any race. NA indicates that data are not available.
Sources: U.S. Census Bureau. *American Community Survey* and *Population Estimates*. www.census.gov/ (accessed March 2007).

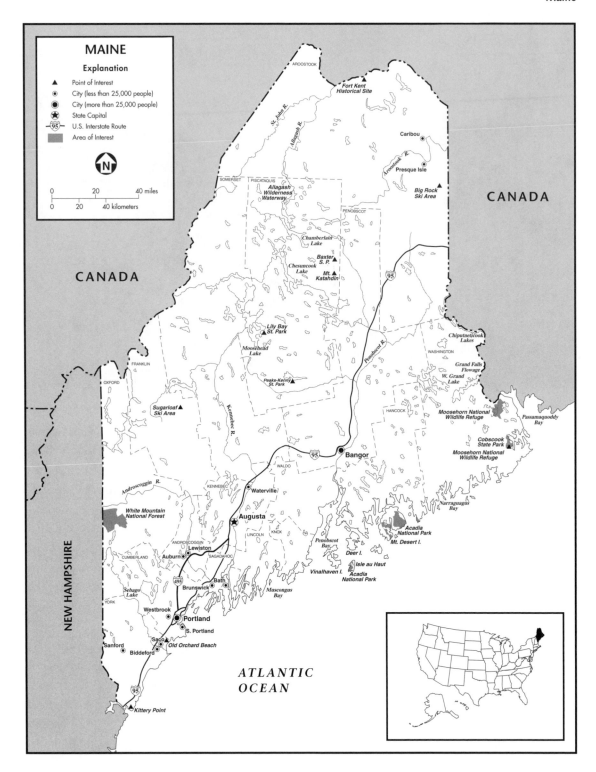

MAINE

Explanation

▲ Point of Interest
⊙ City (less than 25,000 people)
◉ City (more than 25,000 people)
★ State Capital
—95— U.S. Interstate Route
◼ Area of Interest

N

| 0 | 20 | 40 miles |
| 0 | 20 | 40 kilometers |

AROOSTOOK

Fort Kent
Historical Site

St. John R.

Allagash R.

Caribou

Aroostook R.

Presque Isle

Big Rock
Ski Area

CANADA

SOMERSET

PISCATAQUIS

Allagash
Wilderness
Waterway

PENOBSCOT

Chamberlain
Lake

Baxter
S. P.

Chesuncook
Lake

Mt. ▲
Katahdin

CANADA

95

Penobscot R.

Chiputneticook
Lakes

WASHINGTON

Grand Falls
Flowage

W. Grand
Lake

Lily Bay
St. Park

Moosehead
Lake

FRANKLIN

OXFORD

Peaks-Kenny
St. Park

HANCOCK

Moosehorn National
Wildlife Refuge

Passamaquoddy
Bay

Sugarloaf ▲
Ski Area

Kennebec R.

Cobscook
State Park

Moosehorn National
Wildlife Refuge

95

Bangor

WALDO

Narraguagus
Bay

Androscoggin R.

KENNEBEC

Waterville

White Mountain
National Forest

Augusta

LINCOLN

KNOX

Acadia
National Park

Mt. Desert I.

NEW HAMPSHIRE

ANDROSCOGGIN

Lewiston

SAGADAHOC

Auburn

CUMBERLAND

495

Bath

Brunswick

Penobscot
Bay

Deer I.

Isle au Haut

Vinalhaven I.

Acadia
National Park

Sebago
Lake

YORK

Westbrook

Muscongus
Bay

Portland

S. Portland

Saco ▲

Sanford

Old Orchard Beach

Biddeford

ATLANTIC
OCEAN

95

Kittery Point

Bubble Mountain in Acadia National Park. NANCY MARSHALL COMMUNICATIONS.

in temperature year-round than the other two. Annual mean temperatures range from about 40°F (5°C) in the northern zone to 44°F (7°C) in the southern interior and 46°F (8°C) in the coastal zone. Record temperatures for the state are -48°F (-44°C) registered at Van Buren on 19 January 1925, and 105°F (41°C), registered at North Bridgton on 10 July 1911. The mean annual precipitation ranges from 40.2 inches (102 centimeters) in the north to 41.5 inches (105 centimeters) in the southern interior and 45.7 in (116 cm) on the coast. Average annual snowfall is 78 inches (198 centimeters).

4 Plants and Animals

The trees in Maine's forests are largely softwoods, such as red and white spruces, eastern hemlock, and white and red pine. Important hardwoods include beech, white oak, and black willow. Maine is home to most of the flowers and shrubs common to the north temperate zone, including an important commercial resource, the low-bush blueberry. Maine has 17 rare orchid species. Two species, the small whorled pogonia and the eastern prairie fringed orchid, were classified as threatened plant species as of April 2006. The furbish lousewart was classified as endangered that year.

About 30,000 white-tailed deer are killed by hunters in Maine each year, but the herd does not appear to diminish. Moose hunting was banned in Maine in 1935. Other common forest animals include the bobcat, beaver, mink, red fox, and snowshoe hare. Seals and porpoises are found in

Maine Population by Race

Census 2000 was the first national census in which the instructions to respondents said, "Mark one or more races." This table shows the number of people who are of one, two, or three or more races. For those claiming two races, the number of people belonging to the various categories is listed. The U.S. government conducts a census of the population every ten years.

	Number	Percent
Total population	1,274,923	100.0
One race	1,262,276	99.0
Two races	11,987	0.9
White *and* Black or African American	1,914	0.2
White *and* American Indian/Alaska Native	5,387	0.4
White *and* Asian	2,054	0.2
White *and* Native Hawaiian/Pacific Islander	182	—
White *and* some other race	1,598	0.1
Black or African American *and* American Indian/Alaska Native	115	—
Black or African American *and* Asian	87	—
Black or African American *and* Native Hawaiian/Pacific Islander	19	—
Black or African American *and* some other race	245	—
American Indian/Alaska Native *and* Asian	47	—
American Indian/Alaska Native *and* Native Hawaiian/Pacific Islander	11	—
American Indian/Alaska Native *and* some other race	65	—
Asian *and* Native Hawaiian/Pacific Islander	68	—
Asian *and* some other race	183	—
Native Hawaiian/Pacific Islander *and* some other race	12	—
Three or more races	660	0.1

Source: U.S. Census Bureau. *Census 2000: Redistricting Data.* Press release issued by the Redistricting Data Office. Washington, D.C., March, 2001. A dash (—) indicates that the percent is less than 0.1.

coastal waters, along with practically every variety of North Atlantic fish and shellfish, including the famous Maine lobster. Coastal waterfowl include the osprey, great and double-crested cormorants, and herring and great black-backed gulls. Matinicus Rock, an island near Penobscot Bay, is the only known North American nesting site of the common puffin, or sea parrot.

In 2006, a total of 11 Maine animal species were classified as threatened or endangered by the US Fish and Wildlife Service, including the bald eagle, piping plover, Atlantic Gulf of Maine salmon, two species of whale, and the leatherback sea turtle.

5 Environmental Protection

The Department of Environmental Protection is the primary state agency for environmental concerns. The Land Use Regulation Commission extends the principles of town planning and zoning to unorganized townships, "plantations," and numerous coastal islands that have no local government and might otherwise be subject to ecologically unsound development. In 2003, Maine had 59 hazardous waste sites listed in the Environmental Protection Agency's database, 12 of which were on the National Priorities List as of 2006.

6 Population

In 2005, Maine ranked 40th in population in the United States with an estimated total of 1,321,574 residents. The population is projected to grow to 1.41 million by 2025. The population density for 2004 was 42.7 persons per square mile (16.48 persons per square kilometer). More than half the population lives on less than one-seventh of the land within 25 miles (40 kilometers) of the Atlantic coast, and almost half the state is virtually uninhabited. In 2004, the median age was 40.7 years, the highest median in the country. In 2005, of all Maine residents, 14% were age 65 or older, while 22% were 18 or younger. The largest cities are Portland, Bangor, and Lewsiton-Auburn, all of which have populations under 100,000.

7 Ethnic Groups

Maine's population is primarily Yankee, both in its English and Scotch-Irish origins and in its retention of many of the values and folkways of rural New England. As of the 2000 census, a total of 274,423 claimed English ancestry, followed by 192,901 claiming Irish ancestry, 181,663 claiming French ancestry and 110,344 who claimed Canadian or French-Canadian ancestry. The population of Hispanics and Latinos was 9,360. In 2006, Hispanics and Latinos accounted for 0.9% of the population. The Native American population included 7,098 residents. In 2006, Native Americans accounted for 0.5% of the state's population. The leading tribes were the Penobscot, the Aristook Band of Micmac, the Passamaquoddy, and the Houlton Band of Maliseets. Maine in 2000 had 6,760 black American residents and 9,111 Asians, including 2,034 Chinese, 1,159 Filipinos, and 1,021 Asian Indians. Pacific Islanders numbered 382. There were 36,691 foreign-born residents in the state.

8 Languages

Maine English is celebrated as typical Yankee speech. The final /r/ is often absent form a word. A vowel sound between /ah/ and the /a/ is used in words such as *car* and *garden*. Maple syrup comes from *rock* or *sugar maple* trees in a *sap* or *sugar orchard*. Cottage cheese is called *curd cheese* and pancakes are *fritters*. Native Algonkian place-names abound, including Saco, Kennebec, and Skowhegan.

In 2000, of all Maine residents five years old or older, 92.2% reported speaking only English in the home. About 63,640 residents, or 5.3%, spoke French.

9 Religions

In 2004, Maine had about 217,676 Roman Catholics, and an estimated 8,290 Jews in 2000. Leading Protestant denominations were the United Methodist Church, with 31,689 adherents, and the American Baptists USA, with 26,259 members (both as of 2000), and the United Church of Christ with 23,060 followers, as of 2005. The Muslim community had about 800 members. Over 800,000 people (about 63.6% of the population) were not counted as members of any religious organization.

10 Transportation

Railroad development in Maine has declined rapidly since World War II, while passenger service has been nearly dropped altogether. Although Maine had no Class I railroads in 2003, there

Boats in the harbor in Stonington, Maine. © FRANZ-MARC FREI/CORBIS.

were 7 regional and local railroads that operated on 1,148 miles (1,848 kilometers) of railroad track. As of 2006, Amtrak provided service to four stations in Maine via its Downeaster train that ran from Portland to Boston.

About three-quarters of all communities and about half the population depend entirely on highway trucking for the overland transportation of freight. In 2004, Maine had 22,748 miles (36,624 kilometers) of public roads. There were 1.086 million registered motor vehicles, and 984,829 licensed drivers in the same year. The Maine Turnpike and I-95 are the major highways.

River traffic has been central to the lumber industry. Maine has 10 established seaports, with

Portland and Searsport being the main depots for overseas shipping. Portland International Jetport is the largest and most active airport in Maine. In 2004, it had 687,344 passenger boardings. In 2005, Maine had 103 airports, 13 heliports and 37 seaplane bases.

11 History

Sometime around 1600, English expeditions began fishing the Gulf of Maine regularly. By 1630, however, there were permanent English settlements on several islands and at nearly a dozen spots along the coast. In 1652, the government of the Massachusetts Bay Colony began absorbing the small Maine settlements, and in

Maine Governors: 1820–2007

1820–1821	William King	Dem-Rep		1881–1883	Harris Merrill Plaisted	Fusion
1821	William Durkee Williamson	Dem-Rep		1883–1887	Frederick Robie	Republican
1821–1822	Benjamin Ames	Dem-Rep		1887	Joseph Robinson Bodwell	Republican
1822	Daniel Rose	Dem-Rep		1887–1889	Sebastian Streeter Marble	Republican
1822–1827	Albion Keith Parris	Dem-Rep		1889–1893	Edwin Chick Burleigh	Republican
1827–1829	Enoch Lincoln	Republican		1893–1897	Henry B. Cleaves	Republican
1829–1830	Nathan Cutler	Democrat		1897–1901	Llewellyn Powers	Republican
1830	Joshua Hall	Democrat		1901–1905	John Fremont Hill	Republican
1830–1831	Johathan Glidden Hunton	Nat-Rep		1905–1909	William Titcomb Cobb	Republican
1831–1834	Samuel Emerson Smith	Jacksonian		1909–1911	Bert Manfred Fernald	Republican
1834–1838	Robert Pinckney Dunlap	Democrat		1911–1913	Frederick William Plaisted	Republican
1838–1839	Edward Kent	Whig		1913–1915	William Thomas Haines	Republican
1839–1841	John Fairfield	Democrat		1915–1917	Oakley Chester Curtis	Democrat
1841	Richard H. Vose	Democrat		1917–1921	Carl Elias Milliken	Republican
1841–1842	Edward Kent	Whig		1921	Frederic Hale Parkhurst	Republican
1842–1843	John Fairfield	Democrat		1921–1925	Percival Proctor Baxter	Republican
1843–1844	Edward Kavanagh	Democrat		1925–1929	Ralph Owen Brewster	Republican
1844	David Dunn	Democrat		1929–1933	William Tudor Gardiner	Republican
1844	John Winchester Dana	Democrat		1933–1937	Louis Jefferson Brann	Democrat
1844–1847	Hugh Johnston Anderson	Democrat		1937–1941	Lewis Orin Barrows	Republican
1847–1850	John Winchester Dana	Democrat		1941–1945	Sumner Sewall	Republican
1850–1853	John Hubbard	Democrat		1945–1949	Horace Augustus Hildreth	Republican
1853–1855	William George Crosby	Whig		1949–1952	Frederick George Payne	Republican
1855–1856	Anson Peaslee Morrill	Maine Law		1952–1955	Burton Melvin Cross	Republican
1856–1857	Samuel Wells	Democrat		1955–1959	Edmund Sixtus Muskie	Democrat
1857	Hannibal Hamlin	Republican		1959	Robert Nelson Haskell	Republican
1857–1858	Joseph Hartwell Williams	Republican		1959	Clinton Amos Clauson	Democrat
1858–1861	Lot Myrick Morrill	Republican		1959–1967	John Hathaway Reed	Republican
1861–1863	Israel Washburn, Jr.	Republican		1967–1975	Kenneth M. Curtis	Democrat
1863–1864	Abner Coburn	Republican		1975–1979	James Bernard Longley	Independent
1864–1867	Samuel Cony	Republican		1979–1987	Joseph Edward Brennan	Democrat
1867–1871	Jushua Lawrence Chamberlain	Republican		1987–1995	John Rettie McKernan, Jr.	Republican1995
1871–1874	Sidney Perham	Republican		1995–2002	Angus S. King, Jr.	Independent
1874–1876	Nelson Dingley, Jr.	Republican		2002–	John Baldacci	Democrat
1876–1879	Selden Connor	Republican				
1879–1880	Alonzo Garcelon	Democrat			Democratic Republican – Dem-Rep	
1880–1881	Daniel Franklin Davis	Republican			National Republican – Nat-Rep	

1691, Maine became a district of Massachusetts. During the first hundred years of settlement, Maine's economy was based on farming, fishing, trading, and exploitation of the forests.

The first naval encounter of the Revolutionary War occurred in Machias Bay, when, on 12 June 1775, angry colonials captured the British armed schooner *Margaretta*. An expedition through the Maine woods in the fall of 1775 intended to drive the British out of Quebec, but this failed.

Another disaster was a 1779 expedition in which Massachusetts forces, failing to dislodge British troops at Castine, abandoned many of its own ships near the Penobscot River. Popular pressure for separation from Massachusetts mounted after the War of 1812. Admission of Maine to the Union as a free state was joined with the admission of Missouri as a slave state in the Missouri Compromise of 1820.

Textile mills and shoe factories came to Maine between 1830 and 1860. After the Civil War, the revolution in papermaking that substituted wood pulp for rags brought a vigorous new industry to the state. By 1900, Maine was one of the leading papermaking states in the United States, and the industry continues to dominate the state today. The rise of tourism and the conflict between economic development and environmental protection have been central in the postwar period.

In the 1980s, the state government paid $81.5 million to the Penobscot and Passamaquoddy tribes. This settled a suit claiming that a 1794 treaty under which the Passamaquoddy handed over most of its land—amounting to the northern two-thirds of Maine—was illegal and had never been ratified by Congress.

In the late 1990s, Maine's economy experienced strong growth, but in the early 2000s, the state's economy was troubled. By 2003, the state budget was showing a deficit of $24 million. Despite the state's economic woes, in June 2003, Maine's governor signed into law a statewide health plan called Dirigo Health.

By 2005, plans were being made by the state to deal with the closing of military bases, including the Brunswick Naval Air Station.

12 State Government

Maine's constitution was adopted in 1819, and had been amended 169 times as of January 2005. The document sets up a two-house legislature, consisting of a 35-member Senate and a 151-member House of Representatives. The legislature convenes every two years in joint session to elect the secretary of state, attorney general, auditor, and state treasurer. The governor is the

Maine Presidential Vote by Major Political Parties, 1948–2004

YEAR	MAINE WINNER	DEMOCRAT	REPUBLICAN
1948	Dewey (R)	111,916	150,234
1952	*Eisenhower (R)	118,806	232,353
1956	*Eisenhower (R)	102,468	249,238
1960	*Eisenhower (R)	102,468	249,238
1960	Nixon (R)	181,159	240,608
1964	*Johnson (D)	262,264	118,701
1968	Humphrey (D)	217,312	169,254
1972	*Nixon (R)	160,584	256,458
1976	Ford (R)	232,279	236,320
1980	*Reagan (R)	220,974	238,522
1984	*Reagan (R)	214,515	336,500
1988	*Bush (R)	243,569	307,131
1992**	*Clinton (D)	263,420	206,504
1996**	*Clinton (D)	312,788	186,378
2000	Gore (D)	319,951	286,616
2004	Kerry (D)	396,842	330,201

*Won US presidential election.
**Independent candidate Ross Perot received 206,820 votes in 1992 and 85,970 votes in 1996.

only official elected statewide. The governor is limited to two four-year terms. The governor's veto may be overridden by a two-thirds vote of members present and voting in each legislative chamber.

The legislative salary in 2004 was $11,384 for the first year and $8,302 for the second. The governor's salary as of December 2004 was $70,000.

13 Political Parties

The Republican Party dominated Maine politics for 100 years after its formation in the 1850s. The rise of Democrat Edmund S. Muskie, elected governor in 1954 and 1956, and to the first of four terms in the US Senate in 1960, signaled a change. Muskie appealed personally to many traditionally Republican voters, but his party's revival was also the result of demographic changes, especially an increase in the proportion of French-Canadian voters. In 2002 there were 912,092 registered voters. In 1998, of all registered voters in Maine, 32% were Democrats, 29% Republicans, and 39% unaffiliated or members of other parties.

In 2002, Democrat John Baldacci was elected governor; he was reelected in 2006. In 2006 Republican Olympia Snowe won reelection in the US Senate. Republican Susan E. Collins won the seat left vacant by retiring three-term senator William S. Cohen in 1996 (Collins was reelected in 2002). Cohen, a Republican, went on to serve Democratic president Bill Clinton as Secretary of Defense. Both of Maine's seats in the US House of Representatives were held by Democrats following the 2006 mid-term elections. In 2000, Democrat Al Gore won 49% of the presidential vote and Republican George W. Bush received 44%. In the 2004 election, Democrat John Kerry received 53.4% of the presidential vote to George W. Bush's 44.6%. Following the 2006 elections, the state house of representatives had 89 Democrats, 60 Republicans, and 2 independents, while the state senate had 18 Democrats and 17 Republicans. Forty-three women were elected in the state legislature in 2006, or 23.1%.

14 Local Government

The principal units of local government in 2005 included 16 counties, 22 cities, 282 public school districts, and 222 special districts. In 2000, there were 467 townships. As is customary in New England, the basic instrument of town government is the annual town meeting, with an elective board of selectmen supervising town affairs between meetings. Some of the larger towns employ full-time town managers. Maine's counties function primarily as judicial districts.

15 Judicial System

The highest state court is the Supreme Judicial Court, which has statewide appeals jurisdiction in all civil and criminal matters. The 16-member Superior Court has original jurisdiction in cases involving trial by jury and also hears some appeals. The district courts hear non-felony criminal cases and small claims and juvenile cases. In 2004, Maine's violent crime rate (murder/nonnegligent manslaughter, forcible rape, robbery, aggravated assault) was 103.5 incidents per 100,000 persons (the second-lowest in the United States after North Dakota). As of 31 December 2004, there were 2,024 state and federal prisoners held in Maine. The state has not had a death penalty since 1887, but does provide for a life sentence without parole.

16 Migration

Throughout the colonial and early national periods, Maine's population grew primarily by immigration from elsewhere in New England. About 1830, after agriculture in the state had passed its peak, Maine farmers and woodsmen began moving west. Europeans and French Canadians came to the state at about that time.

Between 1990 and 1998, the state had a net loss of 15,000 in domestic migration and a net gain of 3,000 in international migration. In the period 2000–05, some 5,004 people moved into the state from other countries, while 36,804 moved into the state from other states, for a net gain of 41,808 people.

17 Economy

Maine's greatest economic strengths are its forests and waters, yielding wood products, water power, fisheries, and ocean commerce. As of 2005, among the largest industries in the state was paper manufacturing, for which both forests and water power are essential. Maine's greatest current economic weakness is its limited access to the national transportation network that links major production and manufacturing centers with large metropolitan markets. On the other hand, this relative isolation, combined with the state's traditional natural assets, has contributed to Maine's attractiveness as a place for tourism and recreation.

Maine's gross state product (GSP) in 2004 totaled $43.336 billion, of which the real estate sector accounted for the largest portion, by value, at 13.4%, followed by manufacturing at 11.9% of GSP. Of the 40,304 businesses that had employees, an estimated 97.5% were small companies.

18 Income

In 2004, Maine ranked 34th among the 50 states and the District of Columbia with a per capita (per person) income of $30,046, compared to the national average of $33,050. For the three-year period 2002 through 2004, the state's median household income was $39,395, compared to the national average of $44,473. For the same period, 12.2% of the state's residents lived below the federal poverty level, as compared to 12.4% nationwide.

19 Industry

Manufacturing in Maine has always been related to the forests. From the 17th century through much of the 19th, the staples of Maine industry were shipbuilding and lumber. As of 2005, it was papermaking and wood products, but footwear, textiles and apparel, shipbuilding, and electronic components and accessories are also important items.

Maine has the largest paper-production capacity of any state in the nation. There are large papermills and pulpmills in more than a dozen towns and cities. As of 2004, wood-related industries (paper, lumber, wood products) accounted for about 25% of the value of all manufactured product shipments. In 2004, the shipment value of all products manufactured in the state was $13.656 billion. Of that total, paper manufacturing accounted for the largest share at $3.601 billion, followed by transportation equipment at $2.019 billion. In that same year, a total of 57,901 people were employed in the state's manufacturing sector.

20 Labor

In April 2006, the civilian labor force in Maine numbered 716,300, with approximately 30,000 workers unemployed, yielding an unemployment rate of 4.2%, compared to the national average of 4.7% for the same period. In April 2006, early nonfarm employment data indicated that about 5% of the labor force was employed in construction; 9.7% in manufacturing; 20.4% in trade, transportation, and public utilities; 5.5% in financial activities; 8.3% in professional and business services; 18.4% in educational and health services; 9.7% in leisure and hospitality services; and 17.1% in government.

In 2005, a total of 69,000 of Maine's 582,000 employed wage and salary workers were members of a union. This represented 11.9% of those so employed, and below the national average of 12%.

21 Agriculture

Maine's gross farm income in 2005 was $546 million (43rd in the United States). There were 7,200 farms in 2004, with an estimated 1.37 million acres (554,000 hectares) of land.

Maine produces more food crops for human consumption than any other New England state. Maine ranks first in the world in the production of blueberries, producing over 25% of the total blueberry crop and over 50% of the world's wild blueberries. Maine is also home to the largest bioagricultural firm in the world, which produces breeding stock for the broiler industry worldwide. In New England, Maine ranks first in potato production and second in the production of milk and apples. Nationally, Maine ranks third in maple syrup and seventh in potatoes. The greenhouse/nursery and wild blueberry sectors have also shown steady growth in sales since 1990.

22 Domesticated Animals

In 2005, Maine had an estimated 92,000 cattle and calves worth around $101.2 million. Dairy farmers had an estimated 35,000 milk cows, which produced 624 million pounds (283.6 million kilograms) of milk in 2003. Poultry farmers sold an estimated 10.2 million pounds (4.6 million kilograms) of chickens in the same

year. South-central Maine is the leading poultry region.

23 Fishing

Fishing has been important to the economy of Maine since its settlement. In 2004, Maine landings brought a total of 208.4 million pounds (84.3 million kilograms) with a value of $315.8 million (the third highest value in the nation). Rockland and Portland were main ports.

The most valuable Maine fishery product is the lobster. In 2004, Maine led the nation in landings of American lobster for the 23rd consecutive year, with 58.5 million pounds (26.6 million kilograms). Flounder, halibut, scallops, and shrimp were also caught. Maine also was the leading state in soft clams catch, with 2.4 million pounds of meats (1.1 million kilograms) in 2004. In 2003, there were 35 processing and 176 wholesale plants in the state, with a total of about 1,780 employees. The state commercial fleet in 2001 had 5,836 boats and 1,656 vessels.

In 2004, Maine had 15 trout farms. The state also has nine inland fish hatcheries and hosts two national fish hatcheries. In 2004, there were 270,698 licensed sports fishing participants in the state.

24 Forestry

Maine's 17.7 million acres (7.2 million hectares) of forest in 2003 contained over 3.6 billion trees and covered 90% of the state's land area, the largest percentage for any state in the United States. About 16,952,000 acres (6,860,000 hectares) are classified as commercial timberland, over 96% of it privately owned, and half of that by a dozen large paper companies and land managing corporations. Principal commercial hardwood include ash, hard maple, white and yellow birch, beech, and oak; commercially significant softwoods include white pine, hemlock, cedar, spruce, and fir. Total lumber production in 2004 was 964 million board feet, of which 86% was softwood.

25 Mining

The value of nonfuel mineral production in Maine in 2003 was estimated to be $100 million. The mining and production of construction materials accounted for the vast majority of the state's nonfuel mineral production. Construction sand and gravel, and crushed stone, together accounted for about 65% of total nonfuel mineral output by value that year. According to preliminary data, output of construction sand and gravel totaled 9.3 million metric tons, worth $37.9 million, while crushed stone production came to 4.4 million metric tons, and was valued at $26 million. In 2003, portland cement, and dimension granite were also important nonfuel minerals produced in Maine. Gemstone production that same year was valued at $262,000.

26 Energy and Power

In 2003, Maine had a total net summer generating capacity of 4.285 million kilowatts, with output that same year of 18.971 billion kilowatt hours. Natural gas-fueled power plants accounted for 49.8% of all power generated, followed by other renewable sources at 20.6% and hydroelectric plants at 16.7%. Maine no longer generates electricity through nuclear power. As of 2003, Maine's only nuclear plant, the Maine Yankee Atomic Power plant in Wiscasset, was being dismantled after being closed down in 1997.

Maine has no proven reserves or production of crude oil, coal, or natural gas.

27 Commerce

In 2002, Maine's wholesale trade sector had sales of $10.3 billion, while the state's retail sector in that same year had sales of $16.05 billion. Motor vehicle and motor vehicle parts dealers accounted for the largest portion of retail sales at $3.7 billion, followed by food and beverage stores at $2.7 billion. The value of Maine's exports amounted to $2.3 billion in 2005.

28 Public Finance

Maine's biennial budget is prepared by the Bureau of the Budget and submitted by the governor to the legislature for consideration. The fiscal year extends from 1 July to 30 June.

Total revenues for 2004 were $8.3 billion, while total expenditures were $7.3 billion. The largest general expenditures were for public welfare ($2.286 billion), education ($1.65 billion), and highways ($536 million). The state had a total debt of about $4.6 billion, or $3,531.55 per capita (per person).

29 Taxation

As of 1 January 2006, the state's individual income tax had four brackets ranging from 2% to 8.5%. The corporate income tax ranges from 3.5% to 8.93%. The state sales tax is 5% on most goods, although basic foods are tax exempt if consumed off premises (such as at home). Cigarettes and gasoline are subject to state excise taxes

In 2005, Maine collected $3.071 billion in tax revenues, or $2,323 per person, placing the state 19th out of the 50 states in per capita tax burden, compared to the national average of $2,192 per person. Of the tax revenues raised, 42.3% was generated by the state income tax, followed by sales taxes at 30.4%, and state excise taxes at 13.9%. The state's corporate income tax accounted for 4.4% of all tax revenues collected.

30 Health

In 2003, Maine's crude death rate was 9.6 deaths per 1,000 inhabitants. As of October 2005, the state's infant mortality rate was estimated at 6.1 per 1,000 live births. In 2004, about 20.9% of the state's population were smokers. Maine's reported AIDS case rate in 2004 stood at around 4.6 per 100,000 people. The death rates from major causes of death in 2002 (per 100,000 people) were: heart disease at 244.9; cancer at 247.7; cerebrovascular disease at 63.6; chronic lower respiratory diseases at 61.1; and diabetes at 31.2.

Maine's 37 community hospitals had about 3,700 beds in 2003. There were 1,009 nurses per 100,000 people in 2005, while in 2004 there were 302 physicians per 100,000 population in 2004. In that same year, Maine had 629 dentists. The average expense for community hospital care was $1,416 per day in 2003. In 2004, about 10% of the state's population was uninsured.

31 Housing

There were an estimated 676,667 housing units in Maine in 2004. Approximately 534,412 of the total units were occupied, with 72.9% being owner-occupied. About 68.9% of all units are single-family, detached homes. Fuel oils and kerosene are the primary heating fuel for most units. It was estimated that 12,214 units lacked telephone service, 3,771 lacked complete plumbing facilities, and 3,336 lacked complete kitchen facilities. The average household size was 2.39 people.

In 2004, a total of 8,800 privately owned units were authorized for construction. The median home value is $143,182. The median monthly cost for mortgage owners was $1,020. Renters paid a median of $582 per month.

32 Education

Maine has a long and vigorous tradition of education at all levels, both public and private. In 2004, of Maine residents age 25 and older, 87.1% were high school graduates, and 24.2% had obtained a bachelor's degree or higher.

Total public school enrollment was estimated at 200,000 in fall 2003, and was expected to drop to 178,000 by fall 2014. Enrollment in nonpublic schools in fall 2003 was 20,696. Expenditures for public education in 2003/2004 were estimated at $2.2 billion.

As of fall 2002, there were 63,308 students enrolled in institutions of higher education. As of 2005, Maine had 30 degree-granting institutions. Since 1968, the state's public colleges and universities have been incorporated into a single University of Maine System. The original land grant campus is at Orono. The other major campus in the system is the University of Southern Maine at Portland and Gorham. The state also operates the Maine Maritime Academy at Castine and the Maine Technical College System, comprised of seven technical colleges.

Of the state's private colleges and professional schools, Bowdoin College in Brunswick, Colby College in Waterville, and Bates College in Lewiston are the best known.

33 Arts

Maine has long held an attraction for painters and artists, including Winslow Homer and Andrew Wyeth. The state has many summer theaters, the oldest and most famous of which is at Ogunquit, which celebrated its 74th anniversary in 2006.

The Portland Symphony (est. 1923) is Maine's leading orchestra. Augusta and Bangor also host symphonies. The Maine State Ballet Company is based in Westbrook. The Portland Ballet is also well known in the state. The Bossov Ballet Theatre in Pittsfield is part of a boarding school for high school students looking for rigorous pre-professional training in dance. One of the newest additions to Maine's cultural life is the Maine Grand Opera Company (est. 2001), based at the Camden Opera House. There are many local theater groups.

Some well-known festivals include the Arcady Summer Music Festival (est. 1980), specializing in chamber music, and the annual Bowdoin Summer Music Festival (est. 1964), presented at Bowdoin College in Brunswick.

The Maine Arts Commission is an independent state agency funded in part by the Maine State Legislature and the National Endowment for the Arts. The state Department of Educational and Cultural Services has an Arts and Humanities Bureau that provides funds to artists in residence, Maine touring artists, and community arts councils. The Maine Humanities Council, founded in 1975, provides support to about 100 nonprofit art organizations each year. Several ongoing reading programs sponsored in part by MHC include *Born to Read*, for children and youth; *New Books, New Readers*, for adult learners; and *Let's Talk About It*, for adult readers.

34 Libraries and Museums

In 2001, Maine had 280 public libraries, of which 7 were branch libraries. In that same year, the state's libraries had 5,891,000 volumes and a combined circulation of 8,155,000. Leading libraries included the Maine State Library at Augusta, Bowdoin College at Brunswick, and the University of Maine School of Law. Maine has at least 121 museums and historic sites. The Maine State Museum in Augusta houses collections in history, natural history, anthropology, marine studies, mineralogy, science, and technology. The privately supported Maine Historical Society in Portland maintains a research library and the Wadsworth Longfellow House, the boyhood home of Henry Wadsworth Longfellow. The largest of several maritime museums is in Bath.

35 Communications

In 2004, a total of 96.6% of occupied housing units had telephones, while as of June 2004, there were 610,533 mobile telephone service subscribers. In 2003, of all households in the state, 67.8% had a computer, while 57.9% had access to the Internet. Maine had 33 major commercial radio stations (5 AM, 28 FM) in 2005, along with 11 major television stations. Educational television stations broadcast from Augusta, Biddeford, Calais, Orono, and Presque Isle.

Sand Beach, Acadia National Park. NANCY MARSHALL COMMUNICATIONS.

By 2000, a total of 25,583 Internet domain names had been registered in Maine.

36 Press

In 2005, Maine had seven daily newspapers and four Sunday editions. The most widely read newspapers (with their 2005 circulation) were the *Bangor Daily News* (mornings, 62,462; weekend, 74,754) and the *Portland Press Herald* (mornings, 77,788). Maine's largest Sunday newspaper is the *Portland Sunday Telegram* (125,858). The capital is served by the *Augusta Kennebec Journal* (15,167 daily; 14,422 Sundays). Regional interest magazines include *Maine Times* and *Down East*

37 Tourism, Travel & Recreation

In 2004, the state of Maine hosted 43 million travelers who spent $13.6 billion dollars. Though Maine is a year-round resort destination, 59% of travelers arrive during the months of July, August, and September.

Sightseeing and outdoor activities are the primary tourist attractions. In the summer, the southern coast offers sandy beaches, icy surf, and several small harbors for sailing and saltwater fishing. Northeastward, the scenery becomes more rugged and spectacular, and sailing and hiking are the primary activities. Hundreds of lakes, ponds, rivers, and streams offer opportunities for freshwater bathing, boating, and fishing. Whitewater canoeing lures the adventurous along the Allagash Wilderness Waterway in northern Maine. Maine has always attracted hunters, especially during the fall deer season. Wintertime recreation facilities include nearly 60 ski areas and countless opportunities for cross-country skiing.

There are 12 state parks and beaches. Acadia National Park is a popular attraction, along with other wildlife areas, refuges, and forests. The state fair is held at Bangor.

38 Sports

Maine has no major league professional sports team. The Portland Pirates (a minor league hockey team) of the American Hockey League play on their home ice at the Cumberland County Civic Center in Portland. Minor league baseball's Sea Dogs of the AA Eastern League play their games at Hadlock Field, which opened in 1994.

Harness racing is held at Scarborough Downs and other tracks and fairgrounds throughout the state. Sailing is a popular participant sport with a Windsummer Festival held each July at Boothbay Harbor and a Retired Skippers Race at Castine in August.

39 Famous Mainers

The highest federal officeholders born in Maine were Hannibal Hamlin (1809–1891), the nation's first Republican vice-president, under Abraham Lincoln; and Nelson A. Rockefeller (1908–1979), governor of New York State from 1959 to 1973 and US vice-president under Gerald Ford. Margaret Chase Smith (1897–1995) served longer in the US Senate—24 years—than any other woman.

A statue of Paul Bunyon in Bangor, the lumber capital of the world in the 1880s. MAINE OFFICE OF TOURISM.

Maine claims a large number of well-known reformers and humanitarians: Dorothea Lynde Dix (1802–1887), who led the movement for hospitals for the insane; Elijah Parish Lovejoy (1802–1837), an abolitionist killed while defending his printing press from a proslavery mob in St. Louis, Missouri; and Harriet Beecher Stowe (b.Connecticut, 1811–1896), whose novel *Uncle Tom's Cabin* (1852) was written in Maine. Other important writers include poet Henry Wadsworth Longfellow (1807–1882) and Kate Douglas Wiggin (1856–1923), author of *Rebecca of Sunnybrook Farm*. Edwin Arlington Robinson (1869–1935) and Edna St. Vincent

Millay (1892–1950) were both Pulitzer Prize-winning poets. E. B. (Elwyn Brooks) White (1899–1985), *New Yorker* essayist and author of the children's classic *Charlotte's Web*, maintained a home in Maine, which inspired much of his writing. Winslow Homer (b.Massachusetts, 1836–1910) had a summer home at Prouts Neck, where he painted many of his seascapes. Joan Benoit-Samuelson (b.1957), famous distance runner during the 1980s, was born in Cape Elizabeth.

40 Bibliography

BOOKS

Beem, Edgar Allen. *Maine: the Spirit of America*. New York: Harry N. Abrams, 2000.

Bristow, M. J. *State Songs of America*. Westport, CT: Greenwood Press, 2000.

Brown, Jonatha A. *Maine*. Milwaukee, WI: Gareth Stevens, 2007.

Dornfeld, Margaret. *Maine*. New York: Benchmark Books, 2001.

Gale, Robert L. *A Sarah Orne Jewett Companion*. Westport, CT: Greenwood Press, 1999.

McAuliffe, Emily. *Maine Facts and Symbols*. Rev. ed. Mankato, MN: Capstone, 2003.

Murray, Julie. *Maine*. Edina, MN: Abdo Publishing, 2006.

WEB SITES

Official Website of the State of Maine. *Maine.gov*. www.state.me.us (accessed March 1, 2007).

Visit New England. *Maine*. www.visit-maine.com (accessed March 1, 2007).

Maryland

State of Maryland

ORIGIN OF STATE NAME: Named for Henrietta Maria, queen consort of King Charles I of England.

NICKNAME: The Old Line State and the Free State.

CAPITAL: Annapolis.

ENTERED UNION: 28 April 1788 (7th).

OFFICIAL SEAL: REVERSE: A shield bearing the arms of the Calverts and Crosslands is surmounted by an earl's coronet and a helmet and supported by a farmer and fisherman. The state motto (originally that of the Calverts) appears on a scroll below. The circle is surrounded by the Latin legend *Scuto bonæ voluntatis tuæ; coronasti nos,* meaning "With the shield of thy favor hast thou compassed us"; and "1632," the date of Maryland's first charter. OBVERSE: Lord Baltimore is seen as a knight in armor on a charger. The surrounding inscription, in Latin, means "Cecilius, Absolute Lord of Maryland and Avalon New Foundland, Baron of Baltimore."

FLAG: Bears the quartered arms of the Calvert and Crossland families (the paternal and maternal families of the founders of Maryland).

MOTTO: *Fatti maschii, parole femine* (Manly deeds, womanly words).

SONG: "Maryland, My Maryland."

FLOWER: Black-eyed Susan.

TREE: White oak.

CRUSTACEAN: Blue crab.

BIRD: Baltimore oriole.

FISH: Rockfish.

INSECT: Baltimore checkerspot butterfly.

REPTILE: Diamondback terrapin.

DOG: Chesapeake Bay retriever.

BEVERAGE: Milk.

SPORT: Jousting.

LEGAL HOLIDAYS: New Year's Day, 1 January; Birthday of Martin Luther King Jr., 3rd Monday in January; Presidents' day, 3rd Monday in February; Memorial Day, last Monday in May; Independence Day, 4 July; Labor Day, 1st Monday in September; Columbus Day, 12 October; Veterans' Day, 11 November; Thanksgiving Day, 4th Thursday in November plus one day; Christmas Day, 25 December.

TIME: 7 AM EST = noon GMT.

1 Location and Size

Located on the eastern seaboard of the United States in the South Atlantic region, Maryland ranks 42nd in size among the 50 states. The state's total area is 10,460 square miles (27,092 square kilometers), including 9,837 square miles (25,478 square kilometers) of land and 623 square miles (1,614 square kilometers) of inland water. The state extends 199 miles (320 kilometers) east-west and 126 miles (203 kilometers) north-south. The total boundary length of Maryland is 842 miles (1,355 kilometers), including a coastline of 31 miles (50 kilometers). Important islands in Chesapeake Bay, off Maryland's Eastern Shore (part of the Delmarva Peninsula), include Kent, Bloodsworth, South Marsh, and Smith.

2 Topography

Three distinct regions characterize Maryland's terrain. The first and major area is the coastal plain, which is divided by the Chesapeake Bay into Eastern and Western shores. The Piedmont Plateau to the west is a broad, rolling upland with several deep gorges. Farther west is the Appalachian Mountain region, containing the state's highest hills. Backbone Mountain in westernmost Maryland is the state's highest point, at 3,360 feet (1,024 meters).

A few small islands lie in Chesapeake Bay, Maryland's dominant waterway. Principal rivers include the Potomac, the Patapsco, the Patuxent, and the Susquehanna. The state has 23 rivers and other bays, as well as many lakes and creeks, none of any great size.

3 Climate

Despite its small size, Maryland has a diverse climate. Temperatures vary from an annual average of 48°F (9°C) in the extreme western uplands to 59°F (15°C) in the southeast, where the climate is moderated by Chesapeake Bay and the Atlantic Ocean. The mean temperature for Baltimore ranges from 33°F (1°C) in January to 78°F (25°C)

Maryland Population Profile

Total population estimate in 2006:	5,615,727
Population change, 2000–06:	6.0%
Hispanic or Latino†:	5.8%
Population by race	
One race:	98.3%
White:	61.5%
Black or African American:	28.7%
American Indian /Alaska Native:	0.3%
Asian:	4.7%
Native Hawaiian / Pacific Islander:	0.0%
Some other race:	3.1%
Two or more races:	1.7%

Population by Age Group

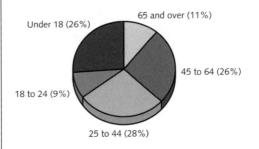

Under 18 (26%)
65 and over (11%)
45 to 64 (26%)
25 to 44 (28%)
18 to 24 (9%)

Major Cities by Population

City	Population	% change 2000–05
Baltimore	635,815	-2.4
Frederick	57,907	9.7
Gaithersburg	57,698	9.7
Rockville	57,402	21.1
Bowie	53,878	7.2
Hagerstown	38,326	4.5
Annapolis	36,300	1.3
Salisbury	26,295	10.7
College Park	25,171	2.1
Greenbelt	22,242	3.7

Notes: †A person of Hispanic or Latino origin may be of any race. NA indicates that data are not available.
Sources: U.S. Census Bureau. *American Community Survey* and *Population Estimates.* www.census.gov/ (accessed March 2007).

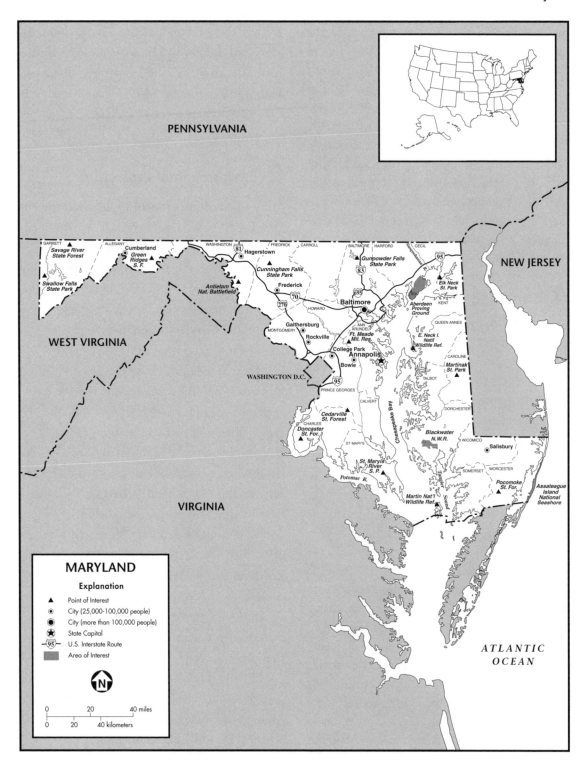

in July. The record high temperature for the state is 109°F (43°C), set on 10 July 1936 in Cumberland and Frederick counties. The record low is -40°F (–40°C), set on 13 January 1912 at Oakland.

Annual precipitation averages 49 inches (124 centimeters) in the southeast, but only 36 inches (91 centimeters) in the Cumberland areas west of the Appalachians. As much as 100 inches (254 centimeters) of snow falls in western Garrett County, while 8–10 inches (20–25 centimeters) is the average annual snowfall for the Eastern Shore.

4 Plants and Animals

Maryland's three life zones (coastal plain, piedmont, and Appalachian) mingle wildlife characteristics of both the North and South. Most of the state lies within a hardwood belt in which red and white oaks, yellow poplar, and beech are represented. Shortleaf and loblolly pines are the leading softwoods. Honeysuckle, Virginia creeper, and wild raspberry are also common. Wooded hillsides are rich with such wildflowers as trailing arbutus, early blue violet, and wild rose. Seven plant species were listed as threatened or endangered in 2006, including Canby's dropwort, sandplain gerardia, northeastern bulrush, and harperella.

The white-tailed (Virginia) deer, eastern cottontail, and raccoon, among others, are native to Maryland, although urbanization has sharply reduced their habitat. Common small mammals are the woodchuck, eastern chipmunk, and gray squirrel. Birds include the cardinal, chestnut-sided warbler, and rose-breasted grosbeak. Among saltwater species, shellfish—especially oysters, clams, and crabs—have the greatest economic importance. As of 2006, 18 Maryland animal species were listed as threatened or endangered, including the Indiana bat, Maryland darter, bald eagle, Delmarva Peninsula fox squirrel, three species of whale, and five species of turtle.

5 Environmental Protection

The Maryland Department of the Environment (MDE) serves as the state's primary environmental protection agency. MDE has broad regulatory, planning, and management responsibility for water quality, air quality, solid and hazardous waste management. MDE also plays a pivotal role in Maryland's initiatives to protect and restore the Chesapeake Bay.

The Maryland Department of Natural Resources (DNR) is responsible for the management, enhancement, and preservation of the state's living and natural resources. Utilizing an ecosystem approach to land, waterway, and species management, DNR programs and services support the health of the Chesapeake Bay and its tributaries, sustainable populations of fishery and wildlife species, and an integrated network of public lands and open space. The Maryland Environmental Service, a quasi-public agency, contracts with local governments to design, construct, finance, and operate wastewater treatment plants, water supply systems, and recycling facilities.

In 2003, Maryland had 168 hazardous waste sites listed in the Environmental Protection Agency's database, 17 of which were on the National Priorities List as of 2006.

Maryland Population by Race

Census 2000 was the first national census in which the instructions to respondents said, "Mark one or more races." This table shows the number of people who are of one, two, or three or more races. For those claiming two races, the number of people belonging to the various categories is listed. The U.S. government conducts a census of the population every ten years.

	Number	Percent
Total population	5,296,486	100.0
One race	5,192,899	98.0
Two races	95,262	1.8
White *and* Black or African American	19,270	0.4
White *and* American Indian/Alaska Native	10,388	0.2
White *and* Asian	15,660	0.3
White *and* Native Hawaiian/Pacific Islander	793	—
White *and* some other race	20,812	0.4
Black or African American *and* American Indian/Alaska Native	6,488	0.1
Black or African American *and* Asian	3,330	0.1
Black or African American *and* Native Hawaiian/Pacific Islander	840	—
Black or African American *and* some other race	10,920	0.2
American Indian/Alaska Native *and* Asian	855	—
American Indian/Alaska Native *and* Native Hawaiian/Pacific Islander	70	—
American Indian/Alaska Native *and* some other race	796	—
Asian *and* Native Hawaiian/Pacific Islander	930	—
Asian *and* some other race	3,827	0.1
Native Hawaiian/Pacific Islander *and* some other race	283	—
Three or more races	8,325	0.2

Source: U.S. Census Bureau. *Census 2000: Redistricting Data.* Press release issued by the Redistricting Data Office. Washington, D.C., March, 2001. A dash (—) indicates that the percent is less than 0.1.

6 Population

In 2005, Maryland ranked 19th in population in the United States with an estimated total of 5,615,727 residents. It is projected that the population will reach 6.2 million by 2015 and 6.7 million by 2025. The population density in 2004 was 572.3 persons per square mile (220.9 persons per square kilometer), the fifth highest among the states. The median age in 2004 was 36.8. In 2005, about 11% of all residents were 65 or older while 26% were 18 or younger.

Baltimore is the state's only major city, with a 2005 estimated population of 635,815. The next-largest city is Frederick, with a 2005 population of 57,907.

7 Ethnic Groups

According to the 2000 census, the largest racial minority in the state was the black Americans, with about 1,477,411 residents. Nearly one-third of all black Marylanders lived in the city of Baltimore. Hispanics and Latinos, mostly from Puerto Rico and Central America, numbered 227,000. The total Asian population was estimated at 210,929 and included 39,155 Koreans, 49,400 Chinese, 26,608 Filipinos, 6,620 Japanese, and 16,744 Vietnamese. Pacific Islanders numbered 2,303.

Foreign-born residents numbered 518,315, representing about 9.8% of the total population. Native Americans, including Eskimos and Aleuts, were estimated at 15,423.

8 Languages

The state's diverse terrain has contributed to unusual diversity in its basic speech. Proximity to Virginia and access to southeastern and central Pennsylvania helped to create a language mixture that now is dominantly Midland and yet reflects earlier ties to Southern English. Regional features occur as well. Special terms in the northeast are *pavement* (sidewalk) and *baby coach* (baby carriage). In the north and west are *poke* (bag) and *sick on the stomach*. In the southern portion are found *light bread* (white bread) and *curtain* (shade). East of Chesapeake Bay are *mosquito hawks* (dragonflies) and *paled fences* (picket fences).

In 2000, 4,322,329 residents, or 87% of the population five years old or older, spoke only English at home. Other languages spoken at home, with the number of speakers, included Spanish, 230,829; French, 42,838; Chinese, 41,883; and Korean, 32,937.

9 Religions

Maryland was founded as a haven for Roman Catholics; but in 1692, Anglicanism (now the Episcopal Church) became the official religion of the colony. The state constitution of 1776, however, placed all Christian faiths on an equal footing.

As of 2000, there were 952,389 Roman Catholics in Maryland. Adherents of the major Protestant denominations (with 2000 data) included United Methodists, 297,729; Southern Baptists, 142,401; Evangelical Lutherans,

103,644; and Episcopalians, 81,061. In 2000, there were an estimated 216,000 Jews and about 52,867 Muslims. The same year, there were about 32 Buddhist congregations and 26 Hindu congregations. Over 3 million people (about 56.7% of the population) were not counted as members of any religious organization.

10 Transportation

Maryland's first railroad, the Baltimore and Ohio (B&O), was started in 1828. In 1835, it provided the first passenger train service to Washington, DC, and Harpers Ferry, Virginia (now West Virginia). By 1857, the line was extended to St. Louis and its freight capacity helped build Baltimore into a major center of commerce.

Today CSX Transportation and Norfolk Southern are the Class I railroads operating in the state, along with one regional, five Local, and two switching and terminal railroads. As of 2003, total rail miles in Maryland amounted to 1,153 miles (1,856 kilometers). The Maryland Transportation Department's Railroad Administration subsidizes four commuter lines in western Maryland and on the Eastern Shore. As of 2006, Amtrak operated six stations.

The Maryland Mass Transit Administration inaugurated Baltimore's first subway line on 21 November 1983. In 1984, the Washington, DC, mass transit system was extended to the Maryland suburbs, including Bethesda and Rockville.

As of 2004, there were 30,809 miles (49,602 kilometers) of public roadway. The major toll road is the John F. Kennedy Memorial Highway (I-95), linking Baltimore with Wilmington, Delaware, and the New Jersey Turnpike. There were 3,594,251 licensed drivers and some

The **Pride of Baltimore II** *under sail in Annapolis.* MARYLAND TOURISM.

4,150,000 motor vehicles registered in Maryland in 2004.

The Delaware and Chesapeake Canal, linking Chesapeake Bay and the Delaware River, opened in 1829. In 2006, the major port was at Baltimore. There are 145 airports in Maryland. The Department of Transportation operates Baltimore-Washington International (BWI) Airport, the major air terminal in the state, which also serves the Washington, DC, area. Another 76 airfields (69 heliports, 1 STOLport—Short Take-Off and Landing, and 6 seaplane bases) also served the state in 2005.

11 History

The Indian tribes living in the region that was to become Maryland were Algonkian-speak-

ers, including the Accomac, Susquehannock, and Piscataway. Although the Algonkian tribes hunted for much of their food, many (including the Susquehannock) also had permanent settlements where they cultivated corn (maize) and other crops. European penetration of the Chesapeake region began early in the 16th century, with the expeditions of Giovanni da Verrazano of Florence and the Spaniard Lucas Vázquez de Ayllón. Captain John Smith was the first English explorer of Chesapeake Bay (1608) and produced a map of the area that was used for years.

Twenty years later, George Calvert received from King Charles I a land grant that embraced not only present-day Maryland but also the present State of Delaware, a large part of Pennsylvania, and the valley between the north

Fort McHenry (on Baltimore's waterfront), birthplace of the national anthem. MARYLAND TOURISM.

and south branches of the Potomac River. When he died in 1632, the title passed to his son, Cecilius Calvert, Second Baron Baltimore, who named the region Maryland after Charles I's queen, Henrietta Maria. Calvert established the first settlement two years later as a refuge for persecuted Roman Catholics.

In 1689, with Protestants in power both in England and Maryland, the British crown took control of the province away from the Catholic Calverts, and in 1692, the Church of England became Maryland's established religion. The Fourth Baron Baltimore regained full hereditary rights—but only because he had embraced the Protestant faith. Rule by the Calvert family through their legitimate heirs continued until the eve of the American Revolution.

Statehood After some initial hesitancy, Maryland cast its lot with the Revolution and sent approximately 20,000 soldiers to fight in the war. On 28 April 1788, it became the seventh state to ratify the federal Constitution. By the early 19th century, Baltimore, founded in 1729, was already the state's major center of commerce and industry. The city and harbor were the site of extended military operations during the War of 1812. It was during the bombardment of Ft. McHenry in 1814 that Francis Scott Key, detained on the British frigate, composed "The Star-Spangled Banner," which became the US national anthem in March 1931.

After the War of 1812, Maryland history was marked by the continued growth of Baltimore and increasing division over immigration, slavery, and secession, which the Maryland house of delegates rejected in 1861. Throughout the Civil War, Maryland was largely occupied by Union troops because of its strategic location. Marylanders fought on both sides during the war, and one major battle took place on Maryland soil—the Battle of Antietam (1862), during which a Union army thwarted a Confederate thrust toward the north, but at an enormous cost to both sides.

The state's economic activity increased during Reconstruction, as Maryland, and especially Baltimore, played a major role in rebuilding the South. Maryland's economic base gradually shifted from agriculture to industry, with shipbuilding, steelmaking, and the manufacture of clothing and shoes leading the way. The decades between the Civil War and World War I were also notable for the philanthropic activities of such wealthy businessmen as Johns Hopkins and George Peabody, who endowed some of the state's most prestigious cultural and educational institutions. Democrat Albert C. Ritchie won election to the governorship in 1919 and served in that office until 1935, stressing local issues, states' rights, and opposition to prohibition.

Post-War Period The decades since World War II have been marked by significant population growth. The state has witnessed the passage of open housing and equal opportunity laws to protect Maryland's black citizens. It has also been rocked by political scandal. Perhaps the most significant occurrence was the redevelopment of Baltimore, which, though still the hub of the state's economy, had fallen into decay. Much of Baltimore's downtown area and harbor were revitalized by urban renewal projects in the late 1970s and 1980s. Although Maryland's economy declined less than those of other states during the recession of the late 1980s and early 1990s, the state suffered from reductions in the defense and technology industries.

Nevertheless, service industry employment, primarily in the Baltimore-Washington, DC corridor, gave Maryland the fifth-highest state income in the country as of the mid-1990s. Federal government and high-tech employment accounted for many of these jobs. As of 2004, Maryland had the third-highest median household income among the states. Maryland had the sixth-lowest poverty rate in the nation in 2004.

Maryland's 370-year history of tobacco farming appeared to be drawing to a close in 2000. The crop that had settled the Chesapeake had become risky, with the tobacco industry under attack for the health hazards of its products. The state had by 2003 implemented a tobacco buyout program, whereby the state agreed to pay farmers $1 per pound of tobacco that they would sell for the following 10 years. Farmers agreed to plant alternative crops instead of tobacco.

The environmental cleanup of Chesapeake Bay, begun in the mid-1980s, continued into the 21st century. The Bay was threatened by an April 2000 oil spill into the Patuxent River, which flows into the Chesapeake. The cleanup continued into the mid-2000s.

12 State Government

The general assembly, Maryland's legislative body, consists of two branches: a 47-member senate and a 141-member house of delegates. All legislators serve four-year terms. Executives elected statewide are the governor and lieutenant governor (who run jointly), the comptroller of

Maryland Governors: 1775–2007

1775–1777	Daniel of St. Thomas Jenifer		1862–1866	Augustus Williamson Bradford	Union-Rep
1777–1779	Thomas Johnson		1866–1869	Thomas Swann	Union-Dem
1779–1782	Thomas S. Lee		1869–1872	Oden Bowie	Democrat
1782–1785	William Paca		1872–1874	William Pinkney Whyte	Democrat
1785–1788	William Smallwood		1874–1876	James Black Groome	Democrat
1788–1791	John Eager Howard	Federalist	1876–1880	John Lee Carroll	Democrat
1791–1792	George Plater	Federalist	1880–1884	William Thomas Hamilton	Democrat
1792	James Brice	Federalist	1884–1885	Robert Milligan McLane	Democrat
1792–1794	Thomas Sim Lee	Federalist	1885–1888	Henry Lloyd	Democrat
1794–1797	John Hoskins Stone	Federalist	1888–1892	Elihu Emory Jackson	Democrat
1797–1798	John Henry	Federalist	1892–1896	Frank Brown	Democrat
1798–1801	Benjamin Ogle	Federalist	1896–1900	Lloyd Lowndes, Jr.	Republican
1801–1803	John Francis Mercer	Dem-Rep	1900–1904	John Walter Smith	Democrat
1803–1806	Robert Bowie	Dem-Rep	1904–1908	Edwin Warfield	Democrat
1806–1809	Robert Wright	Dem-Rep	1908–1912	Austin Lane Crothers	Democrat
1809	James Butcher	Dem-Rep	1912–1916	Phillips Lee Goldsborough	Republican
1809–1811	Edward Lloyd	Dem-Rep	1916–1920	Emerson Columbus Harrington	Democrat
1811–1812	Robert Bowie	Dem-Rep	1920–1935	Albert Cabell Ritchie	Democrat
1812–1816	Levin Winder	Federalist	1935–1939	Harry Whinna Nice	Republican
1816–1819	Charles Carnan Ridgely	Federalist	1939–1947	Herbert Romulus O'Conor	Democrat
1819	Charles Goldsborough	Federalist	1947–1951	William Preston Lane, Jr.	Democrat
1819–1922	Samuel Sprigg	Dem-Rep	1951–1959	Theodore Roosevelt McKeldin	Republican
1822–1826	Samuel Stevens, Jr.	Dem-Rep	1959–1967	John Millard Tawes	Democrat
1826–1829	Joseph Kent	Dem-Rep	1967–1969	Spiro Theodore Agnew	Republican
1829–1830	Daniel Martin	Anti–Jacksonian	1969–1977	Marvin Mandel	Democrat
1830–1831	Thomas King Carroll	Jacksonian	1977–1979	Lee Blair III	Democrat
1831	Daniel Martin	Anti–Jacksonian	1979	Marvin Mandel	Democrat
1831–1833	George Howard	Anti–Jacksonian	1979–1987	Harry R. Hughes	Democrat
1833–1836	James Thomas	Anti–Jacksonian	1987–1995	William Donald Schaefer	Democrat
1836–1839	Thomas Ward Veazey	Whig	1995–2002	Parris N. Glendening	Democrat
1839–1842	William Grason	Democrat	2002–2006	Robert Ehrlich	Republican
1842–1845	Francis Thomas	Democrat	2006–	Martin O'Malley	Democrat
1845–1848	Thomas George Pratt	Whig			
1848–1851	Philip Francis Thomas	Democrat			
1851–1854	Enoch Louis Lowe	Democrat	Democratic Republican – Dem-Rep		
1854–1858	Thomas Watkins Ligon	Democrat	Union Democrat – Union-Dem		
1858–1862	Thomas Holliday Hicks	American	Union Republican – Union-Rep		

the Treasury, and the attorney general. All serve four-year terms.

Bills passed by majority vote of both houses of the assembly become law when signed by the governor, or if left unsigned for six days while the legislature is in session or for 30 days if the legislature has adjourned. The only exception is the budget bill, which becomes effective immediately upon legislative passage. The governor's vetoes may be overridden by three-fifths votes in both houses.

The governor's salary as of December 2004 was $135,000 and the legislative salary was $31,509.

13 Political Parties

In 2004 there were 3,105,000 registered voters. In 1998, 58% of registered voters were Democratic,

Maryland Presidential Vote by Political Parties, 1948–2004

YEAR	MARYLAND WINNER	DEMOCRAT	REPUBLICAN	PROGRESSIVE	DEMOCRAT	STATE'S RIGHTS SOCIALIST
1948	Dewey (R)	286,521	294,814	9,983	2,467	2,941
1952	*Eisenhower (R)	395,337	499,424	7,313	—	—
1956	*Eisenhower (R)	372,613	559,738	—	—	—
1960	*Kennedy (D)	565,808	489,538	—	—	—
1964	*Johnson (D)	730,912	385,495			
				AMERICAN IND.		
1968	Humphrey (D)	538,310	517,995	178,734	—	—
				AMERICAN		
1972	*Nixon (R)	505,781	829,305	18,726	—	—
1976	*Carter (D)	759,612	672,661	—	—	—
					LIBERTARIAN	
1980	Carter (D)	726,161	680,606	—	14,192	—
1984	*Reagan (R)	787,935	879,918	—	5,721	—
1988	*Bush (R)	826,304	876,167	5,115	6,748	—
						IND. (PEROT)
1992	*Clinton (D)	988,571	707,094	2,786	4,715	281,414
1996	*Clinton (D)	966,207	681,530	—	8,765	115,812
					LIBERTARIAN	**REFORM**
2000	Gore (D)	1,144,088	813,827	53,768	5,310	4,248
2004	Kerry (D)	1,334,493	1,024,703	—	6,094	—

* Won US presidential election.

20% Republican, and 12% unaffiliated or members of other parties. Maryland was one of the few states carried by President Jimmy Carter in the November 1980 presidential election, but four years later the state went for President Ronald Reagan in the national Republican landslide. In 2000, Maryland gave 57% of its vote to Democrat Al Gore and 40% to Republican George W. Bush. In 2004, Democratic challenger John Kerry won 55.7% of the vote to incumbent President Bush's 44.6%.

Revelations of corruption afflicted both major parties during the 1970s. In 1973, Republican Spiro T. Agnew, then vice president of the United States, was accused of taking bribes while he was Baltimore County executive and then governor. Agnew resigned from the vice-presidency on 10 October 1973. His guber-natorial successor, Democrat Marvin Mandel, was convicted of mail fraud and racketeering in 1977. He served 20 months of a 36-month prison sentence before receiving a presidential pardon in 1981.

In 1994, the governor's race was one of the closest in Maryland history. Democrat Parris N. Glendening, three-term Prince George's county executive, defeated Ellen R. Sauerbrey, Republican leader of the Maryland House, by a mere 5,993 votes. Glendening was reelected by a comfortable margin in 1998. Republican Governor Robert L. Ehrlich Jr. was elected in 2002. Ehrlich was defeated by Democrat Martin O'Malley in 2006. Democrat Barbara Mikulski was reelected US senator in 2004, and Democrat Ben Cardin was elected senator in 2006, replacing the seat formerly held by Paul Sarbanes, who decided not to run for a sixth term. His son, John Sarbanes, won the seat for Maryland's third congressional district in 2006, the district that Paul Sarbanes represented prior to his election as senator.

As of the November 2006 elections, Maryland's congressional delegation consisted of six Democrats and two Republicans. Following the 2006 elections, there were 33 Democrats and 14 Republicans in the state senate, and 106 Democrats and 35 Republicans in the state house. Sixty-seven women were elected to the state legislature in 2006, or 35.6%, the highest percentage in the nation.

14 Local Government

As of 2005 there were 24 counties and 157 municipal governments in Maryland. Most counties had charter governments, with (in most cases) elected executives and county councils, and other rural counties had elected boards of county commissioners.

Baltimore is the only city in Maryland not contained within a county. It provides the same services as a county, and shares in state aid according to the same allocation formulas. The city (not to be confused with Baltimore County, which surrounds the city of Baltimore but has its county seat at Towson) is governed by a mayor and city council. Other cities and towns are each governed by a mayor and a council, town commissioners, or council and a manager, depending on the local charter. In 2005, Maryland had 25 public school systems.

15 Judicial System

The court of appeals, the state's highest court, comprises a chief judge and six associate judges. Most criminal appeals are decided by the court of special appeals, consisting of a chief judge and 12 associate judges. District courts handle all criminal, civil, and traffic cases. Appeals are taken to one of eight judicial circuit courts. According to the FBI Crime Index for 2004, Maryland had a violent crime rate (murder, rape, robbery, aggravated assault) of 700.5 reported incidents per 100,000 population (third highest in the nation). Crimes against property (burglary, larceny/theft, and motor vehicle theft) totaled 3,640.2 reported incidents per 100,000 people. There were 23,285 prisoners in state and federal prisons as of 31 December 2004. Maryland has a death penalty, with eight persons being held under the sentence of death as of 1 January 2006.

16 Migration

During the 19th century, Baltimore ranked second only to New York as a port of entry for European immigrants. First to come were the Germans, followed by the Irish, Poles, East European Jews, and Italians. A significant number of Czechs settled in Cecil County during the 1860s. After the Civil War, many blacks migrated to Baltimore, both from rural Maryland and from southern states.

Since World War II, both the Baltimore metropolitan area and the Maryland part of the metropolitan Washington, DC, area have experienced rapid growth while the inner cities have lost population. Between 1990 and 1998, Maryland had a net loss of 49,000 in domestic migration and a net gain of 118,000 in international migration. In the period 2000–05, net international migration was 108,972 and net internal migration was 9,752, for a net gain of 118,724 people.

17 Economy

Although manufacturing output continues to rise, the biggest growth areas in Maryland's economy are government, construction, trade, and services. Maryland employees are the best educated in the nation, with more than one-third of those over age 25 possessing a bachelor's degree in 2000. Manufacturing has shifted towards high technology, information, and health-related products. With the expansion of federal employment in the Washington metropolitan area during the 1960s and 1970s, many US government workers settled in suburban Maryland, primarily Prince George's and Montgomery counties. Construction and services in those areas expanded accordingly. Between 1982 and 1992, the number of jobs grew 24% in Maryland, somewhat above the national average of 21% for that period. However, from 1992 to 2000, Maryland lost 17% of its federal employment in Washington, DC.

Fishing and agriculture (primarily dairy and poultry farming) on the Eastern Shore and coal mining in Garrett and Allegheny counties are also important areas of the economy. Although manufacturing output grew from 1997 to 2001, its share of gross state product declined. In contrast, services and wholesale and retail trade grew as a percentage of gross state product (GSP).

As of 2004, real estate accounted for the largest portion of GSP at 15.2%, followed by professional and technical services (9.9%), and

health and social services (7.3%). The GSP that year was $227.9 billion.

18 Income

In 2005, Maryland had a gross state product (GSP) of $245 billion, the 15th highest nationwide. In 2004, Maryland had a per capita (per person) income of $39,631, fifth highest in the nation. The three-year average median household income for 2002–04 was $56,763, compared to the national average of $44,473. During the same period, an estimated 8.6% of the state's residents lived below the federal poverty level, compared with 12.4% among the 50 states and the District of Columbia.

19 Industry

Baltimore is an important manufacturer of automobiles and parts, steel, and instruments. Manufacturing is led by the printing and publishing industry, the food industry, the machinery industry, and the chemical industry. Value of shipments by manufacturers in 2004 was $36.48 billion. About one-third of all manufacturing activity takes place in the city of Baltimore, followed by Baltimore County, Montgomery County, and Prince George's County. Maryland is the headquarters of Lockheed Martin (aerospace), Marriott International (hospitality), Black and Decker (tools), and Giant Food.

20 Labor

As of April 2006, the civilian labor force in Maryland numbered 2,997,700, with approximately 105,700 workers unemployed, yielding an unemployment rate of 3.5%, compared to the national average of 4.7% for the same period. In

2006, 7.3% of the labor force was employed in construction; 5.3% in manufacturing; 18.4% in trade, transportation, and public utilities; 6.2% in financial activities; 15% in business and professional services; 14% in education and health services; 9% in leisure and hospitality services; and 18.2% in government.

The Baltimore Federation of Labor was formed in 1889 and by 1900, the coal mines had been organized by the United Mine Workers. In 1902, Maryland passed the first workers' compensation law in the United States. It was declared unconstitutional in 1904 but was subsequently revived.

In 2005, some 337,000 of Maryland's 2,530,000 employed wage and salary workers were members of unions. This represented 13.3% of those so employed. The national average was 12%.

21 Agriculture

Maryland ranked 36th among the 50 states in agricultural income in 2005, with estimated receipts of $1.66 billion, about 41% of that in crops. In 2004, the state had about 12,100 farms covering 2,050,000 acres (830,000 hectares).

Until the Revolutionary War, tobacco was the state's only cash crop. In 2004, Maryland produced an estimated 1.87 million pounds (848,218 kilograms) of tobacco. Corn and cereal grains are grown mainly in southern Maryland. Main crops include soybeans, wheat, and barley. Commercial vegetables, cultivated primarily on the Eastern Shore, were valued at $36.6 million in 2004. Fruits are also cultivated.

22 Domesticated Animals

The Eastern Shore is an important dairy and poultry region. Cattle are raised in north-central and western Maryland, while the central region is notable for horse breeding. In 2003, poultry farmers produced an estimated 6.4 million pounds (2.9 million kilograms) of chickens and 1.37 billion pounds (0.63 billion kilograms) of broilers for around $494.7 million. Also in 2003, Maryland farmers produced an estimated 813 million eggs worth around $46.2 million.

An estimated 1.2 billion pounds (0.6 billion kilograms) of milk was produced in 2003 from 78,000 dairy cows. Maryland farms and ranches had an estimated 235,000 cattle and calves worth around $237 million in 2005. In 2004, there were an estimated 26,000 hogs and pigs, worth $2.6 million.

23 Fishing

In 2004, Maryland had a total commercial catch of 49.5 million pounds (22.5 million kilograms), valued at $49.2 million. Maryland is a leading source of oysters, clams, and crabs. About 19% of the nation's supply of hard blue crabs comes from Maryland. Ocean City is the state's leading fishing port.

In 2003, the state had 17 processing and 58 wholesale plants with a total of about 1,417 employees. In 2001, the commercial fleet had at least 32 vessels.

The Fisheries Administration of the Department of Natural Resources monitors fish populations and breeds and implants oysters. It also stocks inland waterways with finfish. The state has five cold water and four warm water hatcheries. Maryland had 362,181 licensed sport anglers in 2004.

24 Forestry

Maryland's 2,566,000 acres (1,139,000 hectares) of forestland covers about 40% of the state's land area. More than 90% of that (2,372,000 acres/961,570 hectares) was classified as commercial forest and 90% of it was privately owned. Hardwoods predominate, with red and white oaks and yellow poplar among the leading hardwood varieties. Lumber production in 2004 was 272 million board feet.

Forest management and improvement lie within the jurisdiction of the Maryland Department of Natural Resources Forest Service.

25 Mining

The estimated value of nonfuel mineral production in Maryland in 2003 was $382 million. Maryland ranked 33rd among the states in national nonfuel mineral production value. Crushed stone, cement (portland and masonry), and crushed sand and gravel together accounted for over 95% of the state's total nonfuel mineral value.

According to preliminary figures in 2003, portland cement was the leading nonfuel mineral commodity, totaling 1.9 million tons (valued at $143 million), followed by crushed stone (output 21.8 million metric tons, valued at $138 million), and construction sand and gravel (11.4 million metric tons, $78.1 million). Maryland also produces significant quantities of dimension stone.

26 Energy and Power

In 2003, Maryland's installed electrical capacity (utility and nonutility) was 12.47 million kilowatts. Production of electricity exceeded 52.24 billion kilowatt hours in the same year. More than 99% of the generating capacity was privately owned and about 57.3% of the state's electricity was produced by coal-fired plants. Maryland has one nuclear power generating facility, the Calvert Cliffs nuclear plant in Lusby. In 2003 it produced about 18.9% of the state's electricity. In 2000, Maryland's total per capita energy consumption was 287 million Btu (72.3 million kilocalories), ranking it 40th among the 50 states.

Coal, Maryland's lone fossil fuel resource, is mined in Allegheny and Garrett counties, along the Pennsylvania border. Recoverable coal reserves in 2001 were estimated at 17 million tons. The 2004 output of 19 coal mines totaled 5.2 million tons. Marketed production of natural gas totaled 48 million cubic feet (1.36 million cubic meters) in 2003.

27 Commerce

Maryland had 2002 wholesale sales of $60.6 billion; retail sales totaled $60.0 billion. Most of the state's retail facilities are located in the Baltimore metropolitan area and Montgomery and Prince George's counties surrounding Washington, DC. Foreign exports of Maryland products totaled $7.1 billion in 2005. While most exports still go to such markets as Canada and Europe, strong inroads have been made in targeted trade areas of Latin America and Asia.

28 Public Finance

The state budget is prepared by the Department of Budget and Management and is submitted annually by the governor to the general assembly for amendment and approval. The fiscal year runs from 1 July to 30 June.

The estimated revenues for the fiscal year 2004 were $28.39 billion and expenditures were $25.34 billion. The largest general expenditures were for education ($7.36 billion), public welfare ($5.49 billion), and highways ($1.65 billion). The outstanding state debt exceeded $13.6 billion, or $2,445.74 per capita (per person).

29 Taxation

As of 1 January 2006, individual income taxes in Maryland ranged from 2% to 4.75% on a four-bracket schedule. The corporate income tax rate was 7%. The state general sales and use tax was 5% with exemptions for food and other basic items. No local sales taxes are permitted. The state also imposes a full array of excise taxes covering motor fuels, tobacco products, insurance premiums, public utilities, alcoholic beverages, amusements, pari-mutuels, and other selected items. Maryland has enacted its own estate tax at a maximum rate of 10%. Other state taxes include property taxes including a motor vehicle use tax, various license and franchise fees, and stamp taxes.

All county and some local governments levy property taxes. The counties also tax personal income. Local income tax rates have a cap of 3.1%. In 2002, localities collected 43.6% of total state and local taxes.

The state collected $13.49 billion in taxes in 2005, of which 41.9% came from individual income taxes, 21.4% from the general sales tax, 17.7% from selective sales taxes, 6% from corporate income taxes, 3.9% from property taxes, and 9% from other taxes. In 2005, Maryland ranked 14th among the states in terms of state and local tax burden.

30 Health

As of October 2005, the infant mortality rate was 8.2 per 1,000 live births. The overall death rate was 8.1per 1,000 population in 2003. The leading causes of death were heart disease, cancer, and cerebrovascular diseases. Death from diabetes mellitus and HIV were higher than the national rates in 2000. The death rate from HIV infection was 11.2 per 100,000 people, the second-highest rate in the country, after the District of Columbia. In 2004, the reported AIDS case rate was about 26.1 per 100,000 people, the fourth-highest rate in the nation. Among persons ages 18 and older, 19.5% were smokers in 2004.

Maryland's 51 community hospitals had about 11,600 beds in 2003. The average expense for community hospital care was $1,571 per inpatient day in 2003. There were 389 doctors per 100,000 people in 2004, and 875 nurses per 100,000 in 2005. The state had 4,169 dentists in 2004. In 2004, approximately 14% of the population was uninsured.

Maryland's two medical schools are at Johns Hopkins University, which operates in connection with the Johns Hopkins Hospital, and at the University of Maryland, both located in Baltimore. Federal health centers located in Bethesda include the National Institutes of Health and the National Naval Medical Center.

31 Housing

Maryland has sought to preserve many of its historic houses, especially in Annapolis, which has several ornate mansions. Block upon block of two-story brick row houses fill the older parts of Baltimore, and stone cottages built to withstand rough winters are still found in the western counties.

There were an estimated 2,250,339 housing units in Maryland in 2004, of which 2,077,900 were occupied; 69.5% were owner-occupied. About 51.9% of all units are single-family, detached homes. Most units rely on utility gas and electricity for heating. It was estimated that 61,901 units lacked telephone service, 6,034 lacked complete plumbing facilities, and 5,885 lacked complete kitchen facilities. The average household size was 2.61 people.

In 2004, 27,400 privately owned units were authorized for construction. The median home value was $216,529. The median monthly cost for mortgage owners was $1,406. Renters paid a median of $837 per month.

32 Education

As of 2004, 87.4% of all Marylanders had completed high school and 35.2% had at least four years of college, far surpassing the national average of 26%. Maryland students must pass state competency exams in order to graduate from high school.

Total public school enrollment was estimated at 867,000 in fall 2002 and is expected to drop to 858,000 by fall 2014. Enrollment in nonpublic schools in fall 2003 was 149,253. Expenditures for public education in 2003/04 were estimated at $8.7 billion.

As of fall 2002, there were 300,269 students enrolled in college or graduate school. In the same year. Maryland had 63 degree-granting institutions in 2005. The state's public four-year institutions include the University of Maryland System, Morgan State University, and St. Mary's College of Maryland. The 16 community colleges are two-year, open-admission institutions with courses and programs leading to certificates and associate degrees, as well as career-oriented and continuing education/community service programs. The state provides funding to independent colleges and universities in Maryland under a statutory formula.

St. John's College in Annapolis is known for its unique program that includes study of the ancient Greek and Latin classics in their original languages. The US Naval Academy is also in Annapolis.

Private career schools in Maryland provide job preparatory training for students in a wide variety of fields, including business, computers, travel, truck driving, mechanics, electronics, allied health, cosmetology, and barbering.

33 Arts

Although close to the arts centers of Washington, DC, Maryland has its own cultural attractions. Center Stage in Baltimore is the designated state theater of Maryland and the Olney Theatre in Montgomery County is the official state summer theater.

The state's leading orchestra is the Baltimore Symphony. Baltimore is also the home of the Baltimore Opera Company and its jazz clubs were the launching pads for such musical notables as Eubie Blake, Ella Fitzgerald, and Cab Calloway. Annapolis hosts a symphony, an opera

Graduates of the US Naval Academy in Annapolis celebrate by throwing their hats into the air. JIM WATSON/AFP/GETTY IMAGES.

company, and the Ballet Theatre of Maryland. The National Ballet (est. 1948) is the oldest professional ballet company in the state. One of the newest additions to the arts community is the Maryland Symphony Orchestra in Hagerstown, established in 1982. The Peabody Institute of Johns Hopkins University in Baltimore is one of the nation's most distinguished music schools. Both the Maryland Ballet Company and Maryland Dance Theater are nationally known.

The Maryland State Arts Council was established in 1967. The Maryland Humanities Council (MHC) was founded in 1973. Ongoing programs of the MHC include Family Matters, a family-oriented reading and discussion group, and History Matters!, which promotes heritage tourism. The state makes arts education avail-

able to nearly 170,000 schoolchildren. There are about 1,000 state and 25 local arts associations in Maryland.

34 Libraries and Museums

In 2001, Maryland had 24 public library systems and 175 libraries, of which 158 were branches. The system also had 19 bookmobiles and over 15.3 million volumes and a combined circulation of over 46.59 million. The center of the state library network is the Enoch Pratt Free Library in the city of Baltimore, founded in 1886. Each county also has its own library system. The largest academic libraries are those of Johns Hopkins University in Baltimore and the University of Maryland at College Park. Maryland is also the site of several federal libraries, including the National Agricultural Library, the National Library of Medicine, and the National Oceanic and Atmospheric Administration Library.

Of the approximately 147 museums and historic sites in the state, major institutions include the US Naval Academy Museum in Annapolis and Baltimore's Museum of Art and Maritime Museum. The latter's Peale Museum is the oldest museum building in the United States. Important historic sites include Ft. McHenry National Monument and Shrine in Baltimore (inspiration for "The Star-Spangled Banner") and Antietam National Battlefield Site near Sharpsburg.

35 Communications

In 2004, some 93.4% of Maryland's occupied housing units had telephones. Additionally, by June of that year, there were 3,575,747 mobile telephone subscribers. In 2003, 66% of Maryland households had a computer and 59.2% had Internet access. The state had 12 major AM and 35 major FM radio stations in 2005. Maryland has 13 major television stations, including public broadcasting stations in Annapolis, Baltimore, Frederick, Hagerstown, Oakland, and Salisbury. Maryland also receives the signals of many Washington, DC, broadcast stations. The Baltimore area had almost one million television households, 68% of which received cable.

36 Press

The *Baltimore Sun*, founded in 1837, reached its heyday after 1906, when H. L. Mencken (1880–1956) became a staff writer. Mencken, who was also an important editor and critic, helped found the *American Mercury* magazine in 1924. As of 2005, Maryland had 10 morning and 3 afternoon dailies, and 9 Sunday papers. The most influential newspaper published in Baltimore is the *Sun* (daily, 280,717; Sunday, 454,045). The *Washington Post* is also widely read in Maryland.

37 Tourism, Travel & Recreation

In 2004, the state hosted over 21 million travelers. Total travel expenditures for 2001 were about $8.5 billion, which included support for about 105,400 travel-related jobs.

Attractions include parks, historical sites, and a national seashore (Assateague Island). Annapolis, the state capital, is the site of the US Naval Academy. On Baltimore's waterfront are monuments to Francis Scott Key and Edgar Allan Poe, historic Ft. McHenry, and many restaurants serving the city's famed crab cakes and other seafood specialties. Ocean City is the state's major seaside resort and there are many resort towns along Chesapeake Bay. The Office of Tourism promotes such historical attractions as the Civil War, War of 1812, and National Road. It also is expanding investment in multi-cultural tourism, sports marketing, and nature tourism. There are 19 state parks with camping facilities and 10 recreation areas.

38 Sports

Maryland has two major league professional sports teams: the Baltimore Orioles of Major League Baseball and the Baltimore Ravens of the National Football League. The Ravens (formerly the Browns) moved from Cleveland after the 1995 season and play in a downtown stadium near Oriole Park at Camden Yards. The

Oriole Park is home to the Baltimore Orioles baseball team. JERRY DRIENDL/GETTY IMAGES.

NFL's Washington Redskins play in the Jack Kent Cooke Stadium in Landover, but are still considered to be a team from the District of Columbia.

There are several minor league baseball teams in the state, including teams in Bowie, Frederick, Delmarva, and Hagerstown.

Ever since 1750, when the first Arabian thoroughbred horse was imported by a Maryland breeder, horse racing has been a popular state pastime. The major tracks are Pimlico (Baltimore), Bowie, and Laurel. Pimlico is the site of the Preakness Stakes, the second leg of racing's Triple Crown. Harness racing is held at Ocean Downs in Ocean City. Quarter horse racing takes place at several tracks throughout the state; and several steeplechase events, including the prestigious Maryland Hunt Cup, are held annually.

In collegiate basketball, the University of Maryland won the NCAA Championship in 2002 and the National Invitation Tournament in 1972. The Maryland women's basketball team won the National Championship in 2006. Morgan State University took the NCAA Division II title in 1974. Another major sport is lacrosse. Johns Hopkins University, the Naval Academy, and the University of Maryland all have performed well in intercollegiate competition.

Every weekend from April to October, Marylanders compete in jousting tournaments held in four classes throughout the state. In modern jousting, designated as the official state sport, horseback riders attempt to pick up small rings with long, lancelike poles. The state championship is held in October.

Babe Ruth was one of many star athletes to be born in the state.

39 Famous Marylanders

Maryland has produced no US presidents; its lone vice president was Spiro Theodore Agnew (1918–1996), who served as governor of Maryland before being elected as Richard Nixon's vice-president in 1968. Reelected with Nixon in 1972, Agnew resigned the vice-presidency in October 1973 after a federal indictment had been filed against him.

Roger Brooke Taney (1777–1864) was US chief justice when the Supreme Court heard the *Dred Scott* case in 1856, ruling that Congress could not exclude slavery from any territory. As counsel for the National Association for the

Advancement of Colored People, Thurgood Marshall (1908–1993) argued the landmark *Brown v. Board of Education* school desegregation case before the Supreme Court in 1954. President Lyndon Johnson appointed him to the Court 13 years later.

Lawyer and poet Francis Scott Key (1779–1843) wrote "The Star-Spangled Banner"—now the national anthem—in 1814. The prominent abolitionists Frederick Douglass (Frederick Augustus Washington Bailey, 1817?–1895) and Harriet Tubman (1820?–1913) were born in Maryland. Elizabeth Ann Bayley Seton (b.New York, 1774–1821), canonized by the Roman Catholic Church in 1975, was the first native-born American saint.

Benjamin Banneker (1731–1806), a free black, assisted in surveying the new District of Columbia and published almanacs from 1792 to 1797. Financier-philanthropist Johns Hopkins (1795–1873) was a Marylander. Peyton Rous (1879–1970) won the 1966 Nobel Prize for physiology-medicine.

Maryland's best-known modern writer was H(enry) L(ouis) Mencken (1880–1956), a Baltimore newspaper reporter who was also a gifted social commentator, political wit, and student of the American language. Edgar Allan Poe (b.Massachusetts, 1809–1849), known for his poems and eerie short stories, died in Baltimore. Novelist-reformer Upton Sinclair (1878–1968) was born there, as was Emily Price Post (1873–1960), who wrote about social etiquette. Other writers associated with Maryland include Leon Uris (1924–2003) and John Barth (b.1930). Most notable among Maryland actors are Edwin Booth (1833–1893) and his brother John Wilkes Booth (1838–1865), notorious as the assassin of President Abraham Lincoln.

Edgar Allan Poe (1809–1849) is shown here in a Civil War photograph taken by the Mathew Brady Studio for the US Army. Poe, known for his eerie short stories, died in Baltimore. NATIONAL ARCHIVES.

George Herman "Babe" Ruth (1895–1948), arguably the greatest baseball player of all time, was born in Baltimore. Other prominent ballplayers include Robert Moses "Lefty" Grove (1900–1975) and Cal Ripken Jr. (Calvin Edwin Ripken Jr., b.1960).

40 Bibliography

BOOKS

Bristow, M. J. *State Songs of America*. Westport, CT: Greenwood Press, 2000.

Brown, Jonatha A. *Maryland*. Milwaukee, WI: Gareth Stevens, 2006.

Cohen, Richard M., and Jules Witcover. *A Heartbeat Away: The Investigation and Resignation of Vice President Spiro T. Agnew.*

New York: Viking, 1974.

Coleman, Brooke. *The Colony of Maryland*. New York: PowerKids Press, 1999.

DuBois, Muriel L. *Maryland Facts and Symbols*. Rev. ed. Mankato, MN: Capstone Press, 2003.

Lough, Loree. *Lord Baltimore: English Politician and Colonist*. Philadelphia: Chelsea House, 2000.

Murray, Julie. *Maryland*. Edina, MN: Abdo Publishing, 2006.

Rauth, Leslie. *Maryland*. New York: Benchmark Books, 2000.

WEB SITES

Government of the State Maryland. maryland.gov/portal/server.pt? (accessed March 1, 2007).

Maryland Office of Tourism. www.mdisfun.org (accessed March 1, 2007).

Massachusetts

Commonwealth of Massachusetts

ORIGIN OF STATE NAME: Derived from the name of the Massachusett Native American tribe that lived on Massachusetts Bay; the name is thought to mean "at or about the Great Hill."

NICKNAME: The Bay State.

CAPITAL: Boston.

ENTERED UNION: 6 February 1788 (6th).

OFFICIAL SEAL: Same as the coat of arms, with the inscription *Sigillum Reipublicæ Massachusettensis* (Seal of the Republic of Massachusetts).

FLAG: The coat of arms on a white field.

COAT OF ARMS: On a blue shield, a Native American depicted in gold holds in his right hand a bow, in his left an arrow pointing downward. Above the bow is a five-pointed silver star. The crest shows a bent right arm holding a broadsword. Around the shield beneath the crest is a banner with the state motto in green.

MOTTO: *Ense petit placidam sub libertate quietem* (By the sword we seek peace, but peace only under liberty).

SONG: "All Hail to Massachusetts;" "Massachusetts" (folksong).

FLOWER: Mayflower (ground laurel).

TREE: American elm.

ANIMAL: Right whale (marine mammal); morgan horse (horse).

BIRD: Chickadee.

FISH: Cod.

INSECT: Ladybug.

DOG: Boston terrier.

GEM: Rhodonite.

FOSSIL: Theropod dinosaur tracks.

MINERAL: Babingtonite.

ROCK OR STONE: Roxbury puddingstone; granite; Plymouth Rock (historical rock).

BEVERAGE: Cranberry juice.

LEGAL HOLIDAYS: New Year's Day, 1 January; Birthday of Martin Luther King Jr., 3rd Monday in January; Washington's Birthday, 3rd Monday in February; Patriots' Day, 3rd Monday in April; Memorial Day, last Monday in May; Independence Day, 4 July; Labor Day, 1st Monday in September; Columbus Day, 2nd Monday in October; Veterans Day, 11 November; Thanksgiving Day, appointed by the governor, customarily the 4th Thursday in November; Christmas Day, 25 December. Legal holidays in Suffolk County include Evacuation Day, 17 March; and Bunker Hill Day, 17 June.

TIME: 7 AM EST = noon GMT.

1 Location and Size

Located in the northeastern United States, Massachusetts is the fourth largest of the six New England states. It ranks 45th in size among the 50 states. The total area of Massachusetts is 8,284 square miles (21,456 square kilometers), of which land comprises 7,824 square miles (20,265 square kilometers) and inland water occupies 460 square miles (1,191 square kilometers). Massachusetts extends about 190 miles (306 kilometers) east-west and 110 miles (177 kilometers) north-south. Two important islands lie south of the state's fishhook-shaped Cape Cod peninsula: Martha's Vineyard and Nantucket. The Elizabeth Islands, southwest of Cape Cod and northwest of Martha's Vineyard, consist of 16 small islands separating Buzzards Bay from Vineyard Sound. The total boundary length of Massachusetts is 515 miles (829 kilometers), including a general coastline of 192 miles (309 kilometers).

2 Topography

Massachusetts is divided into four topographical regions: coastal lowlands, interior lowlands, dissected uplands, and residuals of ancient mountains. The coastal lowlands extend about 30–50 miles (48–80 kilometers) inland from the Atlantic Ocean and include Cape Cod and the offshore islands. The northern shoreline of the state is characterized by rugged high slopes, but at the southern end, along Cape Cod, the ground is flatter and covered with grassy heaths.

The Connecticut River Valley, characterized by red sandstone, curved ridges, meadows, and good soil, is the main feature of west-central Massachusetts. East of the Connecticut River

Massachusetts Population Profile

Total population estimate in 2006:	6,437,193
Population change, 2000–06:	1.4%
Hispanic or Latino†:	7.9%
Population by race	
One race:	98.6%
White:	83.4%
Black or African American:	5.9%
American Indian /Alaska Native:	0.2%
Asian:	4.7%
Native Hawaiian / Pacific Islander:	0.0%
Some other race:	4.4%
Two or more races:	1.4%

Population by Age Group

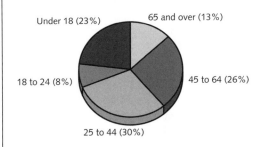

Under 18 (23%)
65 and over (13%)
18 to 24 (8%)
45 to 64 (26%)
25 to 44 (30%)

Major Cities by Population

City	Population	% change 2000–05
Boston	559,034	-5.1
Worcester	175,898	1.9
Springfield	151,732	-0.2
Lowell	103,111	-2.0
Cambridge	100,135	-1.2
Brockton	94,632	0.3
New Bedford	93,102	-0.7
Fall River	91,802	-0.1
Quincy	90,250	2.5
Lynn	88,792	-0.3

Notes: †A person of Hispanic or Latino origin may be of any race. NA indicates that data are not available.
Sources: U.S. Census Bureau. *American Community Survey* and *Population Estimates.* www.census.gov/ (accessed March 2007).

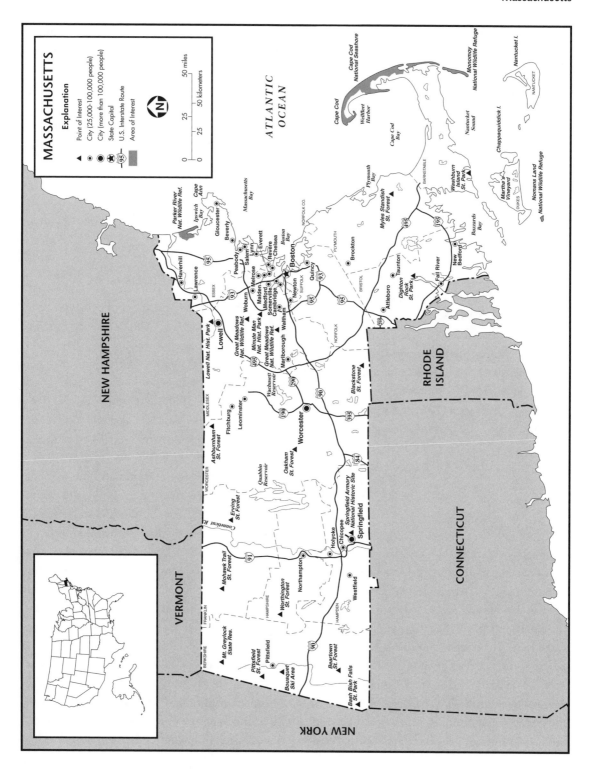

Valley are the eastern uplands, an extension of the White Mountains of New Hampshire. In western Massachusetts, the Taconic Range and Berkshire Hills (which extend southward from the Green Mountains of Vermont) are characterized by numerous hills and valleys. Mt. Greylock, close to the New York border, is the highest point in the state, at 3,487 feet (1,064 meters).

There are more than 4,230 miles (6,808 kilometers) of rivers in the state. The Connecticut River, the longest, runs southward through west-central Massachusetts. The Deerfield, Westfield, Chicopee, and Millers rivers flow into it. Other rivers of note include the Charles, the Mystic, the Taunton, the Blackstone, the Housatonic, and the Merrimack. Over 1,100 lakes dot the state. The largest, the artificial Quabbin Reservoir in central Massachusetts, covers 24,704 acres (9,997 hectares). The largest natural lake is Assawompset Pond in southern Massachusetts, occupying 2,656 acres (1,075 hectares).

Hilly Martha's Vineyard is roughly triangular in shape, as is Nantucket Island to the east. The Elizabeth Islands are characterized by broad, grassy plains.

3 Climate

Although Massachusetts is a relatively small state, there are significant climatic differences between its eastern and western sections. The entire state has cold winters and moderately warm summers. The Berkshires in the west have both the coldest winters and the coolest summers. Normal temperatures for Pittsfield in the Berkshires are 21°F (-5°C) in January and 67°F (19°C) in July. The interior lowlands are several degrees warmer in both winter and summer. The coastal sections are the warmest areas of the state. Normal tem-

peratures for Boston are 30°F (-1°C) in January and 74°F (23°C) in July. The record high temperature in the state was 107°F (42°C) registered at Chester and New Bedford ion 2 August 1975. The record low was -35°F (-37°C), registered at Chester on 12 January 1981. Precipitation ranges from 39 to 46 inches (99 to 117 centimeters) annually. The average snowfall for Boston is 40.9 inches (103 centimeters), with the range in the Berkshires considerably higher. Boston's average wind speed is 13 miles per hour (21 kilometers per hour).

4 Plants and Animals

Maple, birch, beech, hemlock, larch, and other tree species cover the Massachusetts uplands. Common shrubs include rhodora, mountain laurel, and shadbush. Various ferns grow throughout the state. Typical wild flowers include several varieties of orchid, lily, and goldenrod. In 2006, the northeastern bulrush, sandplain gerardia, and small whorled pogonia were listed as threatened or endangered.

Common native mammals include the white-tailed deer, river otter, mink, and porcupine. Among the Bay State's 336 resident bird species are the mallard, ring-necked pheasant, downy woodpecker, and song sparrow. Native inland fish include brook trout, chain pickerel, and yellow perch. Native amphibians include the Jefferson salamander, red-spotted newt, eastern American toad, gray tree frog, and bullfrog. Common reptiles are the snapping turtle and northern water snake. The Cape Cod coasts are rich in a variety of shellfish, including clams, mussels, shrimps, and oysters. As of 2006, some 20 animal species were classified as threatened or endangered, including the American burying

Massachusetts Population by Race

Census 2000 was the first national census in which the instructions to respondents said, "Mark one or more races." This table shows the number of people who are of one, two, or three or more races. For those claiming two races, the number of people belonging to the various categories is listed. The U.S. government conducts a census of the population every ten years.

	Number	Percent
Total population.	6,349,097	100.0
One race	6,203,092	97.7
Two races	138,177	2.2
White *and* Black or African American	19,459	0.3
White *and* American Indian/Alaska Native	12,754	0.2
White *and* Asian	15,769	0.2
White *and* Native Hawaiian/Pacific Islander	1,664	—
White *and* some other race	48,948	0.8
Black or African American *and* American Indian/Alaska Native	3,747	0.1
Black or African American *and* Asian	1,469	—
Black or African American *and* Native Hawaiian/Pacific Islander	915	—
Black or African American *and* some other race	23,362	0.4
American Indian/Alaska Native *and* Asian	727	—
American Indian/Alaska Native *and* Native Hawaiian/Pacific Islander	68	—
American Indian/Alaska Native *and* some other race.	1,330	—
Asian *and* Native Hawaiian/Pacific Islander	1,084	—
Asian *and* some other race.	5,395	0.1
Native Hawaiian/Pacific Islander *and* some other race	1,486	—
Three or more races.	7,828	0.1

Source: U.S. Census Bureau. *Census 2000: Redistricting Data.* Press release issued by the Redistricting Data Office. Washington, D.C., March, 2001. A dash (—) indicates that the percent is less than 0.1.

beetle, the bald eagle, puma, shortnose sturgeon, five species of whale, and four species of turtle.

5 Environmental Protection

All environmentally related programs are administered by the Executive Office of Environmental Affairs (EOEA) and its five agencies: the Department of Environmental Management (DEM); the Department of Environmental Protection (DEP); the Department of Fisheries, Wildlife and Environmental Law Enforcement (DFWELE); the Department of Food and Agriculture (DFA); and the Metropolitan District Commission (MDC).

Since disposal of treated sewage sludge in Boston Harbor was halted in 1991, and with improved sewage treatment, the harbor is now markedly cleaner. In 1988, 10% of the flounder caught in Boston Harbor had liver tumors caused by toxic chemicals. As of 1993, no flounder tested had tumors.

With the adoption of Massachusetts acid rain legislation in 1985, sulfur dioxide output from Massachusetts sources has been cut by 17%. In 2003, Massachusetts had 411 hazardous waste sites listed in the Environmental Protection Agency's database, 31 of which were on the National Priorities List as of 2006.

6 Population

In 2005, Massachusetts ranked 13th in the United States in population with an estimated total of 6,437,193 residents. In 2004, the population density was 818.2 persons per square mile (315.9 persons per square kilometer), making Massachusetts the third most densely populated state. The median age in 2004 was 38.1. In 2005, about 13% of all residents were 65 or older while about 23% were 18 or younger.

The state's largest city is Boston, which ranked 24th among the largest US cities in 2005 with a population of 559,034. Other large cities (with their 2005 populations) are Worcester, 175,898, and Springfield, 151,732. More than two-thirds of all state residents live in the Greater Boston area, which had an estimated metropolitan population of 4,424,649 in 2004.

7 Ethnic Groups

According to the 2000 census, there were 343,454 black Americans in Massachusetts, representing 5.4% of the population (that percentage stood at 5.9% in 2006). Blacks constituted more than 25% of Boston's population. The state also had 428,729 Hispanics and Latinos, predominantly of Puerto Rican and Dominican descent. The total Asian population was estimated at 238,124. Of these, there were 84,392 Chinese, 33,962 Vietnamese, 19,696 Cambodians, 17,369 Koreans, and 10,539 Japanese. Pacific Islanders numbered 2,489. The Native American population, including Eskimos and Aleuts, totaled 15,015. Cape Cod has settlements of Portuguese fishermen, as does New Bedford. As of 2000, the largest groups of people claiming a single ancestry were the Irish (about 22.5% of the population), Italians (13.5%), English (11.4%), French (8%), Polish (5.1%), and Portuguese (4.4%). Also in 2000, about 772,983 residents, or 12.2% of the state's population, were foreign-born.

8 Languages

Massachusetts English is generally classified as Northern, but early migration up the Connecticut River created special variations within the eastern half of the state. Eastern Massachusetts speakers are likely to have the /ah/ sound in the beginning of *orange* and to pronounce *on* and *fog* with the same vowel as in form. A few place-names—such as Massachusetts itself, Chicopee, and Naukeag— are borrowed from the Algonkian-speaking Native American tribes. In 2000, 81.3% of the population five years of age or older spoke only English at home. Other principal languages spoken at home, and number of speakers, were Spanish, 370,011; Portuguese, 159,809; French, 84,484; Chinese, 71,412; and Italian, 59,811.

9 Religions

Both the Pilgrims, who landed on Plymouth Rock in 1620, and the Puritans, who formed the Massachusetts Bay Company in 1629, came to the land to escape harassment by the Church of England. These early communities were based on strict religious principles and forbade the practice of differing religions. Religious tolerance was included in the Charter of 1692, to protect the Baptists, Anglicans, and Catholics who had arrived in the colony.

As of 2004, there were 3,033,367 Roman Catholics in Massachusetts, representing nearly half of the total population. The Roman Catholic Church faced a challenge in the early 2000s, and Cardinal Bernard F. Law, Archbishop of Boston, was among top church officials affected. Law stepped down as archbishop in December 2002 after widespread criticism of his handling of charges that priests sexually abused children and allegations of cover-ups.

The largest Protestant denominations were the United Church of Christ, with 89,264 adherents in 2005; the Episcopal Church, 98,963 in 2000; the American Baptists (USA), 52,716 (2000); and the United Methodist Church, 64,028 (2000). The second largest religious affiliation is Judaism, with about 275,000 adherents in 2000. The Muslim population the same year was about 41,497 people. There were about 57 Buddhist congregations and 20 Hindu congregations throughout the state. About 35% of the population did not specify a religious affiliation.

Although small, the Church of Christ, Scientist is significant to the state's history. Its first house of worship was founded in 1879 in Boston by Mary Baker Eddy, who, four years earlier, had published the Christian Science textbook, *Science and Health with Key to the Scriptures.* In Boston, the church continues to publish an influential newspaper, the *Christian Science Monitor.*

10 Transportation

The first rail line in the United States, a three-mile (five-kilometer) stretch from the Neponset River to the granite quarries in Quincy, was built in 1826. The first steam railroad in New England, connecting Boston and Lowell, was completed seven years later. As of 2003, 10 railroads transported freight through Massachusetts. That year, the state had 1,255 rail miles (2,020 kilometers) of railroad. As of 2006, Boston was the northern terminus of Amtrak's Northeast Corridor, linking New England with Washington, DC, via New York City and Philadelphia. East–west service from Boston to Chicago is also provided by Amtrak.

Commuter service is coordinated by the Massachusetts Bay Transportation Authority (MBTA), formed in 1964 to consolidate bus, commuter rail, high-speed trolley, and subway services to the 79 cities and towns in the Greater Boston area. The Boston subway, which began operation in 1897, is the oldest subway system in the United States. Boston also is one of the few cities in the country with an operating trolley system. About 40% of all Bostonians commute to work by public transportation, the second-highest percentage in the nation, following New York City.

In 2004, 35,783 miles (57,610 kilometers) of public roadways crisscrossed the state. The major highways, which extend from and through Boston like the spokes of a wheel, include I-95, the Massachusetts Turnpike (I-90), I-93, State Highway 3 to Cape Cod, and State Highway 24 to Fall River. The other major road in the state is I-91, which runs north–south through the Connecticut River Valley. In 2004, about 5,532,000 motor vehicles were registered in the state, of which 3,486,000 were automobiles, approximately 1,898,000 were trucks, and 11,000 were buses. There also were 137,000 motorcycles. The state issued 4,645,857 driver's licenses in 2004.

Because it is the major American city closest to Europe, Boston is an important shipping center for both domestic and foreign cargo. All port activity of the Port of Boston is under the jurisdiction of the Massachusetts Port Authority, which also operates Logan International Airport and Hanscom Field in Bedford. Other important ports are Fall River and Salem.

The building housing Quincy Market, the most-visited site in Boston, was constructed in the 1800s. © JAMES CORRIGAN/ EPD PHOTOS.

There were 76 airports and 137 heliports in Massachusetts in 2005. Logan International, near Boston, is the busiest airport in the state, with 12,758,020 passengers in 2004.

11 History

When English settlers arrived in present-day Massachusetts, they encountered five main Algonkian tribes: the Nauset, a fishing people on Cape Cod; the Wampanoag in the southeast; the Massachusetts in the northeast; the Nipmuc in the central hills; and the Pocumtuc in the west. In the wake of John and Sebastian Cabot's voyages (1497 and following), fishermen from England, France, Portugal, and Spain began fishing off the Massachusetts coast. Within 50 years, fur trading with the Native Americans was established.

Permanent English settlement, which would ultimately destroy the Algonkian peoples, began in 1620 when a small band of Puritans left their temporary haven at Leiden in the Netherlands to start a colony in the northern part of Virginia lands, near the Hudson River. Their ship, the *Mayflower*, was blown off course by an Atlantic storm, and they landed on Cape Cod before settling in an abandoned Wampanoag village they called Plymouth. Ten years later, a much larger Puritan group settled the Massachusetts Bay

Colony, to the north in Salem. Between 1630 and 1640, about 20,000 English people, chiefly Puritans, settled in Massachusetts with offshoots moving to Connecticut and Rhode Island.

Farming soon overtook fishing and fur trading in economic importance. After the trade in beaver skins was exhausted, the remaining Native American tribes were devastated in King Philip's War (1675–76). Shipbuilding and Atlantic commerce brought added prosperity to the Massachusetts Bay Colony. In 1692, Massachusetts and the colony of Plymouth were merged under a new charter.

During the 18th century, settlement spread across the entire colony. Boston, the capital, attained a population of 15,000 by 1730. Colonial government provided more advantages than drawbacks for commerce, and supply contracts during the French and Indian War enriched the colony's economy. But the postwar recession after 1763 was accompanied by a new imperial policy that put pressure on Massachusetts as well as other colonies. From 1765, when Bostonians violently protested the Stamp Act, Massachusetts was in the forefront of the resistance.

By December 1773, when East India Company tea was dumped into Boston harbor to prevent its taxation, most of the colony was committed to resistance. When Parliament retaliated for the Tea Party by closing the port of Boston in 1774, Massachusetts was ready to rebel. Battle began at Lexington and Concord on 19 April 1775. By this time, Massachusetts had the backing of the Continental Congress. For Massachusetts, the battlefield experience of the Revolution was largely confined to 1775, after which the fighting shifted southward.

Statehood Massachusetts entered the Union on 6 February 1788. Federalist policies—supporting a strong central government—were dominant, and they were supported by the Whigs in the 1830s and the Republicans from the late 1850s. This political alignment reflected the importance to the state of national commercial and industrial development, as Massachusetts lacked the resources for strong agricultural development.

At Waltham, Lowell, and Lawrence the first large-scale factories in the United States were erected. Massachusetts became a leader in industries including textiles, metalworking, shoes and leather goods, and shipbuilding. By the 1850s, steam engines and clipper ships were both Bay State products. The industrial development of Massachusetts was accompanied by a literary and intellectual flowering centered in Concord, the home of Ralph Waldo Emerson, Henry David Thoreau, and a cluster of others who became known as transcendentalists. Abolitionism found some of its chief leaders in Massachusetts.

Post–Civil War In the years following the Civil War, Massachusetts emerged as an urban industrial state. Its population, fed by immigrants from England, Scotland, Germany, and especially Ireland, grew rapidly in the middle decades of the century. Later, between 1880 and 1920, another wave of immigrants came from French Canada, Italy, Russia, Poland, Scandinavia, Portugal, Greece, and Syria. Still later, between 1950 and 1970, black southerners and Puerto Ricans settled in the cities.

The Massachusetts economy, relatively stagnant between 1920 and 1950, revived in the second half of the 20th century through a combination of university talent, investment, a skilled

Massachusetts Governors: 1775–2007

Years	Governor	Party		Years	Governor	Party
1775–1780	Council of State			1891–1894	William Eustis Russell	Democrat
1780–1785	John Hancock			1894–1896	Frederic Thomas Greenhalge	Republican
1785–1787	James Bowdoin			1896–1900	Roger Wolcott	Republican
1787	Thomas Cushing			1900–1903	Winthrop Murray Crane	Republican
1787–1793	John Hancock	—		1903–1905	John Lewis Bates	Republican
1793–1797	Samuel Adams	Dem-Rep		1905–1906	William Lewis Douglas	Democrat
1797–1799	Increase Sumner	Federalist		1906–1909	Curtis Guild, Jr.	Republican
1799–1800	Moses Gill	Federalist		1909–1911	Eben Sumner Draper	Republican
1800–1807	Caleb Strong	—		1911–1914	Eugene Noble Foss	Democrat
1807–1808	James Sullivan	Dem-Rep		1914–1916	David Ignatius Walsh	Democrat
1808–1809	Levi Lincoln	Dem-Rep		1916–1919	Samuel Walker McCall	Republican
1809–1810	Christopher Gore	Federalist		1919–1921	John Calvin Coolidge	Republican
1810–1812	Elbridge Gerry	Dem-Rep		1921–1925	Channing Harris Cox	Republican
1812–1816	Caleb Strong	Federalist		1925–1929	Alvan Tufts Fuller	Republican
1816–1823	John Brooks	Federalist		1929–1931	Frank G. Allen	Republican
1823–1825	William Eustis	Republican		1931–1935	Joseph Buell Ely	Democrat
1825	Marcus Morton	Republican		1935–1937	James Michael Curley	Democrat
1825–1834	Levi Lincoln, Jr.	Nat-Rep		1937–1939	Charles Francis Hurley	Democrat
1834–1835	John Davis	Whig		1939–1945	Leverett Saltonstall	Republican
1835–1836	Samuel Turell Armstrong	Indep-Whig		1945–1947	Maurice Joseph Tobin	Democrat
1836–1840	Edward Everett	Whig		1947–1949	Robert Fiske Bradford	Republican
1840–1841	Marcus Morton	Democrat		1949–1953	Paul Andrew Dever	Democrat
1841–1843	John Davis	Whig		1953–1957	Christian Archibald Herter	Republican
1843–1844	Marcus Morton	Democrat		1957–1961	Foster Furcolo	Democrat
1844–1851	George Nixon Briggs	Whig		1961–1963	John Anthony Volpe	Republican
1851–1853	George Sewel Boutwell	Democrat		1963–1965	Endicott Peabody	Democrat
1853–1854	John Henry Clifford	Whig		1965–1969	John Anthony Volpe	Republican
1854–1855 Whig	Emory Washburn			1969–1975	Francis Williams Sargent	Republican
1855–1858	Henry Joseph Gardner	Know Nothing		1975–1979	Michael Stanley Dukakis	Democrat
1858–1861	Nathaniel Prentice Banks	Republican		1979–1983	Edward J. King	Democrat
1861–1866	John Albion Andrew	Republican		1983–1991	Michael Stanley Dukakis	Democrat
1866–1869	Alexander Hamilton Bullock	Republican		1991–1996	William Floyd Weld	Republican
1869–1872	William Claflin	Republican		1996–2002	Argeo Paul Cellucci	Republican
1872–1874	William Barrett Washburn	Republican		2002–2006	Mitt Romney	Republican
1874–1875	Thomas Talbot	Republican		2006–	Deval L. Patrick	Democrat
1875–1876	William Gaston	Democrat				
1876–1879	Alexander Hamilton Rice	Republican				
1879–1880	Thomas Talbot	Republican				
1880–1883	John Davis Long	Republican				
1883–1884	Benjamin Franklin Butler	Dem/Green		Democratic/Greenbacker – Dem/Green		
1884–1887	George Dexter Robinson	Republican		Democratic Republican – Dem-Rep		
1887–1890	Oliver Ames	Republican		National Republican – Nat-Rep		
1890–1891	John Quincy Adams Brackett	Republican				

work force, and political clout. As the old industries and the mill cities declined, new high-technology manufacturing developed in Boston's suburbs, led by electronics and defense-related industries. White-collar employment and middle-class suburbs flourished, though run-down mill towns and Yankee dairy farms and orchards still dotted the landscape.

In the 1970s and early 1980s, a revolution in information technology and increased defense

Massachusetts State House. © DAVID SAILORS/CORBIS.

spending fueled a high-technology boom which centered on new manufacturing firms outside Boston along Route 128. Unemployment dropped from 12% in 1978 to 4% in 1987. However, with the beginnings of a nationwide recession in 1989, the Massachusetts economy declined dramatically, losing 14% of its total jobs in three years. The state's economic woes were increased by the collapse in the late 1980s of risky real estate ventures.

By the mid-1990s, the Massachusetts economy was in the midst of a vigorous upturn, due largely to the strength of its leading industries, including software and mutual funds. In 1998, the state's per capita (per person) income was the third highest in the nation. In 2004, per cap-

ita income was $41,801, second highest in the nation behind Connecticut. Despite that record, the thriving economy came to an abrupt halt in 2001, as the United States entered a recession marked by a large increase in job losses. In 2003, Massachusetts had a $3 billion budget deficit.

In November 2003, the Massachusetts supreme court became the first state supreme court to rule that same-sex marriages were legal. Massachusetts became the first state to legally allow gay marriages to take place on 17 May 2004. A ban on smoking in the workplace, including in bars and restaurants—private clubs and cigar bars excepted—came into effect in July 2004.

Boston's multibillion-dollar highway project, dubbed the "Big Dig," was in its final stages in early 2007. However, in July 2006, a ceiling section of a tunnel segment under South Boston collapsed, killing a woman riding as a passenger in a car.

In early 2006, Governor Mitt Romney signed a law that will require all Massachusetts residents to purchase health insurance by 1 July 2007.

12 State Government

The Massachusetts constitution of 15 June 1780 is, according to the state, the oldest written constitution in the world still in effect. As of January 2005, it had been amended 120 times. The legislature of Massachusetts, known as the General Court, is composed of a 40-member senate and 160-member house of representatives, all of whom are elected every two years.

The governor and lieutenant governor are elected jointly every four years. The governor appoints all state and local judges, as well as the heads of the ten executive offices. Other elected officials include the attorney general, secretary of the commonwealth, and treasurer.

To win passage, a bill must gain a majority vote of both houses of the legislature. After a bill is passed, the governor has ten days in which to sign it, return it for reconsideration (usually with amendments), veto it, or refuse to sign it ("pocket veto"). A veto may be overridden by a two-thirds majority in both houses.

The governor's salary as of December 2004 was $135,000, and the legislative salary was $53,379.93.

13 Political Parties

Democrats have, for the most part, dominated state politics in Massachusetts since 1928, when the state voted for Democratic presidential candidate Alfred E. Smith—the first time the Democrats won a majority in a Massachusetts presidential election. In 1960, John F. Kennedy, who had been a popular US senator from Massachusetts, became the first Roman Catholic president in US history. Since then the state has voted for all Democratic presidential candidates except Republican Ronald Reagan in 1980 and 1984. In 1972, it was the only state carried by Democrat George McGovern. Massachusetts chose its native son, Democratic Governor Michael Dukakis, for president in 1988 and voted again for a Democrat in the next four elections: in 1992 and 1996 Massachusetts elected Bill Clinton, in 2000 voted for Al Gore, and in 2004 state voters gave native son John Kerry 53.4% of the vote to incumbent President George W. Bush's 44.6%.

In 2004 there were approximately 3,973,000 registered voters. In 1998, 37% of registered voters were Democratic, 13% Republican, and 50% unaffiliated or members of other parties. In 2006, Democrat Deval Patrick was elected governor, the first African-American elected governor of Massachusetts, and only the second in US history. The US Senate seats were held by Democrats Edward ("Ted") Kennedy and John Kerry in 2006. The US House delegation following the 2006 elections consisted entirely of ten Democrats. Following those elections, the Massachusetts state senate had 35 Democrats and 5 Republicans while the state house of representatives had 141 Democrats and 19 Republicans.

Massachusetts Presidential Vote by Political Parties, 1948–2004

YEAR	MASSACHUSETTS WINNER	DEMOCRAT	REPUBLICAN	SOCIALIST LABOR	PROGRESSIVE
1948	*Truman (D)	1,151,788	909,370	5,535	38,157
1952	*Eisenhower (R)	1,083,525	1,292,325	1,957	4,636
1956	*Eisenhower (R)	948,190	1,393,197	5,573	—
1960	*Kennedy (D)	1,487,174	976,750	3,892	—
1964	*Johnson (D)	1,786,422	549,727	4,755	—
					AMERICAN IND.
1968	Humphrey (D)	1,469,218	766,844	6,180	87,088
				SOC. WORKERS	AMERICAN
1972	McGovern (D)	1,332,540	1,112,078	10,600	2,877
1976	*Carter (D)	1,429,475	1,030,276	8,138	7,555
				LIBERTARIAN	
1980	*Reagan (R)	1,048,562	1,054,213	21,311	—
1984	*Reagan	1,239,600	1,310,936	—	
					NEW ALLIANCE
1988	Dukakis (D)	1,401,415	1,194,635	24,251	9,561
					IND. (PEROT)
1992	*Clinton (D)	1,318,639	805,039	9,021	630,731
1996	*Clinton (D)	1,571,763	718,107	20,426	227,217
				LIBERTARIAN	
2000	Gore (D)	1,616,487	878,502	16,366	173,564
2004	Kerry (D)	1,803,800	1,071,109	15,022	—

*Won US presidential election.

Fifty-one women were elected to the state legislature in 2006, or 25.5%.

14 Local Government

As of 2005, Massachusetts had 14 counties, 45 cities, 306 townships, 349 public school districts, and 403 special districts. In most counties, executive authority is vested in commissioners elected to four-year terms. All Massachusetts cities are governed by mayors and city councils. Towns are governed by selectmen, who are usually elected to either one or two-year terms. Town meetings—a carryover from the colonial period—still take place regularly. By state law, to be designated a city, a place must have at least 12,000 residents. Towns with more than 6,000 inhabitants may hold representative town meetings that are limited to elected officials.

15 Judicial System

The supreme judicial court, composed of a chief justice and six other justices, is the highest court in the state. It has appeals jurisdiction in matters of law and also advises the governor and legislature on legal questions. The superior courts, actually the highest level of trial court, have a chief justice and 79 other justices. These courts hear law, equity, civil, and criminal cases, and make the final determination in matters of fact. The appeals court, consisting of a chief justice and 13 other justices, hears appeals of decisions by district and municipal courts.

Other court systems in the state include the land court, probate and family court, housing court, and juvenile court. Massachusetts had a total violent crime rate (murder, rape, robbery, aggravated assault) of 458.8 reported cases per 100,000 inhabitants in 2004. That year, crimes against property (burglary, larceny/theft, and motor vehicle theft) totaled 2,459.7 reported incidents per 100,000 people. As of 31 December 2004, there were 10,144 prisoners in state and federal correctional institutions in Massachusetts. Massachusetts does not have a death penalty.

16 Migration

Massachusetts was founded by the migration of English religious groups to its shores and for over a century their descendants dominated all activity in the state. The first non-English to enter Massachusetts in significant numbers were the Irish, who migrated in vast numbers during the 1840s and 1850s. Other ethnic groups—such as the Scottish, Welsh, Germans, and Poles—were also entering the state at this time. During the late 1880s and 1890s, another wave of immigrants—from Portugal, Spain, Italy, Russia, and Greece—arrived. Irish and Italians continued to enter the state during the 20th century.

The only significant migration from other areas of the United States to Massachusetts has been the influx of southern blacks since World War II. According to census estimates, between 1990 and 1998, the black population grew from 300,000 to 395,000 persons, mostly in the Boston area.

Between 1990 and 1998, the state had a net loss of 237,000 in domestic migration and a net gain of 135,000 in international migration. In the period 2000–05, net international migration was 162,674 and net internal migration was -236,415, for a net loss of 73,741 people.

17 Economy

From its beginnings as a farming and seafaring colony, Massachusetts became one of the most industrialized states in the country in the late 19th century and, more recently, a leader in the manufacture of high-technology products. Fueled in part by a dramatic increase in the Pentagon's budget that focused on sophisticated weaponry, as well as by significant advances in information technology, high-technology companies rose up around the outskirts of Boston in the 1970s and early 1980s. Wholesale and retail trade, transportation, and public utilities also prospered.

In the late 1980s, the boom ended. The minicomputer industry failed to innovate at the same pace as its competitors as the market became increasingly crowded, and defense contractors suffered from cuts in military spending. Between 1988 and 1991, jobs in both high-technology and non-high technology manufacturing declined by 17%. In addition, the early 1980s had also seen the rise of real estate ventures which collapsed at the end of the decade when the market became saturated. Unemployment rose to 9% in 1991. The economy recovered in the 1990s, as several banks started new lending programs; unemployment was 4% in 1997. Massachusetts benefited from the information technology (IT) and stock market booms of the 1990s. However, Massachusetts was the hardest hit among New England economies in the collapse of the "dot.com" bubble in the national recession of 2001.

As of 2004, real estate accounted for largest portion of gross state product (GSP), at 13.6% of GSP, followed by manufacturing (10.9% of GSP), and healthcare and social assistance (8.2%

of GSP). GSP in 2004 was approximately $317.8 billion.

18 Income

In 2005, Massachusetts had a gross state product (GSP) of $329 billion, 13th highest in the nation. In 2004, Massachusetts ranked third among the 50 states and the District of Columbia with a per capita (per person) income of $42,176. The three-year average median household income for 2002–04 was $52,354, compared to the national average of $44,473. For the period 2002–04, an estimated 9.8% of the state's residents lived below the federal poverty level, as compared to 12.4% nationwide.

19 Industry

Massachusetts is an important manufacturing center. Significant concentrations of industrial machinery employment are in Attleboro, Wilmington, Worcester, and the Springfield area. Much of the manufacturing industry is located along Route 128. This is a superhighway that circles Boston, from Gloucester in the north to Quincy in the south, and is unique in its concentration of high-technology enterprises.

The state's future as a manufacturing center depends on its continued preeminence in the production of computers, optical equipment, and other sophisticated instruments. Among the major computer manufacturers in the state are Digital Equipment Corporation in Maynard, and Data General in Westboro.

In 2004, the value of all products manufactured in the state was $76.5 billion. Of that total, computer and electronic product manufacturing accounted for $20.7 billion, followed by chemi-

cal manufacturing at $9.25 billion, food manufacturing at $6.05 billion, and fabricated metal product manufacturing at $5.8 billion.

20 Labor

In April 2006, the civilian labor force in Massachusetts numbered 3,338,600, with approximately 163,900 workers unemployed, yielding an unemployment rate of 4.9%, compared to the national average of 4.7% for the same period. As of April 2006, 4.4% of the labor force was employed in construction; 9.4% in manufacturing; 17.7% in trade, transportation, and public utilities; 6.9% in financial activities; 14.5% in professional and business services; 18.4% in education and health services; 9.1% in leisure and hospitality services; and 12.7% in government.

Some of the earliest unionization efforts took place in Massachusetts in the early 1880s, particularly in the shipbuilding and construction trades. However, the most important trade unions to evolve were those in the state's textile and shoe industries. After the turn of the century, the state suffered a severe decline in manufacturing, and employers sought to cut wages to make up for lost profits. This resulted in a number of strikes by both the United Textile Workers and the Boot and Shoe Workers Union. The largest strike of the era was at Lawrence in 1912, when textile workers (led by a radical labor group, the Industrial Workers of the World) closed the mills, and the mayor called in troops in an attempt to reopen them. Although the textile and shoe businesses are no longer major employers in the state, the United Shoe Workers of America, the Brotherhood of Shoe and Allied Craftsmen, the United Textile Workers, and the Leather Workers

International Union of America have their headquarters in Massachusetts.

Massachusetts was one of the first states to enact child labor laws. Massachusetts was also the first state to enact minimum wage guidelines (1912). In 2005, some 402,000 of the state's 2,886,000 employed wage and salary workers were members of unions. This represented 13.9% of those so employed. The national average was 12%.

21 Agriculture

As of 2004, there were 6,100 farms in Massachusetts, covering 520,000 acres (210,000 hectares). Farming was mostly limited to the western Massachusetts counties of Hampshire, Franklin, and Berkshire, and southern Bristol County. Total agricultural income for 2005 was estimated at $390 million (47th of the 50 states), of which crops provided 76%. Although the state is not a major farming area, it is the second-largest producer of cranberries in the United States, after Wisconsin. Cranberry production for 2004 was 180.4 million pounds (81.8 million kilograms), about 28% of the US total. Other crops include corn for silage, hay, and tobacco.

22 Domesticated Animals

Massachusetts is not a major producer of livestock. The state had 48,000 cattle and calves, worth around $52.8 million in 2005, and an estimated 12,000 hogs and pigs worth $1.3 million in 2004. Also during 2003, poultry farmers sold 863,000 pounds (392,000 kilograms) of chickens, and the state produced an estimated 73 million eggs, worth around $4.8 million. An estimated 19,000 milk cows produced 332 million pounds (151 million kilograms) of milk in 2003. During 2003, the state produced around 1.8 million pounds (0.8 million kilograms) of turkeys worth $2.7 million.

23 Fishing

The early settlers earned much of their income from the sea. The first shipyard in Massachusetts opened at Salem Neck in 1637 and, during the years before independence, the towns of Salem, Newburyport, Plymouth, and Boston were among the colonies' leading ports. For much of the 19th century, Nantucket and, later, New Bedford were the leading US whaling centers. Whaling declined in importance in the 1920s.

The fishing ports of New Bedford and Gloucester were among the busiest in the United States in 2004. New Bedford ranked first in the nation in catch value at $206.5 million and seventh in the nation for catch volume at 175.1 million pounds (79.6 million kilograms). Gloucester was 12th in the nation in catch value ($42.7 million) and 10th in volume (113.3 million pounds/51.5 million kilograms).

In 2004, Massachusetts ranked second in the nation for total commercial catch value at $326.1 million. The total catch volume that year was 336.9 million pounds (153.1 million kilograms). The quahog catch of 14.1 million pounds (6.4 million kilograms) was the second largest in the nation. The lobster catch was also the second largest with 11.3 million pounds (5.1 million kilograms), valued at $51.5 million. Massachusetts was the leading producer of sea scallops with 28.1 million pounds (12.8 million kilograms). In 2003, there were 232 fish processing and wholesale plants with an annual average of 4,504 employees in the state. The commercial fleet had about 5,235 boats and vessels in 2001.

The state's long shoreline and many rivers make sport fishing a popular pastime for both deep-sea and freshwater fishermen. In 2004, there were 203,139 fishing license holders.

24 Forestry

Forestry is a minor industry in the state. Forested lands cover about 3,126,000 acres (1,265,000 hectares), 76% of which are private lands. Wooded areas lost to urbanization in recent years have been offset by the conversion of inactive agricultural areas into forests. Red oak and white ash are found in the west. Specialty products include maple syrup and Christmas trees. The wood and paper products industries require more pulp than the state currently produces.

Massachusetts has the sixth-largest state park system in the nation, with 38 state parks and 74 state forests totaling some 273,000 acres (110,000 hectares). There are no national forests in Massachusetts.

25 Mining

The value of nonfuel mineral production in Massachusetts 2003 was estimated at $186 million. Crushed stone and construction sand and gravel are the state's two leading mineral commodities. According to preliminary figures, in 2003 there were an estimated 13.2 million metric tons of crushed stone and 111.4 million metric tons of sand and gravel produced. Other mineral commodities produced include common clay, lime, and peat; industrial sand and gravel; and dimension stone. Nationally, the state ranked fifth in dimension stone in 2003.

Industrial minerals processed or manufactured in the state include abrasives, graphite, gypsum, perlite, and vermiculite.

26 Energy and Power

In 2000, the state's total per capita energy consumption was 271 million Btu (68.3 million kilocalories), ranking it 42nd among the 50 states. In 2003, about 48.38 billion kilowatt hours of electric power (utility and nonutility) were generated in state and total installed capacity was over 13.87 million kilowatts. Almost all generating capacity in the state is privately owned.

As of 2006, Massachusetts had one operating nuclear plant, the single-unit Pilgrim plant in Plymouth. There are also four pumped-storage hydroelectric plants and 45 conventional hydroelectric generators. Boston Edison supplies electricity to the city of Boston. The rest of the state is served by 13 other companies, although a few municipalities do generate their own power. Power companies are regulated by the Department of Public Utilities, which establishes rates and monitors complaints from customers.

Massachusetts has no proven oil or coal reserves. Oil exploration off the coast of Cape Cod began in 1979. The state consumes, but does not produce, natural gas. In 2004, about 373 billion cubic feet (10.5 billion cubic meters) of natural gas were delivered.

Private researchers and the state have established demonstration projects for solar energy systems and other alternatives to fossil fuels.

27 Commerce

The machinery and electrical goods industries are important components of the state's wholesale

View of Boston across the Charles River. © KEVIN FLEMING/CORBIS.

trade, along with motor vehicle and automotive equipment, and paper and paper products. State wholesale sales totaled $127.1 billion in 2002; retail sales were $73.9 billion. Foreign exports of Massachusetts products totaled $22.04 billion in 2005 (10th in the United States).

28 Public Finance

The Massachusetts budget is prepared by the Executive Office of Administration and Finance and is presented by the governor to the legislature for revision and approval. The fiscal year runs from 1 July to 30 June.

The estimated revenues for the 2004 fiscal year were $41.6 billion and expenses were $38.4 billion. The largest general expenditures were for public welfare ($10.5 billion), education ($7.58 billion), and highways ($3 billion). The total debt of the state government was more than $50.9 billion, or $7,957.10 per capita (per person).

29 Taxation

The state levies a 12% tax on interest, dividends, and short-term capital gains; a 5% tax rate on capital gains from assets held between one and two years; a 2% rate on capital gains from assets held longer than that, and a flat 5.3% rate in on all other taxable personal income. The corporate income tax rate is 9.5%. Commercial banks and other banking and trust companies pay a 10.5% tax on net income while savings and loans organizations pay 10.91%.

Sales tax is 5%, but such necessities as food, clothing, and home heating fuel are exempt. There is also a wide array of state and local selective (excise) taxes, including a room occupancy tax, a motor vehicle excise tax, taxes covering motor fuels, tobacco products, insurance premiums, alcoholic beverages, amusements, parimutuels, and other selected items. Other state taxes include various license fees, a deeds tax, and a small property tax. Most property taxes are collected at the local level.

The state collected $18.015 billion in taxes in 2005, of which 53.8% came from individual income taxes, 21.6% from the general sales tax, 10.5% from selective sales taxes, 7.4% from corporate income taxes, and 6.7% from other taxes. In 2005, Massachusetts ranked seventh among the states in terms of state and local tax burden, which amounted to $2,815 per person.

30 Health

As of October 2005, the infant mortality was 5 per 1,000 live births. The overall death rate was 8.8 per 1,000 population. The major causes of death were heart diseases, cancer, cerebrovascular diseases, chronic lower respiratory diseases, diabetes, accidents and adverse effects, and suicide. Among persons ages 18 and older, 18.4% were smokers. The rate of HIV-related deaths stood at 3.6 per 100,000 population. In 2004, the reported AIDS case rate was about 8.8 per 100,000 population.

Programs for treatment and rehabilitation of alcoholics are administered by the Division of Alcoholism of the Department of Health, under the Executive Office of Human Services. The Division of Communicable Disease Control operates venereal disease clinics throughout the state and provides educational material to schools and other groups. The Division of Drug Rehabilitation administers drug treatment from a statewide network of hospital agencies and self-help groups. The state also runs a lead-poisoning prevention program.

The state's 79 community hospitals had about 16,000 beds in 2003. That year, the average expense for community hospital care was $1,631 per inpatient day. In 2004, 11% of the population was uninsured; in 2006, the state passed requiring all residents to purchase health insurance by 1 July 2007.

In 2004, Massachusetts had 451 doctors per 100,000 people, and 1,201 nurses per 100,000 people in 2005; these rates are some of the highest healthcare worker-population rates in the nation. In 2004, there were a total of 5,143 dentists in the state. Four prominent medical schools are located in the state: Harvard Medical School, Tufts University School of Medicine, Boston University School of Medicine, and the University of Massachusetts School of Medicine.

31 Housing

The state's older housing stock reflects the state's colonial heritage and its ties to English architectural traditions. Two major styles are common: the colonial style, typified by a wood frame, two stories, center hall entry, and center chimney; and the Cape Cod, one-story houses built by fishermen, with shallow basements, shingled roofs, clapboard fronts, and unpainted shingled sides weathered gray by the salt air. Many new houses are still built in these styles.

As of 2004, there were an estimated 2,672,061 housing units in the state, of which 2,435,421 were occupied; 64.6% were owner-occupied. About 52.5% of all housing units were single-family, detached homes. About 37.1% of all units were built before or during 1939. Nearly 42% of all units rely on utility gas for heating and 33.6% use fuel oil or kerosene. It was estimated that 50,724 units lacked telephone service, 7,775 lacked complete plumbing facilities, and 10,402 lacked complete kitchen facilities. The average household size was 2.55 people.

In 2004, some 22,500 new housing units were authorized for construction. The median home value was $331,200, the fourth highest in the United States. The median monthly cost for mortgage owners was $1,645. Renters paid a median of $852 per month.

32 Education

Massachusetts has a long history of support for education. The Boston Latin School opened in 1635 as the first public school in the colonies. Harvard College was founded in 1636 as the first college in the United States. The drive for quality public education in the state was intensified through the efforts of educator Horace Mann, who during the 1830s and 1840s was also a leading force for the improvement of school systems throughout the United States. Today the state boasts some of the most highly regarded private secondary schools and colleges in the country.

In 2004, 86.9% of state residents age 25 or older were high school graduates and 36.7% had completed four or more years of college. Total public school enrollment was estimated at 983,000 in fall 2002 and was expected to drop to 919,000 by fall 2014. Expenditures for public education in 2003/04 were estimated at $11.7 billion, or $10,693 per student, the sixth highest among the 50 states and the District of Columbia.

The early years of statehood saw the development of private academies, where the students could learn more than the basic reading and writing skills that were taught in the town schools at the time. Some of these private preparatory schools remain, including such prestigious institutions as Andover, Deerfield, and Groton. Enrollment in nonpublic schools in fall 2003 totaled 134,708.

As of fall 2002, there were 431,224 students enrolled in college or graduate school. In 2005, Massachusetts had 122 degree-granting institutions. The major public university system is the University of Massachusetts, with campuses at Amherst, Boston, Dartmouth, and Lowell, and a medical school at Worcester. The state has a total of 15 public colleges and universities, while the Massachusetts Board of Regional Community Colleges has 16 campuses.

Harvard University, which was established in Cambridge originally as a college for clergymen and magistrates, has grown to become one of the country's premier institutions. Also located in Cambridge is the Massachusetts Institute of Technology, or MIT. Mount Holyoke College, the first US college for women, was founded in 1837. Other prominent private schools are Amherst College, Boston College, Boston University, Brandeis University, Clark University, Hampshire College, the New England Conservatory of Music, Northeastern University, Smith College, Tufts University, Wellesley College, and Williams College.

Sculptor Nancy Schon of Newton created this depiction of Mrs. Mallard and her ducklings to celebrate the 150th anniversary of Boston Public Garden in 1987. The sculpture is based on the Caldecott Medal winning book Make Way for Ducklings *(1941) by Robert McCloskey.* EPD PHOTOS.

33 Arts

Boston is the center of artistic activity in Massachusetts. The city is the home of several small theaters, some of which offer previews of shows bound for Broadway. Well-known local theater companies include the American Repertory Theatre and the Huntington Theatre. Of the regional theaters scattered throughout the state, the Williamstown Theater in the Berkshires and the Provincetown Theater on Cape Cod are especially noteworthy.

The Boston Symphony, one of the major orchestras in the United States, was founded in 1881. Emmanuel Church in Boston's Back Bay is known for its early music concerts and chamber music by first-rate local and internationally known performers is presented at the New England Conservatory's Jordan Hall and other venues throughout the city. During the summer, the Boston Symphony is the main attraction of the Berkshire Music Festival at Tanglewood in Lenox. An offshoot of the Boston Symphony, the Boston Pops Orchestra, gained fame under the conductorship of Arthur Fiedler. Its mixture of popular, jazz, and light symphonic music continued under the direction of Fiedler's successors, John Williams and Keith Lockhart. Boston is also the headquarters of the Boston Lyric Opera. Prominent in the world of dance are the Boston Ballet Company and the Jacob's Pillow Dance Festival in the Berkshires.

Ploughshares, a literary journal published through Emerson College in Boston, has become well known nationally as a showplace for new writers.

The Massachusetts Cultural Council provides grants and services to support public programs in the arts, sciences, and the humanities. The Massachusetts Foundation for the Humanities was founded in 1974. In 1979, Massachusetts became the first state to establish a lottery solely for funding the arts.

34 Libraries and Museums

The first public library in the United States was established in Boston in 1653. As of the fiscal year ending June 2001, Massachusetts had 371 public library systems, with a total of 490 libraries, of which 119 were branches. The system served 351 towns and cities, and had over 30.4 million volumes. The major city libraries are in Boston, Worcester, and Springfield. The Boston Athenaeum, with 650,000 volumes, is the most noteworthy private library in the state. Harvard University's library system is one of the largest in the world, with 14.3 million volumes in 1999. Other major academic libraries are those of Boston University, the University of Massachusetts (Amherst), Smith College, and Boston College.

In 2000, the state had over 344 museums. Boston houses a number of important museums, among them the Museum of Fine Arts with vast holdings of artwork. These include extensive Far East and French impressionist collections and

American art and furniture; the Isabella Stewart Gardner Museum, and the Museum of Science. Other museums of note are the Whaling Museum in New Bedford, the Bunker Hill Museum near Boston, and the National Basketball Hall of Fame in Springfield. Plymouth Plantation in Plymouth is a recreation of life in the 17th century and Old Sturbridge Village, a working historical farm, displays 18th- and 19th-century artifacts.

35 Communications

The first American post office was established in Boston in 1639 and Alexander Graham Bell first demonstrated the telephone in Boston in 1876. As of 2004, 93.4% of the state's occupied housing units had telephones. In addition, by June of that year, there were 3,919,139 mobile phone subscribers. As of 2003, 64.1% of Massachusetts households had a computer, and 58.1% had Internet access.

The state had 32 major AM stations and 64 major FM stations in 2005, as well as 10 major television stations. In Boston, WGBH is a major producer of programming for the Public Broadcasting Service. In 2000, the Boston metropolitan area had 2,210,580 television-owning households, 80% of which received cable.

36 Press

Publishing milestones that occurred in the state include the first book printed in the English colonies (Cambridge, 1640); the first regularly issued American newspaper, the *Boston News-Letter* (1704); and the first published American novel, William Hill Brown's *The Power of Sympathy* (Worcester, 1789). During the mid-1840s, two noted literary publications made their debut, the *North American Review* and the *Dial*, the latter under the editorial direction of Ralph Waldo Emerson and Margaret Fuller.

As of 2005, there were 32 daily newspapers in the state (including 14 morning, 18 evening). The *Boston Globe*, the most widely read newspaper in the state, has won numerous awards for journalistic excellence on the local and national levels. The *Christian Science Monitor* is highly respected for its coverage of national and international news.

Major newspapers and their average daily circulations in 2005 were the *Boston Globe* (451,471), the *Boston Herald* (240,759), and the *Christian Science Monitor* (60,723). *The Atlantic* (which began publishing in 1857), *Harvard Law Review, Harvard Business Review*, and *New England Journal of Medicine* are other influential publications. Massachusetts is also a center of book publishing, with more than 100 publishing houses, including Little, Brown and Company; Houghton Mifflin; Merriam-Webster; and Harvard University Press.

37 Tourism, Travel & Recreation

In 2004, there were over 31.2 million travelers to and within the state. The travel industry supports over 125,300 jobs.

The greater Boston area was the most popular area for tourists in 2006. A trip to the city might include visits to such old landmarks as the Old North Church, the USS *Constitution*, Paul Revere's House, and such newer attractions as the John Hancock Observatory, the skywalk above the Prudential Tower, Quincy Market, Faneuil Hall, and Copley Place. Boston Common, one

of the oldest public parks in the country, is the most noteworthy municipal park.

About 19% of all trips are made to Cape Cod (Barnstable County). Among its many attractions are beaches, fishing, good dining spots, artists' colonies with arts and crafts fairs, antique shops, and summer theaters. Beaches, fishing, and quaint villages are also the charms of Nantucket Island and Martha's Vineyard.

The Berkshires are the summer home of the Berkshire Music Festival at Tanglewood and the Jacob's Pillow Dance Festival in Lee. Essex County on the North Shore of Massachusetts Bay offers many seaside towns and the art colony of Rockport. Its main city, Salem, contains the Witch House and Museum as well as Nathaniel Hawthorne's House of Seven Gables. Middlesex County, to the west of Boston, holds the university city of Cambridge as well as the battlegrounds of Lexington and Concord. In Concord are the homes of Henry David Thoreau, Ralph Waldo Emerson, and Louisa May Alcott. Norfolk County, south of Boston, has the homes of three US presidents: John Adams and John Quincy Adams in Quincy and John F. Kennedy in Brookline. Plymouth County offers Plymouth Rock, Plymouth Plantation, and a steam-train ride through some cranberry bogs.

Massachusetts has about 79 state parks.

38 Sports

There are five major league professional sports teams in Massachusetts: the Boston Red Sox of Major League Baseball, the New England Patriots of the National Football League, the Boston Celtics of the National Basketball Association, the Boston Bruins of the National Hockey League, and the New England Revolution of

Young girls perform a traditional Irish dance during the St. Patrick's Day Parade in Boston. AP IMAGES.

Major League Soccer. The Celtics are the winningest team in NBA history. They have won the championship 16 times, including the seemingly unbeatable record of eight consecutive titles from 1959 to 1966. The Bruins won the Stanley Cup five times. Additionally, there are minor league hockey teams in Springfield, Worcester, and Lowell.

Suffolk Downs in East Boston features thoroughbred horse racing. Harness racing takes place at the New England Harness Raceway in Foxboro. Dog racing can be seen at Raynham Park in Raynham, Taunton Dog Track in North Dighton, and Wonderland Park in Revere.

Probably the most famous amateur athletic event in the state is the Boston Marathon, a race of more than 26 miles (42 kilometers) held every Patriots' Day (third Monday in April). It attracts many of the world's top long-distance runners. During the summer, a number of boat races are held. Rowing is also popular. Each October this traditional sport is celebrated in a regatta on the Charles River among college students in the Boston/Cambridge area.

In collegiate sports, the University of Massachusetts has become a nationally ranked basketball power; Boston College has appeared in 12 bowl games and the annual Harvard–Yale football game is one of the traditional rites of autumn.

39 Famous Bay Staters

Massachusetts has produced an extraordinary collection of public figures and leaders of thought. Its four US presidents were John Adams (1735–1826), a signer of the Declaration of Independence; his son John Quincy Adams (1767–1848); John Fitzgerald Kennedy (1917–1963), and George Herbert Walker Bush (b.1924).

Great jurists influential in Massachusetts include US Supreme Court Justices Joseph Story (1779–1845); Oliver Wendell Holmes Jr. (1841–1935); Louis D. Brandeis (b.Kentucky, 1856–1941); and Felix Frankfurter (b.Austria, 1882–1965). David Souter (b.1939), was appointed as a Supreme Court justice in 1990.

Literary genius has flourished in Massachusetts. In the 17th century, the colony was the home of poets Anne Bradstreet (1612–1672) and Edward Taylor (1645–1729) and of the theologian Cotton Mather (1663–1728). During the 1800s, Massachusetts was the home of novelists Nathaniel Hawthorne (1804–1864), Louisa May Alcott (b.Pennsylvania, 1832–1888), and Henry James (b.New York, 1843–1916); essayists Ralph Waldo Emerson (1803–1882) and Henry David Thoreau (1817–1862); and poets Henry Wadsworth Longfellow (b.Maine, 1807–1882) and Emily Dickinson (1830–1886). Among 20th-century notables are novelist and short-story writer John Cheever (1912–1982); and poets Robert Lowell (1917–1977), Anne Sexton (1928–1974), and Sylvia Plath (1932–1963). Henry James's elder brother, William (b.New York, 1842–1910), pioneered psychology; and George Santayana (b.Spain, 1863–1952), philosopher and author, grew up in Boston. Mary Baker Eddy (b.New Hampshire, 1821–1910) founded the Church of Christ, Scientist, during the 1870s.

Reformers have abounded in Massachusetts, especially in the 19th century. William Lloyd

Women's rights activist Susan B. Anthony was born in Massachusetts. EPD PHOTOS.

Garrison (1805–1879) was an outstanding abolitionist. Margaret Fuller (1810–1850), and Susan Brownell Anthony (1820–1906) were leading advocates of women's rights. Horace Mann (1796–1859) led the fight for public education; and Mary Lyon (1797–1849) founded Mount Holyoke, the first women's college in the United States. The 20th century reformer and National Association for the Advancement of Colored People (NAACP) leader William Edward Burghardt (W. E. B.) Du Bois (1868–1963) was born in Great Barrington.

Leonard Bernstein (1918–1990) was a composer and conductor of worldwide fame. Arthur Fiedler (1894–1879) was the celebrated conductor of the Boston Pops Orchestra. Composers include William Billings (1746–1800) and

Alan Hovhaness (1911–2000). Louis Henri Sullivan (1856–1924) was an important architect. Painters include John Singleton Copley (1738–1815), James Whistler (1834–1903), and Winslow Homer (1836–1910).

Among the notable scientists associated with Massachusetts are Samuel F. B. Morse (1791–1872), inventor of the telegraph; Elias Howe (1819–1867), inventor of the sewing machine; and Robert Hutchins Goddard (1882–1945), a physicist and rocketry pioneer.

Massachusetts was the birthplace of television journalists Mike Wallace (b.1918) and Barbara Walters (b.1931). Massachusetts-born show business luminaries include director Cecil B. DeMille (1881–1959); actors Walter Brennan (1894–1974), Jack Haley (1901–1979), Bette Davis (1908–1984), and Jack Lemmon (1925–2001); and singers Donna Summer (b.1948) and James Taylor (b.1948). Outstanding among Massachusetts-born athletes was world heavyweight boxing champion Rocky Marciano (Rocco Francis Marchegiano, 1925–1969), who retired undefeated in 1956.

40 Bibliography

BOOKS

Bristow, M. J. *State Songs of America.* Westport, CT: Greenwood Press, 2000.

Deetz, James. *The Times of Their Lives: Life, Love, and Death in Plymouth Colony.* New York: W.H. Freeman, 2000.

Fairley, Melissa. *Massachusetts.* Milwaukee, WI: Gareth Stevens, 2006.

Leotta, Joan. *Massachusetts.* New York: Children's Press, 2001.

LeVert, Suzanne. *Massachusetts.* New York: Benchmark Books, 2000.

McAuliffe, Emily. *Massachusetts Facts and Symbols.* Rev. ed. Mankato, MN: Capstone Press, 2003.

Murray, Julie. *Massachusetts.* Edina, MN: Abdo Publishing, 2006.

Whitehurst, Susan. *The Colony of Massachusetts.* New York: PowerKids Press, 2000.

WEB SITES

Massachusetts Historical Society. www.masshist.org/welcome (accessed March 1, 2007).

Official Website of the Commonwealth of Massachusetts. *Mass.gov.* www.mass.gov (accessed March 1, 2007).

Visit New England. *Massachusetts.* www.visit-massachusetts.com (accessed March 1, 2007).

Michigan

State of Michigan

ORIGIN OF STATE NAME: Possibly derived from the Fox Indian word *mesikami*, meaning "large lake."

NICKNAME: The Wolverine State.

CAPITAL: Lansing.

ENTERED UNION: 26 January 1837 (26th).

OFFICIAL SEAL: The coat of arms surrounded by the words "The Great Seal of the State of Michigan" and the date "A.D. MDCCCXXXV." (1835, the year the state constitution was adopted).

FLAG: The coat of arms centered on a dark blue field, fringed on three sides.

COAT OF ARMS: In the center, a shield depicts a peninsula on which a man stands, at sunrise, holding a rifle. At the top of the shield is the word "Tuebor" (I will defend), beneath it the state motto. Supporting the shield are an elk on the left and a moose on the right. Over the whole, on a crest, is an American eagle beneath the US motto, *E pluribus unum.*

MOTTO: *Si quaeris peninsulam amoenam circumspice* (If you seek a pleasant peninsula, look about you).

SONG: "Michigan, My Michigan" (unofficial).

FLOWER: Apple blossom.

TREE: White pine.

BIRD: Robin.

FISH: Trout.

REPTILE: Painted turtle.

GEM: Chlorastrolite (Isle Royale Greenstone).

ROCK OR STONE: Petoskey stone.

LEGAL HOLIDAYS: New Year's Day, 1 January; Birthday of Martin Luther King Jr., 3rd Monday in January; Presidents' Day, 3rd Monday in February; Memorial Day, last Monday in May; Independence Day, 4 July; Labor Day, 1st Monday in September; Election Day, 1st Tuesday after the first Monday in November in even-numbered years; Veterans' Day, 11 November; Thanksgiving Day, 4th Thursday in November plus one day; Christmas Day, 25 December.

TIME: 7 AM EST = noon GMT; 6 AM CST = noon GMT.

1 Location and Size

Located in the eastern north-central United States, Michigan is the third-largest state east of the Mississippi River and ranks 23rd in size among the 50 states. The total area of Michigan (excluding Great Lakes waters) is 58,527 square miles (151,585 square kilometers), of which land takes up 56,954 square miles (147,511 square kilometers) and inland water 1,573 square miles

(4,074 square kilometers). The state consists of the Upper Peninsula adjoining three of the Great Lakes (Superior, Huron, and Michigan) and the Lower Peninsula, projecting northward between Lakes Michigan, Erie, and Huron. Michigan has islands in Lakes Superior, Huron, and Michigan, and also in the St. Mary's and Detroit Rivers. The state's total boundary length is 1,673 miles (2,692 kilometers). The total freshwater shoreline is 3,121 miles (5,023 kilometers).

2 Topography

Michigan's two peninsulas are generally level land masses, including flat lowlands in the eastern portion of both peninsulas, higher land in the western part of the Lower Peninsula, and hilly uplands in the Upper Peninsula. The state's highest point, at 1,979 feet (603 meters), is Mt. Arvon, in Baraga County. The state's lowest point, 572 feet (174 meters), is found in southeastern Michigan along Lake Erie.

Michigan's political boundaries extend into four of the five Great Lakes (all but Lake Ontario), giving the state jurisdiction over portions of these lakes. In addition, Michigan has about 35,000 inland lakes and ponds, the largest of which is Houghton Lake, on the Lower Peninsula, with an area of 31 square miles (80 square kilometers).

The state's leading river is the Grand, about 260 miles (420 kilometers) long, flowing through the Lower Peninsula into Lake Michigan. Other major rivers of the Lower Peninsula include the Kalamazoo, Muskegon, Saginaw, and Huron. Most major rivers in the Upper Peninsula (including the longest, the Menominee) flow southward into Lake Michigan. Tahquamenon Falls, in the

Michigan Population Profile

Total population estimate in 2006:	10,095,643
Population change, 2000–06:	1.6%
Hispanic or Latino†:	3.8%
Population by race	
One race:	98.4%
White:	80.0%
Black or African American:	14.0%
American Indian /Alaska Native:	0.6%
Asian:	2.3%
Native Hawaiian / Pacific Islander:	0.0%
Some other race:	1.5%
Two or more races:	1.6%

Population by Age Group

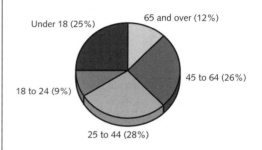

Under 18 (25%)
65 and over (12%)
45 to 64 (26%)
18 to 24 (9%)
25 to 44 (28%)

Major Cities by Population

City	Population	% change 2000–05
Detroit	886,671	-6.8
Grand Rapids	193,780	-2.0
Warren	135,311	-2.1
Sterling Heights	128,034	2.9
Flint	118,551	-5.1
Lansing	115,518	-3.0
Ann Arbor	113,271	-0.7
Livonia	97,977	-2.6
Dearborn	94,090	-3.8
Westland	85,623	-1.1

Notes: †A person of Hispanic or Latino origin may be of any race. NA indicates that data are not available. **Sources:** U.S. Census Bureau. *American Community Survey* and *Population Estimates.* www.census.gov/ (accessed March 2007).

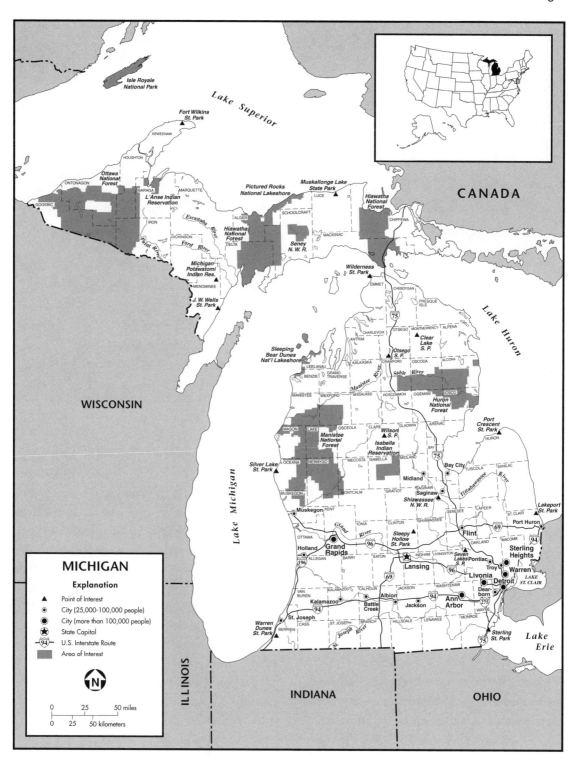

MICHIGAN

Explanation

▲ Point of Interest

◉ City (25,000-100,000 people)

◉ City (more than 100,000 people)

★ State Capital

—94— U.S. Interstate Route

⬛ Area of Interest

N

| 0 | 25 | 50 miles |
| 0 | 25 | 50 kilometers |

Isle Royale National Park

Lake Superior

Fort Wilkins St. Park

KEWEENAW

HOUGHTON

Ottawa National Forest

ONTONAGON

GOGEBIC

BARAGA

MARQUETTE

L'Anse Indian Reservation

Pictured Rocks National Lakeshore

Muskallonge Lake State Park

LUCE

Hiawatha National Forest

CHIPPEWA

CANADA

IRON

DICKINSON

Escanaba River

Ford River

ALGER

SCHOOLCRAFT

Hiawatha National Forest

DELTA

Seney N.W.R.

MACKINAC

Paint River

Michigan Potawatomi Indian Res.

MENOMINEE

J. W. Wells St. Park

Wilderness St. Park

EMMET

CHEBOYGAN

PRESQUE ISLE

Lake Huron

75

CHARLEVOIX

OTSEGO

MONTMORENCY

ALPENA

Clear Lake S. P.

ANTRIM

Otsego S. P.

CRAWFORD

OSCODA

ALCONA

Sleeping Bear Dunes Nat'l Lakeshore

LEELANAU

BENZIE

GRAND TRAVERSE

KALKASKA

Manistee River

Sable River

ROSCOMMON

OGEMAW

IOSCO

Huron National Forest

MANISTEE

WEXFORD

MISSAUKEE

WISCONSIN

Lake Michigan

MASON

LAKE

OSCEOLA

CLARE

GLADWIN

ARENAC

Port Crescent St. Park

HURON

Wilson S. P.

Manistee National Forest

Isabella Indian Reservation

OCEANA

NEWAYGO

MECOSTA

ISABELLA

MIDLAND

BAY

Bay City

TUSCOLA

SANILAC

Silver Lake St. Park

Midland

Tittabawassee River

MUSKEGON

MONTCALM

GRATIOT

Saginaw

Shiawassee N.W.R.

LAPEER

ST. CLAIR

Lakeport St. Park

Muskegon

KENT

IONIA

CLINTON

SHIAWASSEE

GENESEE

Port Huron

69

Grand River

Sleepy Hollow St. Park

Flint

OAKLAND

MACOMB

94

Holland

196

Grand Rapids

ALLEGAN

BARRY

EATON

Lansing

INGHAM

LIVINGSTON

96

Seven Lakes S. P.

Pontiac

Sterling Heights

Troy

Warren

Livonia

Dearborn

Detroit

LAKE ST. CLAIR

VAN BUREN

KALAMAZOO

CALHOUN

JACKSON

WASHTENAW

69

Kalamazoo

Battle Creek

Albion

Jackson

Ann Arbor

94

275

WAYNE

Warren Dunes St. Park

St. Joseph

BERRIEN

CASS

ST. JOSEPH

BRANCH

HILLSDALE

LENAWEE

MONROE

St. Joseph River

Sterling St. Park

75

Lake Erie

ILLINOIS

INDIANA

OHIO

The Sleeping Bear Dunes overlook Lake Michigan. COPYRIGHT © 2006 BY KELLY A. QUIN.

eastern part of the Upper Peninsula, is the largest of the state's more than 150 waterfalls.

Most of the many islands belonging to Michigan are located in northern Lake Michigan and in Lake Huron. In northern Lake Michigan, Beaver Island is the largest, while Drummond Island, off the eastern tip of the Upper Peninsula, is the largest island in the northern Lake Huron area.

3 Climate

Michigan has a temperate climate with well-defined seasons. The warmest temperatures and longest frost-free period are found most generally in the southern part of the Lower Peninsula.

Detroit's temperatures range from 23°F (-5°C) in January to 72°F (22°C) in July. Colder temperatures prevail in the more northerly regions. Sault Ste. Marie has temperature ranges from 13°F (-11°C) in January to 64°F (18°C) in July. The coldest temperature ever recorded in the state was -51°F (-46°C), registered at Vanderbilt on 9 February 1934. The all-time high of 112°F (44°C) was recorded at Mio on 13 July 1936. Both sites are located in the interior of the Lower Peninsula, away from the moderating influence of the Great Lakes.

Detroit has an average annual precipitation of 32.9 inches (83.6 centimeters). Rainfall tends to decrease as one moves northward. The greatest snowfall is found in the extreme north-

Michigan Population by Race

Census 2000 was the first national census in which the instructions to respondents said, "Mark one or more races." This table shows the number of people who are of one, two, or three or more races. For those claiming two races, the number of people belonging to the various categories is listed. The U.S. government conducts a census of the population every ten years.

	Number	Percent
Total population	9,938,444	100.0
One race	9,746,028	98.1
Two races	180,824	1.8
White *and* Black or African American	35,461	0.4
White *and* American Indian/Alaska Native	47,122	0.5
White *and* Asian	20,599	0.2
White *and* Native Hawaiian/Pacific Islander	1,497	—
White *and* some other race	51,880	0.5
Black or African American *and* American Indian/Alaska Native	8,436	0.1
Black or African American *and* Asian	2,360	—
Black or African American *and* Native Hawaiian/Pacific Islander	453	—
Black or African American *and* some other race	6,138	0.1
American Indian/Alaska Native *and* Asian	954	—
American Indian/Alaska Native *and* Native Hawaiian/Pacific Islander	83	—
American Indian/Alaska Native *and* some other race	1,062	—
Asian *and* Native Hawaiian/Pacific Islander	936	—
Asian *and* some other race	3,625	—
Native Hawaiian/Pacific Islander *and* some other race	218	—
Three or more races	11,592	0.1

Source: U.S. Census Bureau. *Census 2000: Redistricting Data.* Press release issued by the Redistricting Data Office. Washington, D.C., March, 2001. A dash (—) indicates that the percent is less than 0.1.

ern areas where cloud cover created by cold air blowing over the warmer Lake Superior waters causes frequent heavy snow along the northern coast. Lake Michigan's water temperatures create a snow belt along the west coast of the Lower Peninsula.

Cloudy days are more common in Michigan than in most states, in part because of the condensation of water vapor from the Great Lakes. The southern half of the Lower Peninsula is an area of heavy thunderstorm activity. Tornados occur from late spring through early summer.

4 Plants and Animals

Maple, birch, hemlock, aspen, spruce, and fir trees predominate in the Upper Peninsula.

Maple, birch, aspen, pine, and beech are common in the lower. Elms have largely disappeared because of disease. The white pine (the state tree) and red pine have been replaced in cutover lands by aspen and birch.

Strawberries, raspberries, blueberries, and cranberries are among the fruit-bearing plants and shrubs that grow wild in many areas of the state, as do mushrooms and wild asparagus. The state flower is the apple blossom. Wild flowers also abound, with as many as 400 varieties found in a single county. As of April 2006, eight Michigan plant species were listed as threatened or endangered, including the American hart's-tongue fern, dwarf lake iris, Michigan Monkey-flower, and Eastern prairie fringed orchid.

Despite intensive hunting, the deer population remains high. Other game animals include the common cottontail, snowshoe hare, and raccoon. In addition to the raccoon, important native furbearers are the river otter and the beaver. Moose are now confined to Isle Royale, as are nearly all the remaining wolves, which once roamed throughout the state. More than 300 types of birds have been observed. The robin is the state bird. Ruffed grouse, bob-white quail, and various ducks and geese are hunted extensively. The most notable bird is Kirtland's warbler, which nests only in a 60-square mile (155 square kilometer) section of jack-pine forest in north-central Michigan.

Reptiles include the massasauga, the state's only poisonous snake. Whitefish, perch, and lake trout (the state fish) are native to the Great Lakes, while perch, bass, and pike are found in inland waters. Rainbow and brown trout have been introduced, and in the late 1960s, the state successfully introduced several species of salmon.

In 2006, the US Fish and Wildlife Service listed 13 Michigan animals as threatened or endangered. These included the Indiana bat, two species of beetle, two species of butterfly, the gray wolf, bald eagle, piping plover, and Kirkland's warbler.

5 Environmental Protection

The Michigan Department of Natural Resources (DNR) is responsible for the administration of hundreds of programs affecting every aspect of the environment. The mission of the department is to conserve and develop the state's natural resources and to protect and enhance the state's environmental quality in order to provide clean air, clean water, productive land, and healthy life. Additionally, the department seeks to provide quality recreational opportunities to the people of Michigan through the effective management of state recreational lands and parks, boating facilities, and population of fish and wildlife.

In 2003, Michigan had 343 hazardous waste sites listed in the Environmental Protection Agency's database, 66 of which were on the National Priorities List, as of 2006.

6 Population

In 2005, Michigan ranked eighth in population in the Untied States with an estimated total of 10,095,643 residents. The population is projected to reach 10.71 million by 2025. The population density in 2004 was 178.5 persons per square mile (68.9 persons per square kilometer). Also in 2004, the median age was 36.6. In 2005, 12% of all residents were 65 or older, while 25% were 18 or younger.

About half the population was concentrated in the Detroit metropolitan area. The 2005 population in Detroit was estimated at 866,671, placing the city as the 11th largest city in the country. Although Detroit's population has been steadily shrinking since it reached about 1.85 million in 1950, the metropolitan population has continued to grow. In 1995, the Detroit metropolitan area had 4.3 million. In 2004 it stood at 4.49 million. Other Michigan cities with their 2005 populations include Grand Rapids, 193,780; Warren, 135,311; Sterling Heights, 128,034; Flint, 118,551; Lansing (the capital), 115,518; and Ann Arbor, 113,271.

7 Ethnic Groups

According to the 2000 census, there were 58,479 American Indian residents in the state, including Eskimos and Aleuts. The Ottawa, Ojibwa, and Potawatomi have been principal groups with active tribal organizations. American Indians accounted for 0.6% of the state's population in 2004. The black population in 2000 totaled about 1,412,742. In 2006 they accounted for 14.0% of the state's population. There were also 323,877 Hispanics and Latinos living in the state, of whom 220,769 were of Mexican descent. In 2006, Hispanics and Latinos accounted for 3.8% of the state's residents. The state's Asian population had a total number of 176,510 people, including 54,631 Asian Indians, 17,377 Filipinos, 33,189 Chinese, 20,886 Koreans, 11,288 Japanese, and 13,673 Vietnamese. Asians in 2006 accounted for 2.3% of the state's resident population. Pacific Islanders numbered 2,692.

Although state residents of first- or second-generation European descent are decreasing in number, there are still active ethnic groups in many cities. Detroit continues to have numerous well-defined ethnic neighborhoods and Hamtramck, a city surrounded by Detroit, is still dominated by its Polish population. Frankenmuth is the site of an annual German festival. In the Upper Peninsula, the Finnish culture dominates in rural areas. In the iron and copper mining regions, descendants of immigrants from Cornwall in England and persons of Scandinavian background predominate. The 2000 census found that 523,589 state residents (5.3% of the population) were foreign born.

8 Languages

Except for the huge industrial area in southeastern Michigan, English in the state is remarkably uniform in its retention of the major Northern dialect features of upper New York and western New England. Common are such Northern terms as *pail, wishbone, darning needle* (dragonfly), and *mouth organ* (harmonica). Common also are such pronunciations as the /ah/ vowel in *fog* and *on* and the /aw/ vowel in *forest* and *orange. Southern blacks have introduced a regional variety of English in the southeast that has become a controversial educational concern. In this dialect pen* and *pin* sound alike. The loss of /r/ after a vowel means that words such as *cart* and *cot* also sound alike.

In 2000, of the state's population five years old or older, 91.6% spoke only English at home. Other languages spoken at home, with the number of speakers, included Spanish, 246,688; Arabic, 75,412; German, 52,366; Polish, 40,372; and French, 38,914.

9 Religions

The Roman Catholic Church was the only organized religion in Michigan until the 19th century. Detroit's St. Anne's parish, established in 1701, is the second-oldest Catholic parish in the country. The Lutheran denomination was introduced by German and Scandinavian immigrants. Dutch settlers were affiliated with the Reformed Church in America.

In 2004, Michigan had 2,265,286 Roman Catholics. Among Protestant denominations, the largest groups were the Missouri Synod Lutherans, with about 244,231 adherents (2000 data), and the United Methodists, with

The Mackinac Bridge in Mackinac City. PHOTOGRAPH BY GARY BASSETT.

about 171,916 adherents, in 2004. Evangelical Lutherans numbered about 160,836 adherents in 2000, while the Christian Reformed Church had about 112,711 members and the Presbyterian Church USA had 104,471 that same year. The Seventh Day Adventists, who had their world headquarters in Battle Creek from 1855 to 1903, numbered 37,712 in 2000. The Jewish community had about 110,000 members. Over 5.7 million people (about 58% of the population) were not counted as members of any religious organization.

10 Transportation

Michigan's inhabitants have always depended heavily on the Great Lakes for transportation. Although extensive networks of railroads and highways now reach into all parts of the state, the Great Lakes remain major avenues of commerce.

The first railroad company in the Midwest was chartered in Michigan in 1830 and six years later the Erie and Kalamazoo, operating between Toledo, Ohio, and Adrian, became the first railroad in service west of the Appalachians. In 2003, Class I railroad trackage totaled 2,752 miles (4,430 kilometers) out of a total of 4,495 miles (7,236 kilometers). Most railroad passenger service is provided by Amtrak. As of 2006, Amtrak provided service to 23 stations in the state, connecting them to Chicago. Freight is carried by the state's 23 railroads, of which four are Class I. Railroads have been used only to a limited degree in the Detroit area as commuter carriers.

As of 2004, the state had 122,382 miles (197,035 kilometers) of roads. Major expressways included I-94 (Detroit to Chicago), I-96 (Detroit to Grand Rapids), and I-75 (from the Ohio border to Sault Ste. Marie). In 2004, there were about 4.632 million registered passenger cars, around 3.613 million trucks, some 10,000 buses, and about 227,000 motorcycles. Licensed drivers numbered 7,103,404 during the same year.

The completion in 1957 of the Mackinac Bridge, the fourth-longest suspension span in the world, eliminated the major barrier to easy movement between the state's two peninsulas. The International Bridge at Sault Ste. Marie, the Blue-Water Bridge at Port Huron, the Ambassador Bridge at Detroit, and the Detroit-Windsor Tunnel all link Michigan with Canada.

The opening of the St. Lawrence Seaway in 1959 made it possible for a large number of oceangoing vessels to dock at Michigan ports. In 2004, major ports were at Detroit, Presque Isle, Escanaba, and Calcite.

The Ford Airport at Dearborn in the 1920s had one of the first air passenger facilities and was the base for some of the first regular airmail service. In 2005, the state had 381 airports, 95 heliports, 2 STOLports (Short Take-Off and Landing), and 7 seaplane bases. The state's major airport is Detroit Metropolitan Wayne County Airport, with 17,046,178 passenger boardings in 2004.

11 History

In the early 17th century, when European exploration began, Michigan's Lower Peninsula was practically uninhabited. The Algonkian-speaking Ojibwa and Menomini inhabited portions of the Upper Peninsula. Other groups, including the Winnebago, Sioux, and Huron, later settled in the area. For two centuries after the first Europeans came to Michigan, the Native Americans remained a vital force in the area's development, providing furs for trade and serving as potential allies in wars between rival colonial powers. However, after the War of 1812, when the fur trade declined and the possibility of war receded, the value of the Indians to the white settlers diminished. Between 1795 and 1842, tribal lands in Michigan were ceded to the federal government, and the Huron, Miami, and many Potawatomi were removed from the area.

The first European explorer known to have reached Michigan was a Frenchman, Etienne Brulé, who explored the Sault Ste. Marie area around 1620. Missionary and fur trading posts—and, later, military forts—were established at Sault Ste. Marie by Father Jacques Marquette in 1668. In 1701, Antoine Laumet de la Mothe Cadillac founded a permanent settlement at the site of present-day Detroit.

Following France's defeat in the French and Indian War, and an unsuccessful Native American rebellion, the British were in firm control of the area by 1764. They continued to occupy it until 13 years after the American Revolution was ended by the Treaty of Paris in

The Grand Traverse Lighthouse, located at the tip of the Leelanau Peninsula, has safely guided ships for 150 years.
COPYRIGHT © 2006 BY KELLY A. QUIN.

1783, which gave Michigan and other territories to the United States. In the summer of 1796, the United States took possession of Michigan.

Statehood However, during the War of 1812, the British captured Detroit, holding the settlement until September 1813, when it was recaptured. But full American control of Michigan would not take place until the Treaty of Ghent was signed at the end of 1814. With the opening in 1825 of the Erie Canal, settlers for the first time pushed into the interior of southern Michigan. By 1833, Michigan had attained a population of 60,000 qualifying it for statehood. After the settlement of boundary disputes with Indiana and Ohio—including the so-called Toledo War, in which no one was killed—Michigan became part of the Union on 26 January 1837.

In July 1854, antislavery Democrats joined with members of the Whig and Free-Soil parties to organize Michigan's Republican Party, which swept into office that year, and except for rare exceptions, controlled the state until the 1930s. Approximately 90,000 Michigan men served in the Union army, taking part in all major actions of the Civil War.

Michigan grew rapidly in economic importance. Agriculture sparked the initial growth of the new state and was responsible for its rapid increase in population. By 1850, the southern half of the Lower Peninsula was filling up. Less than two decades later, exploitation of vast pine forests in northern Michigan had made the state the top lumber producer in the United States. Settlers were also attracted to the area by the discovery of rich mineral deposits.

Industrialization Toward the end of the 19th century, new opportunities in manufacturing opened up. The sudden popularity of Ransom E. Olds's Oldsmobile inspired a host of Michigan residents to produce similar practical, relatively inexpensive automobiles. By 1904, Detroit's Cadillac (initially a cheap car), the first Fords, and the Oldsmobile made Michigan the leading automobile producer in the country—and, later, in the world.

Industrialization brought with it urbanization. The census of 1920 for the first time showed a majority of the state's people living in towns and cities. Nearly all industrial development was concentrated in the southern third of the state, particularly the southeastern Detroit area. The northern two-thirds of the state, where nothing took up the slack left by the decline in lumber and mining output, steadily lost population and became increasingly troubled economically.

The onset of the depression of the 1930s had devastating effects in Michigan. The market for automobiles collapsed. By 1932, half of Michigan's industrial workers were unemployed. The ineffectiveness of the Republican state and federal governments during the crisis led to a landslide victory for the Democrats. Factory workers, driven by the desire for greater job security, joined the recruiting campaign launched by

the new Congress of Industrial Organizations (CIO). By 1941, the United Automobile Workers (UAW) had organized the entire auto industry, and Michigan had been converted to a strongly pro-union state.

By the mid-1950s, the Democrats controlled practically all statewide elective offices. However, Republicans maintained their control of the legislature and frustrated the efforts of Democratic administrations to institute social reforms. In the 1960s, as a result of US Supreme Court rulings, the legislature was reapportioned. This shifted a majority of legislative seats into urban areas and enabled the Democrats generally to control the legislature since that time.

1980s–2000s The nationwide recession of the early 1980s hit Michigan harder than most other states because of its effect on the auto industry. Auto makers had already suffered heavy losses as a result of their inability to foresee the decline of the big luxury cars and because of the increasing share of the American auto market captured by foreign, mostly Japanese, manufacturers. During the late 1970s and the first two years of the 1980s, US automakers were forced to lay off hundreds of thousands of workers, tens of thousands of whom left the state. Many smaller businesses, dependent on the auto industry, closed their doors, adding to the unemployment problem.

When Governor James J. Blanchard took office in 1983, he was faced with the immediate tasks of saving Michigan from bankruptcy and reducing the unemployment rate, which had averaged more than 15% in 1982 (60% above the US average). The new governor was forced to institute budget cuts totaling $225 million and to lay off thousands of government workers.

Michigan Governors: 1835–2007

1835–1840	Stevens Thomson Mason	Democrat	1905–1910	Fred Maltby Warner	Republican
1840–1841	William Woodbridge	Whig	1911–1912	Chase Salmon Osborn	Republican
1841	James Wright Gordon	Whig	1913–1916	Woodbridge Nathan Ferris	Democrat
1842–1846	John Stewart Barry	Democrat	1917–1920	Albert Edson Sleeper	Republican
1846–1847	Alpheus Felch	Democrat	1921–1926	Alexander Joseph Groesbeck	Republican
1847	William L. Greenly	Democrat	1927–1930	Fred Warren Green	Republican
1848–1850	Epaphroditus Ransom	Democrat	1931–1932	Wilber Marion Brucker	Republican
1850–1851	John Stewart Barry	Democrat	1933–1934	William Alfred Comstock	Democrat
1852–1853	Robert McClelland	Democrat	1935–1936	Frank Dwight Fitzgerald	Republican
1853–1854	Andrew Parsons	Democrat	1937–1938	Francis William Murphy	Democrat
1855–1858	Kinsley Scott Bingham	Republican	1939	Frank Dwight Fitzgerald	Republican
1859–1860	Moses Wisner	Republican	1939–1940	Luren Dudley Dickenson	Republican
1861–1864	Austin Blair	Republican	1941–1942	Murray Delos Van Wagoner	Democrat
1865–1868	Henry Howland Crapo	Republican	1943–1946	Harry Francis Kelly	Republican
1869–1872	Henry Porter Baldwin	Republican	1947–1948	Kim Sigler	Republican
1873–1876	John Judson Bagley	Republican	1949–1960	Gerhard Mennen Williams	Democrat
1877–1880	Charles Miller Croswell	Republican	1961–1962	John Burley Swainson	Democrat
1881–1882	David Howell Jerome	Republican	1963–1969	George Wilcken Romney	Republican
1883–1884	Josiah William Begole	Fusion	1969–1983	William Grawn Milliken	Republican
1885–1886	Russell Alexander Alger	Republican	1983–1991	James Johnston Blanchard	Democrat
1887–1890	Cyrus Gray Luce	Republican	1991–2002	John Engler	Republican
1891–1892	Edward Baruch Winans	Democrat	2002–	Jennifer Granholm	Democrat
1893–1896	John Tyler Rich	Republican			
1897–1900	Hazen Stuart Pingree	Republican			
1901–1904	Aaron Thomas Bliss	Republican			

Also, at his urging, the state legislature increased Michigan's income tax by 38%.

By May 1984, Michigan's unemployment rate dropped to 11.3%, but the state faced the difficult task of restructuring its economy to lessen its dependence on the auto industry. By the late 1980s, there were signs of success. Less than 25% of wage earners worked in factories in 1988, a drop from 30% in 1978. Despite continued layoffs and plant closings by auto manufacturers between 1982 and 1988, Michigan added half a million more jobs than it lost. The state established a $100 million job-retraining program to upgrade the skills of displaced factory workers, and contributed $5 million to a joint job-training program created by General Motors and the United Automobile Workers.

Despite moves to modernize and diversify the state's economy, by the mid-1990s Michigan remained heavily dependent upon the automobile industry, which produced 28% of all motor vehicles manufactured within the United States.

By 1999, Michigan's economy was on the rise. Unemployment that year dropped to 3.8%, but new challenges had arisen by 2000, regarding the state's educational system, the preservation of farmland from urban sprawl, and in the cleanup and conservation of the Great Lakes system in cooperation with neighboring states and Canada.

In 2002, the Democrats retook the governorship, with the election of Jennifer Granholm, Michigan's first woman governor. Granholm pledged balance the state's budget and create a region that would attract technology companies

Michigan Presidential Vote by Political Parties, 1948–2004

YEAR	MICHIGAN WINNER	DEMOCRAT	REPUBLICAN	PROGRESSIVE	SOCIALIST	PROHIBITION
1948	Dewey (R)	1,003,448	1,038,595	46,515	6,063	13,052
					SOC. WORKERS	
1952	*Eisenhower (R)	1,230,657	1,551,529	3,922	655	10,331
1956	*Eisenhower (R)	1,359,898	1,713,647	—	—	6,923
				SOC. LABOR		
1960	*Kennedy (D)	1,687,269	1,620,428	1,718	4,347	2,029
1964	*Johnson (D)	2,136,615	1,060,152	1,704	3,817	
						AMERICAN IND.
1968	Humphrey (D)	1,593,082	1,370,665	1,762	4,099	331,968
						AMERICAN
1972	*Nixon (R)	1,459,435	1,961,721	2,437	1,603	63,321
				PEOPLE'S		LIBERTARIAN
1976	Ford (R)	1,696,714	1,893,742	3,504	1,804	5,406
				CITIZENS	COMMUNIST	
1980	*Reagan (R)	1,661,532	1,915,225	11,930	3,262	41,597
1984	*Reagan (R)	1,529,638	2,251,571	1,191	—	10,055
				NEW ALLIANCE	WORKERS LEAGUE	
1988	*Bush (R)	1,675,783	1,965,486	2,513	1,958	18,336
				IND. (PEROT)	TISCH IND. CITIZENS	
1992	*Clinton (D)	1,871,182	1,554,940	824,813	8,263	10,175
1996	*Clinton (D)	1,989,653	1,481,212	336,670	—	27,670
					GREEN	
2000	Gore (D)	2,179,418	1,953,139	—	84,165	16,711
2004	Kerry (D)	2,479,183	2,313,746	—	5,325	10,552

*Won US presidential election

to Michigan, mainly biotechnology and pharmaceutical firms. Granholm was reelected in 2006.

12 State Government

The legislature consists of a senate with 38 members, elected for terms of 4 years, and a house of representatives with 110 members, elected for terms of 2 years. Legislation may be adopted by a majority of each house, but to override a governor's veto, a two-thirds vote of the members of each house is required. Elected executive officials include the governor and lieutenant governor (who run jointly), secretary of state, and attorney general, all serving four-year terms. The governor is limited to two consecutive terms.

Legislative action is completed when a bill has been passed by both houses of the legislature and signed by the governor. A bill also becomes law if not signed by the governor after a 14-day period when the legislature is in session. The governor may stop passage of a bill by vetoing it or, if the legislature adjourns before the 14-day period expires, by refusing to sign it.

The governor's salary, as of December 2004 was $177,000, and the legislative salary was $77,400.

13 Political Parties

From its birth in 1854 through 1932, the Republican Party dominated state politics. But the problems caused by the Great Depression in the 1930s revitalized the Democratic Party and made Michigan a strong two-party state. Most labor organizations, led by the powerful United Automobile Workers union, have generally supported the Democratic Party since the 1930s. But in recent years, moderate Republicans have had considerable success in attracting support among previously Democratic voters.

Ronald Reagan won 49% of the state's popular vote in 1980 and 59% in 1984. Michigan elected Republican George H. W. Bush in 1988, but voted for Democrat Bill Clinton in 1992 and 1996 and Al Gore in 2000. In the latter election, Gore received 51% of the vote and Republican George W. Bush trailed with 47% of the vote. In 2004, John Kerry received 51% of the vote to George W. Bush's 48%. In November 2002, Democrat Jennifer Granholm became Michigan's first female governor. She was reelected in 2006. In 2004 there were 7,164,000 registered voters. There is no party registration in the state. The state's senators are Democrat Carl Levin and Democrat Debbie Stabenow. After the 2006 elections, the state's 15-member US House delegation consisted of six Democrats and nine Republicans. On the state level, following the 2006 elections, there were 17 Democrats and 21 Republicans in the senate, and 58 Democrats and 52 Republicans in the house. Thirty women were elected to the state legislature in 2006; they represented 20.3% of the total.

14 Local Government

In 2005 there were 83 counties, 533 municipal governments, 734 public school districts, and 366 special districts. In 2002 there were also 1,242 townships. Each county is administered by a county board of commissioners. Executive authority is vested in five officers elected for four-year terms: the sheriff, prosecuting attorney, treasurer, clerk, and registrar of deeds. Some counties place overall administrative responsibility in the hands of a county manager or administrator.

Most cities establish their own form of government under an adopted charter. Some charters provide for the election of a mayor; other cities have chosen the council-manager system. Township government, its powers strictly limited by state law, consists of a supervisor, clerk, treasurer, and up to four trustees.

15 Judicial System

Michigan's highest court is the state supreme court, consisting of seven justices elected for eight-year terms. The chief justice is elected by the members of the court. The high court hears cases on appeal from lower state courts and also administers the state's entire court system. Unless the supreme court agrees to review a court of appeals ruling, the latter's decision is final.

The major trial courts in the state as of 1999 were the circuit courts. The circuit courts have original jurisdiction in all felony criminal cases, civil cases involving sums of more than $10,000, and divorces. A special division of the circuit court was created in 1998 to better serve families and individuals. Circuit courts also hear appeals from lower courts and state administrative agencies. Probate courts have original jurisdiction in cases involving juveniles and dependents, and also handle wills and estates, adoptions, and commitments of the mentally ill.

In 2004, Michigan's violent crime rate (murder/nonnegligent manslaughter, forcible rape, robbery, aggravated assault) was 490.2 incidents per 100,000 population. There were 48,883 prisoners in state or federal correctional facilities as of 31 December 2004. In 1846, Michigan became the first state to abolish the death penalty, and subsequent efforts to reinstate it have failed as of 2006.

16 Migration

The earliest European immigrants were the French and English. The successive opening of interior lands for farming, lumbering, mining, and manufacturing proved an irresistible attraction for hundreds of thousands of immigrants after the War of 1812, principally Germans, Canadians, English, Irish, and Dutch. During the second half of the 19th century, lumbering and mining opportunities in northern Michigan attracted large numbers of Cornishmen, Norwegians, Swedes, and Finns. The growth of manufacturing in southern Michigan at the end of the century brought many Poles, Italians, Russians, Belgians, and Greeks to the state. After World War II, many more Europeans immigrated to Michigan, plus smaller groups of Mexicans, other Spanish-speaking peoples from Latin America, and large numbers of Arabic-speaking peoples, particularly in Detroit, who by the late 1970s were more numerous there than in any other US city.

Between 1990 and 1998, Michigan had a net loss of 190,000 in domestic migration and a net gain of 87,000 in international migration. In the period 2000–05, net international migration was 122,901, while net domestic migration for the same period was -165,084, for a net loss of 42,183.

17 Economy

Michigan's dependence on automobile production has caused grave and persistent economic problems since the 1950s. Michigan's unemployment rates in times of recession have far exceeded the national average, since auto sales are among the hardest hit in such periods. Although the state was relatively prosperous during the record automotive production years of the 1960s and 1970s, the high cost of gasoline and the encroachment of imports on domestic car sales had disastrous effects by 1980. By that time it became apparent that the state's future economic health required greater diversification of industry.

Agriculture, still dominant in the rural areas of southern Michigan, remains an important element in the state's economy. In northern Michigan, forestry and mining continue, but generally at levels far below earlier boom periods. By the early 1990s, both the trade and service sectors employed more people than the manufacturing industry. In 2002, Michigan's economy lagged behind that of the nation.

The gross state product (GSP) in 2004 was $372.169 billion, of which manufacturing accounted for the largest portion at 20.4% of GSP, followed by the real estate sector at 11.5%, and professional and technical services at 7.7% of GSP.

Of the state's 213,104 businesses that had employees, 98.4% were small companies.

18 Income

In 2004, Michigan ranked 23rd among the 50 states and the District of Columbia with a per capita (per person) income of $32,079, which

Ford Motor Company plant in Wixom, Michigan. AP IMAGES.

was below the national average of $33,050. The three-year average median household income for 2002 through 2004 was $44,476, compared to the national average of $44,473. For the same period, 12.1% of the state's residents lived below the federal poverty level, compared to the national average of 12.4%.

19 Industry

The rise of the auto industry in the early 20th century completed the transformation of Michigan into one of the most important manufacturing areas in the world. In 2004, the total shipment value of all products manufactured in the state was $220.454 billion. Of that total, the transportation equipment manufacturing sector that same year accounted for $111.568 billion, or 50.6%, followed by machinery manufacturing at $17.549 billion, and fabricated metal product at $14.024 billion. In 2004, motor vehicles and equipment accounted for 39.4% of the state's manufacturing payroll.

The Detroit metropolitan area is the state's major industrial region, which includes not only a heavy concentration of auto-related plants, but also major steel, chemical, and pharmaceutical industries, among others.

In 2004, Michigan's manufacturing sector employed 651,947 people. Of that total, some 202,998 were employed in the transportation equipment manufacturing sector.

20 Labor

In April 2006, the seasonally adjusted civilian labor force in Michigan numbered 5,157,600, with approximately 369,500 workers unemployed, yielding an unemployment rate of 7.2%, compared to the national average of 4.7% for the same period. For that same date, early figures for nonfarm employment showed that: construction accounted for 4.3% of the labor force; 15% was in manufacturing; 18.1% was in trade, transportation, and public utilities; 5% in finance activities; 13.6% in professional and business services; 13% in educational and health services; 9.4% in leisure and hospitality services; and 15.3% in government.

Michigan's most powerful and influential industrial union since the 1930s has been the United Automobile Workers (UAW). Its national headquarters is in Detroit. The union has been a dominant force in the state Democratic Party. The successful sit-down strike by the United Automobile Workers against General Motors in 1936–37 marked the first major victory of the new Congress of Industrial Organizations. Since then, a strong labor movement has provided manufacturing workers in Michigan with some of the most favorable working conditions in the country.

In recent years, as government employees and teachers have been organized, unions and associations representing these groups have become increasingly influential. Certain crafts and trades were organized in Michigan in the 19th century, with one national labor union, the Brotherhood of Locomotive Engineers, founded in 1863, but efforts to organize workers in the lumber and mining industries were generally unsuccessful.

In 2005, a total of 880,000 of Michigan's 4,288,000 employed wage and salary workers were members of unions. This represented 20.5% of those so employed, compared to the national average that year of 12%.

21 Agriculture

In 2005, Michigan's agricultural income was estimated at over $3.9 billion, placing Michigan 22nd among the 50 states. About 60% came from crops and the rest from livestock and livestock products. Dairy products, nursery products, cattle, corn, and soybeans were the principal commodities. In 2004, the state ranked second in output of tart cherries, third in apples, and fourth in prunes and plums.

The southern half of the Lower Peninsula is the principal agricultural region, while the area along Lake Michigan is a leader in fruit growing. Potatoes are profitable in northern Michigan, while eastern Michigan (the "Thumb" area near Lake Huron) is a leading bean producer. The Saginaw Valley leads the state in sugar beets. The south-central and southeastern counties are major centers of soybean production. Leading field crops in 2004 included corn for grain, soybeans, and wheat. Output of commercial apples totaled 720 million pounds (327 million kilograms).

22 Domesticated Animals

The same areas of southern Michigan that lead in crop production also lead in livestock and livestock products, except that the northern counties are more favorable for dairying than for crop production.

In 2005, there were an estimated 1,010,000 cattle and calves, valued at $1.07 billion. The state had an estimated 940,000 hogs and pigs in 2004, valued at $103.4 million. In 2003, dairy farmers had an estimated 302,000 milk cows which produced around 6.36 million pounds (2.89 million kilograms) of milk. Poultry farmers produced nearly 1.89 billion eggs, valued at around $93.7 million.

23 Fishing

In 2004, the commercial catch was 8.4 million pounds (3.8 million kilograms) valued at $6.2 million. Principal species landed were silver salmon and alewives.

Sport fishing continues to flourish and is one of the state's major tourist attractions. A state salmon-planting program, begun in the mid-1960s, has made salmon the most popular game fish for Great Lakes sport fishermen. The state has also sought, through breeding and stocking programs, to bring back the trout, which was devastated by an invasion of lamprey. In 2004, the state issued 1,171,742 sport fishing licenses. There are three national fisheries in Michigan.

24 Forestry

In 2004, Michigan's forestland totaled 19.3 million acres (7.8 million hectares), or more than half the state's total land area. Approximately 96% of it was classified as timberland, and about two-thirds of it was privately owned. The major forested regions are in the northern two-thirds of the state, where great pine forests enabled Michigan to become the leading lumber-producing state in the last four decades of the 19th century. These cutover lands regenerated naturally

or were reforested in the 20th century. Lumber production was 844 million board feet in 2004.

State and national forests covered 6.9 million acres (2.8 million hectares), or about one-fifth of the state's land area.

25 Mining

Nonfuel mineral production in Michigan was valued at an estimated $1.35 billion in 2003. The state ranked seventh nationally in value of nonfuel minerals produced during the same year. Michigan was first nationally in magnesium chloride produced, and ranked second in the production of peat, industrial sand and gravel, bromine, and iron ore. It ranked third in construction sand and gravel, and potash; fourth in portland cement; and seventh in salt, and eighth in masonry cement. According to preliminary figures, in 2003, the state produced 70 million metric tons of construction sand and gravel. Crushed stone production that year totaled 41.2 million metric tons.

The state also produced small quantities of copper, silver, and other mineral specimens for sale to collectors and museums.

26 Energy and Power

In 2003, Michigan's total net summer generating capacity was 30.450 million kilowatts, while total electric power output that same year was 111.347 billion kilowatt hours. Most power (60.9%) was produced by coal-fired steam units, followed by nuclear-powered units at 25.1%, and natural gas-fired generators at 10.2%. Oil-fired plants, hydroelectric sources and other renewable energy sources accounted for the remainder. As of 2006, Michigan had three operating nuclear power plants, the Donald C. Cook plant in Berrion County, the Enrico Fermi plant near Detroit, and the Palisades facility near South Haven.

The two major electric utilities are Detroit Edison, serving the Detroit area and portions of the eastern part of the Lower Peninsula, and Consumers Power, serving most of the remainder of the Lower Peninsula. Rates of the utility companies are set by the Public Service Commission.

Michigan is dependent on outside sources for most of its fossil fuel needs. Petroleum production in 2004 totaled 18,000 barrels per day. Marketed natural gas production in that same year totaled 259.681 billion cubic feet (7.37 billion cubic meters). In 2004, the state's proven crude oil reserves were 53 million barrels, while proven reserves (as of 31 December 2004) of dry or consumer-grade natural gas totaled 3.091 trillion cubic feet (87.8 billion cubic meters). Bituminous coal reserves (estimated at 127.7 million tons) remain in southern Michigan, but production is negligible. In 2004, there was no recorded coal output.

27 Commerce

In 2002, Michigan's wholesale trade sector had sales of $165.9 billion, while the state's retail trade sector had sales that year of $109.3 billion. In the retail sector for 2002, motor vehicle and motor vehicle parts dealers accounted for the largest portion of sales at $31.7 billion, followed by food and beverage stores at $13.1 billion, and building material/garden equipment and supplies dealers at $9.4 billion. With its ports open to oceangoing vessels through the St. Lawrence Seaway, Michigan is a major exporting

and importing state for foreign as well as domestic markets. Exports of Michigan's manufactured goods totaled $37.5 billion in 2005, ranking the state fifth in the United States.

28 Public Finance

The state constitution requires the governor to submit a budget proposal to the legislature each year. This executive budget, prepared by the Department of Management and Budget, is reviewed, revised, and passed by the legislature. The fiscal year extends from 1 October to 30 September.

In 2004, total revenues were $57.46 billion, while total expenditures for that year were $46.5 billion. The largest general expenditures in 2004 were for education ($20.34 billion), public welfare ($9.95 billion), and health ($3.35 billion). The total state debt that year was $20.959 billion, or $2,074.42 per capita (per person).

29 Taxation

In 2005, Michigan collected $24.340 billion in tax revenues, or $2,405 per person, placing the state 15th among the 50 states in per capita tax burden, compared to the national average of $2,192. Sales taxes accounted for the largest portion at 33.2%, followed by personal income taxes at 28.4%, selective sales taxes at 14.2%, property taxes at 8.8%, corporate income taxes at 7.8%, and other taxes at 7.5%.

As of 1 January 2006, the state had a single personal income tax bracket of 3.9%. The state sales and use tax is 6% on most retail purchases. However food is exempt if consumed off premises (such as at home). The state also imposes excise taxes on cigarettes and gasoline.

Downtown Detroit skyline. COPYRIGHT © 2006 BY KELLY A. QUIN.

30 Health

In October 2005, the infant mortality rate was estimated at 7.7 per 1,000 live births. The crude death rate in 2003 was 8.6 per 1,000 population. Major causes of death (per 100,000 people in 2002) included heart disease at 265.3, cancer at 198.8, cerebrovascular diseases at 57.8, chronic lower respiratory diseases at 44.1, and diabetes at 27.7. The HIV-related death rate was 2.4 per 100,000 population. The AIDS case rate in 2004 was at about 6.5 per 100,000 people. About 23.2% of the state's residents were smokers as of 2004.

Michigan's 144 community hospitals had about 25,800 beds in 2003. In 2004, Michigan had 289 physicians for every 100,000 people, and a total of 6,039 dentists in that same year. In 2005, there were 804 nurses per 100,000 population. The average expense for community hos-pital care was $1,382 per day. In 2004, about 11% of the state's population were uninsured.

31 Housing

In 2004, there were an estimated 4,433,482 housing units in Michigan, of which 3,923,135 were occupied. Michigan that year ranked second in the country (after Minnesota) for the number of units (74%) that were owner-occupied. About 70.5% of all units were single-family, detached homes. Most homes rely on utility gas for heating. It was estimated that 218,182 units lacked telephone service, while 8,787 lacked complete plumbing facilities, and 12,705 lacked complete kitchen facilities. The Average household size was 2.51 people.

In 2004, a total of 54,700 privately owned units were authorized for construction. The median home value was $145,177. The median monthly cost for mortgage owners was $1,137. Renters paid a median of $628 per month.

32 Education

Historically, Michigan has strongly supported public education, which helps account for the fact that the percentage of students attending public schools is one of the highest in the United States. In 2004, of Michigan residents age 25 and older, 87.9% were high school graduates and 24.4% had obtained a bachelor's degree or higher.

Total public school enrollment was estimated at 1,786,000 in fall 2003 and is expected to drop to 1,728,000 by fall 2014. Expenditures for public education in 2003/2004 were estimated at $19.2 billion.

Enrollment in private schools in fall 2003 was 160,049. A large percentage of private-school enrollment was in Catholic schools. Lutherans, Seventh-Day Adventists, and Reformed and Christian Reformed churches also maintain schools.

As of fall 2002, there were 605,835 students enrolled in college or graduate school. In 2005, Michigan had 110 degree-granting institutions. The oldest state school is the University of Michigan, originally established in Detroit in 1817. Its Ann Arbor campus was founded in 1835. Other public universities are Michigan State University and Wayne State University. Among the state's private colleges and universities, the University of Detroit Mercy, a Jesuit school, is one of the largest. Kalamazoo College (founded in 1833), Albion College (1835), Hope College (1866), and Alma College (1886) are some of the oldest private liberal arts colleges in the state.

33 Arts

Michigan's major center of arts and cultural activity is the Detroit area. The city's refurbished Orchestra Hall is the home of the Detroit Symphony Orchestra, as well as chamber music concerts and other musical events. The Music Hall and the Masonic Auditorium present a variety of musical productions. The Fisher Theater is the major home for Broadway productions, and the Detroit Cultural Center supports a number of cultural programs. The new Detroit Opera House is sponsored by the Michigan Opera Theatre. Nearby Meadow Brook, in Rochester, has a summer music program. Successful summer theaters include the Cherry County Playhouse at Traverse City, and the Star Theater in Flint.

Programs relating to the visual arts tend to be academically centered. The University of Michigan, Michigan State, Wayne State, and Eastern Michigan University have notable art schools. The Cranbrook Academy of Arts, which was created by the architect Eliel Saarinen, is a significant art center and the Ox-bow School at Saugatuck is also outstanding. The Ann Arbor Art Fair, begun in 1960, is the largest and most prestigious summer outdoor art show in the state, hosting more than 500,000 annual attendees. The Waterfront Film Festival in Saugatuck and the touring Ann Arbor Film Festival promote the art of independent filmmaking.

The Detroit Symphony Orchestra, founded in 1914, is nationally known. Grand Rapids and Kalamazoo have regional orchestras that perform on a part-time, seasonal basis. The National Music Camp at Interlochen is a popular destination for young musicians during the summer and a prestigious private high school for the arts year round.

There are local ballet and opera groups in Detroit and in a few other communities. Michigan's best-known contribution to popular music was that of Berry Gordy Jr., whose Motown recording company in the 1960s popularized the "Detroit sound" and featured such artists as Diana Ross and the Supremes, Smokey Robinson and the Miracles, Aretha Franklin, the Four Tops, the Temptations, and Stevie Wonder, among many others. In the 1970s however, Gordy moved his operations to California.

The Michigan Council for the Arts supports many programs throughout the state with federal and state funding. The Michigan Humanities Council was founded in 1974. One of its ongoing programs is the Great Outdoors Culture Tour, which includes performing artists and cultural interpreters/educators.

34 Libraries and Museums

As of September 2001, Michigan had a total of 654 libraries, of which 278 were branches. In that same year, the state's libraries held 27.188 million volumes, with a circulation of 51,773,000. The largest public library is the Detroit Public Library, which includes the National Automotive History Collection and the E. Azalia Hackley Collection, a notable source for material pertaining to African Americans in the performing arts, especially music. Among academic libraries, the University of Michigan at Ann Arbor is one of the best; in 1980, the Gerald R. Ford Presidential Library was opened on the university campus.

The Detroit Institute of Arts is the largest art museum in the state and has an outstanding collection of African art. The Kalamazoo Institute of Art, the Flint Institute of Art, the Grand Rapids Art Museum, and the Hackley Art Gallery in Muskegon are important art museums. In 1996 the world's largest museum of African American history was established in Detroit. A major Holocaust Memorial Center is located in the West Bloomfield Hills area of metropolitan Detroit.

The Detroit Historical Museum heads the more than 229 museums in the state. In Dearborn, the privately run Henry Ford Museum and Greenfield Village are leading tourist attractions.

35 Communications

In 2004, of all occupied housing units in the state, 93.7% had telephones, and in June of that year, there were 5.43 million wireless telephone service subscribers. In 2003, computers were in 59.9% of all Michigan homes, while 52% had access to the Internet. In 2005, Michigan had 62 major AM radio stations and 110 major FM stations. Radio station WWJ, originally owned by the Detroit News, began operating in 1920 as one of the country's first commercial broadcasting stations, and the News also started Michigan's first television station in 1947. As of 2005 there were 33 major television stations in the state. In the Detroit area, 68% of 1,855,500 television households had cable, while in the Grand Rapids-Kalamazoo-Battle Creek area, 62% of 671,320 television households had cable.

By 2000, a total of 145,596 Internet domain names had been registered in Michigan.

36 Press

The state's oldest paper still being published is the *Detroit Free Press*, founded in 1831. In 2005, there were 48 daily newspapers in Michigan and 27 Sunday editions published in the state. The leading newspapers (and their 2004 circulation rates) are the Detroit *News* (510,736 daily; 710,036 Sunday), the *Grand Rapids Press* (138,126 daily; 189,690 Sunday), and the *Flint Journal* (84,313 daily; 102,154 Sunday).

37 Tourism, Travel & Recreation

In 2003, a total of 150,000 people were employed in Michigan's tourist industry.

The opportunities offered by Michigan's water resources are the number one attraction. No part of the state is more than 85 miles (137 kilometers) from one of the Great Lakes, and most of the population lives only a few miles away from one of the thousands of inland lakes and streams.

Historic attractions have been heavily promoted in recent years, following the success of Dearborn's Henry Ford Museum and Greenfield Village. Tours of Detroit automobile factories and other industrial sites, such as Battle Creek's breakfast-food plants, are also important attractions. The Spirit of Ford, a 50,000 square-foot center in Dearborn, offers a "behind the scenes" look at how the automaker designs, engineers, tests, and produces cars and trucks.

Camping and recreational facilities are provided by the federal government at three national forests, comprising 2.8 million acres (1.1 million hectares). Three facilities are operated by the National Park Service (Isle Royale National Park, the Pictured Rocks National Lakeshore, and Sleeping Bear Dunes National Lakeshore). A wild African-style village covering 70 acres (28.3 hectares) at the Binder Park Zoo in Battle Creek features giraffes, zebras, and ostrich, plus a variety of endangered African species roaming freely on the grassy savannah.

State-operated facilities include 64 parks and recreational areas with 172,343 acres (69,747 hectares), and state forests and wildlife areas totaling 4,250,000 acres (1,720,000 hectares).

38 Sports

Michigan has five major league professional sports teams, all of them centered in Detroit: the Tigers of Major League Baseball, the Lions of the National Football League, the Pistons of the National Basketball Association, the Shock of the Women's National Basketball Association, and the Red Wings of the National Hockey League. The state also has minor league hockey teams in Detroit, Flint, Grand Rapids, Motor City, Muskegon, Kalamazoo, Plymouth, Port Huron and Saginaw, and minor league baseball teams in Grand Rapids, Battle Creek, and Traverse City.

Horse racing, Michigan's oldest organized spectator sport, is controlled by the state racing commissioner, who regulates thoroughbred and harness racing seasons at tracks in the Detroit area and at Jackson. Auto racing is also popular in Michigan. The state hosts four major races, the Detroit Grand Prix, the Michigan 500 Indy car race, and two NASCAR Nextel Cup races.

Interest in college sports centers on the football and basketball teams of the University of Michigan and Michigan State University, which

Gerald R. Ford, the 38th US president, grew up in Grand Rapids. EPD PHOTOS/LBJ PRESIDENTIAL LIBRARY.

usually are among the top-ranked teams in the country. The Michigan State basketball team won the NCAA tournament in 2000.

Other annual sporting events include the Snowmobile Poker Runs in St. Ignace, and in July, the yacht races from Chicago and Port Huron to Mackinac Island.

39 Famous Michiganians

Only one Michiganian has held the offices of US president and vice president: Gerald R. Ford (Leslie King Jr., b.Nebraska, 1913–2006), the 38th US president, who was appointed to the vice presidency by Richard M. Nixon in 1973 upon the resignation of Vice President Spiro T. Agnew. When Nixon resigned on 9 August

1974, Ford became president, the first to hold that post without having been elected to high national office.

Two Michiganians have served as associate justices of the Supreme Court: Henry B. Brown (b.Massachusetts, 1836–1913), author of the 1896 segregationist decision in *Plessy v. Ferguson;* and Frank Murphy (1890–1949), who also served as US attorney general and was a notable defender of minority rights during his years on the court. Another justice, Potter Stewart (1915–1985), was born in Jackson but appointed to the Supreme Court from Ohio.

Other Michiganians who have held high federal office include Robert S. McNamara (b.California, 1916), Secretary of Defense; and W. Michael Blumenthal (b.Germany, 1926), Secretary of the Treasury. Detroit's first black mayor, Coleman A. Young (b.Alabama, 1918–1997), promoted programs to revive the city's tarnished image while in office (1974–93).

The most famous figure in the early development of Michigan is Jacques Marquette (b.France, 1637–1675). Laura Haviland (b.Canada, 1808–1898) was a noted leader in the fight against slavery and for black rights, while Lucinda Hinsdale Stone (b.Vermont, 1814–1900) and Anna Howard Shaw (b.England, 1847–1919) were important in the women's rights movement.

Nobel laureates from Michigan include diplomat Ralph J. Bunche (1904–1971), winner of the Nobel Peace Prize in 1950; and Glenn T. Seaborg (1912–1999), Nobel Prize winner in chemistry in 1951, and for whom element 106, seaborgium, is named.

In the business world, William C. Durant (b.Massachusetts, 1861–1947), Henry Ford (1863–1947), and Ransom E. Olds (b.Ohio

1864–1950) are the three most important figures in making Michigan the center of the American auto industry. Ford's grandson, Henry Ford II (1917–1987), was the dominant personality in the auto industry from 1945 through 1979. Two brothers, John Harvey Kellogg (1852–1943) and Will K. Kellogg (1860–1951), helped make Battle Creek the center of the breakfast-food industry. Pioneer aviator Charles A. Lindbergh (1902–1974) was born in Detroit.

Among prominent labor leaders in Michigan were Walter Reuther (b.West Virginia, 1907–1970), president of the United Automobile Workers, and his controversial contemporary, James Hoffa (b.Indiana, 1913–1975?), president of the Teamsters Union, whose disappearance and presumed murder remain a mystery.

The best-known literary figures who were either native or adopted Michiganians include Ring Lardner (1885–1933), master of the short story; Edna Ferber (1885–1968), best-selling novelist; Howard Mumford Jones (1892–1980), critic and scholar; and Bruce Catton (1899–1978), Civil War historian.

Other prominent Michiganians past and present include Frederick Stuart Church (1842–1924), painter; Albert Kahn (b.Germany, 1869–1942), innovator in factory design; and (Gottlieb) Eliel Saarinen (b.Finland, 1873–1950), architect and creator of the Cranbrook School of Art. Malcolm X (Malcolm Little, b.Nebraska, 1925–1965) developed his black separatist beliefs while living in Lansing.

Popular entertainers born in Michigan include Danny Thomas (Amos Jacobs, 1914–1991); Ed McMahon (b.1923); Julie Harris (b.1925); Ellen Burstyn (Edna Rae Gilhooley, b.1932); Della Reese (Dellareese Patricia Early, b.1932); William "Smokey" Robinson (b.1940);

Diana Ross (b.1944); Bob Seger (b.1945); Stevie Wonder (Stevland Morris, b.1950); and Madonna (Madonna Louise Ciccone, b.1959); along with film director Francis Ford Coppola (b.1939).

Among sports figures who had notable careers in the state were Joe Louis (Joseph Louis Barrow, b.Alabama, 1914–1981), heavyweight boxing champion from 1937 to 1949; "Sugar Ray" Robinson (1921–1989), who held at various times the welterweight and middleweight boxing titles; and baseball Hall-of-Famer Al Kaline (b.Maryland, 1934), a Detroit Tigers star. Basketball star Earvin "Magic" Johnson (b.1959), who broke Oscar Robertson's record for most assists, was born in Lansing.

40 Bibliography

BOOKS

Brill, Marlene Targ. *Michigan.* 2nd ed. New York: Marshall Cavendish Benchmark, 2007.

Bristow, M. J. *State Songs of America.* Westport, CT: Greenwood Press, 2000.

Dubois, Muriel L. *Michigan.* Milwaukee, WI: Gareth Stevens, 2006.

McAuliffe, Emily. *Massachusetts Facts and Symbols.* Rev. ed. Mankato, MN: Capstone Press, 2003.

Murray, Julie. *Michigan.* Edina, MN: Abdo Publishing, 2006.

Wittenberg, Eric J., ed. *One of Custer's Wolverines: the Civil War Letters of Brevet Brigadier General James H. Kidd, 6th Michigan Infantry.* Kent, OH: Kent State University Press, 2000.

WEB SITES

Official Portal for the State of Michigan. *Michigan. gov.* www.michigan.gov (accessed March 1, 2007).

State of Michigan Official Tourism Site. travel. michigan.org (accessed March 1, 2007

Minnesota

State of Minnesota

ORIGIN OF STATE NAME: Derived from the Sioux Indian word *minisota,* meaning "sky-tinted waters."

NICKNAME: The North Star State.

CAPITAL: St. Paul.

ENTERED UNION: 11 May 1858 (32nd).

OFFICIAL SEAL: A farmer, with a powder horn and musket nearby, plows a field in the foreground, while in the background, before a rising sun, a Native American on horseback crosses the plains; pine trees and a waterfall represent the state's natural resources. The state motto is above, and the whole is surrounded by the words "The Great Seal of the State of Minnesota 1858." Another version of the seal in common use shows a cowboy riding across the plains.

FLAG: On a blue field bordered on three sides by a gold fringe, a version of the state seal is surrounded by a wreath with the statehood year (1858), the year of the establishment of Ft. Snelling (1819), and the year the flag was adopted (1893). Five clusters of gold stars and the word "Minnesota" fill the outer circle.

MOTTO: *L'Etoile du Nord* (The North Star).

SONG: "Hail! Minnesota."

FLOWER: Pink and white lady slipper.

TREE: Red (Norway) pine.

BIRD: Common loon.

FISH: Walleye.

INSECT: Monarch butterfly.

GEM: Lake Superior agate.

BEVERAGE: Milk.

LEGAL HOLIDAYS: New Year's Day, 1 January; Birthday of Martin Luther King Jr., 3rd Monday in January; Presidents' Day, 3rd Monday in February; Memorial Day, last Monday in May; Independence Day, 4 July; Labor Day, 1st Monday in September; Veterans' Day, 11 November; Thanksgiving Day, 4th Thursday in November plus one day; Christmas Day, 25 December. By statute, schools hold special observances on Susan B. Anthony Day, 15 February; Arbor Day, last Friday in April; Minnesota Day, 11 May; Frances Willard Day, 28 September; Leif Erikson Day, 9 October.

TIME: 6 AM CST = noon GMT.

1 Location and Size

Situated in the western north-central United States, Minnesota is the largest Midwestern state and ranks 12th in size among the 50 states, with a total area of 84,402 square miles (218,601 square kilometers), of which land accounts for 79,548 square miles (206,029 square kilometers) and inland water 4,854 square miles (12,572 square kilometers). The state extends 406 miles (653 kilometers) north-south and 358 miles (576 kilometers) east-west. Its boundary length totals 1,783 miles (2,870 kilometers).

2 Topography

Minnesota consists mainly of flat prairie. There are rolling hills and deep river valleys in the southeast. The northeast, known as Arrowhead Country, is more rugged and includes the Vermilion Range and the Mesabi Range. Eagle Mountain, in the extreme northeast, rises to a height of 2,301 feet (702 meters), the highest point in the state. The surface of nearby Lake Superior, 601 feet (183 meters) above sea level, is the state's lowest elevation.

With more than 15,000 lakes and extensive wetlands, rivers, and streams, Minnesota has more inland water than any other state except Alaska. Some of the inland lakes are quite large, including Lower and Upper Red Lake, 451 square miles (1,168 square kilometers); Mille Lacs, 207 square miles (536 square kilometers); and Leech Lake, 176 square miles (456 square kilometers). A total of 2,212 square miles (5,729 square kilometers) of Lake Superior lies within Minnesota's jurisdiction.

Lake Itasca, in the northwest, is the source of the Mississippi River, which drains about three-fifths of the state and forms part of the eastern boundary with Wisconsin. The Minnesota River, which flows across the southern part of the state, joins the Mississippi at the Twin Cities. The Red River forms much of the boundary with North Dakota.

Minnesota Population Profile

Total population estimate in 2006:	5,167,101
Population change, 2000–06:	5.0%
Hispanic or Latino†:	3.6%
Population by race	
One race:	98.5%
White:	88.0%
Black or African American:	4.0%
American Indian /Alaska Native:	1.1%
Asian:	3.6%
Native Hawaiian / Pacific Islander:	0.0%
Some other race:	1.8%
Two or more races:	1.5%

Population by Age Group

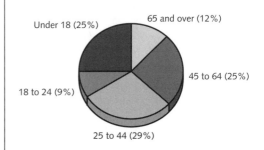

Under 18 (25%)
65 and over (12%)
45 to 64 (25%)
18 to 24 (9%)
25 to 44 (29%)

Major Cities by Population

City	Population	% change 2000–05
Minneapolis	372,811	-2.6
St. Paul	275,150	-4.2
Rochester	94,950	10.7
Duluth	84,896	-2.3
Bloomington	81,164	-4.7
Plymouth	69,701	5.8
Brooklyn Park	68,550	1.7
St. Cloud	65,792	11.3
Eagan	63,665	0.2
Coon Rapids	62,417	1.3

Notes: †A person of Hispanic or Latino origin may be of any race. NA indicates that data are not available. **Sources:** U.S. Census Bureau. *American Community Survey* and *Population Estimates*. www.census.gov/ (accessed March 2007).

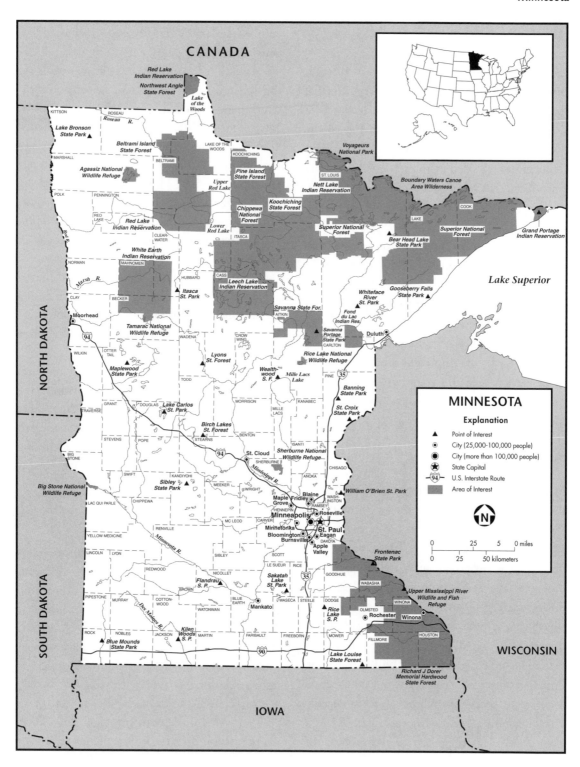

CANADA

Red Lake
Indian Reservation
Northwest Angle
State Forest

Lake
of the
Woods

KITTSON

ROSEAU

Roseau R.

Lake Bronson
State Park ▲

MARSHALL

Beltrami Island
State Forest

LAKE OF THE
WOODS

BELTRAMI

KOOCHICHING

Voyageurs
National Park

ST. LOUIS

Agassiz National
Wildlife Refuge

POLK

PENNINGTON

RED
LAKE

Upper
Red Lake

Pine Island
State Forest

Nett Lake
Indian Reservation

Boundary Waters Canoe
Area Wilderness

COOK

Chippewa
National
Forest

Koochiching
State Forest

Superior National
Forest

LAKE

Superior National
Forest

Grand Portage
Indian Reservation ▲

Red Lake
Indian Reservation

CLEAR-
WATER

Lower
Red Lake

ITASCA

Superior National
Forest

Bear Head Lake
State Park ▲

Lake Superior

NORMAN

HUBBARD

White Earth
Indian Reservation

MAHNOMEN

CASS

Itasca
St. Park ▲

Leech Lake
Indian Reservation

Whiteface
River
St. Park ▲

Gooseberry Falls
State Park ▲

BECKER

Fond
du Lac
Indian Res.

CLAY

Moorhead ⊙

Marsh R.

Tamarac National
Wildlife Refuge

WADENA

CROW
WING

Savanna State For.

AITKIN

Savanna
Portage
State Park ▲

CARLTON

Duluth ⊙

NORTH DAKOTA

94

WILKIN

OTTER
TAIL

Maplewood
State Park ▲

Lyons
St. Forest ▲

TODD

Wealth-
wood
S. F.

Mille Lacs
Lake

PINE

Rice Lake National
Wildlife Refuge

35

Banning
State Park ▲

GRANT

DOUGLAS

Lake Carlos
St. Park ▲

Birch Lakes
St. Forest ▲

MORRISON

MILLE
LACS

KANABEC

St. Croix
State Park ▲

TRAVERSE

STEVENS

POPE

BENTON

STEARNS

94

St. Cloud ⊙

Mississippi R.

Sherburne National
Wildlife Refuge

ISANTI

CHISAGO

William O'Brien St. Park ▲

BIG
STONE

SWIFT

KANDIYOHI

Sibley
State Park ▲

MEEKER

SHERBURNE

⊙ WRIGHT

ANOKA

Maple Fridley
Grove ⊙ Blaine

WASH-
INGTON

Big Stone National
Wildlife Refuge

LAC QUI PARLE

CHIPPEWA

MC LEOD

HENNEPIN

Minneapolis ⊙

CARVER

Roseville ⊙

RAMSEY

★ St. Paul

YELLOW MEDICINE

RENVILLE

Minnetonka ⊙
Bloomington ⊙
Burnsville ⊙

DAKOTA

Eagan ⊙
Apple
Valley ⊙

Minnesota R.

SIBLEY

SCOTT

Frontenac
State Park ▲

LINCOLN

LYON

REDWOOD

NICOLLET

Flandrau
S. P. ▲

LE SUEUR

35

RICE

GOODHUE

WABASHA

Upper Mississippi River
Wildlife and Fish
Refuge

Sakatah
Lake
St. Park ▲

PIPESTONE

MURRAY

COTTON-
WOOD

BROWN

BLUE
EARTH

Mankato ⊙

WASECA

STEELE

DODGE

Rice
Lake
S. P. ▲

OLMSTED

Rochester ⊙

WINONA

Winona ⊙

WATONWAN

Des Moines R.

ROCK

NOBLES

JACKSON

Kilen
Woods
S. P. ▲

MARTIN

FARIBAULT

FREEBORN

MOWER

FILLMORE

HOUSTON

SOUTH DAKOTA

Blue Mounds
State Park ▲

90

Lake Louise
State Forest ▲

Richard J Dorer
Memorial Hardwood
State Forest

WISCONSIN

IOWA

3 Climate

Minnesota has a continental climate with cold, often frigid winters and warm summers. Normal daily mean temperatures range from 12°F (-11°C) in January to 74°F (23°C) in July in the Twin Cities of Minneapolis–St. Paul. The lowest temperature recorded in the state of Minnesota was -60°F (-51°C) at Tower on 2 February 1996. The highest recorded temperature, 114°F (46°C), occured at Moorhead on 6 July 1936.

The mean annual precipitation ranges from 19 inches (48 centimeters) in the northeast to 31 inches (79 centimeters) in the southeast. Heavy snowfalls occur from November to April, averaging 30 inches (76 centimeters) in the southeast and 70 inches (178 centimeters) in the northwest. Blizzards hit Minnesota on an average of twice each winter. There are an average of 18 tornadoes per year in the state, mostly in the south.

4 Plants and Animals

Minnesota is divided into three main life zones: the wooded lake regions of the north and east, the prairie lands of the west and southwest, and a transition zone in between. Oak, maple, elm, birch, pine, ash, and poplar still thrive, although much of the state's woodland has been cut down since the 1850s. Common shrubs include thimbleberry, sweetfern, and several varieties of honeysuckle. There are 1,500 native flowering plants, including prairie phlox and blazing star. Pink and white lady's-slipper is the state flower. Three plant species were listed as threatened in 2006, including Leedy's roseroot, prairie bush-clover, and western prairie fringed orchid; the

Minnesota dwarf trout lily was listed as endangered that year.

Among Minnesota's common mammals are the opossum, little brown bat, striped and spotted skunks, ground squirrels (also known as the Minnesota gopher), raccoon, and white-tailed deer. The western meadowlark, Brewer's blackbird, and Carolina wren are among the 240 resident bird species. Minnesota's many lakes are filled with such game fishes as walleyed pike, northern pike, and rainbow trout. The two poisonous snakes in the state are the timber rattler and the massasauga.

Classification of rare, threatened, and endangered species is delegated to the Minnesota Department of Natural Resources. Among rare species noted by the department are the white pelican, short-eared owl, rock vole, pine marten, American elk, woodland caribou, lake sturgeon, and paddlefish; threatened species include the bobwhite quail and piping plover. In 2006, nine species were listed as threatened or endangered by the US Fish and Wildlife Service, including the gray wolf, bald eagle, piping plover, Topeka shiner, and Higgins' eye pearlymussel.

5 Environmental Protection

Minnesota divides its environmental programs among three agencies: the Minnesota Pollution Control Agency, the Department of Natural Resources, and the Office of Environmental Assistance. The Conservation Department, created in 1931, evolved into the present Department of Natural Resources, which is responsible for the management of forests, fish and game, public lands, minerals, and state parks and waters. The department's Soil and Water Conservation Board has jurisdiction over the

Minnesota Population by Race

Census 2000 was the first national census in which the instructions to respondents said, "Mark one or more races." This table shows the number of people who are of one, two, or three or more races. For those claiming two races, the number of people belonging to the various categories is listed. The U.S. government conducts a census of the population every ten years.

	Number	Percent
Total population	4,919,479	100.0
One race	4,836,737	98.3
Two races	77,732	1.6
White *and* Black or African American	17,700	0.4
White *and* American Indian/Alaska Native	18,793	0.4
White *and* Asian	11,966	0.2
White *and* Native Hawaiian/Pacific Islander	852	—
White *and* some other race	12,015	0.2
Black or African American *and* American Indian/Alaska Native	2,413	—
Black or African American *and* Asian	1,057	—
Black or African American *and* Native Hawaiian/Pacific Islander	191	—
Black or African American *and* some other race	6,054	0.1
American Indian/Alaska Native *and* Asian	812	—
American Indian/Alaska Native *and* Native Hawaiian/Pacific Islander	50	—
American Indian/Alaska Native *and* some other race	675	—
Asian *and* Native Hawaiian/Pacific Islander	1,920	—
Asian *and* some other race	3,091	0.1
Native Hawaiian/Pacific Islander *and* some other race	143	—
Three or more races	5,010	0.1

Source: U.S. Census Bureau. *Census 2000: Redistricting Data.* Press release issued by the Redistricting Data Office. Washington, D.C., March, 2001. A dash (—) indicates that the percent is less than 0.1.

state's 92 soil and water conservation districts. A separate Pollution Control Agency enforces air and water quality standards and oversees solid waste disposal and pollution-related land-use planning. The Environmental Quality Board coordinates conservation efforts among various state agencies.

To control the state's solid waste stream, Minnesotans have established 488 curbside recycling programs. In 1997, the state had some 9.5 million acres (3.8 million hectares) of wetlands. The Wetlands Conservation Act of 1991 set the ambitious goal of no wetland loss in the future.

In 2003, Minnesota had 81 hazardous waste sites listed in the Environmental Protection Agency's database, 24 of which were on the National Priorities List as of 2006.

6 Population

In 2005, Minnesota ranked 21st in population among the 50 states with an estimated total of 5,167,101 residents. The population is projected to reach 6.8 million by 2025. In 2004, the state's population density was 64.1 persons per square mile (24.7 persons per square kilometer). In 2005, approximately 25% of all residents were 18 years of age and younger and 12% were 65 and older. The median age was 36.6 in 2004.

Minneapolis had an estimated 372,811 residents in 2004, while St. Paul had 275,150 people.

Dancers at the Red Lake Native American Pow Wow. The two historic nations in Minnesota were the Dakota and the Ojibwa, or Chippewa. © MINNESOTA OFFICE OF TOURISM.

7 Ethnic Groups

Germans and Scandinavians are the largest groups of first- and second-generation Minnesotans of European origin, The state has more ethnic Norwegians than any other and is second in number of ethnic Swedes (California is first). As of the 2000 census, there were 54,967 Native Americans in Minnesota. Besides those living on reservations and in villages, a cluster of Indian urban dwellers (chiefly Ojibwa) lived in St. Paul. There were 171,731 black Americans in the state, representing about 4% of the population, There were also 141,968 Asian residents, including 41,800 Hmong, 18,824 Vietnamese, 16,887 Asian Indians, 16,060 Chinese, 12,584

Koreans, and 9,940 Laotians. Pacific Islanders numbered 1,979. The Hispanic and Latino population had 143,382 residents, about 2.9% of the population. As of 2000, there were about 260,463 foreign-born residents of Minnesota, or about 5.3% of the population.

8 Languages

English in the state is basically Northern, with minor infiltrations of Midland terms. Among older residents, traces of Scandinavian and Eastern European pronunciation persist. Minnesotans call the grass strip between street and sidewalk the *boulevard* and a rubber band a *rubber binder*. Many say they *cook coffee* when they brew it. Many younger speakers pronounce *caller* and *collar* alike.

In 2000, 91.5% of the population age five years old or older spoke only English at home. Other leading languages spoken at home were Spanish, 132,066; Miao/Hmong, 41,673; German, 35,072; African languages, 24,747; and Vietnamese, 16,503.

9 Religions

Minnesota's first Christian church was organized by Presbyterians in Ft. Snelling in 1835; the first Roman Catholic church, the Chapel of St. Paul, was dedicated in 1841 at a town then called Pig's Eye but now known by the same name as the chapel.

In 2004, Roman Catholics numbered 1,185,980. As of 2000, Protestant groups were predominant with the largest denominations being the Evangelical Lutheran Church in America, with 853,448 adherents, and the Lutheran Church—Missouri Synod, with 203,863 adherents. In 2004, the United Methodist Church had 83,755 adherents. Other Lutheran, Presbyterian, and Baptist denominations were also somewhat prominent. The Episcopal Church had 30,547 adherents in 2000. The Church of Jesus Christ of Latter-day Saints (Mormons) in 2006 had 27,524 members. There were about 42,000 adherents to Judaism and 12,300 adherents of Islam in 2000. Over 1.8 million people (about 38.3% of the population) were not counted as members of any religious organization in 2000.

Minnesota is the headquarters for three national Lutheran religious groups: the American Lutheran Church, the Church of the Lutheran

The headwaters of the Mississippi River at Itasca State Park. © MINNESOTA OFFICE OF TOURISM.

Brethren, and the Association of Free Lutheran Congregations.

10 Transportation

The development of an extensive railroad network after the Civil War was a key factor in the growth of lumbering, iron mining, wheat growing, and other industries. By 2003, Minnesota had a total of 5,923 rail miles (9,536 kilometers). Amtrak serves Minneapolis–St. Paul en route from Chicago to Seattle/Portland. The national Greyhound bus line was founded in Hibbing in 1914.

Minnesota had 131,937 miles (212,418 kilometers) of public roads and streets in 2004. I-35 links Minneapolis–St. Paul with Duluth, and

I-94 connects the Twin Cities with Moorhead and Fargo, North Dakota. In 2004, there were approximately 2,490,000 registered automobiles, 2,046,000 trucks, and some 7,000 buses. There were 3,083,007 licensed drivers in that year.

The first settlements grew up around major river arteries, especially in the southeast. Early traders and settlers arrived first by canoe or keelboat, later by steamer. The port of Duluth-Superior, at the western terminus of the Great Lakes–St. Lawrence Seaway (officially opened in 1959) is a major stop. The ports of Minneapolis and St. Paul are also significant.

As of 2005, the state had 384 airports, 77 seaplane bases, 58 heliports, and 1 STOLport (Short Take-Off and Landing). Minneapolis–St. Paul International is the state's largest and busiest airport, with 17,482,627 passengers in 2004.

11 History

At the time of European penetration in the 17th and early 18th centuries, the two principal Native American nations were the Dakota and, after 1700, the Ojibwa. The first Europeans whose travels through the region have been documented were Pierre Esprit Radisson and his brother-in-law, Médart Chouart, Sieur de Groseilliers, who probably reached the interior of northern Minnesota in the 1650s. In 1679, Daniel Greysolon, Sieur Duluth, formally claimed the region for King Louis XIV of France.

In the two centuries before statehood, French, English, and American explorers, fur traders, and missionaries came to Minnesota. Competition for control of the upper Mississippi Valley ended with the British victory in the French and Indian War, which placed the portion of Minnesota east of the Mississippi under British control. The land west of the Mississippi was ceded by France to Spain in 1762. Although the Spanish paid little attention to their northern territory, the British immediately sent in fur traders and explorers.

US Claims There was little activity in the region during the Revolutionary War, and for a few decades afterward, the British continued to pursue their interests there. After the War of 1812, the US Congress passed an act curbing British participation in the fur trade. Under the Northwest Ordinance of 1787, Minnesota east of the Mississippi became part of the Northwest Territory. Most of western Minnesota was acquired by the United States as part of the Louisiana Purchase of 1803. The Red River Valley became a secure part of the United States after an agreement with England on the northern boundary was reached in 1818.

In 1819, a military post was established on land acquired from the Dakota by Lieutenant Zebulon Pike, on a bluff overlooking the junction of the Mississippi and Minnesota rivers. For three decades, Ft. Snelling served as the principal center of civilization in Minnesota and the key frontier outpost in the northwest.

Beginning in 1837, a series of treaties with the Dakota and Ojibwa transferred large areas of tribal land to the US government, cutting off the profitable relationship between fur traders and Native Americans and opening the land for lumbering, farming, and settlement. In 1849, the Minnesota Territory was established, and in 1851 the legislature named St. Paul as the capital. As lumbering grew and additional treaties

A lighthouse shines a welcome to ships on Lake Superior. DULUTH CVB/SEAQUEST PHOTOGRAPHY.

opened up more land, the population boomed, reaching a total of more than 150,000 by 1857.

Statehood On 11 May 1858, Minnesota officially became the 32d state. In the first presidential election in which Minnesota participated, Abraham Lincoln, the Republican candidate, easily carried the state. When the Civil War broke out, Minnesota was the first state to answer Lincoln's call for troops. In all, Minnesota supplied more than 20,000 men to fight for the Union.

More challenging to the defense of Minnesota was the Dakota uprising of 1862, led by chief Little Crow, in which more than 300 whites and an unknown number of Native Americans were killed. In the aftermath, 38 Dakota captives were hanged and the Dakota remaining in Minnesota were removed to reservations in Nebraska. Also during 1862, Minnesota's first railroad joined St. Anthony (Minneapolis) and St. Paul with 10 miles (16 kilometers) of track.

The railroads soon ushered in an era of large-scale commercial farming. Wheat provided the biggest cash crop, as exports rose from 2 million bushels in 1860 to 95 million in 1890. Meanwhile, the falls of St. Anthony (Minneapolis) became the major US flour-milling center. By 1880, 27 Minneapolis mills were producing more than 2 million barrels of flour annually. Despite these signs of prosperity, discontent grew among Minnesota farmers, who were plagued by high railroad rates and damaging droughts. The first national farmers' movement, the National Grange of the Patrons of Husbandry, was founded in 1867 by a Minnesotan, Oliver H. Kelley, and spread more rapidly in Minnesota than in any other state.

Industrialization Most immigrants during the 1860s and 1870s settled on the rich farmland of the north and west, but after 1880 the cities and industries grew more rapidly. When iron ore was discovered in the 1880s in the sparsely settled northeast, even that part of the state attracted settlers, many of them immigrants from eastern and southern Europe. Before the turn of the century, Duluth had become a major lake port, and by the eve of World War I, Minnesota had become a national iron-mining center.

The economic picture changed after the war. Facing the depletion of their forests and an agricultural depression, Minnesotans adapted to the new realities in various ways. Farmers planted corn, soybeans, and sugar beets along with wheat, and new food-processing industries developed. In 1948, for the first time, the dollar value of all manufactured products exceeded total cash farm receipts. Later were added business machines, electronics, computers, and other high-technology industries.

Economic disruption and the growth of cities and industries encouraged challenges to the Republican leadership from Democrats and third parties. John Johnson, a progressive Democratic governor first elected in 1904, was especially active in securing legislation to regulate the insurance industry. His successor, Republican Adolph Eberhart, promoted numerous progressive measures, including one establishing direct

primary elections. The Farmer-Labor Party had many electoral successes in the 1920s and reached its peak with the election of Floyd B. Olson to the governorship in 1930. Olson introduced a graduated income tax and other progressive measures, but his death in office in 1936 was a crippling blow to the party.

In 1938, the Republicans recaptured the governorship with the election of Harold E. Stassen. However, a successful merger of the Farmer-Labor and Democratic parties was engineered in 1943–44. After World War II, Hubert Humphrey (later a US vice-president) and his colleagues Orville Freeman, Eugene McCarthy, and Eugenie Anderson emerged as leaders of this new coalition. Their political heir, Walter Mondale, was vice-president in 1977–81 but, as the Democratic presidential candidate in 1984, lost the election in a Republican landslide, carrying only his native state and the District of Columbia.

Into the 21st Century In the 1990s, Minnesota continued its economic diversification as service industries, including finance, insurance, and real estate, became increasingly important. Though Minnesota, led by the Twin Cities, enjoyed an unprecedented decade of economic prosperity, it was generally acknowledged that agriculture across the Great Plains was in crisis by the end of the decade.

Many farmers' problems were made worse by weather conditions. In 1998, Minnesota's agricultural producers suffered from the worst drought since the 1930s. As a result of the severe flooding of the Mississippi River in 1993, almost half of Minnesota's counties were designated as disaster areas. Again in 1997, some of the most

Minnesota Governors: 1858–2007

1858–1860	Henry Hastings Sibley	Democrat	1931–1936	Floyd Bjornstjerne Olson	Farmer Laborite
1860–1863	Alexander Ramsey	Republican	1936–1937	Hjalmar Petersen	Farmer Laborite
1863–1864	Henry Adoniram Swift	Republican	1937–1939	Elmer Austin Benson	Farmer Laborite
1864–1866	Stephen Miller	Republican	1939–1943	Harold Edward Stassen	Republican
1866–1870	William Rogerson Marshall	Republican	1943–1947	Edward John Thye	Republican
1870–1874	Horace Austin	Republican	1947–1951	Luther Wallace Youngdahl	Republican
1874–1876	Cushman Kellogg Davis	Republican	1951–1955	Clyde Elmer Anderson	Republican
1876–1882	John Sargent Pillsbury	Republican	1955–1961	Orville Lothrop Freeman	D.F.L.
1882–1887	Lucius Frederick Hubbard	Republican	1961–1963	Elmer Lee Andersen	Republican
1887–1889	Andrew Ryan McGill	Republican	1963–1967	Karl Fritjof Rolvaag	D.F.L.
1889–1893	William Rush Merriam	Republican	1967–1971	Harold LeVander	Republican
1893–1895	Knute Nelson	Republican	1971–1976	Wendell Richard Anderson	D.F.L.
1895–1899	David Marston Clough	Republican	1976–1979	Rudolph George Perpich	D.F.L.
1899–1901	John Lind	Popularist Democrat	1979–1983	Albert Harold Quie	Independent
1901–1905	Samuel Rinnah Van Sant	Republican	Republican		
1905–1909	John Albert Johnson	Democrat	1983–1991	Rudolph George Perpich	D.F.L.
1909–1915	Adolph Olson Eberhart	Republican	1991–1999	Arne Carlson	Republican
1915	Winfield Scott Hammond	Democrat	1999–2002	Jesse Ventura	Reform
1915–1921	Joseph Alfred Arner Burnquist	Republican	2002–	Tim Pawlenty	Republican
1921–1925	Jacob Aall Ottesen Preus	Republican			
1925–1931	Theodore Christianson	Republican	Democrat Farmer Labor – D.F.L.		

severe flooding in the century occurred in the Red River and Minnesota River valleys.

Professional wrestler Jesse Ventura was elected governor as the Reform Party candidate in 1998. He later aligned himself with the Independence Party of Minnesota. Republican Tim Pawlenty was elected governor in 2002. In 2003, the state faced the largest budget deficit in its history, at $4.2 billion. However, by 2005 Pawlenty had balanced the state's budget. Under Pawlenty's leadership, an overhaul of the state's education standards, welfare reform, lawsuit reform, and a large transportation package were passed. Pawlenty won reelection in 2006.

12 State Government

The Minnesota legislature consists of a 67-member senate and a 134-member house of representatives. Senators serve four years and representatives two years. The governor and lieutenant governor are jointly elected for four-year terms. Other constitutional officers are the secretary of state, auditor, and attorney general, all serving for four years.

Once a bill is passed by a majority of both houses, the governor may sign it, veto it in whole or in part, or pocket-veto it by failing to act within 14 days of adjournment. A two-thirds vote of both houses is sufficient to override a veto. Constitutional amendments require the approval of a majority of both houses of the legislature and are subject to ratification by the electorate.

As of December 2004, the legislative salary was $31,140, and the governor's salary was $120,311

13 Political Parties

The two major political parties are the Democratic-Farmer-Labor Party (DFL) and

Minnesota Presidential Vote by Political Parties, 1948–2004

YEAR	MINNESOTA WINNER	DEMOCRAT[1]	REPUBLICAN[2]	PROGRESSIVE	SOCIALIST	SOCIALIST LABOR[3]
1948	*Truman (D)	692,966	483,617	27,866	4,646	2,525
1952	*Eisenhower (R)	608,458	763,211	2,666	—	2,383
					SOC. WORKERS	
1956	*Eisenhower (R)	617,525	719,302	—	1,098	2,080
1960	*Kennedy (D)	779,933	757,915	—	3,077	962
1964	*Johnson (D)	991,117	559,624	—	1,177	2,544
						AMERICAN IND.
1968	Humphrey (D)	857,738	658,643	—	—	68,931
				PEOPLE'S		AMERICAN
1972	*Nixon (R)	802,346	898,269	2,805	4,261	31,407
				LIBERTARIAN		
1976	*Carter (D)	1,070,440	819,395	3,529	4,149	13,592
					CITIZENS	
1980	Carter (D)	954,173	873,268	31,593	8,406	6,136
1984	Mondale (D)	1,036,364	1,032,603	2,996	1,219	—
				MINN. PROG.		SOCIALIST WORKERS
1988	Dukakis (D)	1,109,471	962,337	5,109	5,403	2,155
				IND. (PEROT)		CONSTITUTION
1992	*Clinton (D)	1,020,997	747,841	3,373	562,506	3,363
						GREEN (NADER)
1996	*Clinton (D)	1,120,438	766,476	8,271	257,704	24,908
				REFORM		
2000	Gore (D)	1,168,266	1,109,659	5,282	22,166	1,022
2004	Kerry (D)	1,445,014	1,346,695	4,639	—	—

*Won US presidential election.
1 Called Democratic-Farmer-Labor Party in Minnesota.
2 Since 1976, called Independent-Republican in Minnesota.
3 Appeared as Industrial Government Party on the ballot.

the Republican Party (until 1995 called the Independent-Republican Party). The Republican Party dominated Minnesota politics from the 1860s through the 1920s, except for a period around the turn of the century. The DFL, formed in 1944 by merger between the Democratic Party and the Farmer-Labor Party, rose to prominence in the 1950s under US Senator Hubert Humphrey.

Minnesota is famous as a breeding ground for presidential candidates, who include Republican Governor Harold Stassen (1948, 1952, and later years); and Democrats Vice President Hubert Humphrey (1968), US Senator Eugene McCarthy (1968, 1976), and Walter Mondale

(1976, 1980, 1984). Mondale was chosen in 1976 by Jimmy Carter as his vice-presidential running mate; he again ran with Carter in 1980, when the two lost their bid for reelection. In the 1984 election, Minnesota was the only state to favor the Walter Mondale-Geraldine Ferraro ticket. In the 2000 elections Democrat Al Gore carried the state with 48% of the vote. Republican George W. Bush earned 46%. In 2004, Democratic challenger John Kerry won 51% of the vote to President Bush's 48%.

In 1990, after serving four terms, Democrat Rudy Perpich lost the governorship to Independent-Republican Arne Carlson, who was reelected in 1994. Minnesota's voters stunned the nation in 1998 when they elected Reform Party candidate Jesse Ventura, a former professional wrestler, as governor. After gaining office, Ventura switched allegiances to the Independence Party of Minnesota. Tim Pawlenty, a Republican, won the governorship in 2002 and was narrowly reelected in 2006.

In 2006, Democrat Amy Klobuchar was elected to the US Senate. In 2002 Democratic senator Paul Wellstone died in a plane crash along with his wife and daughter. Republican Norm Coleman won Wellstone's Senate seat in 2002, defeating Walter Mondale, who stepped in to run after Wellstone's death. Following the 2006 elections, Minnesota's delegation to the US House was composed of five Democrats and three Republicans. Following those elections, there were 44 Democrats and 23 Republicans serving in the Minnesota state senate. Party representation in the state house consisted of 85 Democrats and 49 Republicans. Sixty-three women were elected to the state legislature in 2006, or 31.3%.

14 Local Government

Minnesota is divided into 87 counties, 1,793 townships (more than any other state) 854 municipal governments, 415 public school districts, and 403 special districts. Each of Minnesota's counties is governed by a board of commissioners. Other elected officials include the auditor, treasurer, recorder, and sheriff. Regional development commissions, or RDCs, prepare and adopt regional development plans and review applications for loans and grants. The mayor-council system is the most common form of city government. Townships are governed by a board of supervisors and other officials.

15 Judicial System

Minnesota's highest court is the supreme court, consisting of a chief justice and six associate justices. The district court, divided into 10 judicial districts, is the principal court of original jurisdiction. County courts, operating in all counties of the state except two, exercise civil jurisdiction in cases where the amount in contention is $5,000 or less, and criminal jurisdiction in preliminary hearings and misdemeanors. They also hear cases involving family disputes, and have joint jurisdiction with the district court in divorces, adoptions, and certain other proceedings.

The probate division of the county court system presides over guardianship and incompetency proceedings and all cases relating to the disposing of estates. Crime rates are generally below the national average. In 2004, Minnesota's total violent crime rate (murder, rape, robbery, aggravated assault) per 100,000 people was 269.6. Crimes against property (burglary, larceny/theft, and motor vehicle theft) that year totaled 3,039 reported incidents per 100,000 people. Federal and state correctional institutions had a total population of 8,758 as of 31 December 2004. Minnesota has no death penalty law.

16 Migration

A succession of migratory waves began in the 17th and 18th centuries with the arrival of the Dakota and Ojibwa, among other Indian groups, followed during the 19th century by New England Yankees, Germans, Scandinavians, and finally southern and eastern Europeans. Especially since 1920, new arrivals from other states and countries have been relatively few.

Between 1990 and 1998, Minnesota had net gains of 71,000 in domestic migration and 47,000 in international migration. In the period 2000–05, net international migration was 70,800 and net internal migration was 16,768, for a net gain of 54,032 people.

17 Economy

Furs, wheat, pine lumber, and high-grade iron ore were once the basis of Minnesota's economy. As these resources diminished, however, the state turned to wood pulp, dairy products, corn and soybeans, taconite, and manufacturing, often in such food-related industries as meat-packing, canning, and the processing of dairy products.

The leading sources of income in Minnesota have shifted again in recent years. Manufacturing remains central to the state's economy, but finance, real estate, and insurance have also come to play a dominant role. Government and trade activities rose significantly between the late 1960s and early 1980s, while the role played by manufacturing and construction declined. By the mid-1990s, private goods-producing industries accounted for 28% of the state's economic output, while private services-producing industries contributed 61%.

Minnesota's economy grew at a robust rate at the end of the 1990s—it stood at 8.5% in 2000. But in the 2001 national recession, the growth rate dropped to 1%. In 2002, employment declined more rapidly than in the nation as a whole because of the large share of Minnesota workers in areas most affected by the national slowdown: manufacturing, information technology, and airline industries. On the other hand, Minnesota escaped the drought conditions that

afflicted many other states in 2002. The dairy industry has suffered in recent years, however.

As of 2004, manufacturing accounted for 13.7% of gross state product (GSP), followed by the real estate sector at 11.1% of GSP, and healthcare and social assistance at 7.8% of GSP. Minnesota's GSP in 2004 was $223.8 billion, and $233 billion in 2005.

18 Income

In 2005, Minnesota ranked 17th among the 50 states and the District of Columbia with a gross domestic product (GSP) of $233 billion. In 2004, Minnesota had a per capita (per person) income of $36,184, eighth-highest in the nation. The three-year median household income for 2002–04 was $55,914, compared to the national average of $44,473. For the period 2002–04, about 7% of the state's residents lived below the federal poverty level, as compared to 12.4% nationwide.

19 Industry

In the early 20th century, canning and meat-packing were among the state's largest industries. While food and food products remain important, the state's economy has diversified significantly from its early beginnings. Minnesota now has high-technology industries such as computer-manufacturing, scientific instruments, and medical products as well as resource-based industries such as food products and wood products.

The total value of shipments by manufacturers in 2004 exceeded $88.4 billion, with food products accounting for the largest share, at $16.8 billion. Industry is concentrated in the state's southeast region, especially in the Twin

Cities (Minneapolis-St. Paul) area. Among the well-known national firms with headquarters in Minnesota are 3M (Minnesota Mining and Manufacturing), General Mills, Honeywell, and Hormel Foods.

20 Labor

In April 2006, the civilian labor force in Minnesota numbered 2,946,100, with approximately 119,600 workers unemployed, yielding an unemployment rate of 4.1%, compared to the national average of 4.7% for the same period. As of April 2006, 4.7% of the labor force was employed in construction; 12.5% in manufacturing; 19.3% in trade, transportation, and public utilities; 6.6% in financial activities; 11.3% in professional and business services; 14.2% in education and health services; 9.1% in leisure and hospitality services; and 15.2% in government.

The history of unionization in the state includes several long and bitter labor disputes, notably the Iron Range strike of 1916, the Teamsters' strike of 1934, and the Hormel strike of 1985–86. The Knights of Labor were the dominant force of the 1880s. The next decade saw the rise of the Minnesota State Federation of Labor, whose increasing political influence bore fruit in the landmark Workmen's Compensation Act of 1913 and the subsequent ascension of the Farmer-Labor Party.

In 2005, approximately 392,000 of Minnesota's 2,494,000 employed wage and salary workers were members of unions. This represented 15.7% of those so employed. The national average is 12%.

21 Agriculture

Cash receipts from farm marketings totaled over $9 billion in 2005, placing Minnesota sixth among the 50 states. For 2004, Minnesota ranked first in the production of sugar beets, and sweet corn and green peas for processing; second in spring wheat; third in alfalfa hay; fourth in corn, oats, soybeans, and flaxseed; and sixth in barley and durum wheat. As of 2004, the state had 79,800 farms, covering 27,600,000 acres (11,200,000 hectares), or 51% of the state's total land area. The average farm had 346 acres (140 hectares).

The main farming areas are in southern Minnesota, where corn, soybeans, and oats are important, and in the Red River Valley along the western border, where wheat, barley, sugar beets, and potatoes are among the chief crops. Agribusiness is Minnesota's largest basic industry, with about one-fourth of the state's labor force employed in agriculture or agriculture-related industries, most notably food processing.

22 Domesticated Animals

Excluding the northeast, livestock raising is dispersed throughout the state, with cattle concentrated particularly in west-central Minnesota and in the extreme southeast and hogs along the southern border.

In 2005, the state had an estimated 2.4 million cattle and calves, valued at nearly $2.3 billion. The state had 6.5 million hogs and pigs, valued at $780 million in 2004. Minnesota produced more turkey in 2003 than any other state: 1.2 billion pounds (0.55 billion kilograms), worth $425.3 million. Also during 2003, the state produced 13.8 million pounds (6.3 million kilograms) of sheep and lambs, which brought in a total of nearly $13.3 million.

The state's total of 8.3 billion pounds (4 billion kilograms) of milk outproduced all but five states in 2003. Production of broilers in 2003 was 228.5 million pounds (103.4 million kilograms), worth around $77.7 million; and egg output in the same year was 2.9 billion, worth $146.4 million.

23 Fishing

Commercial fishermen in 2004 landed 323,000 pounds (146,800 kilograms) of fish, valued at $187,000. The catch included herring and smelts from Lake Superior, whitefish and yellow pike from large inland lakes, and carp and catfish from the Mississippi and Minnesota rivers. In 2001, the commercial fleet had about 25 boats and vessels.

Sport fishing attracts some 1.5 million anglers annually to the state. Fishing streams are stocked with trout, bass, pike, muskellunge, and other fish by the Division of Fish and Wildlife of the Department of Natural Resources. In 2004, there were 1467,677 sports fishing licenses issued in the state.

24 Forestry

Forests, which originally occupied two-thirds of Minnesota's land area, have been depleted by lumbering, farming, and forest fires. As of 2004, forestland covered 16,230,000 acres (6,568,000 hectares), or over 30% of the state's total land area. Most of the forestland is in the north, especially in Arrowhead Country in the northeast. Of the 14,723,000 acres (5,958,000 hectares) of commercial timberland, less than half

is privately owned and more than one-third is under state, county, or municipal jurisdiction. In 2004, lumber production totaled 265 million board feet, 45% hardwoods and 55% softwoods. Over half of the timber that is harvested is used in paper products and about one-third for wood products. Mills that process raw logs account for half of all forest and forest-product employment in Minnesota.

The state's two national forests are Superior (2,094,946 acres/847,825 hectares) and Chippewa (666,541 acres/269,749 hectares). The Department of Natural Resources, Division of Forestry, promotes effective management of the forest environment and seeks to restrict forest fire occurrence to 1,100 fires annually, burning no more than 30,000 acres (12,000 hectares) in all.

More than 3 million acres (1.2 million hectares) are planted each year with trees by the wood fiber industry, other private interests, and federal, state, and county forest services—more than enough to replace those harvested or destroyed by fire, insects, or disease.

25 Mining

The value of nonfuel mineral production in Minnesota in 2003 was estimated to be about $1.23 billion. Iron ore, Minnesota's leading mineral commodity, accounted for $969 million of this total mineral value. Minnesota in 2003 was the nation's to producer of iron ore, third in peat, and sixth in construction sand and gravel. Iron ore is found along a belt that runs through Itasca and St. Louis counties. The estimated value of construction sand and gravel was $188 million in 2003. The estimated value of crushed stone was

$57.3 million. Michigan's output of common clays and dimension stone is also significant.

26 Energy and Power

Minnesota produced 55.05 billion kilowatt hours of electricity (utility and nonutility) in 2003, when total installed capacity reached 11.48 million kilowatts. Most plants were coal-fired. There are two nuclear power plants (at Monticello, and at the Prairie Island facility). In 2000, Minnesota's total per capita energy consumption was 343 million Btu (86.4 million kilocalories), ranking it 25th among the 50 states.

Minnesota's 7 million acres (2.8 million hectares) of peat lands, the state's only known fossil fuel resource, constitute nearly half of the US total (excluding Alaska). If burned directly, these fuel-quality peat deposits could add to Minnesota's energy needs.

27 Commerce

Access to the Great Lakes, the St. Lawrence Seaway, and the Atlantic Ocean, as well as to the Mississippi River and the Gulf of Mexico, helps make Minnesota a major marketing and distribution center for the upper Midwest. The state's wholesale sales totaled $108.3 billion in 2002; retail sales were $60.01 billion. Exports to foreign countries amounted to $14.71 billion in 2005.

28 Public Finance

The state budget is prepared by the Department of Finance and submitted biennially by the governor to the legislature for amendment and approval. The fiscal year runs from 1 July to 30 June.

Revenues for 2004 were $29.7 billion and expenditures were $28.8 billion. The largest general expenditures were for education ($9.8 billion), public welfare ($8.04 billion), and highways ($1.8 billion). The state's outstanding debt totaled $6.6 billion, or $1,307.76 per capita (per person).

29 Taxation

As of 2006, corporate income tax is at a flat rate of 9.8%. Personal income tax rates were on a three-bracket schedule ranging from 5.35% to 7.85%. The state of Minnesota also levies a 6.5% state sales tax, with local-option sales taxes permitted up to 1%. Food, medicines and other basics are exempted. The state also imposes a full array of excise taxes covering motor fuels, tobacco products, insurance premiums, public utilities, alcoholic beverages, amusements, pari-mutuels, and many other selected items. Other state taxes include per ton severance taxes (for taconite, iron sulphides, agglomerate, and semi-taconite), various license fees, and stamp taxes.

In Minnesota's classified property tax system, commercial, industrial, and rental properties are taxed at considerably higher rates than owned homes. Minnesota's "circuit breaker" system refunds property tax payments to homeowners and renters whose residential property taxes are high relative to their income.

Total state tax collections in Minnesota in 2005 were $15.8 billion, of which 39.9% was generated by the state income tax, 26.5% by the state general sales and use tax, 15.3% by state excise taxes, 3.9% by property taxes, 5.9% by the state corporate income tax, and 8.5% by other taxes. In 2005, Minnesota ranked sixth among the states in terms of state and local tax burden, at $3,094 per capita (per person), compared with the national average of $2,192 per capita.

30 Health

Shortly after the founding of Minnesota Territory, the soothing landscape and cool, bracing climate were trumpeted as a haven for retirees and for those afflicted with malaria or tuberculosis.

As of October 2005, the infant mortality rate was of 5.2 per 1,000 live births. The overall death rate in 2003 was 7.1 per 1,000 population. About 20.6% of Minnesota residents were smokers. The death rates per 100,000 population for heart disease and cerebrovascular disease in 2002 were 171.4 and 53.9 respectively. HIV-related deaths occurred at a rate of 1.1 per 100,000 population.

Minnesota's 131 community hospitals had about 16,400 beds in 2003. The average expense for community hospital care was $1,109 per inpatient day in 2003. In 2004, only 9% of Minnesota residents were uninsured, the lowest percentage in the country. In 2004, Minnesota had 283 doctors per 100,000 residents, and 962 nurses per 100,000 residents in 2005. In 2004, there were 3,069 dentists in the state.

The Mayo Clinic, developed by Drs. Charles H. and William J. Mayo in the 1890s and early 1900s, was the first private clinic in the United States and became a world-renowned center for surgery. Today it is owned and operated by a self-perpetuating charitable foundation. The separate Mayo Foundation for Medical Education and Research, founded and endowed by the Mayo brothers in 1915, was affiliated with the University of Minnesota, which became the first US institution to offer graduate education in surgery and other branches of clinical medicine.

31 Housing

In 2004, Minnesota had 2,212,701 housing units, of which 2,054,900 were occupied. Minnesota had the highest rate of homeownership in the nation with 75.3% of all housing units being owner-occupied. About 68% of all units were single-family, detached homes. Most units relied on utility gas and electricity for heating. It was estimated that 53,332 units lacked telephone service, 9,065 lacked complete plumbing facilities, and 9,270 lacked complete kitchen facilities. The average household size was 2.41 people.

In 2004, 41,800 new units were authorized for construction. The median home value was $181,135. The median monthly cost for mortgage owners was $1,260. Renters paid a median of $673 per month.

32 Education

Minnesota has one of the best-supported systems of public education in the United States. In 2004, 92.3% of Minnesotans age 25 or older were high school graduates and 32.5% had obtained a bachelor's degree or higher.

Total public school enrollment was estimated at 847,000 in fall 2002 but is expected to drop to 826,000 by fall 2014. Enrollment in nonpublic schools in fall 2003 was 93,935. Expenditures for public education in 2003/04 were estimated at $8.6 billion.

As of fall 2002, there were 323,791 students enrolled in college or graduate school. In 2005,

Minnesota had 113 degree-granting institutions. The state university system has campuses at Bemidji, Mankato, Marshall, Minneapolis-St. Paul, Moorhead, St. Cloud, and Winona; there is also a community college system, and a statewide network of area vocational-technical institutes. The University of Minnesota (founded as an academy in 1851) has campuses in the Twin Cities, Duluth, Morris, and Crookston. The state's oldest private college, Hamline University in St. Paul, was founded in 1854 and is affiliated with the United Methodist Church. There are more than 20 private colleges, many of them with ties to Lutheran or Roman Catholic religious authorities. Carleton College, at Northfield, is a notable independent institution.

33 Arts

The Ordway Music Theater which has two concert halls, opened in St. Paul in January 1985. The Ordway is the home of the Minnesota Orchestra, the Minnesota Opera Company, and the St. Paul Chamber Orchestra. In 1999, the Ordway received funding from the National Endowment for the Arts to use interactive video-conferencing technology to develop an "electronic field trip" accessible to student audiences across the state.

The St. Olaf College Choir, at Northfield, has a national reputation. The Guthrie Theater, founded in Minneapolis in 1963, is one of the nation's most prestigious repertory companies; it moved to a new complex overlooking the Mississippi River in 2006. The Minnesota Ballet is based in Duluth.

Literary arts are active in the state. The Loft, founded in 1974 in Minneapolis, is considered to be one of the nation's largest and most com-

prehensive literary centers. Milkweed Editions is a well-known, award-winning, nonprofit literary publisher of books on cultural diversity, environmental stewardship, poetry, and literature for adults and children in the middle grades.

State and regional arts groups as well as individual artists are supported by grants administered through the Minnesota State Arts Board, an 11-member panel appointed by the governor. The state offers arts education to about 50,000 schoolchildren, with approximately 2,500 teachers participating in the programs. The Minnesota Humanities Commission was founded in 1971.

34 Libraries and Museums

In 2001, Minnesota had an estimated 140 public library systems, with a total of 359 libraries, of which 232 were branches. The same year, the total number of books and audiovisual items was over 14.4 million items and total circulation reached more than 43.8 million. The largest single public library system is the Minneapolis Public Library and Information Center. The leading academic library, with over 5.7 million volumes, is maintained by the University of Minnesota at Minneapolis.

There are more than 164 museums and historic sites. In addition to several noted museums of the visual arts, Minnesota is home to the Mayo Medical Museum at the Mayo Clinic in Rochester. In May 1996, the Mille Lacs Indian Museum and Trading Post opened its doors. Historic sites include the boyhood home of Charles Lindbergh in Little Falls and the Sauk Centre home of Sinclair Lewis.

New Guthrie Theater in Minneapolis, Minnesota. AP IMAGES.

35 Communications

As of 2004, 97.1% of Minnesota's occupied housing units had telephones. By June of that year, there were 2,832,079 mobile telephone subscribers. In 2003, 67.9% of Minnesota households had a computer, and 61.6% had Internet access. As of 2005 there were 135 major radio stations—33 AM and 102 FM—and 20 major television stations. The Minneapolis-St. Paul metropolitan area had approximately 1,481,050 television households, 54% of which received cable in 1999.

36 Press

In April 1982, Minneapolis's two daily newspapers were merged into the *Minneapolis Star Tribune*. As of 2005, the state had 15 morn-ing dailies, 10 evening dailies, and 15 Sunday papers. The leading dailies, with their daily circulations in 2005, are the *Minneapolis Star Tribune* (381,094), the *St. Paul Pioneer Press* (191,264), and the *Duluth News-Tribune* (46,460). As of 2005, some 333 weekly newspapers were being published in Minnesota. Among the most widely read magazines published in Minnesota were *Family Handyman*, appearing 11 times a year; *Catholic Digest*, a religious monthly; and *Snow Goer*, published six times a year for snowmobile enthusiasts.

37 Tourism, Travel & Recreation

In 2004, the state hosted about 28.6 million travelers, with about 50% of all tourist activity involving Minnesota residents touring their own state. About 11.7 million visitors were from out of state. Shopping was the most popular tourist activity for out-of-state visitors. Total travel expenditures for 2004 reached about $9.2 billion, which included support for over 233,000 jobs.

With its lakes and parks, ski trails and campsites, and historical and cultural attractions, Minnesota provides ample recreational opportunities for residents and visitors alike.

Besides the museums, sports stadiums, and concert halls in the big cities, Minnesota's attractions include the 220,000-acre (80,000-hectare) Voyageurs National Park, near the Canadian border; Grand Portage National Monument, in Arrowhead Country, a former fur-trading center with a restored trading post; and Lumbertown USA, a restored 1870s lumber community. The US Hockey Hall of Fame is in Eveleth.

The state maintains and operates 66 parks, 9,240 miles (14,870 kilometers) of trails, 10 scenic and natural areas, 5 recreation areas, and 18 canoe and boating routes. Minnesota also has 288 primary wildlife refuges. Many visitors hunt deer, muskrat, squirrel, beaver, duck, pheasant, and grouse. Others enjoy boating each year on Minnesota's scenic waterways. Winter sports have gained in popularity, and many parks are now used heavily all year round. Snowmobiling and cross-country skiing has rapidly accelerated in popularity.

38 Sports

There are five major league professional sports teams in Minnesota: the Minnesota Twins of Major League Baseball, the Minnesota Vikings of the National Football League, the Minnesota Lynx of the Women's National Basketball Association, the Minnesota Timberwolves of the National Basketball Association, and the Minnesota Wild of the National Hockey League.

In collegiate sports, the University of Minnesota Golden Gophers compete in the Big Ten Conference. The university is probably best known for its ice hockey team, which won the NCAA title three times during the 1970s and again in 2002 and 2003, and supplied the coach, Herb Brooks, and many of the players for the gold medal–winning US team in the 1980 Winter Olympics.

Other annual sporting events include the John Beargrease Sled Dog Race between Duluth and Grand Marais in January or early February and auto racing at the Brainerd International Raceway in July and August. Alpine and cross-country skiing are popular.

39 Famous Minnesotans

No Minnesotan has been elected to the US presidency, but several have sought the office, including two who served as vice-president. Hubert Horatio Humphrey (b.South Dakota, 1911–1978) was vice-president under Lyndon Johnson and a serious contender for the presidency in 1960, 1968, and 1972. Humphrey's protégé, Walter Frederick "Fritz" Mondale (b.1928)—after serving as vice-president under Jimmy Carter (and as Carter's running mate in his unsuccessful bid for reelection in 1980)—won the Democratic presidential nomination in 1984. Warren Earl Burger (1907–1995) of St. Paul was named chief justice of the US Supreme Court in 1969. Three other Minnesotans have served on the court: Pierce Butler (1866–1939); William O. Douglas (1898–1980); and Harry A. Blackmun (b.Illinois, 1908–1997).

The first woman ambassador in US history was Eugenie M. Anderson (b.Iowa, 1909–1997).

The Mayo Clinic was founded in Minnesota by Dr. William W. Mayo (b.England, 1819–1911) and developed through the efforts of his sons, Drs. William H. (1861–1939) and Charles H. (1865–1939) Mayo. Oil magnate J. Paul Getty (1892–1976) was a Minnesota native, as was Richard W. Sears (1863–1914), founder of Sears, Roebuck.

The first US citizen ever to be awarded the Nobel Prize for literature was Sinclair Lewis (1885–1951), whose novel *Main Street* (1920) was modeled on life in his hometown of Sauk Centre. Prominent literary figures besides Sinclair Lewis include F. Scott Fitzgerald (1896–1940), well known for his classic novel *The Great Gatsby*. Cartoonist Charles Schulz (1922–2000) and radio personality and author Garrison Keillor (b.1942), were both born in Minnesota.

Minnesota-born entertainers include Judy Garland (Frances Gumm, 1922–1969), Bob Dylan (Robert Zimmerman, b.1941), and Jessica Lange (b.1949). In 1961 Minnesotan Roger Maris (1934–1985) set the record for the most home runs hit in a baseball season; his record stood until 1998. Other notable athletes from Minnesota are Olympic swimmer Tracy Caulkins (b.1963), baseball great Roger Maris (1934–1985), and basketball star Kevin McHale (b.1957).

40 Bibliography

BOOKS

Bristow, M. J. *State Songs of America*. Westport, CT: Greenwood Press, 2000.

Gedatus, Gustav Mark. *Minnesota*. Milwaukee, WI: Gareth Stevens, 2006.

Hintz, Martin. *Minnesota*. New York: Children's Press, 2000.

McAuliffe, Bill. *Minnesota Facts and Symbols*. Rev. ed. Mankato, MN: Capstone Press, 2003.

Sateren, Shelley Swanson, ed. *A Civil War Drummer Boy: the Diary of William Bircher, 1861–1865*. Mankato, MN: Blue Earth Books, 2000.

Uschan, Michael V. *Jesse Ventura*. San Diego: Lucent Books, 2001.

WEB SITES

Minnesota Office of Tourism. *Explore Minnesota*. www.exploreminnesota.com (accessed March 1, 2007).

State of Minnesota. *Minnesota North Star: Official Website for the State of Minnesota*. www.state.mn.us/portal/mn/jsp/home.do?agency=NorthStar (accessed March 1, 2007).

Mississippi

State of Mississippi

ORIGIN OF STATE NAME: Derived from the Ojibwa Indian words *misi sipi,* meaning "great river."

NICKNAME: The Magnolia State.

CAPITAL: Jackson.

ENTERED UNION: 10 December 1817 (20th).

OFFICIAL SEAL: The seal consists of the coat of arms surrounded by the words "The Great Seal of the State of Mississippi."

FLAG: Crossed blue bars, on a red field, bordered with white and emblazoned with 13 white stars—the motif of the Confederate battle flag—cover the upper left corner. The field consists of three stripes of equal width, blue, white, and red.

COAT OF ARMS: An American eagle clutches an olive branch and a quiver of arrows in its talons.

MOTTO: *Virtute et armis* (By valor and arms).

SONG: "Go, Mississippi."

FLOWER: Magnolia.

TREE: Magnolia.

ANIMAL: White-tailed deer (mammal); porpoise (water mammal).

BIRD: Mockingbird; wood duck (waterfowl).

FISH: Largemouth or black bass.

INSECT: Honeybee.

FOSSIL: Prehistoric whale.

ROCK OR STONE: Petrified wood.

BEVERAGE: Milk.

LEGAL HOLIDAYS: New Year's Day, 1 January; Birthdays of Robert E. Lee and Martin Luther King Jr., 3rd Monday in January; Washington's Birthday, 3rd Monday in February; Confederate Memorial Day, last Monday in April; Memorial Day and Jefferson Davis's Birthday, last Monday in May; Independence Day, 4 July; Labor Day, 1st Monday in September; Veterans' Day and Armistice Day, 11 November; Thanksgiving Day, 4th Thursday in November; Christmas Day, 25 December.

TIME: 6 AM CST = noon GMT.

1 Location and Size

Located in the eastern south-central United States, Mississippi ranks 32nd in size among the 50 states. The total area of Mississippi is 47,689 square miles (123,514 square kilometers), of which land takes up 47,233 square miles (122,333 square kilometers) and inland water 456 square miles (1,181 square kilometers). Mississippi's maximum east-west extension is 188 miles (303 kilometers). Its greatest north-south distance is 352 miles (566 kilometers). The total boundary length of Mississippi is 1,015 miles (1,634 kilometers). Several small islands lie off the coast.

2 Topography

Mississippi lies entirely within two lowland plains: the Mississippi Alluvial Plain, popularly known as the Delta, and the Gulf Coastal Plain. Mississippi's generally hilly landscape ascends from sea level at the Gulf of Mexico to reach its maximum elevation, 806 feet (246 meters), at Woodall Mountain, in the extreme northeastern corner of the state.

The state's largest lakes, Grenada, Sardis, Enid, and Arkabutla, are all manmade. Numerous smaller lakes, called oxbow lakes because of their curved shape, extend along the western edge of the state. Once part of the Mississippi River, they were formed when the river changed its course. Mississippi's longest inland river, the Pearl, flows about 490 miles (790 kilometers) from the eastern center of the state to the Gulf of Mexico. The Big Black River, some 330 miles (530 kilometers) long, begins in the northeast and cuts diagonally across the state. The Yazoo flows 189 miles (304 kilometers) southwest to the Mississippi just above Vicksburg.

3 Climate

Mississippi has short winters and long, humid summers. Summer temperatures vary little from one part of the state to another, averaging around 80°F (27°C). During the winter, however, because of the temperate influence of the Gulf of Mexico, the southern coast is much warmer than the north. In January, Biloxi averages 52°F (11°C), while Oxford averages 41°F (5°C). The lowest temperature ever recorded in Mississippi

Mississippi Population Profile

Total population estimate in 2006:	2,910,540
Population change, 2000–06:	2.3%
Hispanic or Latino†:	1.5%
Population by race	
One race:	99.1%
White:	60.8%
Black or African American:	36.5%
American Indian /Alaska Native:	0.4%
Asian:	0.8%
Native Hawaiian / Pacific Islander:	0.0%
Some other race:	0.6%
Two or more races:	0.9%

Population by Age Group

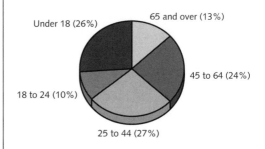

Under 18 (26%)
65 and over (13%)
45 to 64 (24%)
18 to 24 (10%)
25 to 44 (27%)

Major Cities by Population

City	Population	% change 2000–05
Jackson	177,977	-3.4
Gulfport	72,464	1.9
Biloxi	50,209	-0.9
Hattiesburg	47,176	5.4
Southaven	38,840	34.0
Greenville	38,724	-7.0
Meridian	38,605	-3.4
Tupelo	35,673	4.3
Olive Branch	27,964	32.8
Clinton	26,017	11.4

Notes: †A person of Hispanic or Latino origin may be of any race. NA indicates that data are not available.
Sources: U.S. Census Bureau. *American Community Survey* and *Population Estimates*. www.census.gov/ (accessed March 2007).

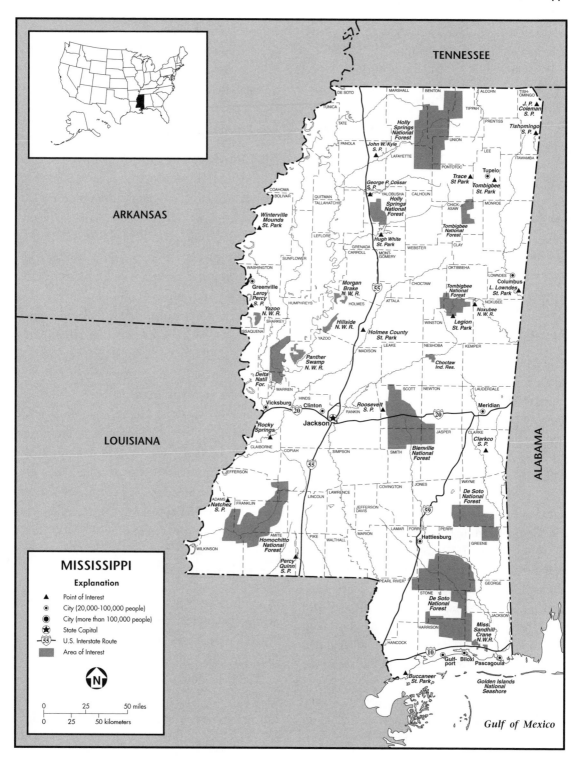

TENNESSEE

ARKANSAS

LOUISIANA

ALABAMA

MISSISSIPPI

Explanation

▲ Point of Interest

⊙ City (20,000-100,000 people)

◉ City (more than 100,000 people)

★ State Capital

〜55〜 U.S. Interstate Route

▨ Area of Interest

N

| 0 | 25 | 50 miles |
| 0 | 25 | 50 kilometers |

DE SOTO
MARSHALL
BENTON
ALCORN
TISH-OMINGO
TUNICA
TIPPAH
J. P. Coleman S. P. ▲
TATE
PRENTISS
Holly Springs National Forest
UNION
Tishomingo S. P. ▲
PANOLA
John W. Kyle S. P. ▲
LAFAYETTE
PONTOTOC
LEE
ITAWAMBA
COAHOMA
BOLIVAR
QUITMAN
George P. Cossar S. P. ▲
Tupelo ▲
Trace ▲ St. Park
Tombigbee St. Park ▲
YALOBUSHA
CALHOUN
MONROE
TALLAHATCHIE
Holly Springs National Forest
CHICK-ASAW
Winterville Mounds St. Park
LEFLORE
GRENADA
Hugh White St. Park
WEBSTER
CLAY
Tombigbee National Forest
CARROLL
MONT-GOMERY
WASHINGTON
SUNFLOWER
OKTIBBEHA
LOWNDES
Columbus ◉
Greenville ⊙
Morgan Brake N. W. R.
CHOCTAW
Tombigbee National Forest
L. Lowndes St. Park ▲
Leroy Percy S. P. ▲
HUMPHREYS
HOLMES
Noxubee N. W. R. ▲
NOXUBEE
Yazoo N. W. R.
Hillside N. W. R.
Holmes County St. Park ▲
WINSTON
Legion St. Park ▲
SHARKEY
ISSAQUENA
YAZOO
ATTALA
LEAKE
NESHOBA
KEMPER
Panther Swamp N. W. R.
MADISON
Choctaw Ind. Res.
Delta Natl For.
WARREN
HINDS
SCOTT
NEWTON
LAUDERDALE
Vicksburg ⊙
Clinton ⊙
Roosevelt S. P. ▲
Meridian ⊙
RANKIN
Jackson ★
20
Rocky Springs ▲
Bienville National Forest
JASPER
CLARKE
Clarkco S. P. ▲
CLAIBORNE
COPIAH
SIMPSON
SMITH
JEFFERSON
COVINGTON
JONES
WAYNE
De Soto National Forest
Natchez S. P. ▲
LINCOLN
LAWRENCE
ADAMS
FRANKLIN
JEFFERSON DAVIS
59
Homochitto National Forest
AMITE
PIKE
WALTHALL
MARION
LAMAR
FORREST
PERRY
GREENE
WILKINSON
Percy Quinn S. P. ▲
Hattiesburg ⊙
PEARL RIVER
STONE
GEORGE
De Soto National Forest
Miss. Sandhill Crane N.W.R.
HARRISON
JACKSON
HANCOCK
Gulf-port ◉
Biloxi ⊙
Pascagoula ⊙
10
Buccaneer St. Park ▲
Golden Islands National Seashore

Gulf of Mexico

was -19°F (-28°C) at Corinth on 30 January 1966. The highest temperature, 115°F (46°C), was set on 29 July 1930 at Holly Springs.

Precipitation in Mississippi increases from north to south. The north-central region averages 53 inches (135 centimeters) of precipitation a year. The coastal region averages 62 inches (157 centimeters) annually. Some snow falls in northern and central sections. Mississippi lies in the path of hurricanes moving northward from the Gulf of Mexico during the late summer and fall. Two tornado alleys cross Mississippi from the southwest to northeast, one from Vicksburg to Oxford and the other from McComb to Tupelo.

4 Plants and Animals

Post and white oaks, hickory, and magnolia grow in the forests of the uplands. Various willows and gums (including the tupelo) are in the Delta and longleaf pine is in the Piney Woods. Wildflowers include the black-eyed Susan and Cherokee rose. In April 2006, Price's potato-bean was listed as a threatened plant species. The Louisiana quillwort, pondberry, and American chaffseed were listed as endangered.

Common among the state's mammals are the opossum, armadillo, and coyote. Birds include varieties of wren, thrush, and hawk, along with numerous waterfowl and seabirds. Black bass, perch, and mullet are common freshwater fish. Rare species in Mississippi include the hoary bat, American oystercatcher, mole salamander, pigmy killifish, Yazoo darker, and five species of crayfish.

In 2006, a total of 30 animal species were listed as threatened or endangered, including the American and Louisiana black bears, eastern

indigo snake, Indiana bat, Mississippi sandhill crane, bald eagle, Mississippi gopher frog, brown pelican, red-cockaded woodpecker, five species of sea turtle, and the bayou darter.

5 Environmental Protection

The Mississippi Department of Environmental Quality (MDEQ) is responsible for environmental regulatory programs in the state, excluding the drinking water program, and the regulation of noncommercial oil field waste disposal. MDEQ regulates surface and groundwater withdrawals through its Office of Land and Water Resources and surface mining reclamation through its Office of Geology. All other environmental regulatory programs are administered through MDEQ's Office of Pollution Control. MDEQ implements one of the premier Pollution Prevention programs in the nation.

In 2003, Mississippi had 83 hazardous waste sites listed in the Environmental Protection Agency's database, three of which were on the National Priorities List, as of 2006. In 1996, wetlands accounted for 13% of the state's lands. The Natural Heritage Program identifies and inventories priority wetlands.

6 Population

In 2005, Mississippi ranked 31st in population among the 50 states with an estimated total of 2,910,540 residents. The population is projected to reach 3.01 million by 2015 and 3.06 million by 2025. In 2004, the population density was 61.9 persons per square mile (23.9 persons per square kilometer). In that same year, the median age of all residents was 34.9. In 2005, of all resi-

Mississippi Population by Race

Census 2000 was the first national census in which the instructions to respondents said, "Mark one or more races." This table shows the number of people who are of one, two, or three or more races. For those claiming two races, the number of people belonging to the various categories is listed. The U.S. government conducts a census of the population every ten years.

	Number	Percent
Total population	2,844,658	100.0
One race	2,824,637	99.3
Two races	18,382	0.6
White *and* Black or African American	3,462	0.1
White *and* American Indian/Alaska Native	5,259	0.2
White *and* Asian	2,402	0.1
White *and* Native Hawaiian/Pacific Islander	287	—
White *and* some other race	2,885	0.1
Black or African American *and* American Indian/Alaska Native	1,372	—
Black or African American *and* Asian	802	—
Black or African American *and* Native Hawaiian/Pacific Islander	230	—
Black or African American *and* some other race	785	—
American Indian/Alaska Native *and* Asian	131	—
American Indian/Alaska Native *and* Native Hawaiian/Pacific Islander	13	—
American Indian/Alaska Native *and* some other race	186	—
Asian *and* Native Hawaiian/Pacific Islander	169	—
Asian *and* some other race	344	—
Native Hawaiian/Pacific Islander *and* some other race	55	—
Three or more races	1,639	0.1

Source: U.S. Census Bureau. *Census 2000: Redistricting Data.* Press release issued by the Redistricting Data Office. Washington, D.C., March, 2001. A dash (—) indicates that the percent is less than 0.1.

dents in the state, 13% were 65 or older, and 26% were 18 or younger.

Mississippi is one of the most rural states in the United States. Mississippi's largest city, Jackson, had an estimated 2005 population of 177,977. The Jackson metropolitan area that year had an estimated population of 517,275. Other major cities include Gulfport, 72,464, and Biloxi, 50,209.

7 Ethnic Groups

According to the 2000 census, the state had 1,746,099 whites, 1,033,809 blacks, 39,569 Hispanics and Latinos, 11,652 Native Americans, and 667 Pacific Islanders. There were also 18,626 Asians, that same year, including 5,387 Vietnamese and 2,608 Filipinos. Mississippi had the lowest percentage of foreign-born residents in the country with 39,908 people, or 1.4% in 2000.

8 Languages

English in the state is largely Southern, with some South Midland speech in northern and eastern Mississippi. The absence of the final /r/ sound in a word is typical. South Midland terms in northern Mississippi include *tow sack* (burlap bag), *snake doctor* (dragonfly), and *stone wall* (rock fence). In the eastern section are found *jew's harp* (harmonica) and *croker sack* (burlap bag). Southern speech in the southern half features the terms *gallery* for porch and *mosquito hawk* for dragonfly. Louisiana French has contributed *armoire* for wardrobe.

In 2000, of all Mississippi residents five years old and older, 96.4% spoke only English in the home. Other languages spoken at home, and the number of people who spoke them, included Spanish, 50,515, and French, 10,826.

9 Religions

Protestants have dominated Mississippi since the late 18th century. The Baptists are the leading denomination and many adherents are fundamentalists. Partly because of the strong church influence, Mississippi was among the first states to enact prohibition and among the last to repeal it.

In 2000, the two principal Protestant denominations were: the Southern Baptist Convention, with 916,440 adherents, and the United Methodist Church with 189,149 adherents in 2004. There were about 124,150 Roman Catholics in 2004. In 2000, there were an estimated 3,919 Muslims, and about 1,400 Jews. Over 1.2 million people (about 45.4% of the population) did not claim any religious affiliation.

10 Transportation

At the end of 2003, there were 2,658 miles (4,279 kilometers) of mainline railroad track in the state. Class I railroads included the Burlington Northern, CSX, Illinois Central Gulf, Kansas City Southern, and Norfolk Southern lines. As of 2006, rail passenger service was provided by Amtrak via its City of New Orleans train, which connected six cities in Mississippi with Chicago and New Orleans, and the Crescent, which connected four cities in the state with New Orleans and Atlanta.

In 2004, Mississippi had 74,129 miles (119,347 kilometers) of public roads. Major interstate highways are I-55, I-59, I-20, I-220, I-10, and I-110. Mileage of four-lane highways is increasing daily under a "pay-as-you-go" public works program passed by the Mississippi legislature in 1987 to provide a four-lane highway within 30 minutes or 30 miles (48 kilometers) of every citizen in the state. In 2004, there were 1,896,008 licensed drivers in Mississippi and 1.159 million registered motor vehicles, including 1.113 million automobiles and 815,000 trucks.

Mississippi's ports and waterways serve a surrounding 16-state market. Mississippi has two deepwater seaports, Gulfport and Pascagoula, both located on the Gulf of Mexico. Other ports located on the Gulf include Port Bienville in Hancock County, and Biloxi in Harrison County. The Mississippi River flows along the western border of the state, linking the Gulf of Mexico to inland river states as far away as Minneapolis, Minnesota. The Mississippi is the largest commercial river in the country and the third-largest river system in the world. It carries the majority of the nation's inland waterway tonnage. Mississippi River ports within the states are at Natchez, Vicksburg, Yazoo County, Greenville, and Rosedale.

To the east of Mississippi lies the Tennessee-Tombigbee (Tenn-Tom) Waterway, completed in 1984, which links the Tennessee and Ohio rivers with the Gulf of Mexico. The Tenn-Tom Waterway's overall length is 232 miles (373 kilometers). Five local ports are located on the waterway: Yellow Creek, Itawamba, Amory, Aberdeen, and Columbus-Lowndes County.

In 2005, there were 191 airports in Mississippi, 51 heliports, and 1 STOLport (Short Take-Off and Landing). The state's main airport is Jackson-Evers International Airport. In 2004, the airport had 639,947 passenger boardings.

11 History

Upon the appearance of the first Spanish explorers in the early 16th century, Mississippi's Native Americans numbered some 30,000 and were divided into 15 tribes. Soon after the French settled in 1699, however, only three large tribes remained: the Choctaw, the Chickasaw, and the Natchez. The French destroyed the Natchez in 1729–30 in retaliation for the massacre of a French settlement.

Spaniards, of whom Hernando de Soto in 1540–41 was the most notable, explored the area that is now Mississippi in the first half of the 16th century. The French explorer Robert Cavelier, Sieur de la Salle, entered the lower Mississippi Valley in 1682 and named the entire area Louisiana in honor of the French King, Louis XIV. Soon the French opened settlements at Biloxi Bay (1699), Mobile (1702), Natchez (1716), and finally New Orleans (1718). After losing the French and Indian War, France ceded Louisiana to Spain, which ceded the portion of the colony east of the Mississippi to England, which governed the new lands as West Florida.

During the Revolutionary War, Spain once again seized West Florida, which it continued to rule almost to the end of the century, although the United States claimed the region after 1783. The US Congress organized the Mississippi Territory in 1798. The territory's large size convinced Congress to organize the eastern half as the Alabama Territory in 1817. Congress then offered admission to the western half, which became the nation's 20th state—Mississippi—on 10 December.

State Development After the opening of fertile Choctaw and Chickasaw lands for sale and settlement in the 1820s, cotton agriculture increased. Slavery was used to make farming profitable. As the profitability and number of slaves increased, so did attempts by ruling white Mississippians to justify slavery morally, socially, and economically. After Lincoln's election to the US presidency, Mississippi became, on 9 January 1861, the second southern state to secede. Union forces maneuvered before Vicksburg for more than a year before Grant besieged the city and forced its surrender on 4 July 1863. Along with Vicksburg went the western half of Mississippi. Of the 78,000 Mississippians who fought in the Civil War, nearly 30,000 died.

Reconstruction was a tumultuous period during which the Republican Party encouraged blacks to vote and hold political office, while the native white Democrats resisted full freedom for their former slaves. The era from the end of Reconstruction (1875) to World War II was a period of economic, political, and social stagnation for Mississippi. White Mississippians discriminated against blacks through segregation laws and customs and a new state constitution that removed the last vestiges of their political rights. Mississippi's agricultural economy, dominated by cotton and tenant farming, provided little economic opportunity for landless black farm workers. According to the Tuskegee

The cemetery at Vicksburg National Military Park where soldiers from the Battle of Vicksburg are buried. © ETHEL DAVIES/ ROBERT HARDING WORLD IMAGERY/CORBIS.

Institute, 538 blacks were lynched in Mississippi between 1883 and 1959, more than in any other state.

The Great Depression of the 1930s drove the state's agricultural economy to the brink of disaster. In 1932, cotton sank to five cents a pound, and one-fourth of the state's farmland was forfeited for nonpayment of taxes. World War II brought the first prosperity in a century to Mississippi. The war stimulated industrial growth and agricultural mechanization. By the early 1980s, Mississippi had become an industrial state.

Post-War Politics Politics in Mississippi have also changed considerably since World War II.

Within little more than a generation, legal segregation was destroyed, and black people exercised full political rights for the first time since Reconstruction. However, the "Mississippi Summer" campaign that helped win these rights also resulted in the abduction and murder of three civil rights activists in June 1964, in Philadelphia, Mississippi.

As of 1990, the Mississippi Legislature was nearly 23% black in a state in which blacks constitute 33% of the population. In 1998, African Americans accounted for 36% of the state's population.

In 1987, Mississippi elected a young reformist governor, Ray Mabus, who enacted the nation's largest teacher pay increase in 1988. Nevertheless, teacher salaries in 1992, were still, on average, the second-lowest in the nation. Democratic Governor Ronnie Musgrove, elected in 2000, was able to win additional teacher pay increases from the legislature in 2001. Improving the educational system was a state priority in the mid-2000s.

Former chairman of the Republican National Committee, Haley Barbour, was elected governor in 2003. Barbour launched "Momentum Mississippi," a long-range economic development strategy group composed of the state's business and community leaders. In 2005, he introduced comprehensive education reform legislation to reward teacher and school performance, reduce state bureaucracy, and strengthen discipline in the state's public schools.

Southern Mississippi was devastated by Hurricane Katrina in August 2005. A 30-foot (10-meter) storm surge came ashore, destroying 90% of buildings along the Biloxi-Gulfport coastline. Casino barges were washed ashore, and about 800,000 people suffered power outages in Mississippi in the aftermath of the storm. Mississippi is one of the nation's poorest states. This only exacerbated the problems facing residents as they tried to rebuild their lives and homes in Katrina's aftermath.

12 State Government

Mississippi's two-chamber legislature includes a 52-member Senate and a 122-member House of Representatives. All state legislators are elected to four-year terms. The governor, lieutenant governor, secretary of state, attorney general, state treasurer, state auditor, commissioner of insurance, and the commissioner of agriculture and commerce are independently elected for four-year terms. The governor is limited to two consecutive terms. The governor's vote can be overridden by a two-thirds vote of the members of both legislative chambers.

The legislative salary in 2004 was $10,000, and the governor's salary was $122,160.

13 Political Parties

Mississippi was traditionally a Democratic state during most of the period since the end of Reconstruction. However, its Democratic Party splintered along racial lines. During the 1950s and early 1960s, the segregationist White Citizens' Councils were so widespread and influential in the state as to rival the major parties in political importance.

In 1980, Ronald Reagan edged Jimmy Carter by a plurality of fewer than 12,000 votes. In 1984, however, Reagan won the state by a landslide, polling 62% of the vote. In the 2000 election, Republican George W. Bush won 57% of the vote and Democrat Al Gore received 42%. In 2004, President Bush won 59.6% of the vote, while John Kerry won 39.6%.

In 2003, Haley Barbour, a Republican, was elected to the state governorship. As of 2006, Mississippi's two senators, Thad Cochran and Trent Lott, were also Republicans. Following the 2006 midterm elections, the state's delegation to the US House of Representatives consisted of two Democrats and two Republicans. Following the 2006 elections, the state senate comprised 27 Democrats, 23 Republicans, and 2 Independents, while in the state's house there were 74 Democrats, 46 Republicans, and 2 Independents. Twenty-four women were elected to the state legislature in 2006, or 13.8%. In

The Mississippi state capitol building in Jackson. AP IMAGES.

2002 there were 1,754,560 registered voters. There is no party registration in the state.

14 Local Government

Each of Mississippi's 82 counties are divided into five districts, each of which elects a member to the county board of supervisors. As of 2005, Mississippi had 296 municipal governments. Most cities, including most of the larger ones, have a mayor and a city council, but some smaller cities are run by a commission or by a city manager. In 2005, there were 152 public school districts, and 458 special districts.

15 Judicial System

The Mississippi supreme court consists of a chief justice, two presiding justices, and eight associ-

ate justices. A new court of appeals was created in 1995. It consists of one chief judge, two presiding judges, and seven judges. The principal trial courts are the circuit courts, which try both civil and criminal cases. Small-claims courts are presided over by justices of the peace, who need not be lawyers.

In 2004, Mississippi's violent crime rate (murder/nonnegligent manslaughter, forcible rape, robbery, aggravated assault) was 295.1 incidents per 100,000 population. There were 20,983 prisoners in state and federal prisons in Mississippi as of 31 December 2004. The death penalty was reinstated in 1977, with lethal injection the sole method of execution. As of 1 January 2006, there were 65 inmates on death row.

16 Migration

In the late 18th century, most Mississippians were immigrants from other parts of the South and predominantly of Scotch-Irish descent. The opening of lands ceded by the Indians beginning in the 1820s brought tens of thousands of settlers into northern and central Mississippi. After the Civil War, there was little migration into the state, but much out-migration, mainly of blacks. The exodus from Mississippi was especially heavy during the 1940s and 1950s, when at least 720,000 people, nearly three-quarters of them black, left the state. During the 1960s, between 267,000 and 279,000 blacks departed while net white out-migration came to an end. Black out-migration slowed considerably during the 1970s.

Between 1990 and 1998, Mississippi had net gains of 43,000 in domestic migration and 6,000 in international migration. In the period 2000–

Mississippi Governors: 1817–2007

1817–1820	David Holmes	Dem-Rep		1896–1900	Anselm Joseph McLaurin	Democrat
1820–1822	George Poindexter	Dem-Rep		1900–1904	Andrew Houston Longino	Democrat
1822–1825	Walter Leake	Republican		1904–1908	James Kimble Vardaman	Democrat
1825–1826	Gerard Chittoque Brandon	Jacksonian		1908–1912	Edmond Favor Noel	Democrat
1826	David Holmes	Dem-Rep		1912–1916	Earl LeRoy Brewer	Democrat
1826–1832	Gerard Chittoque Brandon	Jacksonian		1916–1920	Theodore Gilmore Bilbo	Democrat
1832–1833	Abram Marshall Scott	Nat-Rep		1920–1924	Lee Maurice Russell	Democrat
1833	Charles Lynch	Whig		1924–1927	Henry Lewis Whitfield	Democrat
1833–1835	Hiram George Runnels	Jacksonian		1927–1928	Heron Dennis Murphree	Democrat
1835–1836	John Anthony Quitman	Democrat		1928–1932	Theodore Gilmore Bilbo	Democrat
1836–1838	Charles Lynch	Whig		1932–1936	Martin Sennett Conner	Democrat
1838–1842	Alexander Gallatin McNutt	Democrat		1936–1940	Hugh Lawson White	Democrat
1842–1844	Tilghman Mayfield Tucker	Democrat		1940–1943	Paul Burney Johnson	Democrat
1844–1848	Albert Gallatin Brown	Democrat		1943–1944	Herron Dennis Murphree	Democrat
1848–1850	Joseph W. Matthews	Democrat		1944–1946	Thomas Lowry Bailey	Democrat
1850–1851	John Anthony Quitman	Democrat		1946–1952	Fielding Lewis Wright	Democrat
1851	John Isaac Guion	Democrat		1952–1956	Hugh Lawson White	Democrat
1851–1852	James Whitfield	Democrat		1956–1960	James Plemon Coleman	Democrat
1852–1854	Henry Stuart Foote	Democrat		1960–1964	Ross Robert Barnett	Democrat
1854	John Jones Pettus	Democrat		1964–1968	Paul Burney Johnson, Jr.	Democrat
1854–1857	John Jones McRae	Democrat		1968–1972	John Bell Williams	Democrat
1857–1859	William McWillie	Democrat		1972–1976	William Lowe Waller	Democrat
1859–1863	John Jones Pettus	Democrat		1976–1980	Charles Clifton Finch	Democrat
1863–1865	Charles Clark	Democrat		1980–1984	William Forrest Winter	Democrat
1865	William Lewis Sharkey	Provisional		1984–1988	William A. Allain	Democrat
1865–1868	Benjamin Grubb Humphreys	Democrat		1988–1992	Ray Mabus, Jr.	Democrat
1868–1870	Adelbert Ames	Military		1992–2000	Kirk Fordice	Republican
1870–1871	James Lusk Alcorn	Republican		2000–2004	Ronnie Musgrove	Democrat
1871–1874	Ridgley Ceylon Powers	Republican		2004–	Haley Barbour	Republican
1874–1876	Adelbert Ames	Republican				
1876–1882	John Marshall Stone	Democrat		Democratic Republican – Dem-Rep		
1882–1890	Robert Lowry	Democrat		National Republican – Nat-Rep		
1890–1896	John Marshall Stone	Democrat				

05, net international migration was 10,653 people, while net domestic migration was -10,578, for a net gain of 75 people.

17 Economy

Once the social turmoil of the 1950s and early 1960s had subsided, the impressive industrial growth of the immediate postwar years resumed. By the mid-1960s, manufacturing—attracted to the state, in part, because of low wage rates and a weak labor movement—surpassed farming as a source of jobs. During the following decade, the balance of industrial growth changed somewhat. The relatively low-paying garment, textile, and wood-products industries, based on cotton and timber, grew less rapidly than a number of heavy industries, including transportation equipment, and electric and electronic goods. The debut of casino gambling in the state in 1992 stimulated Mississippi's economy. Still, Mississippi remains a poor state. Mississippi's gross state product (GSP) in 2004 was $76.166 billion. Of that amount, manufacturing accounted for the largest share at 15.9% of GSP. It was followed by the

Mississippi Presidential Vote by Political Parties, 1948–2004

YEAR	MISSISSIPPI WINNER	DEMOCRAT	REPUBLICAN	STATES' RIGHTS DEMOCRAT	SOCIALIST WORKERS	LIBERTARIAN
1948	Thurmond (SRD)	19,384	4,995	167,538	—	—
1952	Stevenson (D)	172,553	112,966	—	—	—
				INDEPENDENT		
1956	Stevenson (D)	144,453	60,683	42,961	—	—
				UNPLEDGED		
1960	Byrd**	108,362	73,561	116,248	—	—
1964	Goldwater (R)	52,616	356,512	—	—	—
				AMERICAN IND.		
1968	Wallace (AI)	150,644	88,516	415,349	—	—
				AMERICAN		
1972	*Nixon (R)	126,782	505,125	11,598	2,458	—
1976	*Carter (D)	381,309	366,846	6,678	2,805	2,788
				WORKERS' WORLD		
1980	*Reagan (R)	429,281	441,089	2,402	2,240	4,702
1984	*Reagan (R)	352,192	582,377	—	—	2,336
1988	*Bush (R)	363,921	557,890			3,329
				IND. (PEROT)	NEW ALLIANCE	
1992	Bush (R)	400,258	487,793	85,626	2,625	2,154
1996	Dole (R)	394,022	439,838	52,222	—	2,809
				PROGRESSIVE (NADER)		
2000	*Bush, G. W. (R)	404,614	572,844	8,122	613	2,009
2004	*Bush, G. W. (R)	458,094	684,981	—	—	1,793

* Won US presidential election.
** Unpledged electors won plurality of votes and cast Mississippi's electoral votes for Senator Harry F. Byrd of Virginia.

real estate sector at 9.4%, and by healthcare and social assistance at 7.2%.

Of the 54,117 businesses in Mississippi that had employees, an estimated 96.8% were small companies.

18 Income

In 2004, Mississippi ranked 51st among the 50 states and the District of Columbia with a per capita (per person) income of $24,518, compared to the national average of $33,050. Median household income for the three-year period 2002 through 2004 was $33,659, compared to the national average of $44,473. For that same period, an estimated 17.7% of the

state's residents lived below the federal poverty level, compared to 12.4% nationwide.

19 Industry

In 2004, the shipment value of all goods manufactured in Mississippi totaled $43.862 billion. Of that total, transportation equipment manufacturing accounted for the largest share at $7.694 billion, followed by food manufacturing at $5.798 billion, and chemical manufacturing at $4.832 billion.

In 2004, a total of 169,947 people were employed in the state's manufacturing sector. Of that total, food manufacturing accounted for the largest portion at 28,815, followed by furniture

Aerial view of the Nissan manufacturing plant that opened in Canton in May 2003. Five models, including the Altima and the Quest minivan, are manufactured there. COURTESY OF MISSISSIPPI DEVELOPMENT AUTHORITY.

and related products manufacturing at 26,292 people, and transportation equipment manufacturing at 25,689.

20 Labor

In April 2006, the seasonally adjusted civilian labor force in Mississippi numbered 1,314,300, with approximately 101,000 workers unemployed, yielding an unemployment rate of 7.7%, compared to the national average of 4.7% for the same period. According to nonfarm employment data released in April 2006, construction accounted for 4.8% of the labor force; manufac-

turing, 15.5%; trade, transportation, and public utilities, 19.8%; professional and business services, 7.9%; education and health services, 10.8%; leisure and hospitality services, l0.2%; and government, 21.4%. Data was not available for financial activities.

In 2005, a total of 77,000 of Mississippi's 1,089,000 employed wage and salary workers were members of a union. This represented 7.1% of those employed, up from 4.9% in 2004, but still below the national average of 12%.

21 Agriculture

In 2005, Mississippi ranked 26th among the states in income from agriculture, with marketings of over $3.85 billion. Crops accounted for $1.24 billion, with livestock and livestock products at $2.61 billion.

The history of agriculture in the state is dominated by cotton, which from the 1830s through World War II was Mississippi's principal cash crop. During the postwar period, however, as mechanized farming replaced the sharecropper system, agriculture became more diversified. During the period 2000–04, Mississippi ranked third in cotton and fourth in rice production among the 50 states.

Federal estimates for 2004 showed some 42,200 farms with a total area of 11 million acres (4.5 million hectares. The richest soil is in the Delta, where most of the cotton is raised. Livestock has largely taken over the Black Belt, a fertile area in the northwest.

22 Domesticated Animals

Cattle are raised throughout the state, though principally in the Black Belt and Delta regions. The main chicken-raising area is in the eastern hills.

In 2005, there were around 1.07 million cattle and calves, valued at $834.6 million. In 2004, there were around 315,000 hogs and pigs, valued at $34.6 million. Mississippi is a leading producer of broilers, ranking fifth in 2003, with some 4.3 billion pounds (2 billion kilograms) of broilers worth $1.51 billion, were produced that year.

23 Fishing

In 2004, Mississippi ranked ninth among the 50 states in size of commercial fish landings, with a total of 183.7 million pounds (83.5 million kilograms) valued at $43.8 million. Of this total, 162.8 million pounds (74 million kilograms) were landed at Pascagoula-Moss Point, the nation's eighth-largest port for commercial landings. Shrimp and blue crab made up the bulk of the commercial landings. The saltwater catch also includes mullet and red snapper. The freshwater catch is dominated by buffalo fish, carp, and catfish. In 2003, the state had 35 processing and 31 wholesale plants employing about 2,706 people. In 2002, the commercial fishing fleet had 1,365 boats and vessels.

Mississippi is one of the leading states in catfish farming, mostly from ponds in the Yazoo River basin. There are 410 catfish farms in operation. In 2004, the state issued 369,252 sport fishing licenses. The Mississippi Department of Wildlife, Fisheries and Parks operates 21 fishing lakes.

24 Forestry

Mississippi had approximately 18,605,000 acres (7,529,000 hectares) of forested land in 2004, about 60% of the state's total land area. Six national forests extend over 1.1 million acres (445,000 hectares). The state's most heavily forested region is the Piney Woods in the southeast. Of the state's total commercial timberland, 90% is privately owned. Some of this land was also used for agricultural purposes (grazing). Lumber production in 2004 totaled 2.74 billion board feet (sixth in the United States).

25 Mining

Mississippi's nonfuel mineral production in 2003 was valued at $174 million. Construction sand and gravel was the leading nonfuel mineral in 2003, accounting for about 40% of the state's total nonfuel mineral production, by value, followed by fuller's earth, crushed stone, portland cement, and industrial sand and gravel. According to preliminary figures for 2003, the state produced 12.8 million metric tons of construction sand and gravel, and 2.5 million metric tons of crushed stone.

By volume, Mississippi ranked second among the states in the production of fuller's earth, third in bentonite, and fourth in ball clay.

26 Energy and Power

In 2003, Mississippi's net summer electric power generating capacity stood at 17.282 million kilowatts, with total production in that same year at 40.148 billion kilowatt hours. The largest portion of all electricity generated came from coal-fired plants at 42.5%, with nuclear power generation accounting for 27.2% of output, and natural gas plants accounting for 23.6%. The remaining output came from plants using other renewable sources, petroleum, or other types of gases. As of 2006, the Grand Gulf Nuclear Station, built by Mississippi Power Company in Claiborne County, was the state's sole nuclear power facility.

Mississippi is a major petroleum producer. As of 2004, the state ranked 14th in proven reserves and 13th in output among the 31 oil producing states. In that same year, the state had 1,412 producing wells. Production of crude oil in 2004 averaged 47,000 barrels per day, while the state had proven reserves of 178 million barrels, that year. Natural gas production by Mississippi in 2004 totaled 145.692 billion cubic feet (4.13 billion cubic meters). As of 31 December 2004, the state's proven reserves of consumer-grade natural gas stood at 995 billion cubic feet (28.2 billion cubic meters). Most production comes from the south-central part of the state.

In 2004, Mississippi had only one producing coal mine. Production that year totaled 3.586 million tons.

27 Commerce

In 2002, Mississippi's wholesale trade sector had sales of $19.2 billion, while the state's retail trade sector that year had sales of $25.01 billion. Motor vehicle and motor vehicle parts dealers accounted for the largest portion of retail sales in 2002 at $6.4 billion, followed by general merchandise stores at $5.1 billion. Exports of goods produced in Mississippi totaled $4 billion in 2005.

28 Public Finance

Two state budgets are prepared each year, one by the State Department of Finance and Administration, which represents the governor's office, and one by the Joint Legislative Budget Committee, which represents the legislature. Both are submitted to the legislature for reconciliation and approval of a final plan. The fiscal year runs from 1 July through 30 June.

Total revenues for 2004 were $15.35 billion, while total expenditures that year totaled $14.33 billion. The largest general expenditures were for education ($4.3 billion), public welfare ($4.04 billion), and highways ($1.01 billion). The state's outstanding debt in 2004 was $4.27 billion, or $1,473.62 per capita (per person).

29 Taxation

The state income tax for both individuals and corporations ranges from 3% to 5%. Mississippi also imposes severance taxes on oil, natural gas, timber and salt. A 7% retail sales tax is levied, with local-option sales taxes permitted only up to 0.25%. The state also imposes a full array of excise taxes covering motor fuels, tobacco products, insurance premiums, public utilities, alcoholic beverages amusements, pari-mutuels, and many other selected items. Other state taxes include various license fee and state property taxes, though most property taxes are collected at the local level.

The state collected $5.432 billion in taxes in 2005, of which 47.6% came from the general sales tax, 21.6% from individual income taxes, 17.2% from selective sales taxes, and 5.2% from corporate income taxes. The remainder came from property and various other taxes. In 2005, Mississippi ranked 39th among the states in terms of combined state and local tax burden, which amounted to $1,860 per person, compared to the per capita national average of $2,192.

30 Health

In October 2005, Mississippi's infant mortality rate was estimated at 9.6 per 1,000 live births, the second-highest in the United States (followed by the District of Columbia). The overall rate of death in 2003 stood at 9.9 per 1,000 population. Leading causes of death were heart disease, cancer, cerebrovascular diseases, chronic lower respiratory diseases, and diabetes. Mississippi had the nation's third-highest death rates from heart disease and homicides, as well as one of the highest accidental death rates. The HIV-related death rate was 6.4 per 100,000 population. In 2004, the reported AIDS case rate was around 16.5 per 100,000 people. In that same year, about 24.4% of the state's population were smokers.

Mississippi's 93 community hospitals had about 13,000 beds in 2003. In 2005 there were 889 nurses per 100,000 people, while in 2004, there were 182 physicians per 100,000 population, and 1,159 dentists in the state. The average expense for community hospital care was $882 per day in 2003. In 2004, approximately 18% of the state's adult population had no health insurance.

31 Housing

In 2004, Mississippi had 1,221,240 housing units, of which 1,074,503 were occupied, and 69.6% were owner-occupied. About 69.4% of all units were single-family, detached homes, while 13.7% were mobile homes. Utility gas and electricity were the most common energy sources to all units. It was estimated that 92,908 units lacked telephone service, 8,325 lacked complete plumbing facilities, and 9,387 lacked complete kitchen facilities. The average household size was 2.61 people.

In 2004, a total of 14,500 privately owned units were authorized for construction. The median home value was $79,023, the second lowest in the country (above Arkansas). The median monthly cost for mortgage owners was $843. Renters paid a median of $529 per month.

32 Education

In 2004, of all Mississippians age 25 and older, 83% had completed high school, while only 20.1% had obtained a bachelor's degree or higher.

Mississippi's reaction to the US Supreme Court decision in 1954 mandating public school desegregation was to repeal the constitutional requirement for public schools and to foster the development of segregated private schools. In 1964, the state's schools did begin to integrate. In 1982, a system of free public kindergartens was established for the first time.

Total public school enrollment was estimated at 489,000 in fall 2003 and is expected to total 469,000 by fall 2014. Enrollment in private schools in fall 2003 was 49,729. Expenditures for public education in 2003/2004 were estimated at $3.4 billion.

As of fall 2002, there were 147,077 students enrolled in college or graduate school. In 2005, Mississippi had 40 degree-granting institutions including 9 public 4-year institutions, 17 public 2-year institutions, and 11 nonprofit private 4-year schools. Important institutions of higher learning in Mississippi include the University of Mississippi (established in 1844), Mississippi State University, and the University of Southern Mississippi. Predominantly black institutions include Tougaloo College, Alcorn State University, Jackson State University, and Mississippi Valley State University.

33 Arts

Jackson has two ballet companies, a symphony orchestra, and two opera companies. Opera South, an integrated but predominantly black company, presents free operas during its summer tours, and two major productions yearly. The Mississippi Opera instituted a summer festival during its 1980/81 season. There are local symphony orchestras in Meridian, Starkville, Tupelo, and Greenville.

Professional theaters in the state include the Sheffield Ensemble in Biloxi and the New Stage in Jackson. The Greater Gulf Coast Arts Center has been very active in bringing arts programs into the coastal area.

A distinctive contribution to US culture is the music of black sharecroppers from the Delta, known as the blues. The Delta Blues Museum in Clarksdale has an extensive collection documenting blues history. The annual Mississippi Delta Blues and Heritage Festival is held in Greenville.

The Mississippi Arts Commission oversees many arts programs throughout the state.

34 Libraries and Museums

As of September 2001, there were 237 libraries in the state, of which 189 were branches. In that same year, the state's libraries had 5.6 million volumes, and a total circulation of 8.898 million. In the Vicksburg-Warren County Public Library are collections on the Civil War, state history, and oral history. Tougaloo College has special collections of African materials, civil rights papers, and oral history. The Gulf Coast Research Library of Ocean Springs has a marine biology collection.

There are 65 museums, including the distinguished Mississippi State Historical Museum at Jackson, the Mississippi Blues Museum at Clarksdale, and the Lauren-Rogers Museum of Art in Laurel. Beauvoir, Jefferson Davis's home at

Biloxi, is a state shrine and includes a museum. The Mississippi Museum of Natural Science in Jackson has been designated as the state's official natural science museum by the legislature. In Meridian is a museum devoted to country singer Jimmie Rodgers. The Mississippi governor's mansion, said to be the second-oldest executive residence in the United States, is a National Historical Landmark.

35 Communications

In 2004, only 89.6% of the state's occupied housing units had telephones, the second-lowest rate in the United States. In June of that same year, Mississippi had over 1.4 million wireless telephone service subscribers. In 2003, computers were in 48.3% of all households in the state, while 38.9% had access to the Internet. In 2005, the state had 64 major operating radio stations (7 AM, 57 FM), and 14 major television stations. A total of 17,234 Internet domain names had been registered in Mississippi by the year 2000.

36 Press

In 2005, Mississippi had 23 daily newspapers, which included 8 morning dailies and 15 evening dailies. In addition there were 18 Sunday papers in the state. The state's leading newspaper is the Jackson *Clarion–Ledger*, with a weekday circulation of 94,938 (107,865 Sunday) in 2004. A monthly, *Mississippi Magazine*, is published in Jackson.

37 Tourism, Travel & Recreation

In 2004, there were 30 million overnight travelers in Mississippi, with about 83% of all visitors traveling from out of state. In 2002, total travel

Nobel Prize-winning author William Faulkner lived in this home in Oxford, Mississippi, for 32 years. AP IMAGES.

expenditures reached about $6.4 billion, which supported more than 126,500 travel-related jobs.

Among Mississippi's major tourist attractions are its riverboat casinos, mansions and plantations, of which many of the latter two are located in the Natchez area. At Greenwood is the Florewood River Plantation, a museum re-creating 19th-century plantation life. The Natchez Trace Parkway, Gulf Islands National Seashore, and Vicksburg National Military Park attract the most visitors annually. There are also 6 national forests and 24 state parks.

In 2005, many of the state's attractions were damaged by Hurricane Katrina, and as of 2006, had not fully recovered.

38 Sports

Although there are no professional major league sports teams in Mississippi, Jackson does have a minor league baseball team, the Senators, of the Central League. There is also a minor league hockey team in Biloxi, as well as teams in Jackson and Tupelo. The University of Mississippi has long been prominent in college football. "Ole Miss" teams have won six bowl games. The Ole Miss Rebels play in the Southeastern Conference, as do the Mississippi State Bulldogs. The University of Southern Mississippi is a member of Conference USA.

Other annual sporting events of interest include the Dixie National Livestock Show and Rodeo, held in Jackson in February, and the Southern Farm Bureau Classic, held in Madison in October and November.

39 Famous Mississippians

Mississippi's most famous political figure, Jefferson Davis (b.Kentucky, 1808–1889), was president of the Confederacy from 1861 until the defeat of the South in 1865. Imprisoned for two years after the Civil War (though never tried), Davis lived the last years of his life at Beauvoir, an estate on the Mississippi Gulf Coast. Lucius Quintus Cincinnatus Lamar (b.Georgia, 1825–1893), who served as Confederate minister to Russia, was appointed secretary of the interior in 1885 and later named to the US Supreme Court.

Some of the foremost authors of 20th-century America had their origins in Mississippi. Supreme among them is William Faulkner (1897–1962), whose novels included such classics as *The Sound and the Fury* (1929) and *Light*

Jefferson Davis (b .Kentucky, 1808–1889) was president of the Confederacy from 1861 until the defeat of the South in 1865. EPD PHOTOS/NATIONAL ARCHIVES.

in August (1932). Faulkner received two Pulitzer Prizes, and in 1949 was awarded the Nobel Prize for literature. Richard Wright (1908–1960), a powerful writer and leading spokesperson for the black Americans of his generation, is best remembered for his novel *Native Son* (1940) and for *Black Boy* (1945), an autobiographical account of his Mississippi childhood.

Other native Mississippians of literary renown (and Pulitzer Prize winners) are Eudora Welty (1909–2001); Tennessee Williams (Thomas Lanier Williams, 1911–1983); and playwright Beth Henley (b.1952). Other Mississippi authors are Shelby Foote (1916–2005); Walker Percy (b.Alabama, 1916–1990); and Willie Morris (1934–1999).

Among the state's numerous musicians are Leontyne Price (Mary Violet Leontine Price, b.1927), a distinguished opera soprano born in Laurel, Mississippi; famous blues singers Muddy Waters (McKinley Morganfield, 1915–1983); John Lee Hooker (1917–2001); and Riley "B. B." King (b.1925). Mississippi's contributions to music also include Jimmie Rodgers (1897–1933), Bo Diddley (Ellas McDaniels, b.1928), Conway Twitty (1933–1994), and Charley Pride (b.1939). Elvis Presley (1935–1977), born in Tupelo, was one of the most popular singers in US history. Other entertainers from Mississippi include Muppet creator Jim Henson (1936–1990) and Oprah Winfrey (b.1954).

Football greats Walter Payton (1954–1999) and Jerry Rice (b.1962), along with boxing legend Archie Moore (1916–1998), were born and raised in Mississippi.

40 Bibliography

BOOKS

Ballard, Michael B. *Civil War Mississippi: A Guide.* Jackson: University Press of Mississippi, 2000.

Bristow, M. J. *State Songs of America.* Westport, CT: Greenwood Press, 2000.

Brown, Jonatha A. *Mississippi.* Milwaukee, WI: Gareth Stevens, 2006.

Gibson, Karen Bush. *Mississippi Facts and Symbols.* Rev. ed. Mankato, MN: Capstone, 2003.

Harmon, Daniel E. *La Salle and the Exploration of the Mississippi.* Philadelphia: Chelsea House, 2000.

Isaacs, Sally Senzell. *Life on a Southern Plantation.* Chicago: Heinemann, 2001.

Lourie, Peter. *Mississippi River: A Journey Down the Father of Waters.* Honesdale, PA: Boyds Mills Press, 2000.

Mudd-Ruth, Maria. *The Mississippi River.* New York: Benchmark Books, 2001.

Murray, Julie. *Mississippi.* Edina, MN: Abdo Publishing, 2006.

Siebert, Diane. *Mississippi.* New York: HarperCollins Publishers, 2001.

WEB SITES

Mississippi Welcome Centers. *Mississippi.* www.visitmississippi.org (accessed March 1, 2007).

State of Mississippi. *Mississippi.gov.* www.mississippi.gov/index.jsp (accessed March 1, 2007).

Missouri

State of Missouri

ORIGIN OF STATE NAME: Probably derived from the Iliniwek Indian word *missouri,* meaning "owners of big canoes."

NICKNAME: The Show Me State.

CAPITAL: Jefferson City.

ENTERED UNION: 10 August 1821 (24th).

OFFICIAL SEAL: The coat of arms is surrounded by the words "The Great Seal of the State of Missouri."

FLAG: Three horizontal stripes of red, white, and blue, with the coat of arms encircled by 24 white stars on a blue band in the center.

COAT OF ARMS: Two grizzly bears stand on a scroll inscribed with the state motto and support a shield portraying an American eagle and a constellation of stars, a grizzly bear on all fours, and a crescent moon, all encircled by the words "United We Stand, Divided We Fall." Above are a six-barred helmet and 24 stars; below is the Roman numeral MDCCCXX (1820), when Missouri's first constitution was adopted.

MOTTO: *Salus populi suprema lex esto* (The welfare of the people shall be the supreme law).

SONG: "Missouri Waltz."

FLOWER: White Hawthorn blossom.

TREE: Flowering dogwood.

BIRD: Bluebird.

INSECT: Honeybee.

FOSSIL: Crinoid.

MINERAL: Galena.

ROCK OR STONE: Mozarkite (chert or flint rock).

LEGAL HOLIDAYS: New Year's Day, 1 January; Birthday of Martin Luther King Jr., 3rd Monday in January; Lincoln's Birthday, 12 February; Washington's Birthday, 3rd Monday in February; Harry S. Truman's Birthday, 8 May; Memorial Day, last Monday in May; Independence Day, 4 July; Labor Day, 1st Monday in September; Columbus Day, 2nd Monday in October; Veterans' Day, 11 November; Thanksgiving Day, 4th Thursday in November; Christmas Day, 25 December. Though not a legal holiday, Missouri Day, the 3rd Wednesday in October, is commemorated in schools each year.

TIME: 6 AM CST = noon GMT.

1 Location and Size

Located in the western north-central United States, Missouri ranks 19th in size among the 50 states. The total area of Missouri is 69,697 square miles (180,516 square kilometers), of which land takes up 68,945 square miles (178,568 square kilometers) and inland water 752 square miles

(1,948 square kilometers). Missouri extends 284 miles (457 kilometers) east-west and 308 miles (496 kilometers) north-south. The total boundary length of Missouri is 1,438 miles (2,314 kilometers).

2 Topography

Missouri is divided into four major land regions: the dissected Till Plains, lying north of the Missouri River; the Osage Plains, covering the western part of the state; the Mississippi Alluvial Plain, in the southeastern corner; and the Ozark Plateau, which comprises most of southern Missouri and extends into northern Arkansas and northeastern Oklahoma. The Ozarks contain Taum Sauk Mountain, which at 1,772 feet (540 meters) is the highest elevation in the state. Along the St. Francis River, near Cardwell, is the state's lowest point, 230 feet (70 meters).

Missouri has more than 1,000 miles (1,600 kilometers) of navigable waterways. The Mississippi and Missouri rivers, the two largest in the United States, form the state's eastern border and part of its western border. The White, Grand, Chariton, St. Francis, Current, and Osage are among the state's other major rivers. The largest lake is the artificial Lake of the Ozarks, covering a total of 93 square miles (241 square kilometers).

Missouri's exceptional number of caves and caverns were formed during the last 50 million years through the erosion of limestone and dolomite by melting snows.

3 Climate

Missouri has a continental climate with considerable local and regional variation. The average

Missouri Population Profile

Total population estimate in 2006:	5,842,713
Population change, 2000–06:	4.4%
Hispanic or Latino†:	2.6%
Population by race	
One race:	98.5%
White:	84.5%
Black or African American:	11.2%
American Indian /Alaska Native:	0.4%
Asian:	1.4%
Native Hawaiian / Pacific Islander:	0.1%
Some other race:	1.0%
Two or more races:	1.4%

Population by Age Group

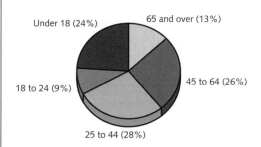

Under 18 (24%)
65 and over (13%)
18 to 24 (9%)
45 to 64 (26%)
25 to 44 (28%)

Major Cities by Population

City	Population	% change 2000–05
Kansas City	444,965	0.8
St. Louis	344,362	-1.1
Springfield	150,298	-0.8
Independence	110,208	-2.7
Columbia	91,814	8.6
Lee's Summit	80,338	13.6
St. Joseph	72,661	-1.8
O'Fallon	69,694	51.0
St. Charles	62,304	3.3
St. Peters	54,209	5.5

Notes: †A person of Hispanic or Latino origin may be of any race. NA indicates that data are not available. **Sources:** U.S. Census Bureau. *American Community Survey* and *Population Estimates*. www.census.gov/ (accessed March 2007).

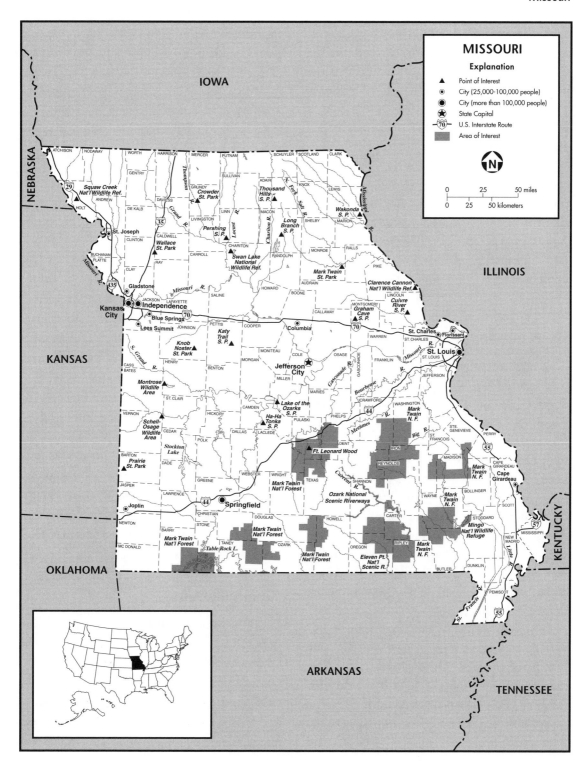

annual temperature is 50°F (10°C) in the north-west, and about 60°F (16°C) in the southeast. The coldest temperature ever recorded in Missouri was -40°F (-40°C) at Warsaw on 13 February 1905. The hottest temperature, 118°F (48°C), was recorded at Warsaw and Union on 14 July 1954.

The heaviest precipitation is in the south-east, where rainfall averages 48 inches (122 centimeters) per year. The northwest usually receives about 35 inches (89 centimeters) of rain per year. Annual snowfall averages 20 inches (51 centimeters) in the north and 10 inches (25 centimeters) in the southeast. Springtime is the peak tornado season.

4 Plants and Animals

Common trees of Missouri include the shortleaf pine, scarlet oak, peachleaf willow, pecan, and dogwood (the state tree). Various types of wild grasses proliferate in the northern plains region. Missouri's state flower is the hawthorn blossom. Other wildflowers include Queen Anne's lace, meadow rose, and white snakeroot. The American elm, common throughout the state, is considered endangered because of Dutch elm disease. In 2006, there were eight threatened or endangered plant species, including the decur-rent false aster, running buffalo clover, pond-berry, Missouri bladderpod, and western prairie fringed orchid.

Native mammals include the common cot-tontail, muskrat, and white-tailed deer. The state bird is the bluebird. Other common birds are the cardinal and solitary vireo. A characteris-tic amphibian is the plains leopard frog. Native snakes include garter, ribbon, and copperhead. Bass, carp, perch, jack salmon (walleye), and

crayfish abound in Missouri's waters. The chig-ger, a minute insect, is a notorious pest. In 2006, 17 species were listed as threatened or endan-gered in Missouri, including three species of bat (Ozark big-eared, gray, and Indiana), bald eagle, pallid sturgeon, gray wolf, and three varieties of mussel.

5 Environmental Protection

Missouri's principal environmental protection agencies are the Department of Conservation and the Department of Natural Resources. The State Environmental Improvement and Energy Resources Authority, within the Department of Natural Resources, is empowered to offer finan-cial aid to any individual, business, institution, or governmental unit seeking to meet pollution control responsibilities.

An important environmental problem is soil erosion. The state loses 71 million tons of topsoil each year.

In 2003, Missouri had 503 hazardous waste sites listed in the Environmental Protection Agency's database, 26 of which were on the National Priorities List in 2006. In 1996, it had 643,000 acres (260,000 hectares) of wetlands, or about 1.4% of the state's lands.

6 Population

In 2005, Missouri ranked 18th in population among the 50 states with an estimated total of 5,842,713 residents. The population is projected to reach 5.7 million by 2005 and 6.3 million by 2025. In 2004, the population density was at 83.5 persons per square mile (32.2 persons per square kilometer). The median age in 2004 was

Missouri Population by Race

Census 2000 was the first national census in which the instructions to respondents said, "Mark one or more races." This table shows the number of people who are of one, two, or three or more races. For those claiming two races, the number of people belonging to the various categories is listed. The U.S. government conducts a census of the population every ten years.

	Number	Percent
Total population	5,595,211	100.0
One race	5,513,150	98.5
Two races	77,339	1.4
White *and* Black or African American	15,566	0.3
White *and* American Indian/Alaska Native	27,998	0.5
White *and* Asian	9,387	0.2
White *and* Native Hawaiian/Pacific Islander	1,192	—
White *and* some other race	12,957	0.2
Black or African American *and* American Indian/Alaska Native	3,161	0.1
Black or African American *and* Asian	1,109	—
Black or African American *and* Native Hawaiian/Pacific Islander	243	—
Black or African American *and* some other race	2,678	—
American Indian/Alaska Native *and* Asian	271	—
American Indian/Alaska Native *and* Native Hawaiian/Pacific Islander	57	—
American Indian/Alaska Native *and* some other race	507	—
Asian *and* Native Hawaiian/Pacific Islander	920	—
Asian *and* some other race	1,166	—
Native Hawaiian/Pacific Islander *and* some other race	127	—
Three or more races	4,722	0.1

Source: U.S. Census Bureau. *Census 2000: Redistricting Data.* Press release issued by the Redistricting Data Office. Washington, D.C., March, 2001. A dash (—) indicates that the percent is less than 0.1.

37.3. In 2005, about 13% of all residents were 65 and older while 24% were 18 and younger.

More than half of all residents live in urban areas. The largest cities and their 2005 populations were Kansas City, 444,965, and St. Louis, 344,362.

7 Ethnic Groups

According to the 2000 census, Missouri had 629,391 black American residents. There were also 118,592 Hispanics and Latinos, including 77,887 of Mexican ancestry. The total Asian population was 61,595, including 13,667 Chinese, 7,735 Filipinos, 6,767 Koreans, 3,337 Japanese, and 12,169 Vietnamese. Pacific Islanders numbered 3,178. The Native American population included 25,076 residents. Of those Europeans claiming descent from one specific ancestry group, 1,313,951 were German, 528,935 English, and 711,995 Irish. The state had 151,196 foreign-born residents in 2000.

8 Languages

Northern and North Midland speakers settled north of the Missouri River and in the western border counties, bringing the Northern terms *pail* and *sick to the stomach* and the North Midland terms *fishworm* (earthworm), *gunnysack* (burlap bag), and *sick at the stomach*. South of the Missouri River, and notably in the Ozark Highlands, South Midland dominates with a few Southern forms, especially in the cotton-growing floodplain of the extreme southeast. *Wait on* (wait for), *light bread* (white bread), and *pully-bone* (wishbone) are terms specific to this area, as are *redworm* (earthworm), *towsack* (burlap bag), and *snap beans* (string beans). In the eastern half of the state, a soft drink is generally called *soda* or *sody*. In the western half, a soft drink is called *pop*.

In 2000, some 94.9% of state residents five years old or older spoke only English at home. Of those who claimed to speak another language at home, the leading languages and number of speakers were Spanish, 110,752; German, 30,680; and French, 30,680.

9 Religions

The first permanent Roman Catholic church was built about 1755 at St. Genevieve. Baptist preachers crossed the Mississippi River into Missouri in the late 1790s. The state's first Methodist church was organized about 1806. Conservative Lutheran immigrants from Germany organized the Lutheran Church—Missouri Synod in 1847.

In 2004, Missouri had 844,102 Roman Catholics. The next largest religious groups were the Southern Baptist Convention, with 797,732 adherents in 2000; the United Methodist Church, 176,022 adherents in 2004; the Lutheran Church—Missouri Synod, 140,315 adherents in 2000; and the Christian Church (Disciples of Christ), 105,583 in 2000. In 2000, the estimated number of Jews was 62,315 and Muslims numbered about 19,359. About 2.7 million people (48.3% of the population) were not counted as members of any religious organization.

10 Transportation

Centrally located, Missouri is the leading US transportation center. Both St. Louis and Kansas City are hubs of rail, truck, and airline transportation. In 2003, there were 4,791 rail miles (7,713 kilometers) of track in the state. In 2006, Amtrak provided passenger train service running directly from Chicago to St. Louis and to Kansas City, en route to San Antonio and Los Angeles, to 11 stations in Missouri.

A two-level cantilever bridge—the first in the world to have a steel superstructure—spanning the Mississippi at St. Louis was dedicated on 4 July 1874. In 2004, there were 125,923 miles (202,736 kilometers) of public roads in Missouri. The main interstate highways were I-70, I-44, I-55, I-35, and I-29. In 2004, there were some 4,855,000 motor vehicles registered in the state, including 2,690,000 passenger cars, 2,084,000 trucks, and 4,000 buses. There were 4,047,652 driver's licenses in force during the same year.

The Mississippi and Missouri rivers have long been important transportation routes. Pirogues, keelboats, and flatboats plied these waterways for more than a century before the first steamboat, the *New Orleans*, traveled down the Mississippi in 1811. The Mississippi still serves considerable barge traffic, making metropolitan St. Louis an active inland port area.

Pioneering aviators in Missouri organized the first international balloon races in 1907 and the first US-sponsored international aviation meet in 1910. Five St. Louis pilots made up the earliest US Army air corps, and a barnstorming pilot named Charles A. Lindbergh, having spent a few years in the St. Louis area, had the backing of businessmen from that city when he flew his *Spirit of St. Louis* across the Atlantic in 1927. As of 2006, Kansas City International Airport and Lambert-St. Louis Municipal Airport were among the busiest airports in the country.

11 History

When the first Europeans arrived in the late 17th century, most of the few thousand Native Americans living in Missouri belonged to two main linguistic groups: Algonkian-speakers, mainly the Sauk, Fox, and Iliniwek (Illinois) in the northeast; and a Siouan group, including the Osage, Missouri, Iowa, Kansas, and other tribes, to the south and west. The flood of white settlers into Missouri after 1803 forced the Native Americans to move into Kansas and into what became known as Indian Territory (present-day Oklahoma). During the 1820s, the US government negotiated treaties with the Osage, Sauk, Fox, and Iowa tribes whereby they surrendered all their lands in Missouri. By 1836, few Native Americans remained.

The first Europeans to pass through land that was eventually included within Missouri's boundaries were Jacques Marquette and Louis Jolliet, who in 1673 passed the mouth of the Missouri River on their journey down the Mississippi. Robert Cavelier, Sieur de la Salle, claimed the entire Mississippi Valley for France in 1682. Missouri passed into Spanish hands with the rest of the Louisiana Territory in 1762. In 1764, the French fur trader Pierre Laclède established a trading post on the present site of St. Louis.

Although the Spanish did not attempt to settle Missouri, they did allow Americans to migrate freely into the territory. Spanish authorities granted free land to the new settlers, relaxed their restrictions against Protestants, and welcomed slave-holding families from southern states. Spanish rule ended abruptly in 1800 when Napoleon forced Spain to return Louisiana to France. Included in the Louisiana Purchase, Missouri then became part of the United States in 1803.

Statehood Missouri was part of the Louisiana Territory until 1 October 1812, when the Missouri Territory (including present-day Arkansas) was established. A flood of settlers between 1810 and 1820 more than tripled Missouri's population from 19,783 to 66,586, leading Missourians to petition the US Congress for statehood as early as 1818. But Congress, divided over the slavery issue, withheld permission for three years, finally approving statehood for Maine and Missouri under the terms of the Missouri Compromise (1820), which sanctioned slavery in the new state but banned it in the rest of the former Louisiana Territory north of Arkansas. Missouri became the 24th state on 10 August 1821.

Aided by the advent of steamboat travel on the Mississippi and Missouri rivers, settlers continued to arrive in the new state, whose population surpassed one million by 1860. There was a great deal of proslavery sentiment in the state, and thousands of Missourians crossed into neighboring Kansas in the mid-1850s to help elect a proslavery government in that territory. During the Civil War, Missouri remained loyal to the Union, though not without difficulty, supplying some 110,000 soldiers to the Union and 40,000 to the Confederacy. At a constitutional convention held in January 1865, Missouri became the first slave state to free all blacks.

The Modern Era In addition to conflicts caused by the Republican Reconstruction government, the 1870s saw a period of lawlessness, typified by the exploits of Jesse and Frank James, that earned Missouri the epithet of the "robber state." Of more lasting importance were the closing of the frontier in Missouri, the decline of the fur trade and steamboat traffic, and the rise of the railroads. The state's economy increasingly shifted from agriculture to industry, and Missouri's rural population declined from about three-fourths of the total in 1880 to less than one-third by 1970. Although the overall importance of mining declined, Missouri remained the world's top lead producer, and the state has emerged as second only to Michigan in US automobile manufacturing.

Postwar prosperity was threatened beginning in the 1960s by the deterioration of several cities, notably St. Louis, which lost 47% of its population between 1950 and 1980. Both St. Louis and Kansas City undertook urban renewal programs to cope with the serious problems of air pollution, traffic congestion, crime, and substandard housing. During the early 1980s, millions of dollars in federal, state, and private funds were used to rehabilitate abandoned and dilapidated apartment buildings and houses.

Missouri was affected by the farm crisis of the 1980s, and many farms in the state failed. With the weakening of trade restrictions, the state's industries also suffered during this period. However, Missouri's economy improved in the 1990s, initially at a rate that outpaced much of the country. Due largely to the weak US economy in the early 2000s, Missouri's unemployment rate rose to 5.8% in July of 2003, albeit below the national average of 6.2%. However,

from September 2004 to September 2005, the state's unemployment rate declined from 5.9% to 4.8%, when it stood below the national average of 5.1%.

In the spring and summer of 1993, Missouri was hit by devastating floods. Over half of the state was declared a disaster area and 19,000 people were evacuated from their homes. Damage to the state was estimated at $3 billion.

In 2000, the state's popular governor, Mel Carnahan, died in a plane crash while running for the US Senate. He was replaced as governor by Democrat Bob Holden. Republican Matt Blunt was elected governor in 2004. He campaigned on a platform pledging to make education the state's top priority, to reform the state's social welfare programs, to address the state's health care crisis, to improve the entrepreneurial climate, and to hold the line on taxes.

12 State Government

Missouri's current constitution has been in force since 1945, and it had a total 105 amendments as of January 2005. A reorganization of state government took place in 1974, which replaced some 90 independent agencies with 13 cabinet departments and the Office of Administration.

The legislative branch, or general assembly, consists of a 34-member senate and a 163-seat house of representatives. Senators are elected to staggered four-year terms; representatives for two. The state's elected executives are the governor and lieutenant governor (who run separately), secretary of state, auditor, treasurer, and attorney general. All serve four-year terms.

A bill becomes law when signed by the governor within 15 days of legislative passage. A two-thirds vote by both houses is required to over-

Missouri Governors: 1820–2007

1820–1824	Alexander McNair	Dem-Rep		1901–1905	Alexander Monroe Dockery	Democrat
1824–1825	Frederick Bates	Democrat		1905–1909	Joseph Wingate Folk	Democrat
1825–1826	Abraham J. Williams	Dem-Rep		1909–1913	Herbert Spencer Hadley	Republican
1826–1832	John Miller	Jacksonian		1913–1917	Elliot Woolfolk Major	Democrat
1832–1836	Daniel Dunklin	Democrat		1917–1921	Frederich D. Gardner	Democrat
1836–1841	Lilburn W. Boggs	Democrat		1921–1925	Arthur Mastik Hyde	Republican
1841–1844	Thomas Reynolds	Democrat		1925–1929	Samuel Aaron Baker	Republican
1844–1845	Meredith Miles Marmaduke	Democrat		1929–1933	Henry Stewart Caulfield	Republican
1845–1848	John Cummins Edwards	Democrat		1933–1937	Guy Brasfield Park	Democrat
1848–1852	Austin Augustus King	Democrat		1937–1941	Lloyd Crow Stark	Democrat
1852–1856	Sterling Price	Democrat		1941–1945	Forrest C. Donnell	Republican
1856–1857	Trusten Polk	Democrat		1945–1949	Phil Matthew Donnelly	Democrat
1857	Hankock Lee Jackson	Democrat		1949–1953	Forrest Smith	Democrat
1857–1861	Robert Marcellus Stewart	Democrat		1953–1957	Philip Matthew Donnelly	Democrat
1861	Claiborne Fox Jackson	Democrat		1957–1961	James Thomas Blair, Jr.	Democrat
1861–1864	Hamilton Rowan Gamble	Unionist		1961–1965	John Montgomery Dalton	Democrat
1864	Willard Preble Hall	Unionist		1965–1973	Warren E. Hearnes	Democrat
1865–1869	Thomas Clement Fletcher	Union-Rep		1973–1977	Christopher S. Bond	Republican
1869–1871	Joseph Washington McClurg	Republican		1977–1981	Joseph P. Teasdale	Democrat
1871–1873	Benjamin Gratz Brown	Liberal-Rep		1981–1985	Christopher S. Bond	Republican
1873–1875	Silas Woodson	Democrat		1985–1993	John Ashcroft	Republican
1875–1877	Charles Henry Hardin	Democrat		1993–2000	Mel Eugene Carnahan	Democrat
1877–1881	John Smith Phelps	Democrat		2000–2004	Bob Holden	Democrat
1881–1885	Thomas Theodore Crittenden	Democrat		2004–	Matt Blunt	Republican
1885–1887	John Sappington Marmaduke	Democrat				
1887–1889	Albert Pickett Morehouse	Democrat		Democratic Republican – Dem-Rep		
1889–1893	David Rowland Francis	Democrat		Liberal Republican – Liberal-Rep		
1893–1897	William Joel Stone	Democrat		Union Republican – Union-Rep		
1897–1901	Lon Vest Stephens	Democrat				

ride a gubernatorial veto. Constitutional amendments require a majority vote of both houses of the legislature and ratification by the voters.

The legislative salary as of December 2004 was $31,561, and the governor's salary was $120,087.

13 Political Parties

Except for the Civil War and Reconstruction periods, the Democratic Party held the governorship from the late 1820s to the early 1900s. The outstanding figures of 20th century Missouri politics were both Democrats: Thomas Pendergast, the Kansas City political boss; and

Harry S. Truman, who began his political career as a Jackson County judge in the Kansas City area and in 1945 became the 33rd president of the United States.

Between 1980 and 1988, the state voted consistently for Republican presidential candidates. However, in 1992 and 1996 Democrat Bill Clinton carried the state. In the 2000 elections, Missouri returned to favoring the Republican candidate. George W. Bush won 50% of the vote and Democrat Al Gore received 47%. In the 2004 presidential election, President Bush garnered 53.4% of the vote to Democratic challenger John Kerry's 46.1%. Republican Matt Blunt was elected governor in 2004. Republican

Christopher Bond was first elected US senator in 1986 and reelected in 1992, 1998, and 2004. Democrat Claire McCaskill was elected senator in 2006 in a closely watched race, defeating incumbent Republican Jim Talent. Following the 2006 elections, four of the state's representatives to the US House were Democrats and five were Republicans. In the state senate following those elections, there were 13 Democrats and 21 Republicans; in the state house, there were 71 Democrats and 92 Republicans. Forty-two women were elected to the state legislature in 2006, or 21.3%. In 2004, there were 4,194,000 registered voters in the state; there is no party registration in the state.

14 Local Government

As of 2005, Missouri had 115 counties, 946 municipalities, 524 school districts, and 1,514 special districts. In 2002, there were also 312 townships. Elected county officials generally include commissioners, a public administrator, prosecuting attorney, sheriff, assessor, and treasurer. The city of St. Louis, which is administratively independent of any county, has an elected mayor, a comptroller, and a board of aldermen (including the president). Most other cities are governed by an elected mayor and council. The state was the first in the union to grant home rule to cities.

15 Judicial System

The supreme court, the state's highest court, consists of seven judges and three commissioners. The court of appeals consists of 32 judges in three districts. The circuit courts are the only trial courts and have original jurisdiction over all cases and matters, civil and municipal. Many circuit courts have established municipal divisions, presided over by judges paid locally. The 2004 violent crime rate (murder, rape, robbery, aggravated assault) for the state was 490.5 per 100,000 people. Crimes against property (burglary, larceny/theft, and motor vehicle theft) totaled 3,903.5 reported incidents per 100,000 people. As of 31 December 2004, there were 31,081 inmates in Missouri federal and state prisons. Missouri has a death penalty law, and from 1976 through 5 May 2006, had executed 66 persons. As of 1 January 2006, 53 prisoners were under sentence of death.

16 Migration

Missouri's first European immigrants, French fur traders and missionaries, began settling in the state in the early 18th century. Under Spain, Missouri received few Spanish settlers but many immigrants from the eastern United States. During the 19th century, newcomers continued to arrive from the South and the East slave-owning southerners (with their black slaves) as well as New Englanders opposed to slavery. They were joined by a wave of European immigrants, notably Germans and, later, Italians. By 1850, one out of three St. Louis residents was German-born.

The dominant intrastate migration pattern has been the concentration of blacks in the major cities, especially St. Louis and Kansas City, and the exodus of whites from those cities to the suburbs and, more recently, to small towns and rural areas.

Between 1990 and 1998, Missouri had net gains of 94,000 in domestic migration and 34,000 in international migration. In the period

Missouri Presidential Vote by Political Parties, 1948–2004

YEAR	MISSOURI WINNER	DEMOCRAT	REPUBLICAN	PROGRESSIVE	SOCIALIST
1948	*Truman (D)	917,315	655,039	3,998	2,222
1952	*Eisenhower (R)	929,830	959,429	—	—
1956	Stevenson (D)	918,273	914,289	—	—
1960	*Kennedy (D)	972,201	962,218	—	—
1964	*Johnson (D)	1,164,344	653,535	—	—
				AMERICAN IND.	
1968	*Nixon (R)	791,444	811,932	206,126	—
1972	*Nixon (R)	698,531	1,154,058	—	—
1976	Carter (D)	998,387	927,443	—	—
				LIBERTARIAN	**SOC. WORKERS**
1980	*Reagan (R)	931,182	1,074,181	14,422	1,515
1984	*Reagan (R)	848,583	1,274,188	—	—
					NEW ALLIANCE
1988	*Bush (R)	1,001,619	1,084,953	434	6,656
					IND. (PEROT)
1992	*Clinton (D)	1,053,873	811,159	7,497	518,741
1996	*Clinton (D)	1,025,935	890,016	10,522	217,188
					GREEN
2000	*Bush, G. W. (R)	1,111,138	1,189,924	7,436	38,515
2004	*Bush, G. W. (R)	1,259,171	1,455,713	9,831	—

* Won US presidential election.

2000–05, net international migration was 42,690, and net internal migration was 26,979, for a net gain of 69,669 people.

17 Economy

Missouri's central location and access to the Mississippi River contributed to its growth as a commercial center. The state's economy is diversified, with manufacturing, farming, trade, tourism, services, government, and mining as prime sources of income. Today, automobile and aerospace manufacturing are the state's leading industries, while soybeans and meat and dairy products are the most important agricultural commodities. The state's historic past, varied physical terrain, and modern urban attractions—notably the Gateway Arch in St. Louis—have made tourism a growth industry in recent decades.

Manufacturing output fell in the late 1990s and early 2000s, while output from financial services, including insurance and real estate, increased. In addition to being negatively affected by the 2001 national recession, Missouri was afflicted by drought conditions in 2002. In 2004, Missouri's gross state product (GSP) was $203.29 billion, of which manufacturing accounted for the largest share ($31.48 billion, or 15.4% of GSP), followed by the real estate sector at $19.53 billion (9.6% of GSP), and healthcare and social assistance at $15.15 billion (7.4% of GSP).

18 Income

In 2005, Missouri had a gross state product (GSP) of $216 billion, 20th among the 50 states and the District of Columbia. In 2004,

Missouri ranked 31st among the 50 states and the District of Columbia with a per capita (per person) income of $30,475; the national average was $33,050. The three-year average median household income for 2002–04 was $43,988 compared to the national average of $44,473. During the same period, 10.9% of the state's residents lived below the federal poverty level, compared to 12.4% nationwide.

19 Industry

The leading industry groups, by value of shipments, are transportation equipment (mainly automobiles, aircraft, and rockets and missiles); food and food products; chemicals; electric and electronic equipment; and fabricated metal products. Shipments by Missouri manufacturers during 2004 amounted to $102.8 billion. McDonnell Douglas, with headquarters in St. Louis, is a leading manufacturer of aerospace products, including all the Mercury and Gemini space capsules, DC-9 and DC-10 commercial jet aircraft, and Tomahawk cruise missiles.

20 Labor

As of April 2006, the civilian labor force in Missouri numbered 3,057,200, with approximately 141,700 workers unemployed, yielding an unemployment rate of 4.6%, compared to the national average of 4.7% for the same period. In April 2006, 5.2% of the labor force was employed in construction; 11% in manufacturing; 19.8% in trade, transportation, and public utilities; 6% in financial activities; 11.7% in professional and business services; 13.5% in education and health services; 10% in leisure and hospitality services; and 15.6% in government.

As early as the 1830s, journeyman laborers and mechanics in St. Louis, seeking higher wages and shorter hours, banded together to form trade unions and achieved some of their demands. Attempts to establish a workingman's party were unsuccessful, however, and immigration during subsequent decades ensured a plentiful supply of cheap labor. Union activity increased in the 1870s, partly because of the influence of German socialists. The Knights of Labor took a leading role in the labor movement from 1879 to 1887, the year that saw the birth of the St. Louis Trades and Labor Assembly. The Missouri State Federation of Labor was formed in 1891, at a convention in Kansas City.

By 1916, the state had 915 unions. Union activity in Missouri declined in the 1990s and early 2000s. In 2005, 290,000 of Missouri's 2,532,000 employed wage and salary workers were members of unions. This represented 11.5% of those so employed. The national average was 12%.

21 Agriculture

In 2004, Missouri had 106,000 farms (second in the United States) covering 30.1 million acres (12.2 million hectares). Missouri's agricultural income reached $5.57 billion in 2005, 15th among the 50 states. In 2004, Missouri was fourth among the states in grain sorghum production, fifth in soybean, and sixth in rice production. Soybean production is concentrated mainly in the northern counties and in the extreme southeast, with Mississippi County a leading producer. Stoddard County is a major source for corn and wheat production, as is New Madrid for grain sorghum.

In 2004, farmers harvested 223.2 million bushels of soybeans, 466 million bushels of corn, 48.4 million bushels of wheat, 15.7 million bushels of grain sorghum, 820,000 bales of cotton, and 9.4 million tons of hay. Tobacco, oats, rye, apples, peaches, grapes, watermelons, and various seed crops are also grown in commercial quantities.

22 Domesticated Animals

In Missouri, hog raising is concentrated north of the Missouri River, cattle raising in the western counties, and dairy farming in the southwest.

In 2005, Missouri farms and ranches had an estimated 4.5 million cattle and calves, valued at $3.8 billion. In 2004, there were around 2.9 million hogs and pigs, valued at $246.5 million. During 2003, Missouri farmers produced 816.2 million pounds (371 million kilograms) of turkey (ranked third in the nation), valued at around $285.7 million. Also in 2003, poultry farmers produced 1.9 million eggs, valued at $100 million. The state's 129,000 milk cows yielded nearly 1.9 million pounds (0.86 million kilograms) of milk in 2003.

23 Fishing

Commercial fishing takes place mainly on the Mississippi, Missouri, and St. Francis rivers. Sport fishing is enjoyed throughout the state, but especially in the Ozarks, whose waters harbor walleye, rainbow trout, bluegill, and largemouth bass. In 2004, Missouri issued 844,318 sport fishing licenses. The Neosho National Fish Hatchery stocks rainbow trout to Lake Taneycomo, as well as sites in Kansas and Iowa.

There are eleven state hatcheries, four of which include trout parks.

24 Forestry

At one time, Missouri's forests covered 30 million acres (12 million hectares), more than two-thirds of the state. As of 2004, Missouri had 15,010,000 acres (6,075,000 hectares) of forestland (about 30% of the land area in the state), of which more than 95% was commercial forest, 82% of it privately owned. Most of Missouri's forestland is in the southeastern third of the state. Of the commercial forests, approximately three-fourths are of the oak/ hickory type; short-leaf pine and oak/pine forests comprise about 5%, while the remainder consists of cedar and bottomland hardwoods.

Missouri leads the United States in the production of charcoal, red cedar novelties, gunstocks, and walnut bowls and nutmeats; railroad ties, hardwood veneer and lumber, wine and bourbon casks, and other forest-related items are also produced. Lumber production in 2004 totaled 575 million board feet, 97% of it hardwoods.

Conservation areas managed by the Forestry Division are used for timber production, wildlife and watershed protection, hunting, fishing, and other recreational purposes. Missouri's one national forest, Mark Twain in the southeast, encompassed 1,489,000 acres (603,000 hectares) of National Forest System lands as of 2005.

25 Mining

Nonfuel mineral production in Missouri was estimated at over $1.29 billion in 2003. In the same year, crushed stone, portland cement, lead,

The St. Louis Gateway Arch. AP IMAGES.

and lime accounted for 88% of the total value. Crushed stone, by value, has been Missouri's leading nonfuel mineral commodity since 1997. Portland cement and lead were the state's second and third top minerals in 2003. In 2003, Missouri was the nation's top lead producer, contributing well over half the lead produced in the United States. The state also ranked first in lime and fire clay production, third in zinc and fuller's earth, fifth in portland cement and crushed stone, and sixth in silver. Missouri ranked eighth nationally in nonfuel mineral value.

26 Energy and Power

Missouri's electric power plants had an installed generating capacity (utility and nonutility) of 19.9 million kilowatts in 2003. Electrical output totaled 87.2 billion kilowatt hours in the same year. Coal-fired plants accounted for 85.1% of all power production and nuclear plants for 11.1%.

Fossil fuel resources are limited. Reserves of bituminous coal totaled 6 billion tons in 1998, but only a small portion (3 million tons) was considered recoverable. About 578,000 tons were mined in 2004, all from three surface mines. Small quantities of crude petroleum are also produced commercially. In 2004, production was 241 barrels per day. In 2000, Missouri's total per capita energy consumption was 296 million Btu (74.6 million kilocalories), ranking it 38th among the 50 states.

27 Commerce

Missouri has been one of the nation's leading trade centers ever since merchants in Independence began provisioning wagon trains for the Santa Fe Trail. The state's wholesale sales totaled $95.6 billion in 2002; retail sales were $61.8 billion. Foreign exports of Missouri products exceeded $10.4 billion in 2005.

28 Public Finance

The Missouri state budget is prepared by the Office of Administration's Division of Budget and Planning and submitted annually by the governor to the general assembly for amendment and approval. The fiscal year runs from 1 July to 30 June.

The revenues for 2004 were $26.3 billion and expenditures were $22.0 billion. The largest general expenditures were for education ($6.8 billion), public welfare ($5.6 billion), and highways ($1.8 billion). The debt of Missouri state government was $16.2 billion, or $2,815.69 per capita (per person).

29 Taxation

Missouri's 10-bracket personal income tax schedule ranges from 1.5% to 6%. Individuals may deduct up to $5,000 of federal taxes paid from their state liability. The corporate tax rate is 6.25% of net income, with 50% of federal corporate taxes paid deductible. The basic state sales tax is 4.225%, but is lowered to 1.225% for food and beverages. Prescription drugs are exempt. Local-option sales taxes can reach up to 4.5%. The state also imposes a full array of excise taxes covering motor fuels, tobacco products, insurance premiums, public utilities, alcoholic beverage, amusements, and other selected items. Other state taxes include an assessment on surface mining, various license fees and franchise taxes, and state property taxes, although most property taxes are collected locally. Property and sales taxes are the leading sources of local revenue.

The state collected $9.544 billion in taxes in 2005, of which 42.1% came from individual income taxes, 31.8% came from the general sales tax, 16.4% from selective sales taxes, 2.3% from corporate income taxes, 0.2% from property taxes, and 7.2% from other taxes. In 2005, Missouri ranked 46th among the states in terms of per capita (per person) tax burden, at $1,645 per capita. The national average was $2,192 per capita.

30 Health

In October 2005, the infant mortality rate in Missouri was 7.6 per 1,000 live births. The over-all death rate was 9.7 per 1,000 population in 2003, one of the highest in the country. Deaths from heart disease, cerebrovascular disease, accidents and adverse effects, and motor vehicle accidents were all above the national rate. About 24.1% of Missouri residents were smokers. The rate of death from HIV-related infection stood at 2.2 per 100,000 population. A total of 9,654 AIDS cases was reported in Missouri through 2001.

Missouri's 119 community hospitals had about 19,300 beds in 2003. The average expense for community hospital care was $1,403 per inpatient day in 2003. As of 2004, there were 241 doctors per 100,000 residents and 940 nurses per 100,000 residents. In 2004, at least 12% of Missouri's adult population was uninsured.

31 Housing

In 2004, Missouri had an estimated 2,564,340 housing units, of which 2,309,205 were occupied; 70.8% were owner-occupied. About 69.3% of all units were single-family, detached homes. Utility gas and electricity were the most common energy sources for heating. It was estimated that 89,522 units lacked telephone services, 11,971 lacked complete plumbing facilities, and 12,264 lacked complete kitchen facilities. The average household size was 2.42 people.

In 2004, 32,800 new privately owned units were authorized for construction. The median home value was $117,033. The median monthly cost for mortgage owners was $954. Renters paid a median of $567 per month.

32 Education

Although the constitution of 1820 provided for the establishment of public schools, it was not until 1839 that the state's public school system became a reality through legislation creating the office of state superintendent of common schools and establishing a permanent school fund. Missouri schools were officially segregated from 1875 to 1954, when the US Supreme Court issued its landmark ruling in *Brown v. Board of Education of Topeka, Kansas*. The state's school segregation law was not taken off the books until 1976.

In 2004, an estimated 87.9% of all Missourians 25 years of age or older were high school graduates and 28.1% had obtained bachelor's degrees or higher. Total public school enrollment was estimated at 924,000 in fall 2002 but expected to drop to 910,000 by fall 2014. Enrollment in private schools in fall 2003 was 119,812. Expenditures for public education in 2003/04 were estimated at $7.8 billion.

As of fall 2002, there were 348,146 students enrolled in college or graduate school. Missouri has 14 public 4-year schools, 20 public 2-year schools, and 54 private institutions of higher education. The University of Missouri, established in 1839, was the first state-supported university west of the Mississippi River. It has four campuses: Columbia, Kansas City, Rolla, and St. Louis. Lincoln University, a public university for blacks until segregation ended in 1954, is located in Jefferson City. There are five regional state universities and three state colleges. Two leading independent universities, Washington and St. Louis, are located in St. Louis, as is the Concordia Seminary, an affiliate of the Lutheran Church-Missouri Synod.

33 Arts

Theatrical performances are offered throughout the state, mostly during the summer. In Kansas City, productions of Broadway musicals and light opera are staged at the Starlight Theater, which seats 7,860 in an open-air setting. The Missouri Repertory Theater, on the University of Missouri campus in Kansas City, also has a summer season. In St. Louis, the 12,000-seat Municipal Opera puts on outdoor musicals. The Goldenrod, built in 1909 and said to be the largest showboat ever constructed (seating capacity 289), is used today for vaudeville, melodrama, and ragtime shows. Other notable playhouses are the 8,000-seat Riverfront Amphitheater in Hannibal and the 344-seat Lyceum Theater in Arrow Rock (population 89).

Leading orchestras are the St. Louis Symphony and Kansas City Symphony. Independence, Liberty, Columbia, Kirksville, St. Joseph, and Springfield also have orchestras. The Opera Theatre of St. Louis and the Lyric Opera of Kansas City are distinguished musical organizations. Springfield has a regional opera company.

Between World Wars I and II, Kansas City was the home of a thriving jazz community that included Charlie Parker and Lester Young. Leading bandleaders of that time were Benny Moten, Walter Page, and Count Basie. Country music predominates in rural Missouri in places like the Ozark Opry at Osage Beach. There are over 40 performing venues in Branson.

There are about 350 arts associations and over 50 local associations in Missouri. The state provides arts education in all of the approximately 550 public school districts. In 1994, the Missouri General Assembly established the

Missouri Cultural Trust, a state endowment for the arts, with the goal of building it into a $200 million operational endowment in 10 years. The Trust is one of only a few such trusts in the nation and the only one that receives dedicated annual tax revenues. The Missouri Humanities Council sponsors an annual weeklong summer history festival on various themes. The festival is generally held in a different community each year.

34 Libraries and Museums

In June 2001, Missouri had 150 public library systems with a total of 363 libraries, of which 216 were branches. That year, the state's public libraries had a combined book stock of 18.7 million and a circulation of 38.7 million. The Missouri State Library, in Jefferson City, is the center of the state's interlibrary loan network. The University of Missouri-Columbia has the leading academic library. The federally-administered Harry S. Truman Library and Museum is at Independence.

Missouri has well over 162 museums and historic sites. The William Rockhill Nelson Gallery/Atkins Museum of Fine Arts in Kansas City and the St. Louis Art Museum both house distinguished general collections. The Mark Twain Home and Museum in Hannibal has a collection of manuscripts and other memorabilia. Also notable are the Pony Express Stables Museum, Missouri Botanical Garden, St. Louis Center Museum of Science and Natural History, and McDonnell Planetarium.

35 Communications

The first experiment in airmail service took place at St. Louis in 1911; Charles Lindbergh was an airmail pilot on the St. Louis-Chicago route in 1926.

As of 2004, about 93.7% of all state households had telephone service. By June of that year, there were 2,859,953 mobile telephone subscribers. In 2003, 60.7% of Missouri households had a computer and 53% had Internet access. The voice of a US president was heard over the air for the first time on 21 June 1923, when Warren G. Harding gave a speech in St. Louis. As of 2005, there were 36 major commercial AM stations and 97 major FM stations in service. There were also 25 major television stations. The St. Louis area had 1,114,370 television households, but only 56% of those received cable in 1999. Kansas City had a 65% subscription rate in 802,580 television households.

36 Press

Many Missouri journalists have achieved national recognition. The best known is Samuel Clemens (later Mark Twain), who started out as a "printer's devil" in Hannibal at the age of 13. Hungarian-born Joseph Pulitzer created the *St. Louis Post–Dispatch* in 1878 and established the Pulitzer Prizes, which annually honor journalistic and artistic achievement.

As of 2005, Missouri had 13 morning newspapers, 29 evening dailies, and 23 Sunday papers. The leading dailies with their 2005 daily circulations were the *St. Louis Post-Dispatch* (286,310) and the *Kansas City Star* (275,747). Periodicals include the St. Louis-based *Sporting News*, a popular bimonthly publication for baseball fans;

Busch Stadium houses the St. Louis Cardinals baseball team. AP IMAGES.

and *VFW Magazine*, put out monthly in Kansas City by the Veterans of Foreign Wars.

37 Tourism, Travel & Recreation

In 2004, the state hosted about 37.7 million domestic travelers, with 69% of all visitors coming from out-of-state. Total travel revenues were at about $8.3 billion dollars and the industry supported over 284,916 jobs.

The most popular vacation areas are the St. Louis region (40% of all visits) and the Kansas City area (23%). The principal attraction in St. Louis is the Gateway Arch. At 630 feet (192 meters) it is the tallest man-made national monument in the United States. In the Kansas City area are the Truman Sports Complex, Jesse

James's birthplace near Excelsior Springs, and Harry Truman's hometown of Independence. Branson is considered the "Live Music Show Capital of the World."

Memorabilia of Mark Twain are housed in and around Hannibal. The birthplace and childhood home of George Washington Carver is in Diamond. The Lake of the Ozarks, with 1,375 miles (2,213 kilometers) of shoreline, is one of the most popular vacation spots in mid-America. Other attractions are the Pony Express Stables and Museum at St. Joseph and the "Big Springs Country" of the Ozarks, in the southeast.

Missouri has 27 state parks. Lake of the Ozarks State Park is the largest, covering 16,872 acres (6,828 hectares). There are also 27 historic sites. State parks and historic sites covered

Missouri's most popular author is Mark Twain (Samuel Langhorne Clemens, 1835–1910), whose Adventures of Tom Sawyer *(1876) and* Adventures of Huckleberry Finn *(1884) evoke his boyhood in Hannibal.* EPD PHOTOS.

105,000 acres (43,050 hectares). Hunting and fishing are popular recreational activities.

38 Sports

There are six major league professional sports teams in Missouri: the Kansas City Royals and the St. Louis Cardinals of Major League Baseball, the Kansas City Chiefs and St. Louis Rams of the National Football League, the St. Louis Blues of the National Hockey League, and the Kansas City Wizards of Major League Soccer. The Rams moved to St. Louis from Los Angeles after the 1994 season and now play in the 66,000-seat Trans World Dome, which opened in 1995. They won the Super Bowl in 2000.

Horse racing has a long history in Missouri. In 1812, St. Charles County sportsmen held two-day horse races. By the 1820s, racetracks were laid out in nearly every city and in crossroads villages.

In collegiate sports, the University of Missouri competes in the Big Twelve Conference.

39 Famous Missourians

Harry S. Truman (1884–1972) has been the only native-born Missourian to serve as US president or vice president. Missouri's best-known senator was Thomas Hart Benton (b. North Carolina, 1782–1858), who championed the interests of Missouri and the West for 30 years.

Meriwether Lewis (b. Virginia, 1774–1809) and William Clark (b. Virginia, 1770–1838) explored Missouri and the West during 1804–06. Lewis later served as governor of Louisiana Territory, with headquarters at St. Louis, and Clark was governor of Missouri Territory from 1813 to 1821. Dred Scott (b. Virginia, 1795–1858), a slave owned by a Missourian, figured in a Supreme Court decision that set the stage for the Civil War. Missourians with unsavory reputations include such desperadoes as Jesse James (1847–1882), his brother Frank (1843–1915), and Cole Younger (1844–1916), also a member of the James gang.

Distinguished scientists include agricultural chemist George Washington Carver (1864–1943) and astronomer Edwin P. Hubble (1889–1953). Charles A. Lindbergh (b. Michigan 1902–1974) was a pilot and aviation instructor in the St. Louis area during the 1920s before winning worldwide acclaim for his solo New York-Paris flight.

Prominent Missouri businessmen include Joseph Pulitzer (b.Hungary, 1847–1911), who established the *St. Louis Post-Dispatch* (1878) and later endowed the journalism and literary prizes that bear his name; and James Cash Penney (1875–1971), founder of the J. C. Penney Company.

Noteworthy journalists from Missouri include newspaper and magazine editor William M. Reedy (1862–1920) and television newscaster Walter Cronkite (b.1916). Missouri's most popular author is Mark Twain (Samuel Langhorne Clemens, 1835–1910). Poet-critic T(homas) S(tearns) Eliot (1888–1965), awarded the Nobel Prize for literature in 1948, was born in St. Louis but became a British subject in 1927. Other Missouri-born poets include Sara Teasdale (1884–1933), Marianne Moore (1887–1972), and Langston Hughes (1902–1967).

Distinguished painters who lived in Missouri include James Carroll Beckwith (1852–1917). Among the state's important musicians are ragtime pianist-composer Scott Joplin (b.Texas, 1868–1917); composer-critic Virgil Thompson (1896–1989); and jazzman Coleman Hawkins (1907–1969).

Missouri-born entertainers include actors Vincent Price (1911–1993), and Edward Asner (b.1929); actresses Jean Harlow (Harlean Carpenter, 1911–1937), Betty Grable (1916–1973), and Shelley Winters (1922–2006); actress-dancer Ginger Rogers (1911–1995); and film director John Huston (1906–1984). In popular music, the state's most widely known singer-songwriter is Charles "Chuck" Berry (b.California, 1926), whose works had a powerful influence on the development of rock music.

St. Louis Cardinals stars who became Hall of Famers include Jerome Herman "Dizzy" Dean (b.Arkansas, 1911–1974), Stanley Frank "Stan the Man" Musial (b.Pennsylvania, 1920), Robert "Bob" Gibson (b.Nebraska, 1935), and Louis "Lou" Brock (b.Arkansas, 1939). Among the native Missourians who achieved stardom in the sports world are baseball manager Charles Dillon "Casey" Stengel (1890–1975), catcher Lawrence Peter "Yogi" Berra (b.1925), sportscaster Joe Garagiola (b.1926), and golfer Tom Watson (b.1949).

40 Bibliography

BOOKS

Bennett, Michelle. *Missouri.* New York: Benchmark Books, 2001.

Boekhoff, P. M. *Missouri.* Milwaukee, WI: Gareth Stevens, 2006.

Bristow, M. J. *State Songs of America.* Westport, CT: Greenwood Press, 2000.

Crawford, Mark. *Confederate Courage on Other Fields: Four Lesser-known Accounts of the War Between the States.* Jefferson, NC: McFarland, 2000.

Gaskell, Richard. *The Missouri State Fair: Images of a Midwestern Tradition.* Columbia: University of Missouri Press, 2000.

Gibson, Karen Bush. *Missouri Facts and Symbols.* Rev. ed. Mankato, MN: Capstone, 2003.

McAuliffe, Emily. *Missouri Facts and Symbols.* Rev. ed. Mankato, MN: Capstone, 2003.

Murray, Julie. *Missouri.* Edina, MN: Abdo Publishing, 2006.

WEB SITES

Government of Missouri. *Show-me Missouri.* www.state.mo.us (accessed March 1, 2007).

Missouri Division of Tourism. *Missouri: Have You visit MO Lately?* www.missouritourism.org (accessed March 1, 2007).

Montana

State of Montana

ORIGIN OF STATE NAME: Derived from the Latin word meaning "mountainous."

NICKNAME: The Treasure State.

CAPITAL: Helena.

ENTERED UNION: 8 November 1889 (41st).

OFFICIAL SEAL: In the lower center are a plow and a miner's pick and shovel; mountains appear above them on the left, the Great Falls of the Missouri River on the right, and the state motto on a banner below. The words "The Great Seal of the State of Montana" surround the whole.

FLAG: A blue field, fringed in gold on the top and bottom borders, surrounds the center portion of the official seal, with "Montana" in gold letters above the coat of arms.

MOTTO: *Oro y Plata* (Gold and silver).

SONG: "Montana."

FLOWER: Bitterroot.

TREE: Ponderosa pine.

ANIMAL: Grizzly bear.

BIRD: Western meadowlark.

FISH: Black-spotted (cutthroat) trout.

GEM: Yogo sapphire and Montana agate.

FOSSIL: Duck-billed dinosaur.

GRASS: Bluebunch wheatgrass.

LEGAL HOLIDAYS: New Year's Day, 1 January; Birthday of Martin Luther King Jr., 3rd Monday in January; Presidents' Day, 3rd Monday in February; Memorial Day, last Monday in May; Independence Day, 4 July; Labor Day, 1st Monday in September; Columbus Day, 2nd Monday in October; State Election Day, 1st Tuesday after the 1st Monday in November in even-numbered years; Veterans' Day, 11 November; Thanksgiving Day, 4th Thursday in November; Christmas Day, 25 December.

TIME: 5 AM MST = noon GMT.

1 Location and Size

Located in the northwestern United States, Montana is the largest of the eight Rocky Mountain states and ranks fourth in size among the 50 states. The total area of Montana is 147,046 square miles (380,849 square kilometers), of which land takes up 145,388 square miles (376,555 square kilometers) and inland water 1,658 square miles (4,294 square kilometers). The state's maximum east-west extension is 570 miles (917 kilometers). Its extreme north-south distance is 315 miles (507 kilometers). Its total boundary length is 1,947 miles (3,133 kilometers).

2 Topography

Montana has an approximate mean elevation of 3,400 feet (1,000 meters). The Rocky Mountains cover the western two-fifths of the state, with the Bitterroot Range along the Idaho border. The high, gently rolling Great Plains occupy most of central and eastern Montana. The highest point in the state is Granite Peak, at an elevation of 12,799 feet (3,904 meters). The lowest point, at 1,800 feet (549 meters), is in the northwest, where the Kootenai River leaves the state at the Idaho border. The Continental Divide passes through the western part of the state. Ft. Peck Reservoir is Montana's largest body of inland water, covering 375 square miles (971 square kilometers). Flathead Lake is the largest natural lake. The state's most important rivers are the Missouri and the Yellowstone.

3 Climate

The Continental Divide separates the state into two distinct climatic regions. The west generally has a milder climate than the east, where winters can be especially harsh. Montana's maximum daytime temperature averages 27°F (-2°C) in January and 85°F (29°C) in July. The all-time low temperature in the state, -70°F (-57°C) at Rogers Pass on 20 January 1954, is also the lowest temperature ever recorded in the continental United States. The all-time high, 117°F (47°C), was set at Medicine Lake on 5 July 1937. Great Falls receives an average annual precipitation of 15 inches (38 centimeters), but much of north-central Montana is arid. About 58.5 inches (148.6 centimeters) of snow descends on Great Falls each year.

Montana Population Profile

Total population estimate in 2006:	944,632
Population change, 2000–06:	4.7%
Hispanic or Latino†:	2.2%
Population by race	
One race:	98.3%
White:	90.6%
Black or African American:	0.5%
American Indian /Alaska Native:	6.0%
Asian:	0.6%
Native Hawaiian / Pacific Islander:	0.1%
Some other race:	0.5%
Two or more races:	1.7%

Population by Age Group

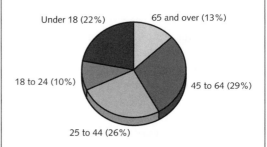

Under 18 (22%)
65 and over (13%)
18 to 24 (10%)
45 to 64 (29%)
25 to 44 (26%)

Major Cities by Population

City	Population	% change 2000–05
Billings	98,721	9.9
Missoula	62,923	10.3
Great Falls	56,338	-0.6
Bozeman	33,535	21.9
Butte-Silver Bow	32,282	-4.8
Helena	27,383	6.2
Kalispell	18,480	29.9
Havre	9,390	-2.4
Anaconda-Deer Lodge	8,948	-5.0
Miles	8,162	-3.8

Notes: †A person of Hispanic or Latino origin may be of any race. NA indicates that data are not available.
Sources: U.S. Census Bureau. *American Community Survey* and *Population Estimates*. www.census.gov/ (accessed March 2007).

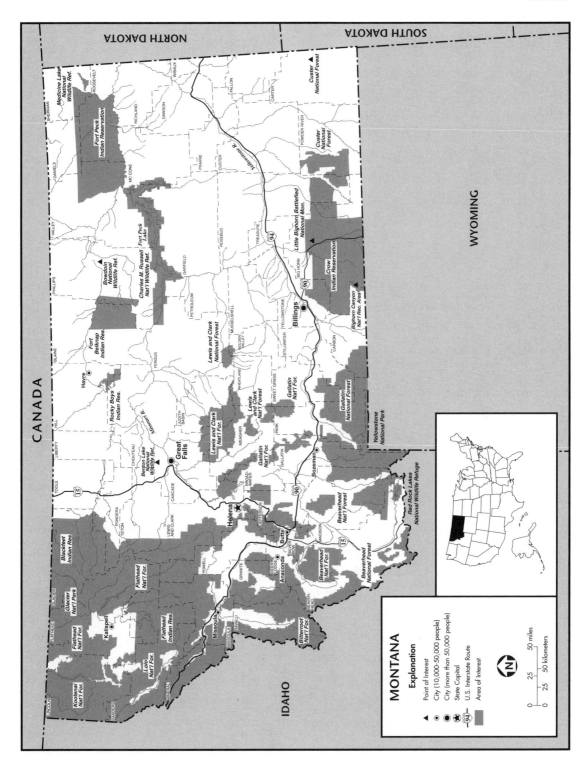

MONTANA

Explanation

Point of Interest
City (10,000–50,000 people)
City (more than 50,000 people)
State Capital
U.S. Interstate Route
Area of Interest

50 miles
0   25   50
0   25   50 kilometers

4 Plants and Animals

The subalpine region, in the northern Rocky Mountains, is rich in wildflowers during a short midsummer growing season. The plants of the montane zone consists largely of coniferous forests, principally alpine fir, and a variety of shrubs. The plains are characterized by an abundance of grasses, cacti, and sagebrush species. Three plant species were threatened as of April 2006: Ute ladies'-tresses, Spalding's catchfly, and water howellia.

Game animals of the state include elk, moose, pronghorn antelope, and mountain goat. Notable among the amphibians is the axolotl. Rattlesnakes and other reptiles occur in most of the state. As of 2006, eleven species were listed as threatened or endangered, including the grizzly bear, black-footed ferret, Eskimo curlew, two species of sturgeon, the gray wolf, and the whooping crane.

5 Environmental Protection

Montana's major environmental concerns are management of mineral and water resources and reclamation of strip-mined land. In 2003, Montana had 71 hazardous waste sites listed in the Environmental Protection Agency's database, 14 of which were on the National Priorities List as of 2006. Only a tiny fraction of the state's lands are wetlands. The Water Quality Bureau of the Montana Department of Health and Environmental Sciences is responsible for managing wetlands.

6 Population

In 2005, Montana ranked 44th in population in the United States with an estimated total of 944,632 residents. The population is projected to reach 999,489 by 2015 and 1.03 million by 2025. In 2004, Montana's population density of 6.4 persons per square mile (2.47 persons per square kilometer) was one of the lowest in the country. In 2005, 13% of the all residents were 65 years of age and older, while 22% were 18 and younger. The median age was about 39.6 in 2004. The largest metropolitan area in 2005 was Billings, with an estimated 98,721 residents. The Missoula metropolitan area had an estimated population of 62,923.

7 Ethnic Groups

According to the 2000 census, there were approximately 56,068 Native Americans in Montana, of whom the Blackfeet and Crow are the most numerous. In 2006, American Indians accounted for 6.0% of the state's population. In 2000, there were also 2,692 black Americans and 4,691 Asians. In 2006, blacks accounted for 0.5% of the population, while Asians accounted for 0.6%. There were 18,081 Hispanic or Latino residents in 2000, accounting for 2% of the population. In 2006, Hispanic or Latino residents accounted for 2.2% of the state's population. In 2000, a total of 16,396 residents in Montana were foreign born. Canada, Germany, the United Kingdom, and Mexico were the leading places of origin.

Montana Population by Race

Census 2000 was the first national census in which the instructions to respondents said, "Mark one or more races." This table shows the number of people who are of one, two, or three or more races. For those claiming two races, the number of people belonging to the various categories is listed. The U.S. government conducts a census of the population every ten years.

	Number	Percent
Total population	902,195	100.0
One race	886,465	98.3
Two races	15,003	1.7
White *and* Black or African American	1,016	0.1
White *and* American Indian/Alaska Native	9,116	1.0
White *and* Asian	1,710	0.2
White *and* Native Hawaiian/Pacific Islander	268	—
White *and* some other race	1,945	0.2
Black or African American *and* American Indian/Alaska Native	300	—
Black or African American *and* Asian	40	—
Black or African American *and* Native Hawaiian/Pacific Islander	7	—
Black or African American *and* some other race	50	—
American Indian/Alaska Native *and* Asian	117	—
American Indian/Alaska Native *and* Native Hawaiian/Pacific Islander	34	—
American Indian/Alaska Native *and* some other race	196	—
Asian *and* Native Hawaiian/Pacific Islander	91	—
Asian *and* some other race	95	—
Native Hawaiian/Pacific Islander *and* some other race	18	—
Three or more races	727	0.1

Source: U.S. Census Bureau. *Census 2000: Redistricting Data*. Press release issued by the Redistricting Data Office. Washington, D.C., March, 2001. A dash (—) indicates that the percent is less than 0.1.

8 Languages

English in Montana fuses Northern and Midland features, with the Northern influence declining from east to west. In 2000, the number of Montanans who spoke only English at home was 803,031, representing about 95% of the resident population five years of age or older. Other languages spoken at home, and number of speakers, included Spanish, 12,953; German, 9,416; and various Native American languages, 9,234.

9 Religions

In 2000, there were nearly an equal number of Protestants and Roman Catholics within the state. In 2004, there were about 103,351 adherents to the Roman Catholic faith. Leading Protestant denominations (with 2000 data) were the Evangelical Lutheran Church in America, 50,287; the United Methodist Church, 17,993; Assemblies of God, 16,385; the Lutheran Church—Missouri Synod, 15,441 and the Southern Baptist Convention, 15,318. There were about 850 Jews and 614 Muslims in the state in 2000. In 2006, the Church of Jesus Christ of the Latter-day Saints (Mormons) reported a statewide membership of 13,384 adherents.

About 493,703 people (55% of the population) were not counted as members of any religious organization in 2000.

10 Transportation

Montana's first railroad, the Utah and Northern, entered the state in 1880. Today, Montana is served by two Class I railroads (the Burlington Northern Santa Fe, and the Union Pacific), plus two regional railroads, and two local railroads, operating on 3,291 miles (5,326 kilometers) of track. As of 2006, Amtrak operated one long-distance route (Chicago–Seattle/Portland) through the state, which served 12 stations.

Because of its large size, small population, and difficult terrain, Montana was slow to develop a highway system. In 2004, the state had 69,452 miles (111,817 kilometers) of public roads, streets, and highways. There were about 1.031 million registered motor vehicles in that same year, including some 427,000 automobiles, around 555,000 trucks, and some 1,000 buses. There were 712,880 licensed drivers in 2004.

Montana had 241 airports, 31 heliports, 2 STOLports (Short Take-Off and Landing), and 2 seaplane bases in 2005. The leading airport is Billings-Logan International Airport, which had 395,086 passenger boardings in 2004.

11 History

Montana's first European explorers were probably French traders and trappers from Canada who arrived during the 17th and 18th centuries. It was not until 1803, however, that the written history of Montana began. In that year, the Louisiana Purchase gave the United States most of Montana, and the Lewis and Clark expedition, dispatched by President Thomas Jefferson in 1804, added the rest. Soon afterwards, the first American trappers, traders, and settlers entered Montana.

The fur trade dominated Montana's economy until 1858, when gold was discovered east of the present-day community of Drummond, bringing with it a temporary gold boom. In 1863, the eastern and western sectors of Montana were joined as part of Idaho Territory. On 26 May 1864, President Abraham Lincoln signed the Organic Act, which created the Montana Territory.

The territorial period was one of rapid and profound change. By the time Montana became a state on 8 November 1889, the remnants of Montana's Native American culture had been largely confined to federal reservations, following the surrender of the Nez Perce tribe to federal forces. As the Native American threat subsided, cattle ranchers wasted little time in putting the seemingly limitless open range to use. The "hard winter" of 1886/87, when perhaps as many as 362,000 head of cattle starved, marked the end of a cattle frontier based on the "free grass" of the open range and taught the stockmen the value of a secure winter feed supply.

Modern Times Construction of Montana's railroad system between 1880 and 1909 breathed new life into mining as well as the livestock industry. By 1890, the Butte copper pits were producing more than 40% of the nation's copper requirements. The struggle to gain financial control of the enormous mineral wealth of Butte Hill led to the "War of the Copper Kings," whose victor, Anaconda Copper Mining, practically controlled the press, politics, and governmental processes of Montana until the 1940s and 1950s.

The railroads also brought an invasion of agricultural homesteaders. Montana's popula-

The Last Stand Monument commemorates those who died in the Battle of Little Bighorn (1876). © CONNIE RICCA/ CORBIS.

tion doubled between 1900 and 1920, while the number of farms and ranches increased form 13,000 to 57,000. Drought and a sharp drop in wheat prices after World War I brought an end to the homestead boom. Conditions worsened with the drought and depression of the early 1930s. Then the New Deal—enormously popular in Montana—helped revive farming and silver mining, and financed irrigation and other public works projects.

The decades since the end of World War II have seen moderate growth in Montana's population, economy, and social services. Although manufacturing developed slowly, the state's fossil fuels industry grew rapidly during the national energy crisis of the 1970s. However, production of coal, crude oil, and natural gas leveled off after the crisis and even declined in the early 1980s.

In 1983 the Anaconda Copper Mining Company shut down its mining operations in Butte. Farm income declined in the late 1980s as a result of falling prices, drought, and insect damage. By the early 1990s, growth in manufacturing and construction and recovery in agriculture improved the state's economy. Nevertheless, the state had the eighth-highest unemployment rate in the nation, 5.2% as of 1999. US Senator Max Baucus urged a special session of the state legislature to address unemployment and convened a Montana Economic Development Summit in June 2000. By September 2005, the state's economic picture improved, with unemployment falling to 4.5%. However the number of Montana residents living below the federal poverty line remained high at 14.3% in 2004.

Tourism, air quality, and wildlife in parts of Montana were affected by forest fires. In 1988 forest fires burned for almost three months in Yellowstone National Park, and some Montana residents had to be evacuated from their homes. In 2000, Montana was again among the states afflicted by raging wildfires. By the end of July, 3.5 million acres had burned across the West. In August 2003, wildfires burned more than 400,000 acres, an area large enough to cover about half of Rhode Island.

In 1992 Montana's delegation to the US House of Representatives was reduced from two members to one, based on the results of the 1990 Census. As of the 2004 election, the state was still represented in the US House of Representatives by a single member. In that election, Democrat

The statue Montana sits atop the dome of the Montana state capitol building in Helena. AP IMAGES.

Brian Schweitzer retook the governorship, which had been held by Republicans since 1988.

12 State Government

Montana's original constitution, dating from 1889, was revised by a 1972 constitutional convention, effective in 1973. That document had been amended 30 times by January 2005.

The state legislature consists of 50 senators, elected to staggered four-year terms, and 99 representatives, who serve for two years. Elected officers of the executive branch include the governor and lieutenant governor (who run jointly), secretary of state, attorney general, auditor, and superintendent of public instruction. Each serves a four-year term. To become law, a bill must pass both houses by a simple majority and be signed by the governor, or remain unsigned for five days, or be passed over the governor's veto by a two-thirds vote of both houses.

In 2004, legislators received $78.60 per day during regular legislative sessions, while the governor received $93,089 per year, as of December 2004.

13 Political Parties

Since statehood, Democrats have generally dominated in contests for the US House and Senate, while Republicans led in elections for state and local offices, and in national presidential campaigns (except during the New Deal years). In 2000, Montanans gave Republican George W. Bush 58% and Democrat Al Gore 34%. In 2004, President Bush took 59% of the vote, compared to 39% for challenger John Kerry.

Democrat Brian Schweitzer became governor in 2004. Democratic challenger Jon Tester defeated incumbent senator Conrad Burns, a Republican, in the 2006 US Senate race. Democrat Max Baucus won reelection to his seat in the US Senate in 2002. The state's sole seat in the US House was retained by a Republican in the 2006 election.

Following the 2006 midterm elections, there were 24 Republicans and 26 Democrats in the state senate, while there were 50 Democrats,

49 Republicans, and 1 Independent in the state house. Thirty-seven women were elected to the state legislature in 2006, or 24.7%.

In 2004 there were 638,000 registered voters in Montana. The state does not require party registration.

14 Local Government

As of 2005, Montana had 56 counties, 129 municipalities, 592 special districts, and 453 public school districts. Typically, elected county officials consist of three county commissioners, an attorney, a sheriff, a clerk and recorder, school superintendent, treasurer, assessor, and coroner.

15 Judicial System

Montana's highest court, the Montana Supreme Court, consists of a chief justice and six associate justices. District courts are the courts of general jurisdiction. There are 37 district court judges. Justice of the peace courts are essentially county courts whose jurisdiction is limited to minor civil cases, misdemeanors, and traffic violations.

Montana's violent crime (murder/nonnegligent manslaughter, forcible rape, robbery, aggravated assault) rate in 2004 was 293.8 incidents per 100,000 people. The state has a death penalty, for which lethal injection is the sole method of execution. However, the state rarely enforces the death penalty. Between 1976 and 5 May 2006, only two people have been executed. As of 1 January 2006, there were four inmates on death row. There were 3,877 inmates in Montana's state and federal prisons as of 31 December 2004.

Montana Governors: 1889–2007

1889–1893	Joseph Kemp Toole	Democrat
1893–1897	John Ezra Rickards	Republican
1897–1901	Robert Burns Smith	Populist, Democrat
1901–1908	Joseph Kemp Toole	Democrat
1908–1913	Edwin Lee Norris	Democrat
1913–1921	Sam Vernon Stewart	Democrat
1921–1925	Joseph Moore Dixon	Republican
1925–1933	John Edward Erickson	Democrat
1933–1935	Frank Henry Cooney	Democrat
1935–1937	William Elmer Holt	Democrat
1937–1941	Roy Elmer Ayers	Democrat
1941–1949	Samuel Clarence Ford	Republican
1949–1953	John Woodrow Bonner	Democrat
1953–1961	John Hugo Aronson	Republican
1961–1965	Donald Grant Nutter	Republican
1965–1969	Tim M. Babcock	Republican
1969–1973	Forest Howard Anderson	Democrat
1973–1981	Thomas Lee Judge	Democrat
1981–1989	Ted Schwinden	Democrat
1989–1993	Stan Stephens	Republican
1993–2000	Marc Francis Racicot	Republican
2000–2004	Judy Martz	Republican
2004–	Brian Schweitzer	Democrat

16 Migration

Montana's first great migratory wave brought Indians from the east during the 17th and 18th centuries. The gold rush of the 1860s, and a land boom between 1900 and 1920 resulted in surges of white settlement. The economically troubled 1920s and 1930s produced a severe wave of out-migration that continued through the 1960s. The trend began reversing between 1970 and 1980. Between 1990 and 1998, Montana had net gains of 48,000 in domestic migration and 3,000 in international migration. In the period 2000–05, net international migration was 2,141, while net domestic migration for that same period was 18,933 people, giving the state a net gain of 21,074 people.

Montana Presidential Vote by Major Political Parties, 1948–2004

YEAR	MONTANA WINNER	DEMOCRAT	REPUBLICAN
1948	*Truman (D)	119,071	96,770
1952	*Eisenhower (R)	106,213	157,394
1956	*Eisenhower (R)	116,238	154,933
1960	Nixon (R)	134,891	141,841
1964	*Johnson (D)	164,246	113,032
1968	*Nixon (R)	114,117	138,835
1972	*Nixon (R)	120,197	183,976
1976	Ford (R)	149,259	173,703
1980	*Reagan (R)	118,032	206,814
1984	*Reagan (R)	146,742	232,450
1988	*Bush (R)	168,936	190,412
1992**	*Clinton (D)	154,507	144,207
1996**	Dole (R)	167,922	179,652
2000	*Bush, G. W. (R)	137,126	240,178
2004	*Bush, G. W. (R)	173,710	266,063

*Won US presidential election.
** Independent candidate Ross Perot received 107,225 votes in 1992 and 55,229 votes in 1996.

17 Economy

Agriculture, mining, and lumbering traditionally dominated Montana's economy. In the early 21st century, tourism was of increasing importance. A lawsuit with the federal government over the federal lands that have supplied much of the state's timber has placed the timber industry's future in question. Employment in the services industries overtook manufacturing and mining during the 1990s. Business, engineering, and health services stimulated the economy, in addition to tourism.

The state economy was little affected by the national recession of 2001, and employment increased in construction, financial, and general services, and fell slightly in manufacturing, transportation, and utilities in 2002. Farming in Montana was hard-hit by drought conditions in the early 2000s. Wheat crop yields in 2002 were the lowest since 1988.

Montana's gross state product (GSP) in 2004 was $27.482 billion, of which real estate accounted for the largest share of GSP at $3.229 billion or 11.7%. It was followed by healthcare and social assistance at 9% of GSP, and construction at 5.9% of GSP. Of the 33,801 businesses that have employees, 97.8% are small companies.

18 Income

In 2004, Montana ranked 42nd among the 50 states and the District of Columbia with a per capita (per person) income of $27,657, compared to the national average of $33,050. Montana's median household income for the three-year period 2002 through 2004 was $35,201, compared to the national average of $44,473. For the same period, 14.3% of the state's residents lived below the federal poverty level, compared to 12.4% nationwide.

19 Industry

Montana's major manufacturing industries process raw materials from mines, forests, and farms. In 2004, the total shipment value of all products manufactured in the state totaled $6.468 billion. Of that total, wood product manufacturing accounted for the largest share at $960.445 million, followed by food manufacturing at $666.718 million, and nonmetallic mineral product manufacturing at $216.365 million.

In 2004, a total of 17,311 people were employed in Montana's manufacturing sector. Of that total, the wood product manufacturing sector accounted for the largest portion, with 4,109 workers, followed by food manufacturing at 2,464, and miscellaneous manufacturing at 1,447.

20 Labor

In April 2006, the seasonally adjusted civilian labor force in Montana numbered 502,800, with approximately 18,300 workers unemployed, yielding an unemployment rate of 3.6%, compared to the national average of 4.7% for the same period. April 2006 data for nonfarm employment showed that about 6.9% of the labor force was employed in construction; 4.5% in manufacturing; 4.5% in trade, transportation, and public utilities; 5% in financial activities; 8.4% in professional and business services; 13% in leisure and hospitality services; and 20.2% in government. Data was unavailable for education and healthcare services.

In 2005, a total of 42,000 of Montana's 391,000 employed wage and salary workers were members of a union. This represented 10.7% of those so employed, and was below the national average of 12%.

21 Agriculture

Montana's farms numbered 28,000 in 2004. Farm income totaled almost $2.38 billion in 2005. In 2004, Montana was the nation's third-leading wheat producer. Other major crops were barley (third in the United States), sugarbeets (sixth), and hay. Oats, potatoes, flax, and dry beans are also grown.

22 Domesticated Animals

In 2005, Montana's farms and ranches had around 2.4 million cattle and calves, valued at $2.5 million. There were an estimated 165,000 hogs and pigs, valued at $18.2 million in 2004. During 2003, Montana farmers produced around 24.6 million pounds (11.2 million kilograms) of sheep and lambs that grossed $22.6 million in income.

23 Fishing

Montana's designated fishing streams offer some 10,000 miles (16,000 kilometers) of good to excellent freshwater fishing. In 2004, the state issued 379,252 sport fishing licenses.

Montana is home to the Creston and Ennis National Fish Hatcheries as well as the Bozeman Fish Technology Center and the Bozeman Fish Health Center. Creston specializes in rainbow trout, westslope cutthroat trout, kokanee salmon, and bull trout. Ennis works as part of the National Broodstock Program, producing about 20 million rainbow trout eggs annually for research facilities, universities and federal, state and tribal hatcheries in 23 states.

24 Forestry

In 2004, a total of 23,500,000 acres (9,510,000 hectares) in Montana were classified as forestland. There were 11 national forests, comprising 16,932,447 acres (6,852,561 hectares) in 2005. The lumbering industry produced 1.09 billion board feet in 2004.

25 Mining

The estimated value of nonfuel mineral production for Montana in 2003 was $492 million. Metallic minerals accounted for 63% of the state's total nonfuel mineral production by value. Montana ranked 26th nationally in the value of nonfuel minerals produced.

Gold was Montana's leading mineral by value in 2003, followed by platinum, construction sand and gravel, cement (portland and masonry), and bentonite. Montana is the only state to produce primary platinum and palladium. The state is first in the production of talc; second in bentonite; fourth in gold, zinc and lead, and seventh in silver. According to preliminary figures, production and value in 2003 included construction sand and gravel, 18 million metric tons ($81.9 million); palladium, 14,600 kilograms ($98.3 million); and platinum, 4,100 kilograms ($86.5 million)

26 Energy and Power

In 2003, Montana generated 26.268 billion kilowatt hours of electricity, of which 64.9% came from coal-fired plants, 33.1% from hydropower, and 1.5% from petroleum-fueled plants. Total net summer generating capacity was 5.210 million kilowatts in 2003.

In 2004, the state produced an average of 68,000 barrels per day of crude oil. Proven reserves in that same year totaled 364 million barrels. Marketed natural gas production in 2004 totaled 96.762 billion cubic feet (2.74 billion cubic meters), with proven reserves of consumer-grade natural gas of 995 billion cubic feet (28.2 billion cubic meters), as of 31 December 2004. In 2004, Montana had six producing coal mines (five surface operations and one underground). In that same year, coal output totaled 39.989 million tons. Recoverable coal reserves totaled 1.14 billion tons in 2004.

27 Commerce

In 2002, Montana's wholesale trade sector had sales totaling $7.2 billion, while the retail trade sector had sales of $10.1 billion. Motor vehicle and motor vehicle parts dealers accounted for the largest portion of retail sales at $2.7 billion, followed by general merchandise stores at $1.6 billion, and food and beverage stores at $1.3 billion. In 2005, Montana's foreign exports totaled $710 million.

28 Public Finance

The Montana state budget is prepared biennially by the Office of Budget and Program Planning and submitted by the governor to the legislature for amendment and approval. The fiscal year runs from 1 July to 30 June.

In 2004, Montana had total revenues of $5.45 billion, while total expenditures that year totaled $4.69 billion. The largest general expenditures were for education ($1.377 billion), public welfare ($762 million), and highways ($537 million). The state's debt in 2004 totaled $3.048 billion, or $3,288.96 per capita (per person).

29 Taxation

As of 1 January 2006, Montana had a seven-bracket personal income tax that ranged from 1% to 6.9%. The corporate income tax was a flat rate of 6.75%. There is no state sales and use tax, but Montana imposes excise taxes covering such products as motor fuels, and tobacco products. There are also state and local property taxes.

The state collected $1.788 billion in taxes in 2005, of which 39.9% came from individual income taxes, 25.5% from selective sales taxes,

10.4% from state property taxes, and 5.5% from corporate income taxes. The per capita (per person) tax burden in 2005 amounted to $1,910, compared to the national average of $2,192, which ranked the state 35th among the 50 states in terms of individual tax burden.

30 Health

In October 2005, the infant mortality rate was estimated at 6.7 per 1,000 live births. The overall death rate was 9.2 per 1,000 people in 2003. Major causes of death were heart disease, cancer, cerebrovascular diseases, chronic lower respiratory diseases, and diabetes. About 20.3% of the population were smokers in 2004. Montana has one of the lowest AIDS rates in the country. In 2004, the state's AIDS case rate was about 0.8 per 100,000 people.

Montana's 53 community hospitals had about 4,300 beds in 2003. In 2005, Montana had 800 nurses per 100,000 population, while in 2004, there were 224 physicians per 100,000 population, and a total of 513 dentists in the state. The average expense for community hospital care was $733 per day. In 2004, about 19% of Montana's residents were uninsured.

31 Housing

In 2004, Montana had an estimated 423,262 housing units, of which 368,530 were occupied, and 68.5% were owner-occupied. About 69.8% of all units were single-family, detached homes, while about 12.8% were mobile homes. Utility gas and electricity were the most common energy sources for heating. It was estimated that 18,156 units lacked telephone service, 1,780 lacked complete plumbing facilities, and 2,143 lacked complete kitchen facilities. The average household size was 2.45 people.

In 2004, a total of 5,000 new privately owned units were authorized for construction. The median home value was $119,319. The median monthly cost for mortgage owners was $974. Renters paid a median of $520 per month.

32 Education

In 2004, of all Montana residents age 25 and older, 91.9% were high school graduates and 5.5% had obtained a bachelor's degree or higher.

Total public school enrollment was estimated at 147,000 in fall 2003, and expected to total 141,000 by fall 2014. Enrollment in nonpublic schools in fall 2003 was 8,924. Expenditures for public education in 2003/2004 were estimated at $1.2 billion.

As of fall 2002, there were 45,111 students enrolled in college or graduate school. In 2005, Montana had 23 degree-granting institutions. The University of Montana has campuses at Missoula, Montana Tech, and Western Montana College. Montana State University encompasses the Bozeman, Billings, and Northern campuses.

33 Arts

The state capitol in Helena is home to Charles Russell's mural *Lewis and Clark Meeting the Flathead Indians*. Orchestras are based in Billings and Bozeman. The Equinox Theater Company is also a popular attraction in Bozeman.

The Montana Arts Council supports many programs with state and federal funds. The Montana Committee for the Humanities (MCH) was founded in 1972. In 2000, the MCH sponsored its first annual Montana Festival of the Book in downtown Missoula, bringing together writers, readers, and entertainers from across the state.

34 Libraries and Museums

In 2001, Montana had 107 public libraries, of which 28 were branches. The combined book stock of all Montana public libraries was 2.625 million volumes and their combined circulation was 4.8 million. Distinguished collections include those of the University of Montana (Missoula) and Montana State University (Bozeman).

Among the state's 74 museums are the Montana Historical Society Museum in Helena, the World Museum of Mining in Butte, and the Museum of the Plains Indian in Browning. The C. M. Russell Museum in Great Falls honors the work of Charles Russell, whose mural *Lewis and Clark Meeting the Flathead Indians* adorns the capitol in Helena. Other fine art museums include the Museum of the Rockies in Bozeman, the Yellowstone Art Center at Billings, and the Missoula Museum of the Arts.

35 Communications

In 2004, of all the state's households, 93.5% had telephone service, and as of December 2003, there were 373,947 wireless telephone service subscribers. In 2003, computers were in 59.5% of all Montana households, while 50.4% had Internet access. There were 43 major commercial radio stations (14 AM, 29 FM) in 2005, and 16 major television stations. A total of 15,300 Internet domain names were registered in Montana in 2000.

36 Press

As of 2005, Montana had eight morning dailies, three evening dailies, and seven Sunday newspapers. The leading papers and their circulations were the *Billings Gazette* (47,105 mornings, 52,434 Sundays), the *Great Falls Tribune* (33,434 mornings, 36,763 Sundays), and the *Missoulian* (30,466 mornings, 34,855 Sundays).

37 Tourism, Travel & Recreation

In 2002, about 10 million nonresident travelers spent $1.8 billion dollars on visits to the state. The tourist industry sponsors over 33,500 jobs for the state.

Many tourists seek out the former gold rush camps, ghost towns, and dude ranches. Scenic wonders include Glacier National Park in the northwest, and Yellowstone National Park, which also extends into Idaho and Wyoming. Bighorn Canyon National Recreation Area is another popular destination.

38 Sports

Although there are no professional major league sports teams in Montana, there are minor league baseball teams in Billings, Great Falls, Helena, and Missoula. The University of Montana Grizzlies and Montana State University Bobcats both compete in the Big Sky Conference. Skiing is a very popular participation sport. The state has world-class ski resorts in Big Sky. Other annual sporting events include the Seeley-Lincoln 100/200 Dog Sled Race between Seely Lake and Lincoln in January, and many rodeos statewide.

39 Famous Montanans

Prominent national officeholders from Montana include US Senator Thomas Walsh (b. Wisconsin, 1859–1933), who directed the investigation that uncovered the Teapot Dome scandal; Jeannette Rankin (1880–1973), the first woman member of Congress and the only US representative to vote against American participation in both world wars. Crazy Horse (1849?–1877) led a Sioux-Cheyenne army in battle at Little Big Horn. The town of Bozeman is named for explorer and prospector John M. Bozeman (b. Georgia, 1835–1867).

Creative artists from Montana include Alfred Bertram Guthrie Jr. (b. Indiana, 1901–1991), author of *The Big Sky* and the Pulitzer Prize-winning *The Way West*; and Charles Russell (b. Missouri, 1864–1926), Montana's foremost painter and sculptor. Hollywood stars Gary Cooper (Frank James Cooper, 1901–1961) and Myrna Loy (1905–1993) were also from Montana.

40 Bibliography

BOOKS

Bennett, Clayton. *Montana*. New York: Benchmark Books, 2001.

Bristow, M. J. *State Songs of America*. Westport, CT: Greenwood Press, 2000.

Brown, Jonatha A. *Montana*. Milwaukee, WI: Gareth Stevens, 2007.

George, Charles. *Montana*. New York: Children's Press, 2000.

Murray, Julie. *Montana*. Edina, MN: Abdo Publishing, 2006.

Sateren, Shelley Swanson. *Montana Facts and Symbols*. Mankato, MN: Capstone, 2003.

Sullivan, Gordon. *Beautiful America's Montana*. Woodburn, OR: Beautiful America, 2000.

WEB SITES

State of Montana. *mt.gov: Montana's Official State Website*. mt.gov (accessed March 1, 2007).

Travel Montana, Department of Commerce, and State of Montana. *Montana: Big Sky Country*. www.visitmt.com/index.htm (accessed March 1, 2007).

Nebraska

State of Nebraska

ORIGIN OF STATE NAME: Derived from the Oto Indian word *nebrathka*, meaning "flat water" (for the Platte River).

NICKNAME: The Cornhusker State.

CAPITAL: Lincoln.

ENTERED UNION: 1 March 1867 (37th).

OFFICIAL SEAL: Agriculture is represented by a farmer's cabin, sheaves of wheat, and growing corn; the mechanic arts, by a blacksmith. Above is the state motto; in the background, a steamboat plies the Missouri River and a train heads toward the Rockies. The scene is surrounded by the words "Great Seal of the State of Nebraska, March 1st 1867."

FLAG: The great seal appears in the center, in gold and silver, on a field of blue.

MOTTO: Equality Before the Law.

SONG: "Beautiful Nebraska."

FLOWER: Goldenrod.

TREE: Western cottonwood.

ANIMAL: White-tailed deer.

BIRD: Western meadowlark.

INSECT: Honeybee.

GEM: Blue agate.

FOSSIL: Mammoth.

ROCK OR STONE: Prairie agate.

GRASS: Little bluestem.

LEGAL HOLIDAYS: New Year's Day, 1 January; Birthday of Martin Luther King Jr., 3rd Monday in January; Presidents' Day, 3rd Monday in February; Arbor Day, last Friday in April; Memorial Day, last Monday in May; Independence Day, 4 July; Labor Day, 1st Monday in September; Columbus Day, 2nd Monday in October; Veterans' Day, 11 November; Thanksgiving, 4th Thursday in November and following Friday; Christmas Day, 25 December. Other days for special observances include Pioneers' Memorial Day, 2nd Sunday in June; Nebraska Czech Day, 1st Sunday in August; and American Indian Day, 4th Monday in September.

TIME: 6 AM CST = noon GMT; 5 AM MST = noon GMT.

1 Location and Size

Located in the western north-central United States, Nebraska ranks 15th in size among the 50 states. The total area of the state is 77,355 square miles (200,349 square kilometers), of which land takes up 76,644 square miles (198,508 square kilometers) and inland water 711 square miles (1,841 square kilometers). Nebraska extends about 415 miles (668 kilometers) from east to west and 205 miles (330 kilometers) from north to south. The boundary length of Nebraska totals 1,332 miles (2,143 kilometers).

2 Topography

Most of Nebraska is prairie, since more than two-thirds of the state lies within the Great Plains. The elevation slopes upward gradually from east to west, from a low of 840 feet (256 meters) in the southeast to 5,424 feet (1,654 meters) in Kimball County. The Sand Hills of the north-central plain is an unusual region of sand dunes anchored by grasses that cover about 18,000 square miles (47,000 square kilometers).

The Sand Hills region is dotted with small natural lakes, but in the rest of the state, the main lakes are artificial. The Missouri River forms the eastern part of the northern boundary of Nebraska. Three rivers cross the state from west to east: the wide, shallow Platte River; the Niobrara River; and the Republican River.

3 Climate

Nebraska has a continental climate with highly variable temperatures. The central region has a normal monthly maximum of 76°F (24°C) in July and a minimum of 22°F (-6°C) in January. The record low for the state is -47°F (-44°C), registered in Morrill County on 12 February 1899. The record high of 118°F (48°C) was recorded at Minden on 24 July 1936. Normal yearly precipitation ranges from 17 inches (43 centimeters) in the west to 30 inches (76 centimeters) in the southeast. Snowfall in the state varies from about 21 inches (53 centimeters) in the southeast to about 45 inches (114 centimeters) in the northwest corner. Blizzards, drought, and wind-

Nebraska Population Profile

Total population estimate in 2006:	1,768,331
Population change, 2000–06:	3.3%
Hispanic or Latino†:	7.2%
Population by race	
One race:	98.5%
White:	89.6%
Black or African American:	4.0%
American Indian / Alaska Native:	0.8%
Asian:	1.5%
Native Hawaiian / Pacific Islander:	0.0%
Some other race:	2.6%
Two or more races:	1.5%

Population by Age Group

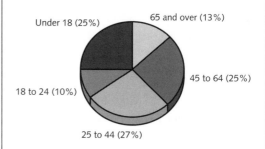

Under 18 (25%)
65 and over (13%)
45 to 64 (25%)
18 to 24 (10%)
25 to 44 (27%)

Major Cities by Population

City	Population	% change 2000–05
Omaha	414,521	6.3
Lincoln	239,213	6.0
Bellevue	47,334	6.7
Grand Island	44,546	3.7
Kearney	28,958	5.6
Hastings	25,437	5.7
Fremont	25,314	0.6
North Platte	24,324	1.9
Norfolk	23,946	1.8
Columbus	20,909	-0.3

Notes: †A person of Hispanic or Latino origin may be of any race. NA indicates that data are not available. **Sources:** U.S. Census Bureau. *American Community Survey* and *Population Estimates*. www.census.gov/ (accessed March 2007).

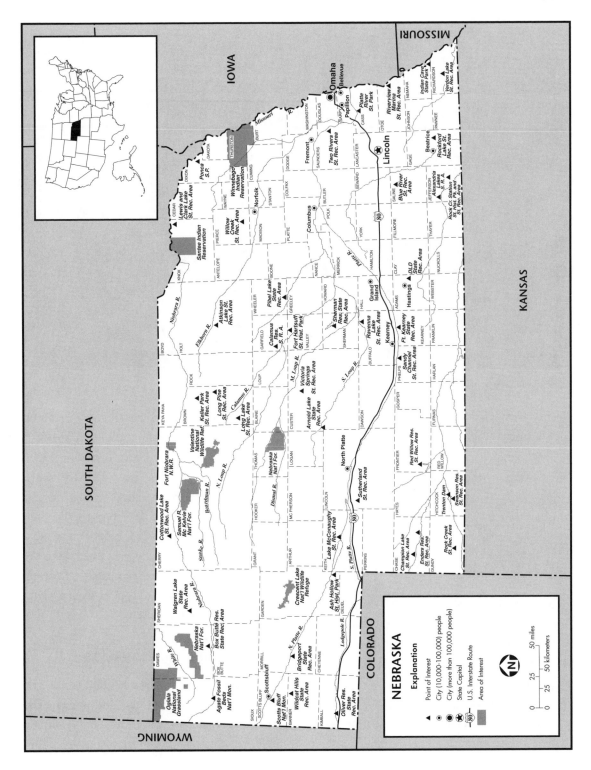

NEBRASKA

Explanation

▲ Point of Interest

◉ City (10,000–100,000) people

◉ City (more than 100,000 people)

✪ State Capital

80 U.S. Interstate Route

▨ Area of Interest

N

0   25   50 miles

0   25   50 kilometers

Chimney Rock on the Oregon Trail. NEBRASKA DIVISION OF TRAVEL AND TOURISM.

storms have plagued Nebraskans throughout their history.

4 Plants and Animals

Nebraska's deciduous forests are generally oak and hickory. Conifer forests are dominated by western yellow (ponderosa) pine. Slough grasses, needlegrasses, western wheatgrass, and buffalo grass are found in the prairies. Common Nebraska wildflowers include wild rose, columbine, and sunflower. Three plant species were threatened as of 2006, Ute ladies'-tresses, western prairie fringed orchid, and Colorado butterfly plant. The blowout penstemon was listed as endangered that same year.

Common mammals native to the state include the pronghorn sheep, white-tailed and mule deer, and coyote. There are more than 400 kinds of birds, the mourning dove and the western meadowlark (the state bird) among them. Carp, catfish, and trout are fished for sport. Rare animal species include the least shrew, least weasel, and bobcat. In 2006, the US Fish and Wildlife Service listed nine animal species as threatened or endangered, including the American burying beetle, bald eagle, whooping crane, black-footed ferret, Topeka shiner, pallid sturgeon, and Eskimo curlew.

5 Environmental Protection

The Department of Environmental Quality was established in 1971 to protect and improve the quality of the state's water, air, and land resources. In 2003, Nebraska had 255 hazardous waste sites

Nebraska Population by Race

Census 2000 was the first national census in which the instructions to respondents said, "Mark one or more races." This table shows the number of people who are of one, two, or three or more races. For those claiming two races, the number of people belonging to the various categories is listed. The U.S. government conducts a census of the population every ten years.

	Number	Percent
Total population	1,711,263	100.0
One race	1,687,310	98.6
Two races	22,591	1.3
White *and* Black or African American	4,651	0.3
White *and* American Indian/Alaska Native	5,285	0.3
White *and* Asian	3,344	0.2
White *and* Native Hawaiian/Pacific Islander	310	—
White *and* some other race	6,057	0.4
Black or African American *and* American Indian/Alaska Native	704	—
Black or African American *and* Asian	302	—
Black or African American *and* Native Hawaiian/Pacific Islander	50	—
Black or African American *and* some other race	669	—
American Indian/Alaska Native *and* Asian	113	—
American Indian/Alaska Native *and* Native Hawaiian/Pacific Islander	15	—
American Indian/Alaska Native *and* some other race	356	—
Asian *and* Native Hawaiian/Pacific Islander	181	—
Asian *and* some other race	461	—
Native Hawaiian/Pacific Islander *and* some other race	93	—
Three or more races	1,362	0.1

Source: U.S. Census Bureau. *Census 2000: Redistricting Data.* Press release issued by the Redistricting Data Office. Washington, D.C., March, 2001. A dash (—) indicates that the percent is less than 0.1.

listed in the Environmental Protection Agency's database, 12 of which were on the National Priorities List as of 2006.

The state has three wetlands of international importance as migrational and breeding grounds for waterfowl and nongame birds. While these areas are protected, the state has lost about 1 million acres (405,000 hectares) of wetlands since pre-European settlement times.

6 Population

In 2005, Nebraska ranked 38th in population in the United States with an estimated total of 1,768,331 residents. The population is projected to reach 1.78 million by 2015 and 1.81 million by 2025. The population density in 2004 was 22.7 persons per square mile (8.76 persons per square kilometer). The median age of the state's population was 36 for that same year. In 2005, of all Nebraska residents, 13% were 65 or older, while 25% were 18 or younger.

The largest cities in 2005 were Omaha, with an estimated population of 414,521, and Lincoln, with 239,213 residents.

7 Ethnic Groups

According to the 2000 census, the population of Nebraska included 94,425 Hispanics and Latinos, 68,541 black Americans, 21,931 Asians, and 836 Pacific Islanders. There were 14,896 Native Americans residing in the state, primarily from the Omaha, Winnebago, and Santee Sioux tribes. Among those of European descent who reported at least one specific ancestry 661,133 were German, 163,651 were English, 229,805 were Irish, 93,286 were Czech, and 84,294 were Swedish. About 74,638 residents, or 4.4% of the total population, were foreign born.

In 2006, black Americans accounted for 4.0% of the state's population, while 1.5% were Asian, and 7.2% were Hispanic or Latino.

8 Languages

Nebraska English is almost pure North Midland, except for slight South Midland and Northern influences. A few words, mostly food terms like *kolaches* (fruit-filled pastries), are derived from the language of the large Czech population. Usual pronunciation features *cot* and *caught* as soundalikes and a strong final /r/. *Fire* sounds almost like *far*, and *our* like *are*. *Greasy* is pronounced *greezy*.

In 2000, of the resident population five years old or older, 92.1% spoke only English at home. The number of residents who spoke other languages at home included Spanish, 77,655 and German, 8,865.

9 Religions

Nebraska's religious history derives from its patterns of immigration. German and Scandinavian settlers tended to be Lutheran, while Irish, Polish, and Czech immigrants were mainly Roman Catholic. Methodism and other Protestant religions were spread by settlers from other Midwestern states.

Although Protestants outnumber Catholics, the Roman Catholic Church was the largest single Christian denomination in the state with about 376,843 adherents in 2004. As of 2000, Lutherans constituted the largest Protestant group with 117,419 adherents of the Missouri Synod, while there were 128,570 members of the Evangelical Lutheran Church in America, and 5,829 belonged to the Wisconsin Evangelical Lutheran Synod. In 2004, a total of 84,337 people were United Methodists. In 2000, there were 39,420 Presbyterians–USA. The Jewish population was estimated at 7,100 in 2000, and Muslims numbered about 3,115. There were 704,403 people (about 41% of the population) who were not counted as members of any religious organization.

10 Transportation

Nebraska's development was profoundly influenced by two major railroads, the Union Pacific and the Burlington Northern Santa Fe, both of which were major landowners in the state in the late 1800s. As of 2003, these railroads still operated in the state. In that same year, there were 11 railroads operating in Nebraska, with 3,548 miles (5,712 kilometers) of track in the state. As of 2006, Amtrak provided east-west service to Chicago or Emeryville/San Francisco, to five stations in Nebraska

In 2004, the state's road system totaled 93,245 miles (150,124 kilometers), and is dominated by Interstate 80, the major east–west route, and the largest public investment project in the state's history. A total of 1.678 million motor vehicles were registered in 2004, of which 829,000 were automobiles and about 820,000 were trucks. A total of 1,315,819 people held driver's licenses in that same year.

In 2005, there were 266 airports in the state, along with 36 heliports and 1 seaplane base.

A tornado touches down less than two miles from this farm. AP IMAGES.

Eppley Airfield, Omaha's airport, is by far the busiest in the state, with 1,892,379 passenger boardings in 2004.

11 History

By 1800, the Pawnee, Ponca, Omaha, and Oto tribes, along with several others, were living in what became present-day Nebraska. The area was claimed by both Spain and France and was French territory at the time of the Louisiana Purchase in 1803, when it came under US jurisdiction. During the first half of the 19th century, the area was explored by Lewis and Clark, Zebulon Pike, and others.

Military forts were established in the 1840s to protect travelers from attack by Native Americans. The Kansas-Nebraska Act of 1854 established the Nebraska Territory, which assumed its present shape in 1861. Still sparsely populated, Nebraska escaped the violent clash over slavery that afflicted Kansas. From 1860 to the late 1870s, however, western Nebraska was a battleground for US soldiers and Native Americans, who were moved to reservations in Nebraska, South Dakota, and Oklahoma by 1890.

Statehood Settlement of Nebraska Territory was rapid, escalated by the Homestead Act of 1862, under which the US government provided 160 acres (65 hectares) to a settler for a small fee. On 1 March 1867, Nebraska became the 37th state to join the Union. Farming and ranching developed as the state's two main enterprises. However, by 1890, depressed farm prices, high railroad

Nebraska Governors: 1867–2007

1867–1871	David C. Butler	Republican	1923–1925	Charles Wayland Bryan	Democrat
1871–1873	William Hartford James	Republican	1925–1929	Adma McMullen	Republican
1873–1875	Robert Wilkinson Furnas	Republican	1929–1931	Arthur J. Weaver	Republican
1875–1879	Silas Garber	Republican	1931–1935	Charles Wayland Bryan	Democrat
1879–1883	Albinus Nance	Republican	1935–1941	Robert LeRoy Cochran	Democrat
1883–1887	James William Dawes	Republican	1941–1947	Dwight Palmer Griswold	Republican
1887–1891	John Milton Thayer	Republican	1947–1953	Val Frederick Demar Peterson	Republican
1891	James E. Boyd	Democrat	1953–1955	Robert Berkey Crosby	Republican
1891–1892	John Milton Thayer	Republican	1955–1959	Victor Emanuel Anderson	Republican
1892–1893	James E. Boyd	Democrat	1959–1960	Ralph Gilmour Brooks	Democrat
1893–1895	Lorenzo Crounse	Republican	1960–1961	Dwight Willard Burney	Republican
1895–1899	Silas Alexander Halcomb	Populist	1961–1967	Frank Brenner Morrison	Democrat
1899–1901	William Amos Poynter	Fusion	1967–1971	Norbert Theodore Tiemann	Republican
1901	Charles Henry Dietrich	Republican	1971–1979	John James Exon	Democrat
1901–1903	Ezra Perin Savage	Republican	1979–1983	Charles Thone	Republican
1903–1907	John Hopwood Mickey	Republican	1983–1987	Robert Kerrey	Democrat
1907–1909	George Lawson Sheldon	Republican	1987–1991	Kay A. Orr	Republican
1909–1911	Ashton Cockayne Shallenberger	Democrat	1991–1999	Earl Benjamin Nelson	Democrat
1911–1913	Chester Hardy Aldrich	Republican	1999–2005	Michael Johanns	Republican
1913–1917	John Henry Morehead	Democrat	2005–	Dave Heineman	Republican
1917–1919	M. Kieth Neville	Democrat			
1919–1923	Samuel Roy McKelvie	Republican			

shipping charges, and rising interest rates were hurting the state's farmers, and a drought in the 1890s worsened their plight.

When the dust storms of the 1930s began, thousands of people fled Nebraska for the West Coast. The onset of World War II, however, brought prosperity in many areas. Military airfields and war industries were placed in the state because of its safe inland location, bringing industrial growth that extended well into the postwar years. Much of the new industry developed since that time is agriculture-related, including the manufacture of farm machinery and irrigation equipment.

Farm output and income increased dramatically into the 1970s. Many farmers took on large debt burdens to finance expanded output, with their credit supported by strong farm-product prices and exports. When prices began to fall in the early 1980s, many found themselves in

trouble. A 1982 state constitutional amendment prohibits the sale of land used for farming or ranching to anyone other than a Nebraska family farm corporation.

The average farm income in Nebraska rose more than 10% between 1989 and the mid-1990s. Farms in the state were fewer in number by the late 1990s, but they were larger and more mechanized. But farmers were struggling again by June 2000, when drought struck and most of the corn crop was lost. Some areas of the state had received no substantial rain in a year. The previous autumn and winter were the driest on record. Water conservation to avoid depletion of the state's aquifers for irrigation purposes remained a major priority into 2004, as the state faced its fifth straight year of severe drought conditions.

Although the state's farm sector was being hit by drought and falling farm prices, Nebraska's nonfarm sector saw the growth of small industries and tourism, which acted to bolster the state's economy.

In January 2005, Lieutenant Governor Dave Heineman became governor, following the resignation of Governor Mike Johanns, who left to become the US Secretary of Agriculture. In the 2006 election, Heineman retained the governorship.

12 State Government

Nebraska's legislature is unique among the states. It is a single-chamber body of 49 members not elected by political party. Members go by the title of senator, and are elected for four-year terms. In 2002, there was one African American and one Latino senator serving in the state legislature. Elected executives are the governor, lieutenant governor, secretary of state, auditor, treasurer, and attorney general. They all serve four-year terms. The governor is limited to two consecutive terms, after which the governor is ineligible to serve in office for four years. A bill becomes law when passed by a majority of the legislature and signed by the governor. If the governor does not approve, the bill is returned with objections, and a three-fifths vote of the legislature is required to override a veto. A bill automatically becomes law if the governor does not take action within five days after receiving it.

The legislative salary in 2004 was $12,000 and the governor's salary was $85,000.

The current state constitution was adopted in 1875. As of January 2005, it had been amended 222 times.

Nebraska Presidential Vote by Major Political Parties, 1948–2004

YEAR	NEBRASKA WINNER	DEMOCRAT	REPUBLICAN
1948	Dewey (R)	224,165	264,774
1952	*Eisenhower (R)	188,057	421,603
1956	*Eisenhower (R)	199,029	378,108
1960	Nixon (R)	232,542	380,553
1964	*Johnson (D)	307,307	276,847
1968	*Nixon (R)	170,784	321,163
1972	*Nixon (R)	169,991	406,298
1976	Ford (R)	233,692	359,705
1980	*Reagan (R)	166,424	419,214
1984	*Reagan (R)	187,866	460,054
1988	*Bush (R)	259,235	397,956
1992**	Bush (R)	217,344	344,346
1996**	Dole (R)	236,761	363,467
2000	*Bush, G. W. (R)	231,780	433,862
2004	*Bush, G. W. (R)	254,328	512,814

* Won US presidential election.
** Independent candidate Ross Perot received 174,687 votes in 1992 and 71,278 votes in 1996.

13 Political Parties

In 2004 there were 1,160,000 registered voters. In 1998, 37% of registered voters were Democratic, 49% Republican, and 14% unaffiliated or members of other parties. In the 2000 presidential election, Republican candidate George W. Bush secured 63% of the vote while Democrat Al Gore received a 33% share. In the 2004 presidential election, Bush carried the state with 66% of the vote to John Kerry's 33%. In the 2006 elections, Democrat Ben Nelson was reelected to the US Senate, while Republican Chuck Hagel was reelected to the US Senate in 2002. In that same year, Republican Mike Johanns was reelected governor. However in January 2005, Lieutenant Governor Dave Heineman became governor after Johanns resigned to become the US Secretary of Agriculture. Heineman was elected governor in his own right in 2006.

In the 2006 election, all three of the state's seats in the US House of Representatives were won by Republicans. Nebraska's unicameral state legislature is nonpartisan. Twelve women were elected to the state legislature in 2006, or 24.5%.

14 Local Government

In 2005, Nebraska had 93 counties, 531 municipalities, and 575 public school districts. In 2002, the state had 446 townships. Municipalities are governed by a mayor (or city manager) and a council. Counties are administered by elected boards of supervisors or commissioners.

15 Judicial System

The state's highest court is the Nebraska Supreme Court, which consists of a chief justice and six other justices. Below the supreme court are the district courts, which are the trial courts of general jurisdiction. County courts handle criminal misdemeanors and civil cases involving less than $5,000. Nebraska's crime rate is well below the national average. In 2004, the state's rate for violent crime (murder/nonnegligent manslaughter, forcible rape, robbery, aggravated assault) was 308.7 incidents per 100,000 people. As of 31 December 2004, a total of 4,130 prisoners were being held in Nebraska's state and federal prisons. Nebraska has a death penalty law, for which electrocution is the sole method of execution. As of 1 January 2006, there were 10 inmates on death row.

16 Migration

The pioneers who settled Nebraska in the 1860s consisted mainly of Civil War veterans from the North and foreign-born immigrants. The Union Pacific and Burlington Northern Santa Fee railroads, which sold land to the settlers, actively recruited immigrants in Europe. Germans were the largest group to settle in Nebraska, then Czechs from Bohemia, and Scandinavians from Sweden, Denmark, and Norway. The Irish came to work on the railroads in the 1860s and stayed to help build the cities. Another wave of Irish immigrants in the 1880s went to work in the packinghouses of Omaha. The city's stockyards also attracted Polish workers. By the 1900 census, over one-half of all Nebraskans were either foreign-born or the children of foreign-born parents.

For much of the 20th century, Nebraska was in a period of out-migration. Between 1990 and 1998, the state had net gains of 2,000 in domestic migration and 14,000 in international migration. In the period 2000–05, net international migration was 22,199, while net domestic migration was -26,206, for a net loss of 4,007 people.

17 Economy

Agriculture remains the backbone of Nebraska's economy. Cattle, corn, hogs, and soybeans lead the state's list of farm products, and the largest portion of the state's workforce is either directly employed in agriculture as farm workers, or indirectly as workers in the farm equipment and food processing industries. However in more recent years, the state has attempted to diversify its economy and has been successful in attracting new business, in large part because of its location near western coal and oil deposits.

Nebraska's agricultural sector has been deeply affected by consolidation, technical advances in farming and transportation, and a prolonged drought. As of 2004, the drought was in its fifth consecutive year. Although water conservation was imposed to avoid depletion of the state's aquifers, it appears likely that the state is facing long-term water shortages. In addition to the drought, the state's rural counties have been steadily losing population since the 1970s, a trend that increased in the 1990s. In 2002, of the state's 93 counties, 66 had lost population.

Nebraska's gross state product (GSP) in 2004 was $68.183 billion, of which manufacturing accounted for the largest share of GSP at $8.305 billion, or 12.1%, and was followed by real estate at 8.6% of GSP, and by health care and social assistance at 7.2%. Of the 46,161 businesses in Nebraska that had employees, 96.8% were small companies.

18 Income

In 2004, Nebraska ranked 21st among the 50 states and the District of Columbia with a per capita (per person) income of $32,341, compared to the national average of $33,050. For period 2002–04, the median household income was $44,623 compared to the national average of $44,473. In that same period, 9.9% of the state's residents lived below the federal poverty level, compared to 12.4% nationwide.

19 Industry

Nebraska has a small but growing industrial sector. In 2004, the shipment value of all goods manufactured in the state was $34.433 billion. Of that total, food manufacturing accounted for the largest portion at $19.037 billion, followed by machinery manufacturing at $2.061 billion,

and transportation equipment manufacturing at $2.034 billion.

20 Labor

In 2004, a total of 99,706 people were employed in the state's manufacturing sector, of which food manufacturing accounted for the largest portion at 36,190. The largest portion of the state's manufacturing is concentrated in the Omaha metropolitan area. Other industrial centers are Lincoln, and in the portion of the Sioux City, Iowa metropolitan area that is in Nebraska.

In April 2006, the labor force in Nebraska numbered 988,200, with approximately 33,700 workers unemployed, yielding an unemployment rate of 3.4%, compared to the national average of 4.7% for the same period. In April 2006, nonfarm employment data showed that about 4.9% of the labor force was employed in construction; 10.9% in manufacturing; 21.2% in trade, transportation, and public utilities; 6.9% in financial activities; 10.4% in professional and business services; 13.7% in educational and health services; 8.5% in leisure and hospitality services; and 17.1% in government.

In 2005, a total of 69,000 of Nebraska's 830,000 employed wage and salary workers were members of a union, representing 8.3% of those so employed, compared to the national average of 12%.

21 Agriculture

With total cash receipts from farm marketings at over $11.2 billion in 2005, Nebraska ranked fourth among the 50 states. About $7.3 billion of all farm marketings came from livestock production, and $3.9 billion from cash crops. In 2004, corn accounted for 22% of farm receipts.

Crop production in 2004 (in bushels) included: corn, 1.3 billion; sorghum grain, 33.6 million; wheat, 61 million; oats, 3.7 million; and barley, 162,000. Hay production was 6.1 million tons; and potato production, 9.3 million hundredweight, (422 million kilograms). In the period 2000–04, Nebraska ranked third among the states in the production of corn and sorghum for grain, and fifth in sorghum for beans.

Nebraska farms still tend to be owned by single persons or families rather than by large corporations. The strength of state support for the family farm was reflected in the passage of a 1982 constitutional amendment, initiated by petition, prohibiting the purchase of Nebraska farm and ranch lands by any group other than a Nebraska family farm corporation.

22 Domesticated Animals

In 2005, Nebraska ranked third behind Texas and Kansas in the total number of cattle on farms (6.35 million), including 61,000 milk cows. Nebraska farmers had around 2.85 million hogs and pigs, valued at $313.5 million in 2004. During 2003, the state produced an estimated 10.3 million pounds (4.7 million kilograms) of sheep and lambs, which grossed $10.8 million in income for Nebraska farmers. Dairy products included 1.13 billion pounds (0.51 billion kilograms) of milk produced.

23 Fishing

Commercial fishing is negligible in Nebraska. The US Fish and Wildlife Service maintains 87 public fishing areas. In 2004, the state issued

176,619 fishing licenses. There are five state hatcheries producing a variety of stock fish that include largemouth bass, bluegill, black crappie, channel catfish, yellow perch, walleye, trout, and tiger musky

24 Forestry

Arbor Day, now observed throughout the United States, originated in Nebraska in 1872 as a way of encouraging tree planting in the sparsely forested state. Forestland occupies 1,275,000 acres (516,000 hectares), or 2.6% of the state. Ash, boxelder, hackberry, cottonwood, honey locust, red and bur oaks, walnut, elm, and willow trees are common to eastern and central Nebraska, while ponderosa pine, cottonwood, eastern red cedar, and Rocky Mountain juniper prevail in the west. The state's two national forests, Nebraska and Samuel R. McKelvie, are primarily grassland and are managed for livestock grazing. In 2005, the National Forest Service maintained 257,628 acres (104,262 hectares) of forestland. Lumber production in 2004 totaled 15 million board feet.

25 Mining

The value of nonfuel mineral production in Nebraska in 2003 was estimated at $94.2 million. All minerals produced in Nebraska, with the exception of gemstones, were basic construction materials. Most clay mining occurs in the southeast region, but sand and gravel mining takes place throughout the state. Industrial sand was used in the production of glass and had some applications outside of construction activities. In 2003, the top minerals were, in descending order of value, cement (portland and masonry), crushed stone, and construction sand and gravel.

26 Energy and Power

Nebraska is the only state with an electric power system owned by the public through regional, cooperative, and municipal systems. The state's net summer generating capacity in 2003 was 6.685 million kilowatts. Total electricity output in that same year was 30.455 billion kilowatt hours. Electricity from coal accounted for 68.8% of the total (20.954 billion kilowatt hours), followed by nuclear power at 26.3% (7.996 billion kilowatt hours), and hydropower at 3.2%. The remaining 1.7% came from natural gas or oil fired plants, and from other renewable fuel sources.

As of 2006, there were two operating nuclear power plants in Nebraska, the Cooper plant in Brownsville and the Fort Calhoun Station near Omaha.

Crude oil production for 2004 in Nebraska averaged 8,000 barrels per day. In that same year Nebraska had proven crude oil reserves of 15 million barrels. In 2004, marketed natural gas production in Nebraska totaled 1.454 billion cubic feet (0.041 billion cubic meters). Nebraska has no commercial coal industry, nor any crude oil refineries.

27 Commerce

In 2002, Nebraska's wholesale trade sector had sales totaling $26.1 billion, while the state's retail trade sector that year had sales totaling $20.2 billion. Motor vehicle and motor vehicle parts dealers accounted for the largest share of retail sales in 2002, at $5.07 billion, followed by general merchandise stores at $2.8 billion, and food and beverage stores at $2.4 billion. Nebraska's exports of goods produced within the state totaled $3 billion in 2005.

28 Public Finance

The Nebraska state budget is prepared by the Budget Division of the Department of Administrative Services and is submitted annually by the governor to the legislature. The fiscal year runs from 1 July to 30 June.

Total revenues for the year 2004 were $8.3 billion, while total expenditures that year were $6.979 billion. The largest general expenditures were for education ($2.3 billion), public welfare ($1.899 billion), and highways ($595 million). The state's outstanding debt in 2004 was $1.949 billion, or $1,115.36 per capita (per person).

29 Taxation

As of 1 January 2006, Nebraska had a state personal income tax with tax brackets ranging between 2.56% to 6.84%. The corporate tax rate ranges from 5.58% to 7.81%. The state sales tax rate was 5.5%. Food consumed off premises (such as at home) is exempt from the sales tax. Local sales taxes range from 0 to 1.5%. The state imposes excise taxes on gasoline and on cigarettes. Property taxes are collected locally and by the state.

The state collected $3.797 billion in taxes in 2005, of which 36.7% came from individual income taxes, 39.9% from the general sales tax, 12% from selective sales taxes, 5.2% from corporate income taxes, 0.1% from property taxes, and 6% from other types of taxes. In 2005, Nebraska ranked 24th among the states in terms of its combined state and local tax burden, which came to $2,158 per person, compared to the national average of $2,192.

30 Health

In October 2005, Nebraska's infant mortality rate was estimated at 5.7 per 1,000 live births. The crude death rate in 2003 was 8.9 per 1,000 population. Major causes of death in 2002 were heart disease, cancer, cerebrovascular diseases, chronic lower respiratory diseases, and diabetes. About 20.2% of the state's residents were smokers in 2004. The rate of HIV-related deaths was 1.2 per 100,000. The reported AIDS case rate in 2004 was around 3.9 per 100,000 people.

University Hospital and the University of Nebraska Medical Center are in Omaha. Nebraska's 85 community hospitals in 2003 had about 7,500 beds. In 2004, there were 243 physicians per 100,000 people, and a total of 1,114 dentists in Nebraska. In 2005, the state had 936 nurses per 100,000 population. The average expense for community hospital care was $1,043 per day. In 2004, about 11% of Nebraskans were uninsured.

31 Housing

In 2004, there were an estimated 757,743 housing units in Nebraska, of which 687,456 were occupied, and 68.4% were owner-occupied. About 73.8% of all units were single-family, detached homes. Utility gas and electricity were the most common heating energy sources. It was estimated that 35,566 units lacked telephone service, 1,426 lacked complete plumbing facilities, and 3,513 lacked complete kitchen facilities. The average household size was 2.47 people.

In 2004, authorization was given to build 10,900 new privately owned units. The median home value was $106,656. The median monthly cost for mortgage owners was $1,051. Renters paid a median of $547 per month.

32 Education

In 2004, of all Nebraskans age 25 and older, 91.3% were high school graduates and 24.8% had obtained a bachelor's degree or higher.

Total public school enrollment was estimated at 282,000 in fall 2003, and was expected to rise to 285,000 by fall 2014. Enrollment in private schools in fall 2003 was 39,454 students. Expenditures for public education in 2003/2004 were estimated at $2.6 billion.

As of fall 2002, there were 116,737 students enrolled in college or graduate school. In 2005, Nebraska had 39 degree-granting institutions, including 7 public four-year colleges, 16 nonprofit, private 4-year colleges and universities, and 8 public 2-year schools. The University of Nebraska is the state's largest postsecondary institution, with campuses in Kearney, Lincoln, and Omaha.

33 Arts

The 15-member Nebraska Arts Council (NAC), appointed by the governor, is empowered to receive federal and state funds, and to plan and administer statewide and special programs in all the arts. Affiliation with the Mid-America Arts Alliance allows the council to help sponsor national and regional events. The Nebraska Humanities Council, founded in 1972, sponsors two annual festivals: The Great Plains Chautauqua and the Nebraska Book Festival.

A librarian at the Nebraska State Library shows off a bookcase with a secret door the leads to a small balcony on the south side of the state capitol building. AP IMAGES.

The Omaha Theater Company for Young People sponsors a number of theatrical performances, as does as the Omaha Theater Ballet Company. The Omaha Symphony was founded in 1921, and Opera Omaha was founded in 1958. The Lied Center for Performing Arts in Lincoln sponsors a wide variety of dance, theater, and musical programs.

34 Libraries and Museums

As of December 2001, the state had 289 libraries, of which 17 were branches. For that same period, there were a total of 6 million volumes and a total circulation of 11.36 million. The Omaha public library system had 916,560

books and 2,471 periodical subscriptions in 9 branches. The state had 107 museums in 2000. The Roslyn Art Museum in Omaha is the state's leading museum. Other important museums include the Nebraska State Museum of History, the Stir Museum of the Prairie Pioneer in Grand Island, and the University of Nebraska State Museum.

35 Communications

In 2004, about 95.7% of the state's occupied housing units had telephones. In June of that same year, there were 984,355 wireless telephone service subscribers, while 66.1% of all households in the state had a computer and

55.4% had access to the Internet, in 2003. In 2005, there were 52 major FM and 19 major AM radio stations in operation. There were eight major network TV stations. A total of 23,752 Internet domain names were registered in the state by 2000.

36 Press

In 2005, Nebraska had 6 morning dailies, 12 evening dailies, and 6 Sunday newspapers.

The leading newspaper in 2005 was the *Omaha World–Herald*, with a daily circulation that year of 192,607 and a Sunday circulation of 242,964. The *Lincoln Journal–Star* had a daily circulation of 74,893 and a Sunday circulation of 84,149.

37 Tourism, Travel & Recreation

Tourism is Nebraska's third largest source of outside revenue (after agriculture and manufacturing). In 2004, the state hosted about 19.6 million travelers. Total travel expenditures came to $2.9 billion. The industry supports nearly 43,000 jobs.

The 8 state parks, 9 state historical parks, 12 federal areas, and 55 recreational areas are main tourist attractions. Fishing, swimming, picnicking, and sightseeing are the principal activities. The most attended Nebraska attractions in 2002 were: Omaha's Henry Dourly Zoo (1,420,556 visitors), Cabala's in Sidney (1,025,000), Eugene T. Mahoney State Park (1,100,000), Lake McDonough State Recreation Area (859,624), Fort Robinson State Park (357,932), Roslyn Art Museum (186,646), Strategic Air and Space Museum (173,889), the Great Platte River Road

Archway Monument (163,000), University of Nebraska State Museum (133,343), and Scotts Bluff National Monument (111,293).

38 Sports

There are no professional major league sports teams in Nebraska. Minor league baseball's Omaha Golden Spikes play in the AAA Pacific Coast League. Equestrian activities, including racing and rodeos, are also popular. Pari-mutuel racing is licensed by the state. Major annual sporting events are the National Collegiate Athletic Association (NCAA) College Baseball World Series at Rosenblatt Stadium, and the River City Roundup and Rodeo, both held in Omaha.

The most popular spectator sport is college football. The University of Nebraska Cornhuskers compete in the Big 12 football conference. The Cornhuskers have won numerous bowl games, including the Fiesta Bowl in 1996 and 2000, and the Alamo Bowl in 2001.

39 Famous Nebraskans

Nebraska was the birthplace of only one US president, Gerald R. Ford (Leslie King Jr., 1913–2006). William Jennings Bryan (b.Illinois, 1860–1925), a US representative from Nebraska, served as secretary of state and was the unsuccessful Democratic candidate for president three times.

Native American leaders important in Nebraska history include Oglala Sioux chiefs Red Cloud (1822–1909) and Crazy Horse (1849?–1877), and Ponca chief Standing Bear (1829–1908). Father Edward Joseph Flanagan (b.Ireland, 1886–1948) was the founder of Boys

Town, a home for underprivileged youth. Two native Nebraskans became Nobel laureates in 1980: Lawrence R. Klein (b.1920) in economics and Val L. Fitch (b.1923) in physics.

Writers associated with Nebraska include Willa Cather (b.Virginia, 1873–1947), who used the Nebraska frontier setting of her childhood in many of her writings, and won a Pulitzer Prize in 1922; Mari Sandoz (1896–1966), who wrote of her native Great Plains; and author Tillie Olsen (1912–2007). Composer-conductor Howard Hanson (1896–1982), born in Wahoo, won a Pulitzer Prize in 1944.

Nebraskans important in entertainment include actor-dancer Fred Astaire (Fred Austerlitz, 1899–1984); actors Henry Fonda (1905–1982), and Marlon Brando (1924–2004); and television star Johnny Carson (b.Iowa, 1925–2005).

40 Bibliography

BOOKS

Bristow, M. J. *State Songs of America.* Westport, CT: Greenwood Press, 2000.

Brown, Jonatha A. *Nebraska.* Milwaukee, WI: Gareth Stevens, 2007.

Heinrichs, Ann. *Nebraska.* Minneapolis, MN: Compass Point Books, 2004.

McAuliffe, Emily. *Nebraska Facts and Symbols.* Rev. ed. Mankato, MN: Capstone, 2003.

Murray, Julie. *Nebraska.* Edina, MN: Abdo Publishing, 2006.

Nichols, John. *Big Red: The Nebraska Cornhuskers Story.* Mankato, MN: Creative Education, 1999.

WEB SITES

Nebraska Division of Travel and Tourism. *Nebraska, possibilities...endless.* visitnebraska.org (accessed March 1, 2007).

State of Nebraska. *Nebraska.gov: The Official Website of Nebraska.* www.state.ne.us (accessed March 1, 2007).

Glossary

alpine: Generally refers to the Alps or other mountains; can also refer to a mountainous zone above the timberline.

ancestry: Based on how people refer to themselves, and refers to a person's ethnic origin, descent, heritage, or place of birth of the person or the person's parents or ancestors before their arrival in the United States. The Census Bureau accepted "American" as a unique ethnicity if it was given alone, with an unclear response (such as "mixed" or "adopted"), or with names of particular states.

antebellum: Before the US Civil War.

aqueduct: A large pipe or channel that carries water over a distance, or a raised structure that supports such a channel or pipe.

aquifer: An underground layer of porous rock, sand, or gravel that holds water.

blue laws: Laws forbidding certain practices (e.g., conducting business, gaming, drinking liquor), especially on Sundays.

broilers: A bird (especially a young chicken) that can be cooked by broiling.

BTU: The amount of heat required to raise one pound of water one degree Fahrenheit.

capital budget: A financial plan for acquiring and improving buildings or land, paid for by the sale of bonds.

capital punishment: Punishment by death.

civilian labor force: All persons 16 years of age or older who are not in the armed forces and who are now holding a job, have been temporarily laid off, are waiting to be reassigned to a new position, or are unemployed but actively looking for work.

Class I railroad: A railroad having gross annual revenues of $83.5 million or more in 1983.

commercial bank: A bank that offers to businesses and individuals a variety of banking services, including the right of withdrawal by check.

compact: A formal agreement, covenant, or understanding between two or more parties.

consolidated budget: A financial plan that includes the general budget, federal funds, and all special funds.

constant dollars: Money values calculated so as to eliminate the effect of inflation on prices and income.

conterminous US: Refers to the "lower 48" states of the continental US that are enclosed within a common boundary.

continental climate: The climate typical of the US interior, having distinct seasons, a wide range of daily and annual temperatures, and dry, sunny summers.

council-manager system: A system of local government under which a professional administrator is hired by an elected council to carry out its laws and policies.

credit union: A cooperative body that raises funds from its members by the sale of shares and makes loans to its members at relatively low interest rates.

current dollars: Money values that reflect prevailing prices, without excluding the effects of inflation.

demand deposit: A bank deposit that can be withdrawn by the depositor with no advance notice to the bank.

electoral votes: The votes that a state may cast for president, equal to the combined total of its US senators and representatives and nearly always cast entirely on behalf of the candidate who won the most votes in that state on Election Day.

endangered species: A type of plant or animal threatened with extinction in all or part of its natural range.

federal poverty level: A level of money income below which a person or family qualifies for US government aid.

fiscal year: A 12-month period for accounting purposes.

food stamps: Coupons issued by the government to low-income persons for food purchases at local stores.

general budget: A financial plan based on a government's normal revenues and operating expenses, excluding special funds.

general coastline: A measurement of the general outline of the US seacoast.

gross state product: The total value of goods and services produced in the state.

growing season: The period between the last 32°F (0°C) temperature in spring and the first 32°F (0°C) temperature in autumn.

Hispanic: A person who originates from Spain or from Spanish-speaking countries of South and Central America, Mexico, Puerto Rico, and Cuba.

home-rule charter: A document stating how and in what respects a city, town, or county may govern itself.

hundredweight: A unit of weight that equals 100 pounds in the US and 112 pounds in Britain.

inpatient: A patient who is housed and fed—in addition to being treated—in a hospital.

installed capacity: The maximum possible output of electric power at any given time.

massif: A central mountain mass or the dominant part of a range of mountains.

mayor-council system: A system of local government under which an elected council serves as a legislature and an elected mayor is the chief administrator.

Medicaid: A federal-state program that helps defray the hospital and medical costs of needy persons.

Medicare: A program of hospital and medical insurance for the elderly, administered by the federal government.

metric ton: A unit of weight that equals 1,000 kilograms (2,204.62 pounds).

metropolitan area: In most cases, a city and its surrounding suburbs.

montane: Refers to a zone in mountainous areas in which large coniferous trees, in a cool moist setting, are the main features.

no-fault insurance: An automobile insurance plan that allows an accident victim to receive payment from an insurance company without having to prove who was responsible for the accident.

nonfederal physician: A medical doctor who is not employed by the federal US government.

northern, north midland: Major US dialect regions.

ombudsman: A public official empowered to hear and investigate complaints by private citizens about government agencies.

per capita: Per person.

personal income: Refers to the income an individual receives from employment, or to the total incomes that all individuals receive from their employment in a sector of business (such as personal incomes in the retail trade).

piedmont: Refers to the base of mountains.

pocket veto: A method by which a state governor (or the US president) may kill a bill by taking no action on it before the legislature adjourns.

proved reserves: The quantity of a recoverable mineral resource (such as oil or natural gas) that is still in the ground.

public debt: The amount owed by a government.

religious adherents: The followers of a religious group, including (but not confined to) the full, confirmed, or communicant members of that group.

retail trade: The sale of goods directly to the consumer.

revenue sharing: The distribution of federal tax receipts to state and local governments.

right-to-walk: A measure outlawing any attempt to require union membership as a condition of employment.

savings and loan association: A bank that invests the savings of depositors primarily in home mortgage loans.

secession: The act of withdrawal, such as a state that withdrew from the Union in the US Civil War.

service industries: Industries that provide services (e.g., health, legal, automotive repair) for individuals, businesses, and others.

short ton: A unit of weight that equals 2,000 pounds.

Social Security: As commonly understood, the federal system of old age, survivors, and disability insurance.

southern, south midland: Major US dialect regions.

subalpine: Generally refers to high mountainous areas just beneath the timberline; can also more specifically refer to the lower slopes of the Alps mountains.

sunbelt: The southernmost states of the US, extending from Florida to California.

supplemental security income: A federally administered program of aid to the aged, blind, and disabled.

tidal shoreline: A detailed measurement of the US seacoast that includes sounds, bays, other outlets, and offshore islands.

time deposit: A bank deposit that may be withdrawn only at the end of a specified time period or upon advance notice to the bank.

value added by manufacture: The difference, measured in dollars, between the value of finished goods and the cost of the materials needed to produce them.

wholesale trade: The sale of goods, usually in large quantities, for ultimate resale to consumers.

ABBREVIATIONS & ACRONYMS

AD—Anno Domini
AFDC—aid to families with dependent children
AFL–CIO—American Federation of Labor–Congress of Industrial Organizations
AI—American Independent
AM—before noon
AM—amplitude modulation
American Ind.—American Independent Party
Amtrak—National Railroad Passenger Corp.
b.—born
BC—Before Christ
Btu—British thermal unit(s)
bu—bushel(s)
c.—circa (about)
C—Celsius (Centigrade)
CIA—Central Intelligence Agency
cm—centimeter(s)
Co.—company
comp.—compiler
Conrail—Consolidated Rail Corp.
Corp.—corporation
CST—Central Standard Time
cu—cubic
cwt—hundredweight(s)
d.—died
D—Democrat
e—evening
E—east
ed.—edition, editor
e.g.—exempli gratia (for example)
EPA—Environmental Protection Agency
est.—estimated
EST—Eastern Standard Time
et al.—et alii (and others)
etc.—et cetera (and so on)
F—Fahrenheit
FBI—Federal Bureau of Investigation
FCC—Federal Communications Commission
FM—frequency modulation
Ft.—fort
ft—foot, feet
GDP—gross domestic products
gm—gram
GMT—Greenwich Mean Time
GNP—gross national product
GRT—gross registered tons
Hist.—Historic
I—interstate (highway)

i.e.—id est (that is)
in—inch(es)
Inc.—incorporated
Jct.—junction
K—kindergarten
kg—kilogram(s)
km—kilometer(s)
km/hr—kilometers per hour
kw—kilowatt(s)
kwh—kilowatt-hour(s)
lb—pound(s)
m—meter(s); morning
m³—cubic meter(s)
mi—mile(s)
Mon.—monument
mph—miles per hour
MST—Mountain Standard Time
Mt.—mount
Mtn.—mountain
mw—megawatt(s)
N—north
NA—not available
Natl.—National
NATO—North Atlantic Treaty Organization
NCAA—National Collegiate Athletic Association
n.d.—no date
NEA—National Education Association or National Endowment for the Arts
N.F.—National Forest
N.W.R.—National Wildlife Refuge
oz—ounce(s)
PM—after noon
PST—Pacific Standard Time
r.—reigned
R—Republican
Ra.—range
Res.—reservoir, reservation
rev. ed.—revised edition
S—south
S—Sunday
Soc.—Socialist
sq—square
St.—saint
SRD—States' Rights Democrat
UN—United Nations
US—United States
USIA—United States Information Agency
w—west

NAMES OF STATES AND OTHER SELECTED AREAS

	Standard Abbreviation(s)	Postal Abbreviation
Alabama	Ala.	AL
Alaska	*	AK
Arizona	Ariz.	AZ
Arkansas	Ark.	AR
California	Calif.	CA
Colorado	Colo.	CO
Connecticut	Conn.	CN
Delaware	Del.	DE
District of Columbia	D.C.	DC
Florida	Fla.	FL
Georgia	Ga.	GA
Hawaii	*	HI
Idaho	*	ID
Illinois	Ill.	IL
Indiana	Ind.	IN
Iowa	*	IA
Kansas	Kans. (Kan.)	KS
Kentucky	Ky.	KY
Louisiana	La.	LA
Maine	Me.	ME
Maryland	Md.	MD
Massachusetts	Mass.	MA
Michigan	Mich.	MI
Minnesota	Minn.	MN
Mississippi	Miss.	MS
Missouri	Mo.	MO
Montana	Mont.	MT
Nebraska	Nebr. (Neb.)	NE
Nevada	Nev.	NV
New Hampshire	N.H.	NH
New Jersey	N.J.	NJ
New Mexico	N.Mex.(N.M.)	NM
New York	N.Y.	NY
North Carolina	N.C.	NC
North Dakota	N.Dak. (N.D.)	ND
Ohio	*	OH
Oklahoma	Okla.	OK
Oregon	Oreg. (Ore.)	OR
Pennsylvania	Pa.	PA
Puerto Rico	P.R.	PR
Rhode Island	R.I.	RI
South Carolina	S.C.	SC
South Dakota	S.Dak. (S.D.)	SD
Tennessee	Tenn.	TN
Texas	Tex.	TX
Utah	*	UT
Vermont	Vt.	VT
Virginia	Va.	VA
Virgin Islands	V.I.	VI
Washington	Wash.	WA
West Virginia	W.Va.	WV
Wisconsin	Wis.	WI
Wyoming	Wyo.	WY

*No standard abbreviation

Indiana

Iowa

Kansas

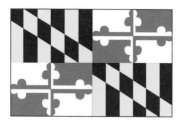

Kentucky

Louisiana

Maine

Maryland

Massachusetts

Michigan

Minnesota

Mississippi

Missouri

Montana

Nebraska